DATE DUE			

German Essays on
Art History

The German Library: Volume 79
Volkmar Sander, General Editor

GERMAN ESSAYS ON ART HISTORY

Edited by Gert Schiff

CONTINUUM • NEW YORK

1988

The Continuum Publishing Company
370 Lexington Avenue, New York, NY 10017

The German Library
is published in cooperation with Deutsches Haus,
New York University.
This volume has been supported by a grant
from The Claus Hueppe Foundation.

Copyright © 1988 by The Continuum Publishing Company
Introduction © 1988 by Gert Schiff

Printed in the United States of America

Library of Congress Cataloging-in-Publication Data

German essays on art history / edited by Gert Schiff.
p. cm. — (The German library; v. 79)
German and English.
Bibliography: p.
ISBN 0-8264-0308-5   ISBN 0-8264-0309-3 (pbk.)
1. Art.   2. Art—Philosophy.   3. Art—Historiography.   I. Schiff,
Gert.   II. Series.
N7443.4.G47 1987   87-18430
700—dc19   CIP

Acknowledgments will be found on page 283,
which constitutes an extension of the copyright page.

For C. H. C.

Contents

Contents

Introduction

The essays presented in this volume are meant to introduce the interested reader to some of those writers who initiated and shaped the study of art in the German-speaking countries. No more than three of these essays have been translated before; some of the authors appear here for the first time ever in English.

In more than one respect the present selection represents a consistent chapter in the history of the discipline. It begins with Winckelmann, who established for several generations the absolute preeminence of Greek art; it ends with Warburg and Panofsky who, at a time of waning interest in the Greek legacy, raised once more the question of the survival of classical antiquity. Moreover, most of the writers who have been brought together here based their work on the presupposition that there are detectable laws underlying the historical development of art. Some embraced the concept of rise and fall, which was first put forth in the sixteenth century by Giorgio Vasari. This holds for Winckelmann, the older Goethe, Wackenroder, Schlegel, Rumohr, Burckhardt, and Wölfflin. Others adopted conceptions which can be traced back to the philosophy of Georg Wilhelm Friedrich Hegel: the idea of continuous, predetermined progress in art (Wickhoff, Riegl), or the assumption that there is a demonstrable interdependence, or even structural unity, linking the art of a given period to all its other manifestations in religion, philosophy, law, government, and so on. This was maintained by Burckhardt, Wölfflin, Wickhoff, Riegl, Dvořák, Warburg, and Panofsky.[1] Only a smaller group (the young Goethe, Heinse, Kolloff, Hetzer, Schlosser) emphasized instead the isolated achievement of autonomous genius.

If this selection does indeed represent a consistent chapter, it does so only in fragmentary form. The required length of the book imposed severe limitations. Not even personal preference explains why Friedrich Schlegel was included and not his brother, August Wilhelm; Burckhardt, and not Schnaase; Wölfflin, and not Schmarsow; Hetzer, and not Vöge, Goldschmidt or Pinder; Riegl, and not Worringer; Warburg and Panofsky, and not Saxl or Wind.

In order to make up in depth for what the selection lacks in breadth, I have endeavored in this introduction to place text and authors in their respective historical contexts. Moreover, I have taken great care to show how each text epitomizes its author's basic views. In a few cases it seemed indispensable to indicate to what extent the factual results or the underlying assumptions have been superseded by more recent research. However, in general I preferred to offer a close textual exegesis — leaving it to the reader to discover what has become more and more evident to myself: that more often than not, these great art historians made their lasting contributions not because, but in spite of, their "systems."

Johann Joachim Winckelmann (1717–1768)[2] was both a leading pioneer of Neoclassicism and, as founder of the scholarly discipline of classical archaeology, the originator of German art history. Born the son of a poor cobbler in the backward March of Brandenburg, he was propelled by his genius through Latin school and the university to the Dresden court of Augustus III, one of the greatest collectors and art lovers among the European monarchs of his day. There in 1755 Winckelmann published the essay that opens the present anthology. The king honored the work with a pension which allowed its author to travel to Rome, where he became prefect of the pontifical antiquities, professor of Greek at the Vatican Library, an authority on ancient art, and a world-famous savant.

In Rome, his daily contact with the statues reinforced the intuitions that Winckelmann had derived from his study of the classical literature on the arts. He thus became capable, in his monumental *History of Ancient Art*,[3] to trace the "origin, growth, transformation, and fall" of Greek art by analogy to biological process, and in connection with the religious, political, and cultural history of Hellas. In this respect, he was the forerunner of Burckhardt. There was no precedent for such an undertaking; Winckelmann was as innovative in his general conception as he was in his individual insights and methods. He tried to impose order on the monuments by distinguishing, in every piece of sculpture, between authentic parts and modern restorations, and by eliminating whatever he recognized as fakes. Of far-reaching consequence was his insight that most of the extant statues were Roman copies of Greek originals; he rarely failed to identify the few authentic Greek works then known. One of Rome's most important collections of antiquities was formed by Cardinal Alessandro Albani with Winckelmann as consultant. It bears lasting testimony to his discerning eye. Mostly by his shrewd reading of ancient historiography, Winckelmann proved the independence of the earliest Greek art from Egypt. By careful comparison, he defined its difference from the more excessive forms of the Etruscans. Using his extensive knowledge of Greek and Roman mythology, he strove to determine the subject of a given work and thus became the father of modern iconography (compare, in this volume, the essays by Warburg and Panofsky). No matter how often Winckelmann may have erred in details, one feature of his *History* retains its validity to the present: his periodization of Greek art. He was, furthermore, far ahead of his time in that he did not concentrate primarily upon the lives of the artists (as had been done by the earlier historiographers of art, Vasari, van Mander, Sandrart), but tried instead to explore the evolution of forms and styles. About 150 years after Winckelmann, similar attempts have been made by scholars such as Wölfflin, Wickhoff, Riegl, and Hetzer. However, more than for all their scholarly merits, it is for their style that Winckelmann's writings are still read. Winckelmann writes as an inspired enthusiast. His language registers the most minute inflections, whether in the continuous contour of the figures on Greek vases or in the heavy volumes of the Torso Belvedere, whose muscles tell him of all the labors of Hercules. His style can be workmanlike, poetic, or briskly polemical. And in his descriptions of those works that he values most, he writes as a lover who perceives in the beloved object a reflection of the eternal idea of beauty.

With the hindsight of history, we recognize in his first work, the short pamphlet *On the Imitation of the Painting and Sculpture of the Greeks,* a faint yet firm sketch for the large historical construct and theoretical edifice of the *History of Ancient Art.* It is Winckelmann's aim to prove that "there is but one way for the moderns to become great, and perhaps unequaled; (namely) by imitating the ancients." He demonstrates this through a discussion of seven points: the beautiful nature of the Greeks; the exquisite outline, drapery, and expression of their statues; their technique of sculpture in marble; their painting; and their allegory. The present selection excludes the last three sections, for they betray the beginner. The technical hypothesis is untenable. Winckelmann's remarks on ancient painting (of which he had seen nothing) prove merely that he was insensitive to the sensuous qualities of painting: color, atmosphere, space; he thinks exclusively in terms of line and plasticity, and although he is aware of the original polychromy of the statues, he prefers their present immaculate whiteness. His thoughts on allegory (or, more broadly, on subject matter in art) had not yet crystallized. It is in the first four sections of his pamphlet that one perceives the earliest flashes of Winckelmann's genius. They make us understand why this first utterance of an obscure writer was instantly accepted, by the most sophisticated audiences in all Europe, as a signpost leading on a new road to refined taste.

How he conceived those ideas remains a mystery. Winckelmann lived amidst the splendors of the most advanced rococo culture, but he rejects the "caricatura carvings" of the rocaille ornament as he rejects the "contortions and strange postures" of baroque sculpture. His eyes are blind to Dresden's noble architecture and his ears are deaf to the Italianate sacred music. Instead, his whole being is pervaded by his conviction of the absolute preeminence of Greek art. Yet at the time of his writing, the Dresden collection of antiquities, later to be so famous, was stashed away in a miserable shack, where the statues stood "packed like herrings"; the only three works that he used in his pamphlet to exemplify the excellence of Greek attitudes and draperies, the so-called *Vestals* from Herculaneum and the *Ariadne* (which he calls "Agrippina"), were indeed the only ones he found "more comfortably placed." All his other knowledge of classical sculpture was derived from engravings. Moreover, here was a man who had toiled his life away in classrooms and libraries, in the sandy plains and fogs of the North; but he writes about the unsurpassed physical beauty of the Greeks, which he explains as resulting from their sunny climate, from the serene freedom of their life-style, from their sportive discipline and enlightened eugenics— he speaks about all this, as his great biographer, Carl Justi, remarks, "as a Greek could have spoken when exiled among barbarians."⁴ Hence, one is led to conclude that, right from the outset, he carried his image of antiquity in his soul.

What, then, was it that Winckelmann found so worthy of imitation in Greek art? The answer is, in the broadest sense, beauty. Why should the modern artist painstakingly select and combine those perfectly shaped limbs and bodily features, which in nature he could find only scattered over a great many individuals, if they were already harmoniously united in every work of classical statuary? Not only were the ancient sculptors inspired by the sight of lovelier bodies than can be found in all the modern world, they were also possessed by a mystical intuition of a higher, ideal beauty, which they bestowed upon their depictions of the gods. Intimately connected, however, with classical beauty is that quality which, according to Winckelmann, constitutes the "last and most eminent characteristic of the Greek works," and which he sums up in the well-known formula *"noble simplicity and sedate grandeur."* Pronounced for the first time in the opening sentence of the section on "Expression," these oft-quoted words both herald and summarize Winckelmann's entire aesthetics. They have given rise to all those qualities of subdued emotion and cool perfection which, in the works of Canova, Mengs, Flaxman, Thorvaldsen, or Ingres, appeared to later generations as frosty and asthenic. Yet, Winckelmann detects this characteristic, to the perennial amazement of all but his most uncritical readers, in the *Laocoon!* Pangs are piercing his every muscle, but Winckelmann perceives his struggling body as kept under control by his stoic mind, and "put . . . into a posture . . . the next to a state of tranquility." His painfully distorted mouth does not howl, but emits "an overloaded, anxious groan."

An interpretation that so obviously runs counter to the visual evidence betrays its origin in an illusion, in illusionary wish fulfillment. In fact, as is well known, Winckelmann's experience of antiquity is not determined by the titanic contortions of the struggling hero, nor by the mellow forms of the Cnidian *Aphrodite.* His entire vision of ancient art is suffused by that ideal that inhabited his soul since his earliest youth, and which dominated all his thinking and feeling: the ephebe, the beautiful adolescent, in whose lithe body the charms of both sexes commingle.[5] He is still all wrapped up in himself, in a state of dreamy inaction: whence Winckelmann's contention that ideal beauty is static and excludes strong emotional expression. Time and again, Winckelmann likens the experience of ideal beauty to the contemplation of a calm sea, or to purest water, "which, the less taste it has, the better it is" — a beauty purged of all the dross of humanity. This erotic ideal, which Winckelmann sometimes links to the mystical tradition of the original bisexuality of the Greek gods,[6] colors all his interpretations of ancient art. It determines his emphasis upon *sedate* grandeur. It explains his need to argue away the violence in the expression of the *Laocoön*; it explains as well his admiration for the *Sistine Madonna,* the only work of Christian art he ever wrote about.

Hence, it was idiosyncrasy that inspired his scholarly achievement. However, this idiosyncrasy proved so potent that it became the aesthetic model for scores of classicizing painters and sculptors well into the early twentieth century. We find it in David's expiring *Joseph Bara,* and in Feuerbach Alcibiades in his *Plato's Repast;* in Girodet's *Endymion* and in Gustave Moreau's *Narcissus;* in Puvis de Chavannes' young fishermen and in Burne-Jones's knights errant; in the Italianate youths of Hans von Marées and in the langorous ephebes of the Belgian symbolist Jean Delville. Thus, Winckelmann's dream lived on, long after he himself had died miserably at the hands of a murderer.

However, Winckelmann's view of Greek art was largely rejected by those poets and free spirits of the following generation whose mentality was aptly conjured up by the phrase "Sturm and Drang." Disciples of Rousseau, they acknowledged only the authority of nature; emphatic believers in original genius, they repudiated any rules that obstructed autonomous creation, hence also the normative validity of Greek art. "All art is human, not Greek," declared J. J. Wilhelm Heinse (1746–1803).[7]

Heinse was above all a sensualist and hedonist. His earliest works include a novel about a hetaera of antiquity and translations of Greek and Roman erotica. The treasures of the Düsseldorf Gallery awakened his love for the arts. His "Descriptions of Paintings," published 1776 and 1777 in the periodical *Teutscher Merkur,* are a landmark in German art criticism. They are the first professional interpretations of paintings in the German language; for Heinse endeavors to recreate in words the visual appearance of pictorial works, instead of merely explaining their intellectual content, as his contemporaries were wont to do. Moreover, he proclaims the singular rank of Rubens and, among his works, the autonomous value of the landscapes. In humanist theory, landscape was an "inferior" category, devoid of the ethical quality of history painting.

The revolutionary character of Heinse's evaluation of Rubens becomes evident in comparison with the opinion of Georg Forster, an otherwise quite perceptive critic, especially of English painting. Says Forster, "In the dithyrambic fury, which permeates everything; in those grape-like clusters of men which, as a disgusting tangle of worms, form a confused mass of limbs and—I describe with shudder what I see—a cannibalistic meat market, one recognized the wild bacchantic maenad who, full of her god, shreds Orpheus, creator of harmony."[8]

Hold against this Heinse's interpretation of the *Battle of the Amazons* (Fig. 1)! The "confused mass of limbs" appears to him as a string of interconnected scenes of combat and pursuit, which he unravels like a strategist overlooking a battlefield. Even Heinse's obsolete habit of denoting right and left as if viewed from inside the picture adds to the liveliness of his description: he experiences the depicted events as if he were part of them. Far from responding with a humanist's shudder to the sight of "blood and wounds, swimming and death, nakedness and torn garments and splendid armour," Heinse perceives nothing but "life at its highest pitch." His observations on color and light are like a painter's. Never at a loss in search of a fitting metaphor—"her body wafts in the air like a rose being plucked"—, he explains the abduction of the beautiful daughters of Leucippus (Fig. 3) as a battle of love, in which the losers gladly surrender. Heinse's description of the *Landscape with a Rainbow* (Fig. 4) grows under his hands into a *Song of the Earth.* Yet it is here that we read his naive confession: "All that I really ask of a painting (is): pleasure and illusion."

Theory—or a systematic foundation of his aesthetic experience—was not among Heinse's aims. During his three years in Italy (1780–1783), his knowledge of art broadened. He studied Michelangelo and Raphael and discovered a connection between the seductive light of Venice and the colorism of Titian and Veronese. He learned to appreciate ancient art; however, in opposition to Winckelmann, he perceived the *Laocoon* as a "tragedy of nature."[9] Heinse even wondered why Winckelmann presented just the *Laocoon* as an instance of the Greek tendency to beautify everything—"as if a body infected and swollen by poison was such a lovely subject."[10] He for one would give a hundred Laocoons for a single Venus like the one by Praxiteles.

In his daily contact with the beautiful children of Rome, in bacchic orgies hosted by the Swedish sculptor Sergel, life and art became one for Heinse. From now on, poetic fiction superseded his verbal recreations of works of art. Upon his return to Germany, Heinse wrote his novel *Ardinghello and the Blessed Islands*. Since the book is constantly shifting from narrative to reflection, it is hardly successful as a work of poetry; but it is remarkable as one of the earliest manifestoes of aesthetic immoralism. The hero is a young painter of the High Renaissance. Ruthless and endowed with all but superhuman strength and beauty, he founds on some Greek islands a republic, which admits as citizens only the young and beautiful. Their religion consists in worship of nature. The civic order serves to restrain merely violence, not the free use of the psychical forces. These, however, consist primarily in the pursuit of pleasure. The strong have in this respect the greatest prerogatives, as they are possessed by the strongest desires. Based on the natural inequality of human beings, this civic order accepts war as the law of life; but within the blessed society, a war of all against all is prevented by the fact that everything is common property—including everyone's person. They live in constant give-and-take of lust, with nobody refusing himself to anyone, for jealousy is an unnatural vice, and "as soon as anything has been enjoyed entirely, let it go." "The secret aim of this state's constitution . . . was to put an end to the rule of the Turks in this happy climate, in order to restore man's original dignity. But after a period of undiminished bliss, this was thwarted by inexorable fate."[11]

The book offers a delightful insight into the working of the creative imagination if one realizes that Heinse found all the elements of this utopia prefigured in his interpretation of Rubens. "The fortifying spirit of ripening fertility," which he finds embodied in the *Land-*

scape with a Rainbow, bespeaks his pantheistic worship of nature. His loving immersion in "the thick of battle" betrays, in both the *Amazons* and the *Sennacherib* (Fig. 2), his joyous affirmation of war. In the *Rape of the Daughters of Leucippus* he sees a forceful demonstration of the right of the strongest in love. And Rubens himself, who appears to Heinse as "strength incarnate" and, moreover, as visible proof of the immanence of God in Man—this Rubens, one is tempted to think, must have been his superb model for the character of Ardinghello.

The history of art history is to a great extent (as the essays in this volume will show) a history of rehabilitations. What Heinse did for Rubens had been done, a few years earlier, by the twenty-three-year old student Johann Wolfgang Goethe[12] for Gothic architecture. Goethe's brief essay "On German Architecture" put an end to a misconception that had lasted for more than four centuries, and which has been described in great detail by Julius von Schlosser.

In April 1770 the young Goethe arrived in Strasbourg and went immediately to see the cathedral, or "Minster" (Fig. 6). Having grown up among detractors of medieval buildings, for whom the term "Gothic" denoted something "undefined, disorganized, unnatural, patched-together, tacked-on, overloaded," Goethe expected to find some "misshapen, curly-bristled monster." Instead, the building appeared to him "whole, great, and with the beauty of necessity in every smallest part, like trees of God." This impression proved strong enough to trigger a whole set of ideas that revolutionized contemporary aesthetics—even if these ideas were based on the young student's rather faulty understanding of historical fact.

Goethe believed that the entire building was the work of one single architect, Erwin von Steinbach. In truth, the structure had had at least four architects. Erwin designed only its west façade, and there is no stylistic coherence, either among façade, nave, and choir, or between the façade and its single north tower, itself the work of yet another master. Furthermore, Gothic architecture appeared to Goethe as the deepest manifestation of the German genius, inaccessible to the "effete" sensibility of the French. He was unaware that the Gothic is a thoroughly French creation, and that Strasbourg Minster is unthinkable without the precedent of Chartres, Saint-Denis, and certain other churches in Burgundy. Nor

German Essays on Art History

could the young Goethe (or, in fact, any of his contemporaries) see
that there was not only polar opposition, but also a secret kinship
between the Gothic of Strasbourg Minster and the Baroque of
Rome's St. Peter's whose colonnades he dismisses as "inappropriate
and unnecessary." He ought to have insisted upon the incompatibili-
ty of the Romance and the Germanic spirit, for his impassioned
pleas for the recognition of Gothic architecture were, in a broader
sense, inspired by the suddenly awakened German need for a national identity. In a narrower sense, it was part and parcel of his
opposition to the classicizing aesthetics of men such as J. G. Sulzer
in Berlin, or the Abbé Laugier in Paris, which ruled the day. In
Sulzer's *General Theory of the Fine Arts* Goethe found the term
"Gothic" defined as denoting everything that was formless, taste-
less, and barbaric. In Laugier's "Essai sur l'architecture," on the
other hand, he could have found a sensitive evaluation of Strasbourg Minster. Yet he read the pamphlet only halfway through and
contented himself to oppose to Laugier's idea of the "classical" hut
as archetypal building, his own of a tentlike shelter—which resembles the Gothic arch.[13]

Goethe's historical conceptions may have been faulty—but what
far-reaching conclusions he was to derive from them! He imagined
Strasbourg Cathedral the work of one single master, and this confirmed his conception of the autonomous genius, above schools and
rules, whose creations are unified because rooted in one single feeling. The "rugged strength" of the Gothic made him realize that in
art, significant form counts for more than beauty, which in the
rococo period had degenerated into mere prettiness. "Art is formative long before it is beautiful"—this profound realization allowed
the young Goethe to recognize the expressive force of primitive art,
to find harmony even in the "fantastical lines, hideous forms, and
gaudy colors" with which "the savage articulates his coconut shells,
his feathers, his body." Almost breathless in enchantment, Goethe
enumerates the individual beauties of the cathedral, and imagines
how recognition of their quality will result in a new blossoming of
the arts, in a rich harvest of living beauty.

If one turns from this youthful essay to the *Observations on the
Laocoön* (1798), it seems hard to believe that both are works by the
same author. Instead of "rugged strength," Goethe here advocates
ideal beauty. The defender of the Gothic postulates, at least tacitly,

the absolute preeminence of Greek art. Even more surprisingly, he renounces the analogy between the work of art and the creations of nature (the cathedral as a "tree of God"). The whole of his penetrating analysis of the Laocoon (Fig. 7) aims to show that "the subject is conceived in an *ideal* and *elevated* manner." Already in 1767, the young Goethe had observed that Laocoon did not cry out; however, he ascribed Laocoon's silent endurance of his pain not, like Winckelmann, to the greatness of his soul, nor, like Lessing, to an aesthetic law that prohibits violent expression, but to a simple physiological fact: "To lessen the pain, the lower part of the torso was drawn in, which made screaming impossible."[14] Now he adds (in contradistinction to Heinse) that we see neither the effect of the poison nor "the agony in a sound, beautiful body." Throughout this essay, Goethe emphasizes symmetry and harmony as hallmarks of the successful work of art, no matter how impassioned its subject. Add to this his insistence upon the idealized human form as the sole end of all artistic endeavors, upon poetic timelessness and the "fruitful moment," and it becomes clear that the panegyrist of autonomous genius has embraced again the time-honored tenets of classicism. In only one respect does Goethe diverge from orthodox classicism: in his reading of the *Laocoon* he stresses that all "that mythology has made of [Laocoon] is done away; he is only now a father with his two sons, menaced with death by the bite of two serpents." This means more than "poetic timelessness" in the sense of suppression of costume realism: it means that classical history and mythology are worthy of representation not in their time-bound particularity but solely as paradigms of the immutable conditions of human experience.

This essay was an outcome of the crisis into which the great revolutions had plunged Western humanity. Deeply aware of the historical exhaustion of Christianity, Goethe reverted back to antiquity as the base of Western civilization. His Italian journey had opened his eyes to the splendors of classical and Renaissance art. It was here, he believed, that he could find the roots of art, and from now on he strove, as theoretician, critic, and, one might almost say, as impresario, to promote an art that was classical in style, yet universally human in spirit. His position as the acknowledged intellectual leader of German-speaking Europe seemed to grant him the necessary authority. His means toward this end were a periodical, the *Propyläen,* whose first issue was headed by the *Observations on the Laocoon,* and the organization of annual art competitions. However, Goethe's originally broad-minded and vital precepts had somewhat hardened in their didactic application, and in the face of rising romanticism, his advocacy of classical art became a hopeless rearguard action. The *Propyläen* ran only through six issues from October 1798 until November 1800. The competitions were held from 1799 until 1805, when they were suspended for lack of entries. They had not succeeded in attracting promising artists.

Yet it would be wrong, on the grounds of these facts, to consider Goethe a disenchanted progressive who at an early age (and irrevocably) went conservative. Seen in the context of his entire career, the essays on *German Architecture* and on the *Laocoön* appear less incompatible, for they are both rooted in that feeling for organic vitality and spiritualized sensuality that informs all of Goethe's manifold activities as poet, naturalist, historian, and critic. Nor were his artistic interests and critical studies limited to classical, or classically inspired, works. His collections included Greek bronzes, Byzantine ivories, Gothic stained glass; drawings by his contemporaries, Carstens, Friedrich, Fuseli, prints by Dürer, Claude, Rembrandt, Tiepolo, John Martin. He wrote perceptively about Leonardo's *Last Supper* and Mantegna's *Triumph of Caesar;* about Ruysdael and Claude, Memling and Cranach and, not least, about those late-medieval paintings which, in the wake of the Napoleonic secularization of Church property, were collected by the brothers Boisserée. When the same brothers campaigned for the restoration of Cologne Cathedral, Goethe's youthful enthusiasm for Gothic architecture reawakened, and he lent them his support. If he had nothing but scorn for the pious medievalizing painting of the Nazarenes, he was all the more receptive to the dark romanticism of Delacroix's illustrations of his own *Faust.* Himself an *artiste manqué,* the old Goethe was sensitive enough to recognize in the works of C. D. Friedrich and P. O. Rungs the dawn of a new art.

Throughout his life, Goethe was an enlightened realist. Therefore, he had little use for the aspirations of the romantics—their desire to transcend the boundaries of the ego and of the known world; their interest in the occult in nature and in the soul; their striving for national unity, and their ensuing search for the mythical origins of the Germanic nation; finally, their wish to escape the harsh realities of the present through immersion in an idealized past.

This last tendency found eloquent expression in a curious little book by the short-lived Wilhelm Heinrich Wackenroder, *Effusions of an Art-Loving Monk* (1797).[15] Given Goethe's rejection of the entire new trend, one can understand his annoyance when some of his younger admirers credited him with the authorship of the anonymously published work. Wackenroder, a Protestant, had a revelation while visiting the Catholic cathedral of Bamberg. Both its architecture and its function as the center of a colorful cult and a joyous religious community convinced him of the still-unbroken vitality of the Christian tradition, which he believed was capable of restoring art to its lost splendor. An emulation of the pious masters of the Middle Ages and, above all, a reestablishment of the union of art and religion should accomplish this end. This was Wackenroder's doctrine. In actual fact, he knew very little medieval art, and what he knew — the Gothic buildings of Nürnberg — he did not approve of. Wackenroder's essays are permeated by a strange paradox: he writes about the artists of the early and High Renaissance, about Piero di Cosimo, Franceso Francia, as well as Leonardo and Raphael, as though they were medieval masters, totally disregarding their classicism, stressing only the Christian character of their art. The same holds for his central chapter on Dürer, which is reprinted here. Ignorant of Dürer's learned humanism, Wackenroder presents him as a simple and untrained craftsman, inspired only by his piety and his honest mind. This wish–image was quickly adopted by the romantics. Witness Friedrich Schlegel's aphorism: "The German artist has no character, or he has the character of an Albrecht Dürer, Kepler, Hans Sachs, of a Luther or Jakob Böhme. Righteous, ingenuous, thorough, precise, and profound is this character, thereby innocent and a little clumsy."[16] The importance of Wackenroder's instantly popular book for the art of the next few decades was enormous. After Wackenroder's death his friend, the poet Ludwig Tieck, edited another manuscript of his, *Phantasies on Art* (1799), and wrote his own novel, *Franz Sternbald's Travels* (1798), about a pupil of Dürer's who travels to Italy in pursuit of religious art and romantic love. With these three books a new creed was born. That its emphasis on religious art and medieval, pre-

Reformation Christianity should bring its Protestant spokesmen close to Catholicism was only natural. The poet Novalis took the lead when, in the hymnic prose of his *Christianity, or Europe* (1799; published 1826), he created a transfigured image of the Christian Middle Ages; the essay ends with a vision of "the holy time of eternal peace, when the New Jerusalem will be the capital of the world," thus anticipating the political aims of the Catholic restoration after 1815.

The Catholic restoration was the cause to which Friedrich Schlegel (1772–1829)[17] devoted his entire intellectual energy—as critic of arts and letters and also, during the Austrian insurrection against Napoleon, as speech writer for the Archduke Karl or, later, as counselor with the Austrian legation at the Diet of the German Confederation in Frankfurt. A native Hanoverian, Schlegel saw in the multinational Austrian Empire the closest paradigm of that universal theocracy envisioned—on the model of the Holy Roman Empire—by Novalis. The French Revolution and the Napoleonic conquest of Germany directed the political orientation of the youthful Schlegel from republicanism to monarchism, from cosmopolitanism to patriotism. The decisive event, however, was his conversion to Catholicism. Wackenroder, Tieck, and Novalis impressed upon his mind that art was inseparable from religion, that the glorification of Christianity was the sole purpose of art. As a critic, Schlegel attempted to prove that this lofty purpose had indeed determined the course of European painting as long as it was good and strong, and that only a return to its sacred roots could result in a renewal of the arts. He thus became both pioneer and spokesman of that new trend of Christian and medievalizing German painting, which is known as the Nazarene movement.

Schlegel acquired his basic art-historical knowledge—and wrote his trailblazing essays—between 1802 and 1804. His "Views and Ideas of Christian Art" are included in five loosely structured essays, united under the heading of "Descriptions of Paintings from Paris and the Netherlands." They were published in Schlegel's periodical, *Europa*. The first three ("Notice of the Paintings in Paris," "On Raphael," and "Supplement of Italian Paintings") were written in Paris, 1802/03, under the impact of the collections in the Louvre, which had been greatly, if only temporarily, enlarged by Napoleon's plundering of Italy, Germany, and the Netherlands. In

September 1803, the Boisserée brothers arrived in Paris and befriended Schlegel. Trained lovers of art, they opened his eyes to the
splendors of Gothic architecture, and took him via Belgium, Aachen,
and Düsseldorf to their home town, Cologne. In the course of this
trip Schlegel gained greatly in firsthand knowledge of art and architecture. He was also present when the Boisserées laid the ground-
work for their collection of early German and Netherlandish paintings. Hence, when he drafted—in the spring and summer of
1804—the *Second* and *Third Supplement of Ancient Paintings*, he
wrote from a comparatively broader and safer basis of scholarship.

As will be seen, Schlegel's views on art are not free from contra-
dictions; yet their outlines are simple enough. Right at the beginning he states that he has a taste for only ancient painting. Among
the Italians, he prefers Masaccio, Perugino, Bellini, and Mantegna
to the masters of the High Renaissance; he likes the early Raphael
better than the mature, classically inspired one, and has little sympathy for Leonardo, even less for Michelangelo. Titian, Correggio,
Giulio Romano, and Andrea del Sarto are for him the "last painters" before the universal decline, which is marked by those extremes of mannerism, Reni and Rubens. However, since Schlegel
writes as a German critic with the express aim of establishing guidelines for German artists, he saves his loving empathy for the artists
of the Old German and Old Netherlandish schools, which he treats
more or less as a unity. The course of development runs from the
quasi-scientific foundation of painting in the works of Jan van Eyck
through the philosophical art of Dürer to the portrait realism of
Holbein. A high point of pious inwardness is marked by the art of
Memling (Schlegel calls him "Hemmelink"). The eccentric works
of Lucas van Leyden are a marginal phenomenon. Even before van
Eyck, however, Schlegel finds in the School of Cologne all those
qualities of devout workmanship, heartfelt simplicity, and naive
piety that are, according to him, the hallmarks of divine inspiration. Though certainly helped by the Boisserées, Schlegel writes
about the Master of the Life of the Virgin ("Israel von Meckenem"),
or about the Adoration altarpiece by Stephan Lochner (which he
mistakenly attributes to Wilhelm von Köln) with the excitement of
an epochal discovery. Those are the artists whom the new generation of painters should emulate—not the Greeks and Romans! The
plastic beauty of the ancients can serve as a model only for the
sculptor. Classical mythology, so inferior to the spiritual beauty of

Christianity, engenders much too readily effete voluptuousness or, as in the case of J. L. David, an odious mixture of theatricality and republicanism.[18]

Schlegel's ideas about the identity of art and religion, and about the superiority of pre-Renaissance art, are expressed with rare clarity in the opening paragraphs of the *Second Supplement,* which precede our excerpts. His interpretations of Sebastiano del Piombo's *Martyrdom of Saint Agatha* (Fig. 9), and Altdorfer's *Battle of Alexander* (Fig. 10) are prime examples of his power of description. Yet they hardly exemplify those values that he upheld so zealously; in fact, they run counter to his most heartfelt views. Concerning the *Battle of Alexander,* Schlegel remarks that "this little Iliad in colors" could teach "the thinking painter . . . the essence of chivalry." For once, the romantic poet in him gains the upper hand over the theologian.

The *Martyrdom of Saint Agatha* presents a more difficult problem. It is a work by a follower of Michelangelo—and the latter, according to Schlegel, was responsible for so much of the ensuing degeneration of the arts. Moreover, he characterizes it as a "classical work," pervaded by that stoicism which, as he well knew, was cherished by the despised school of David. Why, then, did he make this painting the subject of one of his most detailed, and certainly most loving, descriptions? I deny myself the psychohistorian's search for an unconscious motivation, even though the sensual ardor of Schlegel's prose betrays an uncommon degree of emotional participation. As Hans Eichner[19] has shown, it was Schlegel's ideological opposition to Goethe that attracted him to this picture. Goethe's mouthpiece, the art historian Heinrich Meyer, had published in the *Propyläen* an article about suitable subjects for the visual arts which, based on Goethe's own ideas, sharply censured the traditional themes of Christian iconography: "mystical" subjects were "indifferent," the Crucifixion "repellent," and martyrdoms were "uncomfortable, even if a tasteful artist could perhaps treat some of them in a way not offensive to the eye and the feelings." Compare Schlegel's impassioned plea for the depiction of martyrdoms, which in every instance repeat the Passion of Christ! The front lines were clear: on the one side was Goethe's belated battle for an art inspired by classical antiquity and on the other was Schlegel's medievalism, and his unshakable belief in Catholic Christianity as the sole inspiration for modern painting.

The course taken by German art during the following thirty years unequivocally declared Schlegel the winner. Many of Germany's most gifted artists embraced his precepts, which Goethe found sickly and retrogressive; a *passéiste* movement united the German avant-garde. It was a satisfaction to Friedrich Schlegel when, fifteen years after the publication of his essays, he reviewed the exhibition of German artists in Rome's Palazzo Caffarelli, in which the Nazarenes and, among them, his own stepson Philipp Veit, figured so prominently. It was also a satisfaction to see the Boisserées' collection of medieval painting acquired in 1827 by King Ludwig I of Bavaria and made accessible to the public. Schlegel had used the art of the past as an instrument of *propaganda fide*; its scholarly investigation began with Carl Friedrich von Rumohr.

Rumohr (1785–1843)[20] represents the type of the independent scholar–aristocrat. He accomplished his lifework unhampered by career considerations, and helped by the privileged position to which he had been born. He spent his life as a bachelor, "capricious and obstinate like a carriage horse," as he characterized himself. As a landowner, he engaged in economic and agricultural studies, with a special interest in irrigation. As a gourmet, he wrote the most scintillating of all cookbooks. Rumohr's worldly experiences found their way into a manual of good manners and into a novel about the travels of an eighteenth-century diplomat in Germany and France. His immersion in Italian history resulted in translations of Trecento novellas and in historical novellas of his own. However, it was his overriding love of art that triggered his lasting achievements. Rumohr bought paintings and conceived the installation for the Berlin Museum, founded by Frederick William IV. He became a tasteful collector—and the founder of documentary, or philological, art history.

It may be that Rumohr felt frustrated because he himself was denied artistic creativity. Yet he was born with the gift of discerning connoisseurship. He received decisive stimuli for his art-historical work in Rome, in the company of both neoclassical and Nazarene artists. Of crucial importance was his contact with Barthold Georg Niebuhr, for this learned historian introduced him to archival research.

Rumohr's masterpiece, the *Italian Studies* (1827–1831)[21] traces the history of Italian painting (with occasional observations on sculpture and architecture) from early Christian times to the death of Raphael. It was Rumohr's conviction that "one cannot enjoy a work of art without having clarified the circumstances accompanying and conditioning its creation." Hence he thoroughly searched the Italian archives for documents and read critically all the sources. Most notably, he was the first modern scholar to make use of the long-neglected manuscript of Ghiberti's *Commentarii.* However, the historical knowledge gained from these sources provided him with only a base for visual study. The core of Rumohr's method was autopsy, and the careful registration and comparison of all technical, formal, and expressive characteristics of the works under investigation.

Rumohr rejected the romantics' confounding of ideological content and visual fact, as exemplified by Schlegel. For him, its visual appearance is the essence of the work of art. He defines the creative process as determined by *perception* and *representation.* The artist's understanding of nature lends validity to his perception; his originality determines the quality of his representation. In Quattrocento art, representation is more advanced than perception. A perfect balance between the two—and the summit of art—have been reached with Raphael. After Raphael, art deteriorated. Rumohr pays minute attention to the technical aspect of artistic creation; hence his somewhat narrow definition of style as "habitual compliance with the requirements of the material."[22] This concept was later greatly expanded by Semper. It means, in the case of sculpture, that the heaviness of marble requires static, stable, and equilibrated creations, a requirement that Rumohr finds better fulfilled by Thorvaldsen than by Michelangelo.[23] Like Schlegel, Rumohr wants perception to be "honest, accurate, objective, and severe."[24] He therefore rates the Old German masters higher than Rubens. Yet he does not think that the subject alone gives the work its value. Perception and representation can ennoble repellent subjects. There are many individual beauties—not one single Platonic ideal, as in Winckelmann's view. As a historian of style, Rumohr wants to do justice to all schools of all times. Most remarkable in this respect is his positive evaluation of Hellenistic and Roman art; he praises the reliefs on the Arch of Titus for their vital representation of contemporary life.[25] However, Rumohr does not always live up to his principles. In his rejection of the Baroque, in his depreciation of the "raw" energy of Donatello and Michelangelo, and, not least, in his ambivalence toward Giotto, the subject of our excerpt, he appears ensnared in Nazarene prejudice.

Rumohr's discussion of Giotto shows both the progressive and the conservative features of his method. Regardless of the literary tradition, he bases his selection of safely attributable works on the only one that bears Giotto's signature (the Baroncelli polyptych, Fig. 11). He accepts as authentic only works that correspond to the descriptive categories that he derives from the signed one. Among these categories, it is above all his observation on Giotto's color (linked to his use of a new binding medium) that shows Rumohr's astute eye. This approach marks the great advance of Rumohr's method over the methods of his predecessors; it is for this attitude that he is considered the initiator of the scientific study of art. The exactitude of his method by far outweighs his problematic conclusions, which result in an undue reduction of Giotto's oeuvre. After all, most of Rumohr's attributions and misattributions continue to be debated to the present day.[26]

On the other hand, Rumohr's interpretation of Giotto's artistic character will leave the modern reader perplexed. We are used to admiring the abstract qualities in Giotto's painting, and to take them as the expression of a timeless, transcendental spirit. Instead, Rumohr stresses affect and action, and the observation of life as it is, as the essence of Giotto's innovation. Although, Rumohr argues, the artistic standards of his time did not yet allow Giotto to create a physiognomically exact illusion of reality, yet his new naturalness was sufficient to estrange art from that religious austerity which was the essence of older painting. Almost insidiously, Rumohr uses the anecdotal tradition to build up his image of Giotto as a man: He is worldly, jocose, a shrewd businessman, and a cynical critic of the corruptions of monasticism; he is not even loath to poke fun at biblical tradition. With that illegitimate variety of argumentation that seeks to deduce the artistic character of a man from his moral temper, Rumohr concludes that such an artist was by necessity unable to do justice to those holy subjects which he was called upon to glorify with his brush. How could he arrive at this bewildering judgment?

Part of it is tradition. The opinion of Giotto as the initiator of a new truth to nature was a persistent topos from Boccaccio to Vasari, and understandably so. If Giotto's art appears "abstract" as seen against the High Renaissance, it is indeed "closer to nature" than the works of his predecessors, Duccio and Cimabue, let alone the earliest sacred art of Tuscany. Moreover, Rumohr was appalled at the thoroughly etherealized Giotto drawn by his former disciple, the Nazarene critic J. D. Passavant, against whom he strikes out at the end of his discourse.[27] Rumohr despised Nazarene mawkishness. He was not even insensitive to the earthiness of Giotto. Yet there was nonetheless enough of Nazarene idealism in him to find "frivolous" Christ's embroidered sleeves and the noisy angelic music in the Baroncelli polyptych. Under those premises it was inevitable that Rumohr should disattribute the cycle of the Legend of Saint Francis in the Upper Church in Assisi. There is too much here, Rumohr thinks, even for Giotto himself, of that unholy joy in colorful ornament and popular narration, through which Giotto estranged art from its sacred purpose. Hence, the frescoes must date from the first half of the fifteenth century, when art seemed forever tied to that "rather lowly level which Giotto had achieved." It is significant that to the present day, Anglo-Saxon and German scholars have tended to disattribute the Legend of Saint Francis, whereas the Italian critics never questioned Giotto's authorship. Maybe Schlosser is right in assuming that at the root of Rumohr's discomfort with Giotto, there is the Northerner's reluctance to accept the Italians' ease in dealing with both the all-too-human and the supernatural.[28]

The first adequate interpretation of the art and personality of Rembrandt—yet another rehabilitation—is due to an outsider, Eduard Kolloff (1811–1879).[29] I do not know the circumstances that drove this somewhat elusive scholar from Polish Galicia to Paris. It may be that this move was a result of his contact with a group of politically radical writers, called "Young Germany." Some of these, like Heine and Börne, settled after the July Revolution in Paris, and Kolloff dedicated two articles to the memory of Börne. Furthermore, he owed his first appointment at the Louvre to its revolutionary director, Philippe Jeanron, and had to leave with him in 1849. (Kolloff contributed notes and commentaries to Jeanron's translation of Vasari.) However, his political sympathies seem to have changed in his middle years: In his essay on Rembrandt he speaks caustically of the "most undemocratic ink, in which his quill is dipped."[30] From 1853 until 1877 he worked as librarian in the print room of the Bibliothèque Nationale. When in 1872 Wilhelm von Bode offered Kolloff the directorship of the Berlin print room, he declined: slaving away in a subaltern position, which consisted mostly in providing fashion designers with models for their historicizing costumes, he had lost both the drive and the capacity for such a position.

Kolloff wrote a travelers' guide to Paris and essays about the Paris museums, buildings, and art exhibitions. In 1840 he published a paper on "The Development of Modern Art out of the Art of Antiquity until the Epoch of the Renaissance".[31] The importance of this work is twofold: On the one hand, it rejects Winckelmann's concept of harmonious, serene, and undaemonic Greek antiquity, thus anticipating insights of Burckhardt and Nietzsche. On the other, it discards the romantic idea of the "divinely" inspired Middle Ages by stressing that the time from the third to the thirteenth century was far from being an artistic wasteland.[32] Kolloff's observations on Byzantine art anticipate Burckhardt's study of *The Time of Constantine the Great* (1853); his insistence upon the validity of "interim styles" paved the way toward Riegl's assertion that there are no periods of decline (see below, pp. xlvi).

In his essay on Rembrandt, Kolloff had, first of all, to do away with misconceptions and slander. He cleansed Rembrandt's memory from the accusations of avarice, vulgarity, ignorance, blasphemy, and alchemy. Rembrandt's bankruptcy was due not so much to his collector's mania as to the dismal economic situation in Holland. Kolloff dispels the notion of the plebeian Rembrandt, ridden by a republican's resentment against the patrician royalist and Catholic Rubens, as well as the image of Rembrandt as a "cunning fanatic, who . . . at times with covert irony, at times with undisguised passion, attacked all higher tendencies in art, and debased and ridiculed with his burlesque especially the classical and biblical subjects."[33] Instead, Kolloff intends to base his interpretation on a dispassionate study of Rembrandt's paintings.

Almost all the works he discusses have until very recently been accepted as genuine. In a number of cases, Kolloff corrects the traditional identifications of their subjects. In masterful descriptions of Rembrandt's biblical paintings he proves that the allegedly ignorant artist was well versed in the Scriptures, and brought to their pictorial interpretation an understanding that was both profoundly religious and humanely sensitive. Against the aesthetics of romanticism, Kolloff maintains that Rembrandt's time was a time of religious controversy, and pervaded by Renaissance naturalism and scepticism, hence no longer able to produce devotional images in the style of Memling or Fra Angelico. Rembrandt was "the most notable and original among the Dutch masters of the seventeenth century,"[34] yet he did not appear like a meteor in the sky of art. Kolloff traces the origins of his style via Lastman to Elsheimer (*not* via Honthorst to Caravaggio, who for him is still a "vulgar" naturalist), and points at his borrowings from Lucas van Leyden, Schongauer, and Dürer.

Kolloff devotes special attention to Rembrandt's fantastic costumes (which he relates to the international exchange in the Amsterdam harbor) and to his portrayal of the biblical patriarchs in the persons of his Jewish friends. At this point it becomes evident to what extent Kolloff's art-historical study was linked to his contact with the most recent art of France. He points out that the Protestant exegesis of the Bible, with its emphasis upon the Jewishness of the Old Testament, influenced seventeenth-century Dutch painting in much the same way as the conquest of Algeria influenced the French painters of Kolloff's own day. As the Dutch artists found their biblical models among the Jews, so did the French find theirs among the Bedouins, "where the drapery folds still pleat in the same way as in the days of Jacob and Abraham."[35] This theory of the immutability of Arab (or Semitic) life had been promoted in the 1830s by the history painter Horace Vernet.[36]

Kolloff's high estimation of Rembrandt's art has its limit in his discomfort with his "coarse" human types. He speaks of Rembrandt's female nudes with the revulsion of an aesthete. On the other hand, he finds moving words for Rembrandt's landscapes in their entirely new reduction to broad lines and masses. In addition, he derives his most sensitive observations from his study of Rembrandt's color and light. These are the subject of our excerpt, and may speak for themselves.

Jacob Burckhardt (1818–1879)[37] is represented here by a text, drafted shortly after he had finished his university studies, and "published" in a journal that circulated in only one handwritten copy among a handful of friends. Until recently this text was practically inaccessible even in German. To be sure, Burckhardt, who was a conservative at heart, was soon to sever his ties with this circle and its head, the radical Gottfried Kinkel. In later years he even declared his (mostly poetical) contributions to the journal as "trash," and protested "for all time" against their publication.[38] Yet his diary notes "On Murillo" anticipate essential features of his mature approach to art and history. They thus offer an astonishing example of how the mind of a genius can be perfectly formed, even before he embarks on his life's work.

Political conflict looms already in the lead paragraph in Burckhardt's jibe against the liberal regent of Spain, Espartero, who was the leader in the struggle against the absolutist Carlists. Burckhardt's thoughts are drawn to Seville, where the internecine battle rages, because it was in Seville that Murillo found the model for his *Immaculate Conception,* whose artistic quality touches the young scholar at his core, for the model's beauty fills his soul with erotic enchantment. Little does it matter that the work triggering Burckhardt's far-reaching observations was in all probability not that crown of Murillo's Madonnas, the *Immaculada Soult* (which found its way into the Louvre only in 1852), but the work of an imitator, perhaps from the beginning of the eighteenth century; this latter painting belonged to Louis Philippe and was part of his *Musée espagnol* in the Louvre (Fig. 12).[39]

Already Burckhardt's characterization of Murillo the man (which might remind readers of this anthology of Heinse's description of Rubens), sounds a leitmotif of his interpretation of history. Murillo is a *Gewaltmensch,* a term for which there is no precise equivalent in English, and which has been translated here, rather unsatisfactorily, as "a force of nature." It means Man in the all but superhuman development of his faculties of soul, mind, and body; a personality, free from intellectual bondage, religious mania, guilt, and fear; self-possessed, master of his own reason and sensuality, hence capable of mastering and enjoying life. This is the description of that new humanity which, according to Burckhardt, came into being in the Italian Renaissance; this is how he would characterize, in *The Civilization of the Renaissance in Italy* (1860),[40] the princes, condottieri, humanists, and majestic women of the period. In terms such as these Burckhardt was to define for several generations their conception of the Renaissance.

German Essays on Art History

Burckhardt writes about Murillo; but his musings engender the outlines of an entire schema of the development of art between Jan van Eyck and the Baroque, with polemical sidelights on the art of his own time. In the Northern countries, the discovery of reality through van Eyck infused painting with a palpable sense of contemporary life at the expense of that wonderful naive idealism which permeated the older schools. In the South, the awakening of realism occurred one century later, yet it was inseparable from the discovery of antiquity. Hence, during the "Medicean epoch," Italian art reached its summit (which Burckhardt finds embodied in Raphael's *Sistine Madonna*) in a thorough interpenetration of idealism and realism, while in the North, the Reformation prevented a thorough reception of the new spirit. After that brief period of unparalleled blossoming, Italian art degenerates in Rome and Florence "into a hopelessly insipid, one-sided idealism," whereas the sensuous art of Venice experiences, in the late works of Titian, the gradual ascent of realism, which then "runs away in large leaps" with Caravaggio and his offshoot, the Neapolitan school, from which Murillo's art derives.

Burckhardt, who is so deeply moved by the down-to-earth loveliness of Murillo's *Immaculada,* must come to terms with the lack of idealism in his art. He explains the Spaniard's gloomy landscapes as an outcome of his need for solitude. But his observation that Murillo fails whenever he has to depict the ideality of Christ, whereas all his passion goes into his maidenly Virgins, his ecstatic saints, his Prodigal Son, and his beggar boys—this observation requires a supra-individual explanation. Burckhardt was at the time collecting material for a projected history of the Counter-Reformation; thus he found the explanation in the spiritual conditions of that period: In counterreformatory art, the expressive emphasis shifts from the object of adoration to the adoring subject, from the holy persons to the martyrs, ecstatic visionaries, and sufferers for their faith. This whole complex of concepts was to reappear in Burckhardt's later writings—in his addenda to the art-historical handbooks of his teacher Franz Kugler (1847–1848), in his own lectures on the Counter-Reformation (1863–1864), finally in his posthumously published *Reminiscences of Rubens* (1898).[41] Another insight, namely, that the blossoming of art is independent of economic misery and political corruption, heralds again *The Civilization of the Renaissance in Italy,* and so does Burckhardt's burning love for the Mediterranean, its sensuality and beauty. His tendency toward universal history expresses itself in his wish that one should "give every age its due"; in his recognition of the "idealism" in Oriental and Mexican art (reminiscent of the young Goethe's defense of primitive artifacts); and finally, in his comprehension of the spirituality in Rubens's and Rembrandt's painting. With these notions he bolsters his opposition to the Nazarenes' attempt at reviving the pious art of the Middle Ages. As a historian, Burckhardt writes "with a constant eye on the present world."

Thus, his spontaneous jottings on Murillo read like a prelude to his later works. Burckhardt's aims were twofold. As a historian of art, he wanted to describe, without undue emphasis on national schools, the independent development and mutations of forms and styles. As a historian of culture, he intended the same with regard to the development of the human spirit. *The Time of Constantine the Great* (1853)[42] paints a (quite somber) picture of the intellectual history of that period, whose art-historical rehabilitation had been first envisioned by Kolloff. *The Cicerone* (1855)[43] is a most spirited "guide to the enjoyment of the artworks of Italy," from antiquity to the eighteenth century, written in an unorthodox mix of biographical, topographical, historical, and aesthetic information. *The Civilization of the Renaissance in Italy* is unsurpassed for the plasticity of its narration. However, its sequel, *The History of the Renaissance in Italy* (1867)[44] is in actual fact a history of Renaissance architecture. Concentrating with unusual rigidity on the autonomous development of architectural forms (and their purposes), it anticipates in many ways the methods of Wölfflin, Wickhoff, and Riegl.

This was the last book published by Burckhardt. Free from that craving for fame that he had described as one of the moving forces in Renaissance individualism, he lived for the rest of his life exclusively for his teaching at Basel University, which pursuit gave him personal fulfillment and happiness. In addition, he delivered, during the remaining thirty years, approximately 170 public lectures dealing with every possible aspect of Western culture. Only after his death were the magnificent fruits of his later research published. The latter include *Reminiscences of Rubens,* unforgettable for the intensity of its compositional analyses. Then came his *History of*

Greek Civilization (1898–1902),[45] which definitely demolished Winckelmann's concept of the "harmonious" Greek character—through its stress on the cruelly undemocratic class structure of the *polis,* on the ingrained pessimism of the Greeks, and on the predominance of the tragic element in Greek myth and history. A similar lack of illusions permeates the *Reflections on Universal History* (1868–1873),[46] however, with even stronger emphasis on the redeeming faculty of art.

Burckhardt's successor in his Basel chair was Heinrich Wölfflin (1864–1945).[47] Throughout his career, Wölfflin was concerned with the analysis of forms and styles, and their transformations. He was not interested in synthesizing the entire intellectual history of an epoch, as Burckhardt had done; nor was it his aim to add new material to the canon of known works. His research centered on two epochs, the Renaissance and the Baroque, and within these he dealt mostly with masterpieces, for only a masterpiece could yield those insights that he attempted to systematize. Wölfflin's theoretical conclusions have hardly stood the test of time. Yet his visual analyses are still the prime models for all similar endeavors. Wölfflin taught in Basel, Berlin, Munich, and Zurich. Personally reticent, he was a disciplined and demanding teacher. When his critics called him a "formalist," he accepted this as a title of honor.

His essay on "The Classical Triumphal Arches in Italy" (1893) is an offshoot of his book, *Renaissance and Baroque,* of 1888.[48] In the latter, Wölfflin had attempted to describe the genesis of baroque architecture as a transformation of High Renaissance forms in the direction of painterliness, grandeur, massiveness, and movement. In the essay he was to trace the development of the triumphal arches in order to find out whether Roman art followed the same course. To this task Wölfflin brings an exquisite sense of proportion, economy, and functional logic in architecture, recreating verbally every shift in the articulation of the buildings and judging their success and failure with unerring taste. As soon as a similar pattern of development has been established, Wölfflin draws those parallels that are his principal concern. The Arch of Aosta (Fig. 13) corresponds to the early Renaissance architecture of Brunelleschi; the Arch of Titus (Fig. 14), to the Cancelleria (which he still ascribes entirely to Bramante); the Arch of Septimius Severus (Fig.

16), to Michelangelo. (In *Renaissance and Baroque,* Wölfflin had attempted to show the roots of the Baroque in Michelangelo, whose genius he acknowledges, in spite of his misgivings concerning the "oppressive, unredeemed" character of his forms: "Michelangelo never embodied a happy existence.")[49]

Evidently, Wölfflin conceives both the development of Roman art and the evolution of art from the fifteenth to the seventeenth century in terms of "rise and fall," and he postulates "that a rise and fall in just about the same sense can be traced in every style in the history of art." It needs hardly to be argued that this is not the case. Concerning Renaissance and Baroque, Wölfflin's schema has been overthrown by our recognition of Mannerism as a separate, intermediary style; nor does the scheme apply to the art before, or after, the periods that he studies. Michael Podro, who has written the most penetrating recent critique of Wölfflin, points to one more problematic feature of our essay — its teleological concept of artistic evolution. In other words, Wölfflin describes the evolution of the triumphal arches as if in each consecutive monument the architects had solved a problem, or eliminated a defect which, they felt, was present in the preceding one. This, of course, would presuppose "that there was an ideal to which all artists working in the genre were striving."[50] In a somewhat different form, this concept would reappear in the writings of Riegl. Wölfflin abandoned this concept. But he continued to treat the visual tradition as autonomous, in isolation from all other historical manifestations: new forms are always transformations of older forms.

In his *Classic Art, An Introduction to the Italian Renaissance* (1899),[51] Wölfflin describes the transformation that painting and sculpture underwent from the fifteenth to the sixteenth century. He concentrates on the works of Leonardo, Michelangelo, Raphael, Fra Bartolommeo, and Andrea del Sarto, largely excluding biographical detail. Wölfflin's demonstration consists largely of comparisons. In describing the differences between two childbed scenes, the *Birth of the Baptist* by Domenico Ghirlandajo and the *Birth of Mary* by Andrea del Sarto, he describes the shift from the "philistine" attitude of the Quattrocento to the "noble nonchalance" of the Cinquecento.[52] However, if this reflects the new intellectual and social climate of the High Renaissance, there are other redirections of a formal nature, namely, the clarification of the composition, the enrichment of its visual content, and the integration of its components in a "necessary" unity. These factors cannot be derived from the temper of the time; they are "in themselves inexpressive and belong to a development of a purely optical kind."[53]

Wölfflin's interpretations of classic art derive much of their passion from a Northerner's hankering after the Italians' seemingly inborn poise, sense of form, and gift for the unaffected grand gesture. He interprets *The Art of Albrecht Dürer* (1905) as a synthesis of Northern naturalism and Southern idealism. It was "the craving for a beauty which keeps one spellbound like a mathematical deduction, the longing . . . to ascend to the 'pure forms,'"[54] that drove Dürer to Italy. Wölfflin defends Dürer against certain nationalistic allegations, which implied that the artist had endangered his German identity through his concern with measure and proportion. Yet Wölfflin hints how much energy Dürer lost in his struggle to resolve the conflict between Italian form and German late-Gothic feeling for nature.[55] At the end of his life, Wölfflin deemed the art of the South to be limited by its anthropocentrism, as opposed to the pantheism of Germanic art.[56]

In evaluating the *Principles of Art History* (1915),[57] one must recognize that in using the term "*Grund*begriffe," Wölfflin aimed at a primary level of "imaginative beholding" which, according to him, underlies, and precedes, all individual expression. He thus refuted the objection that he disregarded the significance of the artistic personality. It is on this fundamental level, he thought, that changes in style can best be grasped. Again he dwells on the transformation of Renaissance into Baroque, which he describes as a transformation of "linear" into "painterly," "planimetric" into "recessional," "closed" into "open" forms, and so on. Again, he postulates an autonomous visual tradition and leaves it to the parallel development of general culture to account for those changes in the modes of representation not covered by his categories—mostly the spiritual, emotional, iconological approach to subject matter. In this book, Wölfflin's art of descriptive analysis reaches its ultimate refinement. Even if its universal validity cannot be accepted, *Principles of Art History* offers a unique school of seeing. As one of his students, Wilhelm Waetzoldt, put it: "In Wölfflin's lecture rooms there blows the wind of the studios."[58] His isolating of the formal aspect in art found an answer in the emergence, after 1910, of an art of pure form.

Theodor Hetzer (1890–1946)[59] studied with Wilhelm Vöge and Wölfflin, but his real teacher was Friedrich Rintelen, who impressed on him the unique artistic accomplishment of Giotto. Hetzer taught from 1934 onward in Leipzig, but his scholarly career was cut short by frequent illnesses and an untimely death. He continued the predominantly formal art history of Wölfflin, yet with a difference: If Wölfflin treated form as an exclusively optical phenomenon, Hetzer attached a transcendental significance to form.

The following is a summary of Hetzer's basic ideas.[60] According to him, there was one continuous period of highest achievement in European painting; it lasted from 1300 to 1800, and its founder was Giotto, for he created a new type of pictorial representation that underlies all great art during those five centuries. Hetzer's term for this type of representation is "Bild," a word which, like many German words, is sufficiently vague to cover a whole hierarchy of meanings—from the portrait snapshot to the sacred icon. For the sake of convenience, we translate Hetzer's term as "image." The meaning he attaches to it can only be inferred from his consistent use of the term in all his books; for he gives nowhere an explicit definition. The "image" results from a composition in which every element, figures, objects, landscape, and architecture, conform to those lines and planimetric segments that form the natural subdivisions of the picture plane. The predominance of planar values was by no means invalidated by the Renaissance conquest of space through perspective; in any accomplished later painting, the spatial relations evolve in accordance with those planimetric divisions. Hetzer likes to speak of the "mathematical" element in pictorial composition; it is for him equivalent to a higher reality, underlying appearances. In a mathematically ordered composition, all elements are related to the frame; hence, such a composition appears self-contained, and its order epitomizes the divinely ordered universe. Hetzer finds a profound significance in the original meaning of the Greek word "cosmos" = decoration: the decorative is another form of universal order. The perfect mathematical shapes of haloes, mandorlas, quatrefoils, and so forth enact a "sacralization of the 'image.'" Giotto was the first artist to make pictorial representation conform to those mathematical ground patterns. No matter how thoroughly in his paintings the living form is determined by the spirit of the narration, it is still shaped by contours, lines, and planes which in their generality come close to mathematical form. Giotto derived his sense of order from the spirit of Gothic architecture; the cathedral itself was a symbol of the order of the universe. If Giotto's figures radiate a spiritual beauty, this is not so much because of their well-shaped bodies and faces, but is the result of the well-ordered relations between figuration, picture-plane, and frame.

Evidently, the evaluation of Giotto has come a long way since Rumohr! It may be noted, in parenthesis, that in Hetzer's abstract and transcendental conception of Giotto's art, there is, as with Rumohr, "not the tiniest place" for the frescoes of the Life of Saint Francis in Assisi. If Hetzer's ideas may seem rather high flown (especially in this oversimplified summary), every reader of his works will agree that he uses them ingeniously. Hetzer's interpretative endeavors aim invariably at the highest achievements in history. His aesthetic ideal is ethically determined and forces him into opposition to the art of his own time. This can be seen in the following excerpt from his essay on *Veronese*:

> A time, which recognized genius merely in its creative isolation, and in its creative violence . . ., a time, which therefore downgraded Ghiberti in favor of Donatello, Raphael in favor of Michelangelo, Dürer in favor of Grünewald and finally, most inappropriately, Velázquez in favor of Greco, such a time must also make its choice in Venice and opt for Tintoretto instead of Veronese.[61]

Eminently civilized, Hetzer himself concentrated on artists whose achievements belong in the Apollonian realm: Giovanni Bellini, Raphael, Dürer, Titian, Tiepolo. He finds them all united by that secret (not to say, sacred) geometry which originated in Giotto. In one of his boldest essays, Hetzer detects even in the late works of Rembrandt an underlying structure that links him to Giotto—or rather, since Rembrandt could not possibly know Giotto, to those basic laws of creation which Giotto and, independent of him, Rembrandt himself had detected.[62] It is easy to see that in such observations, Hetzer relies exclusively on his own highly refined sensorium for the formal and spiritual irradiations of works of art, and this leads him into a realm beyond scientific demonstrability. The same holds for his essay in the present collection. Although Hetzer's deductions there are clearly derived from a wealth of carefully studied facts, he adopts such a bird's-eye view that *The Creative Union of Classical and Northern Elements in the High Renaissance* appears as a fusion of two near-abstract artistic principles. When he goes into detail, he does not show demonstrable borrowings by Dürer from Raphael, or by Titian from Dürer, but points to a *rhythmic* kinship between Titian's *Bacchus and Ariadne* and Dürer's *Apocalyptic Riders*. There is obviously no place for such "sweeping statements" in any positivistic art history; from an artistic point of view, they shed unexpected light on the works in question. With Hetzer as with Wölfflin, it is not so much the "system" that matters, but the emphatic and almost poetic recreation in words of works of art. Hetzer had a singular gift for that most elusive of tasks, to write about color. His book on *Titian* (1935) is designated in its subtitle as a *History of His Color*;[63] in actual fact, it is a history of European colorism.

That unified epoch of painting that started with Giotto, ended with Tiepolo; it was "destroyed" (Hetzer's term) by Goya. "Francisco Goya and the Crisis in Art Around 1800" (1950)[64] is one of Hetzer's most brilliant essays. This has to be admitted, even if one disagrees with its all too negative characterization of Goya (which does not admit the artist's compassion or his enlightened humanism) and with its gloomy view of nineteenth-century art. What is most interesting in the present context is *how*, in Hetzer's description, Goya destroyed the tradition of the "image." Hetzer demonstrates it by comparing a handful of little-known, and marginal, early works by Goya, etchings after Velázquez, with their models. In the case of the dwarf, *Don Sebastian de Morra,* Goya isolates the figure against its background, he dissolves Velázquez's sense of order, and creates a tension between the figure and its surroundings. "In Goya, the background does not evoke a sensation of shelter but is turned into something inimical; *lacking compositional coordinates,* it suggests an engulfing infinity." (Italics mine.)[65]

In Hetzer's view, the precious legacy of the Renaissance, its combination of vitality with beauty and classical form, disintegrated in the nineteenth century. "After 1800, on the one hand we find the anaemic, smooth, and frigid beauty of classicism and on the other a cult of the ugly, the forceful, and the demythicized."[66] It is understandable that Hetzer, possessed of an overrefined sensibility and a marvelously unified worldview, should arrive at such conclusions.

But it is regrettable that a scholar of his stature provided ideologues from right and left with arguments for their later warfare against modern art. He himself recognized only one modern artist, who inspired him with lasting enthusiasm: Cézanne. Yet Cézanne "stood alone in front of the eternal; he could no longer connect it with forms of objective character and general validity."[67]

The following essays were written by some of the principal members of the "Viennese School":[68] Wickhoff, Riegl, Dvořák, and Schlosser. The first three of these scholars excelled in "rehabilitations"; they stressed the continuity of art in all its manifestations, to the point of eliminating any notion of "periods of decline." The fourth, Schlosser, was, at least in theory, much more concerned with the singular achievement of individual genius. Several factors account for the broad and unprejudiced approach of this school. In Vienna the contact between university and museums was closer than elsewhere. Outstanding collections directed the attention of scholars to the applied arts, both Western and non-Western, and to the hitherto neglected study of drawings. There were strong traditions of art topography, of the protection of monuments, and of the study of the literature of the arts. The "ancestor" of this school, Rudolf Eitelberger von Edelberg (1817–1885) founded the Austrian Museum of Art and Industry, and saw to the publication of *Sources for Art History and Artistic Techniques of the Middle Ages and the Renaissance.* Moritz Thausing (1835–1884) made the Albertina the foremost institution for the study of drawings and prints.

Franz Wickhoff (1853–1909)[69] was a student of both Eitelberger and Thausing. He was a scholar of universal orientation and a partisan of modern art. With the authority of his office as holder of the chair in art history, he opted against the historicizing architecture of his time, and for the iron constructions of modern engineering.[70] He defended Gustav Klimt and the Impressionists, and asked in a public lecture whether a Millet or a Bastien-Lepage should be ranked below a Raphael or a Titian![71] Wickhoff was fascinated by the reception of Japanese art in Art Nouveau and Impressionism. Many of his studies dealt with Renaissance topics; but his major revolutionary deed was the discovery of Roman art,[72] which up until then had been downgraded as a mere corruption of Hellenistic painting and sculpture. Instead, Wickhoff points at the gradual perfection of the Roman vault, from the Pantheon to the Basilica of Constantine, and at the undisputed physiognomic intensity of Roman busts, from Vespasian to Trajan. Wickhoff's view of Roman art from Augustus to Constantine is colored by his notion of Impressionism. "Illusionism" is the first, and almost the last, word of his analysis.

In 1895, Wickhoff wrote an introduction to a facsimile edition of the *Vienna Genesis,* an early Christian manuscript of the fourth century. He found the style of its illustration determined by two factors: In an illusionistic setting, the incidents are depicted in *continuous narration:* Contrary to experience, the same persons appear repeatedly, in consecutive phases of their actions, within the same setting. This mode of representation persisted, off and on, until the High Renaissance, when in Michelangelo's Sistine ceiling God appears twice in one and the same Creation fresco. By the end of the first century, continuous narration (prime example: the reliefs on the Column of Trajan) and illusionism (the reliefs on the Arch of Titus) had become the constituents of the official art of the Roman Empire. Wickhoff traces the persistent use of these combined principles in Roman painting through the following three centuries; in his view, the development leads without a break into early Christian art.

Thus Wickhoff's introduction grew under his hands into the first outline of the history of Roman art. His is a forceful, yet biased view: He does not mention the reappearance of classicism in the Hadrianic period. Wickhoff shows the gradual ascent of illusionism not only in portraits and narrative reliefs, but also in sculptural ornament as, for instance, in a pillar adorned with roses branching out around high and narrow vases, from the tomb of the Haterii in the Lateran Museum (end of the first century A.D.).[73] In these decorative reliefs, the sculptors did not copy minutely every branch and leaf from nature; they emphasized only those elements that enhance the impression of sprouting and blossoming in a rosebush trembling in the air. Here, Wickhoff points to a profound analogy between this mode of ornamentation and the vegetal ornament of the Japanese, which likewise consists of illusionistically rendered plants and flowers in decorative (asymmetrical) arrangement. He hints ever so cautiously at the possibility that the art of the Far East might have been fertilized by classical influences, transmitted via India. What matters to Wickhoff is that the artistic currents of East and West, which had taken their separate courses through two millennia, are joined again in the art of his own time. The designers of Art Nouveau dare again to use illusionistically rendered natural forms in their vegetal ornament; there is much in plein-air painting and Impressionism that originated in the Far East. Conversely, these modern manifestations help us in appreciating neglected periods such as the art of Rome.

In the essay reprinted here, Wickhoff returns to the cross-fertilization of East and West. This opusculum, which so boldly postulates "The Historical Unity in the Universal Evolution of Art" (1898), is both progressive and retardatory. On the one hand it is a belated manifestation of that belief in the absolute preeminence of Greek art, which had inspired the entire humanist tradition since the Renaissance, but which by now was thrust aside by Realism and Impressionism, and by the dispassionate study of non-Western cultures. On the other, it is an outgrowth of Wickhoff's enthusiasm for precisely these advanced trends in art and research. We have seen how much importance he attached to the analogy between Western and Japanese illusionism. Now he sets out to prove that both Western and Far-Eastern art have their common root in the art of Greece. Wickhoff's test piece is a Chinese bronze vessel from the Chou Dynasty (Fig. 23), on which he detects indigenous Greek ornaments: the meander, parts of a palmette, and the so-called eye motif, well known from Greek vases of the second half of the sixth century B.C. (see Fig. 24). Wickhoff assumes that such motifs made their way to China at precisely this time, which was a period of massive exportation of Attic pottery. That such migrations of Greek forms to China occurred repeatedly, also in Hellenistic and Roman times, is undisputed; but that the assumed first wave "*gave this distant nation its style*," and that this proves the Greek origin of *all* art — these bold generalizations can hardly be maintained. For, to take up only one line of Wickhoff's argument: The eye motif in its specific Chinese form appears already on Chinese vessels of the twelfth and eleventh centuries B.C. Moreover, it is not even a Greek invention; witness those "eye idols," which recently have been found in great numbers, embedded in the platform of the Eye Temple in Tell Brak, Syria; they date from 3500 to 3300 B.C.[74] The occurrence of the eye motif in the most disparate cultures (Mexico, New Guinea, Nubia, and so forth) makes it much more plausible to assume, with Emanuel Loewy and E. H. Gombrich,[75] that it is apotropaic, destined to ward off evil influences. Hence, its ubiquity is not due to transcultural migration, but to a deep-seated need of the human soul.

This essay is an art-historical counterpart to the various forms of philosophical Monism, which all claim one single absolute principle as the basis of reality. In terms of Wickhoff's own work, it bears witness to his conviction that the secret goal of the entire evolution of art was the illusionistic rendition of the visible. He found this goal achieved in the art of his own time. This belief was shared by his colleague Alois Riegl.

Riegl (1858–1905)[76] taught during the last six years of his life side by side with Wickhoff at Vienna University. He came to art history via the study of law and "universal history" (Universalgeschichte). Riegl spent the crucial years of his career, from 1887 to 1897, as head of the textile department at the Austrian Museum for Art and Industry. When he was forced to renounce his museum work in favor of teaching, he sorely missed his daily contact with objects; yet he found an outlet in his work for the Central Commission for Art and Historical Monuments, which he thoroughly reformed. His draft of a law for the protection of monuments established far-reaching guidelines for this field.[77] Riegl achieved his life's work in constant struggle against illness. His death cut short a career of international consequence.

Riegl's first book, on *Ancient Oriental Rugs* (1891),[78] succeeds, in a limited area, where Wickhoff's essay "On the Historical Unity in the Universal Evolution of Art" fails. He could prove that one of the motifs most frequently used in Oriental rugs, a kind of pomegranate linked by leaves, as well as its more abstract version, the Islamic arabesque, were both transformations of a Greek ornament, the palmette linked by a vegetal scroll. Now it happened that at the time of his writing, the Egyptologist W. H. Goodyear was able to demonstrate that the palmette itself was a transformation of the Egyptian lotus. Hence, the development of one particular ornament could be traced through five thousand years! This realization induced Riegl to treat the history of ornament on a global scale in his following book, *Questions of Style* (1893).[79] His first task was to find out where and how the isolated lotus became incorporated in the continuous geometric or vegetal scroll. He found the link in Mycenaean pottery. Next, Riegl succeeded in demonstrating that the other, most widely used Greek vegetal ornament, the acanthus, was likewise an adaptation of the palmette in the shape of a leaf. He followed the transformations of the acanthus from the Corinthian capital through its Byzantine, Sassanian, and Syrian versions into its most complicated variant in Moorish art. (As E. H. Gombrich has noticed, this line of development could well be pursued further through medieval and Renaissance Europe, India, the South Seas, and China.[80]) For Riegl himself, the importance of his discovery surpassed the mere notions of continuity or of the interdependence of all Old World civilizations. In tracing the metamorphosis of the stylized palmette into the acanthus, which only gradually assumed the actual shape of the botanical species, he recognized that changes in style are not dependent upon external stimuli (the accidental discovery of a particular weed), but upon an inner dynamism that directs the evolution of forms.

It was in the light of this concept that Riegl reevaluated the hitherto neglected and disdained art of late antiquity in his most famous work, *Late Roman Art Industry* (1901).[81] Riegl had been commissioned by the Austrian Archaeological Institute to publish examples of late antique arts and crafts from the time of Constantine the Great through the so-called Migration period until the accession of Charlemagne, inasmuch as these artifacts had been unearthed in the territories of the Austro-Hungarian Empire. This induced him, taking up where Wickhoff had left off, to research the entire artistic development of the period in architecture, sculpture, painting, and the decorative arts. Late antiquity had hitherto been viewed as a period of decline, its art as the result of a barbarization of the Greco-Roman world by Eastern peoples and Celto-Germanic tribes. In Riegl's view, it was instead an eminently progressive period which, in accordance with the spiritual needs of ascendant Christianity, transformed objective classical form in the direction of modern subjectivism. He thus saw the totality of ancient art—from Egypt through Hellas and Rome to late antiquity—as a unity, its gamut running from a denial of space and the resulting emphasis

upon isolated, self-contained, tactile objects toward their incorporation, still as separate entities, in a continuum of figure and surrounding space, the "optical plane"; this process paved the way for the
spatiality of Romanesque and Gothic architecture, and toward the
Renaissance conquest of perspective. One might notice here a similarity between Riegl's notion of change from a "tactile" (or "haptic")
to an "optical" orientation, and Wölfflin's progression from "linear"
to "painterly" forms. However, in Wölfflin's view, the history of art
consists of cycles, whereas Riegl sees it as a continuous evolution.

Riegl's article "Late Roman or Oriental?" (1902) gives a summary of *Late Roman Art Industry* in the form of a polemic against
Josef Strzygowski. Strzygowski (1862–1941), the outsider within
the Viennese School, opposed what he viewed as a too-exclusive
concentration of art-historical research on the Mediterranean in
order to investigate the vast and hitherto unexplored artistic regions of the Near East, Armenia, Persia, and Russia, as well as
northern Europe. The opposite thrust of Strzygowski's work explains his antagonism to Riegl's conception of late antiquity. Where
Riegl saw a continuous evolution, Strzygowski maintained the old-
line conservative notion of a sudden demise of the classical world,
and the replacement of its artistic tradition by an influx from the
Orient. Riegl defends himself—and every reader of *Late Roman Art
Industry* will agree with him—by stating that he had taken great
care to show whatever features in late antique art did indeed touch
upon ancient Oriental elements. It should also be noted that his
book was only the first of an intended two-volume publication; the
second was to have dealt with the contribution of the newly
emerged "barbarians" to the art of late antiquity. Riegl did not live
to write this volume.

"Late Roman or Oriental?" is a lucid, yet rigorously condensed
summary of a very complex book. It conveys none of the liveliness
of Riegl's analyses of specific works of architecture, sculpture, and
painting, nor does it give an idea of his mastery in describing those
late antique metalworks that formed the starting point of his investigation. In the book he shows the four branches of the arts all
pervaded by that central principle, the isolation of the individual
form in the optical plane. It is largely through Riegl's art of descriptive analysis that one follows, or rather submits to, his sometimes
strained argument as he demonstrates that widely disparate works

such as the mosaics in San Vitale and the reliefs on fourth-century sarcophagi, or the exterior of the so-called Temple of Minerva Medica in Rome and the gold fibula from Apahida all obey the same formal impulse.[82] This underlying "aesthetic urge" is what Riegl calls the *Kunstwollen* of late antiquity. (The term does not occur in "Late Roman or Oriental?".) This is not the place to go into the complexities of this concept, nor to summarize the criticism it has received from later scholars, criticism that ranges from the total rejection by Gombrich[83] to its careful endorsement by Otto Pächt. What seems crucial to the present writer is Pächt's observation that the term *Kunstwollen*, which he translates literally as "that which wills art," implies a double meaning, namely "the seemingly conflicting notions of active volition and passive compulsion." On the one hand, all the artists of a given period, from the secular genius to the humblest craftsmen, are united in their conscious and deliberate choice of certain stylistic modes: "If the late Romans built, painted, and carved differently it was not because they could not do better, but because they wanted something radically different."[84] For Riegl, an analogy that he perceives between the late antique *Kunstwollen* and the aesthetic doctrines of Saint Augustine proves that the artists did indeed work in complete awareness of their common aims.[85] On the other hand, these aims are *imposed* upon the artists; even the greatest cannot evade them, for they are the outcome of some deeper changes in the temper of the times. How these changes come about, how they engender the changed "aesthetic urge" — those questions are not addressed by Riegl; they lie beyond art-historical research.

In his next book, *The Dutch Group Portrait,* Riegl applied his theory of the *Kunstwollen* to an art that was not anonymous — after all, it included some of the greatest works by Rembrandt and Hals — and had a well-researched sociopolitical background. What is obsolete in Riegl's approach is, on the one hand, his linking of the essential differences between "Germanic" and "Romance" art to racial categories; and on the other, his teleological view of art history, which presupposes that the naturalistic and impressionistic art of his own time was the fulfillment of the entire preceding development.[86] In other respects, this book still marks a milestone in the elucidation of the specific character of Dutch painting.

* * *

Max Dvořák (1874–1921)[87] succeeded Wickhoff in the chair of art history at the University of Vienna. At the outset of his tenure, he represented a continuation of Wickhoff and Riegl. Later on, he was to arrive at a highly personal position of his own.

Dvořák's scholarly career falls into two parts. During the first half, which lasted from the turn of the century to the middle of World War One, he subscribed, like his two predecessors, to an evolutionist conception of art history: Art evolves in a continuous flow, without retrogression or decline; its history consists in the development of new modes of representation, which aim at an ever-increasing mastery in the rendition of visible reality; the art historian describes these processes as a geneticist describes evolution in nature.[88] The main work of Dvořák's first phase is *The Riddle of the Art of the Brothers Van Eyck* (1904). Here he endeavored to show that the revolutionary naturalism of Jan van Eyck was nevertheless anchored in preceding developments in French and Italian painting of the fourteenth century. In his attempt to ascertain Hubert van Eyck's contribution to the Ghent altarpiece, Dvořák used to a considerable extent the method of Giovanni Morelli (1816–1891).[89] This connoisseur and collector with a background in medicine and science caused a stir in the European art world when, from circa 1873 onward, he began to challenge traditional attributions and to establish the oeuvres of individual masters as well as entire local and regional schools of Italian painting by comparing inconspicuous elements such as earlobes, fingernails, and the like; for he found in the treatment of such minutiae the safest indication of individual hands, or workshop conventions. Often attacked for his single-mindedness, Morelli nonetheless helped to put connoisseurship, not least in the field of drawing, on a broader and safer basis. Through his contact with Wickhoff he had an impact on the Viennese School.

In his early phase, Dvořák rejected any influence of extra-artistic factors on the formation of style. A fundamental change in his outlook can be detected in his article "An Illustrated Chronicle of War," of 1916.[90] The wartime experience had drawn his attention to Goya's etchings of the *Desastros de la Guerra*. It seemed impossible to interpret these works merely in terms of the artist's optical experience. As a chronicle of the horrors and miseries of war, they broke with the Renaissance idealization of heroic strife and replaced the scientific detachment of Callot's war scenes by compassion and outrage. Dvořák explains this new attitude by reference to a thorough subjectivization of art: disenchanted by the rationalism of the Enlightenment, the artists sought truth and an understanding of life exclusively in their own inner world.

This implied a program, which Dvořák had defined already two years earlier in a lecture on the education in art-historical research: "Art does not consist merely in the solution of formal tasks and problems; it is also always, and in the first place, an expression of ideas which govern mankind, of their history as well as of the history of religion, philosophy, and poetry; it is part of the general history of the human spirit."[91]

All Dvořák's later studies were guided by this conviction. The principal ones were united after his death under the fitting heading *The History of Art as History of Ideas.*[92] In this volume, each of the seven studies (of which the one reprinted here is the last) deals with a moment of historical crisis, and links the resulting redirections in art to spiritual redirections. The first one, "Catacomb Painting: The Beginnings of Christian Art," challenges Riegl's notion of a coherent development in late antique art, which embraced both its pagan and Christian manifestations. The paintings in the Roman catacombs, which in Riegl's time were unpublished and barely accessible, mark in Dvořák's view a total break with the classical legacy. Their formal asceticism — deindividualized figures of reduced corporeality, striking formulaic gestures in undefined space — marks them as symbolical. They are intended to convey the mysteries and certitudes of the new faith: redemption, detachment from the world, the eschatological destiny of mankind. Their ideational character differs radically from the corporeal allegories of classical art and requires a much higher degree of intellectual participation from the viewer. Dvořák finds corroboration for his interpretation and dating of the catacomb paintings in his readings of the church fathers.

This essay links up with the following, "Idealism and Naturalism in Gothic Sculpture and Painting,"[93] for here Dvořák deals with an essential dualism in Christian art, which he first detects in the pictorial cycles of the Constantinian period, where the ascetic spiritualism of the catacomb paintings was largely replaced by historical depictions of biblical events: The transcendental idealism of Christian art does away with the pagan worship of life. Yet, since all life is pervaded by the Divine will, earthly events have a certain dignity of their own inasmuch as they bear witness to this all-pervading higher reality. This in turn enables the art of both Constantinian and Gothic periods to move back toward a greater closeness to nature. This "fundamental conciliation of a transcendental explanation of life with a relative acceptance of life"[94] determines, according to Dvořák, the whole course of Gothic art. His demonstration includes brilliant interpretations of cathedral sculpture and stained-glass windows; it ends with penetrating analyses of the art of Giotto and Jan van Eyck, the latter being now perceived in his spiritual significance. Dvořák's basic assumption that the "worldview" of a period has a decisive influence on the formation of its style is—in this very general formulation—certainly valid. Yet here as elsewhere he establishes the link between religious (or secular) art and thought by way of an almost entirely abstract speculation. "The way that leads" (in the words of Wölfflin) "from the cell of the scholastic philosopher into the architect's lodge"[95] remains, for the most part, elusive.

Two realizations of his later years mark Dvořák's advance over Wickhoff and Riegl. First, he recognized that the gradual conquest of perceived reality was not the sole underlying goal of the entire evolution of art; he now saw that "periods of Naturalism appear almost like islands within a mainstream of artistic thought which regarded the representation of inner emotion as more important than fidelity to nature."[96] Second, Dvořák came to the conclusion that the movement of the human spirit, in art as well as in all its other manifestations, is ultimately determined by the creative activity of great individuals.

Both these ideas are at the root of our essay "On El Greco and Mannerism." It is in actual fact the manuscript of a lecture given in October 1920 at the Austrian Museum for Art and Industry; hence its (for Dvořák) rather informal character, and the compelling immediacy of its prose style. Although at the time of its delivery, Dvořák did not stand alone in his positive evaluation of El Greco and Mannerism, both the master and the period style were only gradually emerging from long periods of misapprehension and contempt. For the style, suffice it to quote from Riegl's lecture courses on Italian Baroque art (1894–1902): "What is it we call Mannerism? Superficial imitation of the characteristic features in the art of Michelangelo, or Raphael in his latest, michelangelesque period;

yet the profound spiritual content has all but vanished."[97] The common estimation of El Greco had for several generations been determined by the authority of Carl Justi, who in his great book on *Velázquez and His Century* (1888) had written: "His amorphous painting can be studied as mirror and compendium of the phenomena of pictorial degeneration. He seems to wield his brush oppressed by heavy dreams, offering the distorted incubus of his heated brain as a revelation."[98] Instead, Dvořák derives El Greco's art from the late works of Michelangelo and Tintoretto and, on the deepest level, from the spiritual crisis into which the collapse of church authority and the disenchantment with Reformation rationalism had plunged contemporary humanity. That he compares the situation during the second half of the sixteenth century to the collapse of antiquity, and the anaturalistic attitude of late Michelangelo to that which was upheld by medieval Christianity, shows the consistency of his historical vision.

And yet, it is this very consistency that makes one doubt it. In voicing my reservations, I do not mean to repeat the cliché that Dvořák's was an "expressionistic" art history, nor do I subscribe to Otto Kurz's spirited but malicious bon mot that "when Dvořák speaks of El Greco, he wants instead to say Kokoschka."[99] Dvořák's characterization of the Greek's spirituality remains valid, and so does his distinction of the two trends in mannerist culture, one realistic and psychological, the other transcendental and emotional. But take another work that Dvořák claims as a "model," or at least as an influence on El Greco's style: Bellange's *Three Maries at the Tomb* (Fig. 28). Can this celebrated print really be interpreted in terms of inwardness and spiritual concentration on the miraculous? Is not its overriding quality one of coquettish formalism, or sophisticated artificiality? All its most artificial features—the flamelike shapes of the puffed-up dresses, the coiling, "serpentine" bodily attitudes—have their precise counterpart in the precepts of mannerist treatises on painting.[100] It is the artificial, virtuosic trend that dominates mannerist theory as it dominates mannerist art. Neglected by Dvořák, this trend nonetheless coexists with the two others. Neither one is entirely free from it, and it may well be at the root of both.

❖   ❖   ❖

Julius von Schlosser (1866–1938), a student of Wickhoff's, succeeded Dvořák in his chair, but it should be mentioned that in 1909 it was Schlosser, eight years older than Dvořák, who voted for this latter's appointment, since he himself preferred his position as head of the department of sculpture and applied arts at the Austrian Museum.

Otto Kurz, a student of Schlosser's and himself an eminent art historian, has left us a penetrating analysis of his teacher's personality, method, and work.[101] Thus we know Schlosser as a gentleman scholar, deeply steeped in the classics, and endowed with an encyclopedic mind; as an aristocrat who kept aloof from professional circles and wrote his difficult works, so densely packed with arcane allusions and learned digressions, "for the happy few," for a handful of kindred spirits in international scholarship. What he wrote went against the grain of the principal currents of his lifetime, expressionist art history and Wölfflinian formalism. Hence it was inevitable, though of little concern to himself, that the public at large (including his colleagues) ignored most of his contributions. A stranger in his own time, Schlosser was indifferent to contemporary art, history, and politics. Born from mixed parentage, he felt more Italian than Austrian.

Schlosser's fame rests primarily on his main work, *The Literature of the Arts* (1924),[102] a bibliography and critical history of art historiography and artistic theory from antiquity to the end of the eighteenth century. With this work, he continued a line of research which had been inaugurated by Eitelberger and reinforced by Wickhoff. Schlosser's first publication in this area, *Sources for the History of Carolingian Art* (1892),[103] is—in accordance with the ahistorical attitude of that period—hardly more than a collection of references to works of art and architecture, gleaned from chronicles, letters, poetry, and theological writings. Yet as he plowed through the ever-increasing mass of writings about art, from the merely technical treatises of the Middle Ages to the theoretical, biographical, and topographical compendia of Renaissance, Mannerism, and Baroque, Schlosser's work changed its character. It became not only a history of artistic thought through the ages and, as such, an eminent key to the *spirit* of every age, but also a history of art history as a nascent and evolving discipline. Much of the bibliographical research was based on the vast holdings of Schlosser's personal library. The final publication presents this immense material for the first time united in one clearly arranged volume. It makes compelling reading.

The essay on the age-old prejudice against "The Gothic" is an early offshoot of these studies. All Schlosser's crown witnesses, from Ghiberti to Vasari, from Francisco da Hollanda to J. G. Sulzer, are discussed extensively in *Die Kunstliteratur*. In fact, Schlosser writes in 1910 as if his magnum opus of 1924 were already finished in his head, or as if he could presuppose that his readers *knew* all these authors. Since the present volume's limitations of space must preclude an exhaustive annotation, *our* readers are referred to that book. "The Gothic" was first published in 1910, together with other *Prolegomena* to Schlosser's edition of Lorenzo Ghiberti's *Commentarii*.[104] This manuscript, which was drafted by the great sculptor during the years preceding his death in 1455, had been used by Rumohr (see p. xxviii). It contains Ghiberti's outline of the history of art, lives of artists (including his own), and unfinished notes about the scientific foundations of the arts in optics, proportion, and so forth. Schlosser researched the manuscript in all its ramifications and established its rank as a major art-historical document. In our essay, Schlosser derives the prejudice against the Gothic—as well as the term itself—convincingly from the Italian resentment against the prolonged foreign rule of Germanic invaders and emperors, as epitomized by the Goths. In every page, the essay reveals Schlosser's passionate identification with Italy. The essay is remarkable also in another respect: Schlosser's tendency to treat the history of art in close parallel with the development of music and language is one of the hallmarks of his method.

Late in his career, in 1935, Schlosser published a "backward glance" over his scholarly life under the title *History of Style and History of Language in the Plastic Arts*.[105] There he relates, in the form of a playful analogy between his own life and Dante's *Divine Comedy,* how he was released from an intellectual midlife crisis by the Italian philosopher Benedetto Croce, who became his "Virgil," and the German scholar Karl Vossler, a specialist in Romance languages and literatures, who became his "Statius." Both men had a decisive influence on Schlosser's art-historical philosophy, as he expounds it in this retrospective essay. For Croce, there is no history of art, only a history of artists. Only the greatest, truly creative artists have their rightful place in this history; they are subject only to their own laws, and entirely independent of one another. The historical elucidation of the "inner history of these insular, creative monads" constitutes, in Schlosser's definition, the "history of style." The use made of their discoveries by "copyists, imitators, industrialists," that is to say, the continuity of art (or, in Croce's radical view, of nonart) as it unfolds around, and below, these summits, all this belongs in the "history of (artistic) language." Karl Vossler distinguished in much the same way between the history of literature and the history of language. It amounts almost to a reversal of the position of the Viennese School, which had labored so hard to cleanse certain periods of the stigma of "decline," when Schlosser assigns the arts of late antiquity, Mannerism, and Baroque each for the most part to the "history of language." Within Riegl's impersonal interpretation of the history of style, it was difficult to account for the *emergence* of great artists; Schlosser was faced with the problem of how to determine their *rank*. In the opening paragraph of his book on medieval art he states that "the separation of the original expression from the work of imitators and bunglers forms the thorny problem of art history of any kind (including literary history)."[106] On the other hand, he found in Vossler's linguistic research an important model for his own endeavors to describe the development and mutations of period styles in their temporal and regional subdivisions.

Given Schlosser's conviction that the elucidation of genius is the supreme task of the art historian, it must strike us as all but tragic that he himself was not gifted for this kind of work. Kurz notes not without regret how Schlosser's attempts in this direction, his monographic essays on Leon Battista Alberti, Paolo Uccello, Piero della Francesca, and, above all, his favorite artist, Ghiberti, all fall short of this great task.[107] In fact, very few of Schlosser's many trailblazing discoveries fall within the "history of style." He would certainly make this claim for some neglected north Italian Trecento painters, whose superior quality he recognized, but who were acknowledged only by the following generation of scholars. About his study of the literature of the arts he said himself that it extended into the "history of style" inasmuch as the critical judgment of past epochs can help us in recognizing the achievement of genius.[108] On the other hand, Schlosser's investigations of the construction principles of early medieval monasteries; of the artistic culture of the international courts around 1400; of collections of art and curiosities in the High Renaissance and — most unusual — of the history of portraiture in waxworks — these are all part of the "history of language."

Schlosser's brief but highly original and illuminating book on *The Art of the Middle Ages* has been rightly singled out by Kurz as the triumph of his "linguistic" method.[109] Not that Schlosser failed to distinguish here between secular achievements and mere workshop traditions. It was rather the suppression of the individual in the Middle Ages, the fact that large parts of this art are indeed anonymous, that invited this particular approach. In tracing the parallel developments of literary and artistic languages in the principal regions of western Europe, Schlosser established something like a "historical grammar" of medieval art; this enabled him to describe the special inflections of every regional "dialect." Above all, the radical transformation that French Gothic underwent in Italy had never been seen before in such sharp focus.

The fame of Aby Warburg (1866–1929) rests equally on his writings and on the research library he founded and which, as the Warburg Institute, is incorporated in the University of London. His writings are slender in bulk yet they constitute not only a new approach to art history, but also an entirely new concept of "cultural psychology." The library was originally a mirror of its founder's highly idiosyncratic interests and methods; it is now an eminent tool for all those whose research transcends the purely formal study of art in the direction of other historical realities.

Warburg was not what popular opinion mistakenly sees in him: the iconographer who disengaged the study of (often esoteric) content from more conventional art history. The essence of his contribution has been laid bare in articles by his closest collaborators, Fritz Saxl and Gertrud Bing.[110] A comprehensive "intellectual biography" by E. H. Gombrich, himself for many years director of the Warburg Institute, allows us to follow the formation of Warburg's mind from his student years to the achievements of his maturity.[111]

Among the formative influences, Gombrich enumerates Darwin's theory of expression, the historian Karl Lamprecht's ambition to interpret the stages of cultural evolution psychologically and the interpretations of the minds of the ancients by Hermann Usener and Tito Vignoli. Usener found ancient myth rooted in primeval man's fear; the Olympians are personifications of the threatening or life-preserving forces of nature. Vignoli traced the path leading from primitive animism to the causal explanation of the universe. A concept of the conquest of fear underlies Warburg's interpretation of cultural progress in the Renaissance. Since he himself was subject to deep-seated, unexplained anxieties that threatened and at one point disrupted his mental balance, there was a personal motivation behind his research.

Collecting material for his dissertation on Botticelli, Warburg discovered that in the early Renaissance depictions of movement are invariably based upon classical prototypes. This holds for the bulging draperies and fluttering hair of Botticelli's Venus, nymphs, and graces—these were based on motifs in neo-Attic sculpture, which had already been recommended as models for painters by L. B. Alberti and Leonardo Da Vinci. The same holds true for the many classical borrowings in the mythological poems by Angelo Poliziano, Botticelli's learned adviser.[112] Every depiction (or description) of life in motion, from the swift bodily movements of the nymphs to the maenads' murderous rage in the killing of Orpheus, could be traced back to classical motifs, which Warburg called "Pathosformeln." This has been translated by Jan Bialostocki as "formulae of expressing pathetic passion."[113] The sheer number of such "Pathosformeln" as well as the fact that they retained their exemplary power, as Warburg has shown, throughout Western art, demonstrates once more how one-sided Winckelmann's understanding of classical antiquity was. Warburg's view of antiquity is closely related to Nietzsche's. His interest in the psychological motivation of such coinages induced him to switch temporarily to the study of psychology on a medical basis. A trip to America in 1896 brought him firsthand experience of a living pagan culture, that of the Pueblo Indians, and of their coinage of religious imagery. Upon his return to Florence, he resumed his previous study with a thorough exploration of the archives. In order to comprehend Renaissance men and women in their totality, Warburg researched their daily lives, their pageants, their theatre, their religious observances, and, not least, the relations between artists and patrons. He examined their use of classical images of life in motion not only in great works of art, but also in the decoration of objects of daily use, tapestries, paintings on wedding caskets, or in the allusive images incised on boxes that lovers gave their beloved. In his study of the will and the sepulchral chapel of a Florentine merchant and partner of the Medici, Francesco Sassetti,[114] Warburg reached the core of his exploration of early Renaissance psychology. Sassetti devotes his chapel in Santa Trinità to his patron, Saint Francis, yet he invokes in his will the goddess Fortuna. The reliefs surrounding the niche holding his sarcophagus are modeled upon the orgiastic lament for Meleager on Roman sarcophagi; but the fresco above depicts the controlled Christian mourning for Saint Francis. The biblical shepherd David appears side by side with Sassetti's personal symbol, the sling-brandishing centaur. In the fresco of *The Pope Approving the Order of Saint Francis,* Domenico Ghirlandajo gives such prominence to the figures of Sassetti and his sons, as well as to Lorenzo de' Medici with his sons and their tutors, that it looks as if these wealthy Florentine merchants patronized the acceptance of the "eternally poor" as vassals of the Church Militant. All this proved to Warburg the psychological polarity of the men of this transitional period, as they tried to strike a balance between Christianity and paganism, between their proud self-assertiveness as Renaissance men and their medieval submission to the will of God, between God and Fortuna. Yet another polarity emerged from Warburg's research into the commercial and artistic exchange between Florence and the Netherlands: the polarity between Northern realism and classical idealization. Florentine merchants on their outposts in Flanders had their portraits painted by Flemish artists. These latter adopted the Italians' classical formulae for the depiction of life in motion, yet rendered the characters of ancient myth in contemporary French court dress. Northern realism in physiognomy and costume was adopted by Florentine painters: in his *Adoration* for Francesco Sassetti, D. Ghirlandajo borrowed the shepherds from the Portinari altarpiece by Hugo van der Goes. How could these conflicting tendencies result in an art as unified as Florentine painting of the early Renaissance?

In order to answer this question, Warburg felt he had to trace the survival of the classical legacy in North and South during the Middle Ages. His extensive research of medieval mythographic manuscripts led to that far-reaching discovery at the root of his article on "Italian Art and International Astrology in the Palazzo Schifanoja in Ferrara": The gods of Greece survived the lasting suppression of the classical legacy by the Church in the guise of astral demons. The

article represents the unchanged text of a lecture delivered by Warburg at an international art historians' congress in Rome in 1912. In
order to understand its central position in Warburg's work, one
must take to heart his affirmation that "the resolution of a pictorial
riddle" was not the sole purpose of his talk. Evidently, Warburg's
elucidation of the impact of astrology on the artistic culture of the
Renaissance (which had already been noticed, in more general
terms, by Burckhardt) is in itself an admirable achievement. No
reader of the article under discussion will be unimpressed by the
assurance with which he uncovers in the Ferrarese frescoes the
Greek core underneath the various layers of Egyptian, Indian, Arabic, Latin, and medieval astro-mythological concepts.[115] But for
Warburg, his astrological research was never an end in itself. In art-
historical terms, the imagery in the Palazzo Schifanoja marked an
important stage within that process of liberation that freed the artists from "medieval illustrative subservience" and enabled them to
create the High Renaissance style of "ideal humanity." In terms of
Warburg's "cultural psychology," astrology stood for all those irrational fears which, in the mental life of the individual as well as in
the web of culture, threaten, time and again, to disrupt the balance
obtained through enlightened humanism. All those conflicts that he
detected in art and psychology of the early Renaissance are present
in the Schifanoja frescoes.

Warburg describes the three pictorial planes dividing the depictions
of the months as "a spherical system projected upon a flat surface"
(see Figs. 31–33). The lowest plane represents life on earth, at the
Ferrarese court. As Fritz Saxl has noticed,[116] Duke Borso and his
courtiers confront—here below as well as on high—the Olympian
gods with the same self-assertiveness as Sassetti and Lorenzo de'
Medici display when they confront the Pope and Saint Francis in the
Approval of the Franciscan Order. Yet they *fear* these same gods—and
the intermediate astral demons, the decans in the middle plane—as
dark and unyielding rulers over their destinies. The Olympians appear in the uppermost plane as protectors of the months, that is, in
the degrading role of projections of man's superstitions and fears.
Yet they are at least the Graeco-Roman gods as described by Manilius. The replacement of the planetary demons of Oriental astrology
by truly classical divinities marks for Warburg the first step in these
latters' recapture of Olympus. However, dressed in Burgundian

court dress, and laden with the learned attributes of the Northern mythographic tradition, these classical gods are still subject to "medieval illustrative subservience." Botticelli frees them from much of this ballast. But it is only Raphael who, in his Farnesina frescoes, restores them to their classical freedom and ideality.

One point in Warburg's ingenious interpretation, criticized already during his lifetime and now largely rejected by specialists, was his identification of the first decan of Aries as a transformation of Perseus. E. H. Gombrich explains why Warburg attached so much importance to this point. If it could be proven, the image would have come full circle, from the mythical hero through his degradation as an astrological phantom to his final restitution as an embodiment of heroic humanity in the High Renaissance: "Maybe the symbol was so important to him because he could see his own destiny reflected in the life history of that hero, bewitched and transformed beyond recognition but returning triumphantly in the end."[117]

The parallel is indeed hard to dismiss. In his following essay, Warburg investigated the ambivalence (and manipulative attitude) of Luther and his circle toward astrology and prophecy, and offered a trailblazing interpretation of Dürer's Melencolia I.[118] Yet a few years later his despair at the universal doom caused by World War I brought about that disruption of his mental balance that Warburg had so long dreaded. Confined to a series of mental hospitals, he recovered only in 1923. As a sign of his recovery, he delivered to his fellow patients a "Lecture on Serpent Ritual,"[119] which was based on his observations with the Pueblo Indians. During his absence, Fritz Saxl carried out what Warburg had long planned. With the help of relatives—the Warburgs were an eminent banking family— Saxl transformed his mentor's private library into a public research institute. Warburg himself spent his remaining years working on a project to incorporate all his finds and speculations: a "picture atlas" illustrating the history of human expression, to be entitled *Mnemosyne*. One of several subtitles sheds light on the concept of this work: "The awakening of the pagan gods in the age of the European Renaissance as the transformation of energy into expressive values." He did not live to complete it.

Warburg's work was carried on most notably by two scholars, the above-mentioned Fritz Saxl and Erwin Panofsky. Saxl saved the library from that destructive rage with which the Nazis assaulted all cultural values and institutions whose creators or leading proponents were Jews. He organized its transfer to England and its incorporation in the University of London. Saxl was head of the Warburg Institute until his death. His own research covered a wide range of subjects: Mithraism, medieval astrology and science, Renaissance humanism, the classical legacy in the works of Rembrandt, and many others.

Panofsky (1892–1968)[120] is the only scholar included in this collection who became an American. He transmitted Warburg's ideas to American scholarship and thus contributed to their worldwide dissemination. However, this should not obscure the fact that in his own work he refined and transformed Warburg's method. Panofsky was always grateful for the extensive classical training he received in high school, at the Joachimsthalsche Gymnasium in Berlin, for this had laid the ground for his future scholarship. He was initially enrolled as a law student at Freiburg University, but when a friend took him to a lecture by Wilhelm Vöge, "the scales fell from his eyes," and he switched to art history. Within a year he was to write a prize-winning essay on Dürer's artistic theory. Panofsky maintained a lifelong admiration for his teacher Vöge.[121] Having earned his degree in 1914, Panofsky spent three years of postdoctoral study in Berlin with Adolph Goldschmidt (1863–1944), a scholar who was less interested in systems than in the precise solution of monographic problems, mostly in medieval art. Panofsky's later book on *German Sculpture from the Eleventh to the Thirteenth Century*[122] is a fruit of his study with both Goldschmidt and Vöge.

In 1921 the young scholar was called to the newly founded University of Hamburg in order to build up a department of art history. Within a few years he became *Ordinarius* (full professor). Panofsky's brilliant teaching soon attracted many students. Outstanding scholars emerged from his school.

Throughout his tenure, Panofsky kept close ties with the *Kulturwissenschaftliche Bibliothek Warburg*, and so did the members of his department; they all contributed to the library's lectures and publications. The philosopher Ernst Cassirer exerted a decisive influence on this whole circle and, not least, on Panofsky himself, through his interest in Neoplatonism and through his "philosophy of symbolic forms." The manifestations of the human spirit in language, art, myth, religion, philosophy, history are described by Cassirer as "symbolic forms," inasmuch as they are understood according to their function within a specific culture. The discovery of the common bond uniting these various manifestations within a given local and temporal setting results in a definition of this specific culture. The search for the basic function of speech, art, myth, and so on *behind* their cultural manifestations aims at an understanding of the structure of the human mind. Both Cassirer and Panofsky lectured in the Warburg Library on related topics—Cassirer on the idea of beauty in Plato's dialogues, Panofsky on the transformation of the Platonic idea in artistic theory from antiquity to the Baroque. This lecture was the starting point for his book *Idea*.[123]

Panofsky's close collaboration with Fritz Saxl resulted in their jointly written book, *Dürer's "Melencolia I,"*[124] which extended and deepened Warburg's interpretation of the print. Both Warburg and his two followers link the work to Renaissance astrology. In Dürer's conception, the evil force of Saturn, demon of melancholy, is counteracted by the beneficent influence of Jupiter. Paralyzing gloom is transformed into creative meditation. Thus in both interpretations the *Melencolia* embodies the temperament of the creative personality, artist, or thinker. However—and this exemplifies an essential difference between Panofsky's and Warburg's approach—Warburg sees Dürer's accomplishment in terms of sociocultural progress: The transformation of a pathological condition into a creative state is possible only through the conquest of superstitious fear. Panofsky and Saxl, on the other hand, stress a different implication of the subject: The melancholy of the creative thinker is due to their awareness that they "cannot extend their thoughts beyond the limits of space."[125]

It may thus be said that Warburg was more concerned with the *process* of intellectual liberation in the early Renaissance, whereas Panofsky, following both Warburg and Cassirer, set out to explore the "cultural cosmos" which the liberated men of the Renaissance created for themselves; he tried to understand their new enthusiasm, as well as, in the case of Dürer, their awareness of the ultimate insufficiency of their rational-geometric tools vis-à-vis the unattainable "ideas" of truth and beauty.

Both Warburg and Panofsky thought continually about their respective methods. However, whereas Warburg's reflections took the

form of sporadic jottings that he never worked into a definite statement, Panofsky wrote profusely about theory and method of art
history, from his early critiques of Wölfflin and Riegl to the defini-
tive formulations of his later years.[126]

The analysis of a work of art consists for Panofsky of three
stages, which can be roughly summarized as follows: (1) mere recording of the visual fact, (2) identification of the subject, (3) recognition of the "intrinsic meaning." The last is "apprehended by ascer-
taining those underlying principles which reveal the basic attitude
of a nation, a period, a class, a religious or philosophical persua-
sion—qualified by one personality and condensed into one
work."[127] Each of these procedures has to be corrected: (1) by our
knowledge of the history of style, (2) by our knowledge of the
history of iconographic types, (3) by "an insight into the manner in
which, under varying historical conditions, the general and essential tendencies of the human mind were expressed by specific
themes and concepts. This means what may be called a history of
cultural symptoms—or 'symbols,' in Ernst Cassirer's sense—in general."[128] Panofsky illustrates his various expositions of this method
by reference to a wide variety of works of art; he takes great care to
demonstrate in what way both the analysis of form and style and
the judgment of quality are included in this approach. All this is
brilliantly exemplified in the essay in our collection, "Eros Bound
(Concerning the Genealogy of Rembrandt's *Danae*)" (Fig. 36).

In this essay it is Panofsky's purpose, first to prove that the painting does indeed represent Danae (and not Hagar, Rahel, Sarah, or
Venus); secondly, to determine the function of the bound Cupid in
Rembrandt's composition; and finally to describe the epiphany of
Danae in the light of Rembrandt's genius. Mere recording of the
visual fact has blinded previous writers to the true meaning of the
painting: Jupiter visits Danae in a rain of gold, yet this golden rain is
missing in the picture. The figure does not seem to look upward. The
Cupid is unexplained. Panofsky counters these arguments first by
pointing out that the rain of gold is replaced by a miraculous burst of
light. Since the mere recording of visual fact has to be corrected by
our knowledge of style, Panofsky adduces that it lies well within
Rembrandt's style to visualize a miracle by way of supernatural
light; witness his *Christ in Emmaus*. With his sharper reading of the
visual evidence, Panofsky notices furthermore that even if the figure's head is not raised sharply, her glance is unquestionably

directed upward; "her eye follows the uplifted hand, which both welcomes the apparition and wards off its blinding brightness."

With his identification of the woman in amorous expectation as Danae and, moreover, of the bound Cupid as *Anteros*, Panofsky enters the second stage of analysis, the identification of the subject. Since this procedure has to be corrected by knowledge of iconographic types, he traces the iconographic traditions in word and image of both Danae and Anteros.

Only the "intrinsic meaning" that links this particular painting to the underlying principles of contemporary culture is nowhere spelled out, and such an ultimate conclusion seems to be absent from this essay—unless we assume that Panofsky finds it implied in the function of Anteros. He shows that this classical godhead of "reciprocated love" was transformed in Renaissance Neoplatonism into the very "opponent of Eros, who quenches the fire of love." He thus stands, in Rembrandt's conception, for the involuntary chastity from which Danaë was redeemed by Jupiter. Are we to take the *defeat* of Anteros, then, as symbolizing the proud assertion of free will and self-determination in seventeenth-century Holland?

A quite unusual postscript has been added to this essay. It originated in the technical laboratories of the Hermitage. Soviet scholars investigated the painting and found underneath the depiction earlier strata which had been thoroughly revised and overpainted by Rembrandt, some dozen or more years after the earliest version. Thus it became apparent that precisely those traditional features which, according to Panofsky's analysis, had been eliminated or transformed by Rembrandt in the picture as we know it, were part and parcel of his original conception. Danaë's gesture was merely functional as she was pulling back the curtain. She looked with her head raised at the (implied) heavenly apparition. The old nurse figured much more prominently in the background; her eagerness was not yet reduced to "quiet, motherly sympathy." And the magical light turned out to be the result of extensive overpainting. Hence, Rembrandt had enacted with paint on canvas that transformation of the pictorial tradition which Panofsky ascribed to him on the grounds of his judicious comparisons! It would be hard to find a more striking corroboration of an art historian's method.

Eros Bound was among the last works written by Panofsky in Germany. Starting in 1931, he taught alternate semesters as a visiting professor at New York University. It was in New York that in 1933 he received notice of his dismissal by the Nazi authorities. As a consequence, Panofsky spent the remainder of his life in the United States, teaching in New York and Princeton, and writing his great later books under the auspices of Princeton's Institute for Advanced Study. These books — on Renaissance iconology, Dürer, early Netherlandish painting, tomb sculpture, Titian, and so forth — were written in English. They belong to American art history.

For the purpose of this introduction, I read all texts used in the German originals; whenever English translations are available, they are indicated in the footnotes. In all quotes except those from the texts reprinted in this volume, the translations are my own. Among the basic books, Udo Kultermann's *Geschichte der Kunstgeschichte* gave me a first orientation in the field. Wilhelm Waetzoldt's *Deutsche Kunsthistoriker* provided reliable guidance for the first half of this introduction. The writings of E. H. Gombrich proved indispensable for the second one. For personal advice, I am grateful to Sir Ernst Gombrich and to my colleagues at the New York University Institute of Fine Arts: Peter Hans von Blanckenhagen, Jonathan Brown, Colin Eisler, Donald Hansen, Evelyn Harrison, Egbert Haverkamp-Begemann, John Hay, James R. McCredie, Donald Posner, Priscilla Soucek, Marvin Trachtenberg. Further thanks go to David Rattray for invaluable assistance with the minutiae of wording in the introduction; to Peter Wortsman for the thorny task of translating some of the most difficult texts in all art history; and to Louise Stern for her sharp eye in the final editing of the manuscript.

G.S.

Notes

1. About the impact of Hegel on art history, see E. H. Gombrich, "In Search of Cultural History," in *Ideals and Idols, Essays on Values in History and in Art* (Oxford: Phaidon 1979), and "The Father of Art History, A Reading of the Lectures on Aesthetics of G. W. F. Hegel (1770–1831)," in *Tributes, Interpreters of Our Cultural Tradition*, Ithaca, New York: Cornell University Press, 1984).

2. The basic monograph is Carl Justi, *Winckelmann und seine Zeitgenossen*, 3 vols. (1866–1872), here used in the 2d ed. (Leipzig: Verlag von F. C. W. Vogel, 1898). See also Wilhelm Waetzoldt, *Deutsche Kunsthistoriker*, I, *Von Sandrart bis Rumohr*, 2d ed. (Berlin: Verlag Bruno Hessling, 1965), pp. 51–73, and Karl Schefold, *Winckelmanns neue Sicht der antiken Kunst*, in Neue Zürcher Zeitung, 10 December 1967, fol. 4.

3. *Geschichte der Kunst des Altertums* (1763– 1768), vols. 3–6 in Johañ Winckelmañs sämtliche Werke, Donauöschingen, Im Verlage deutscher Classiker, 1825–1829, Tr. by G. Henry Lodge as *History of Ancient Art*, 4 vols in 2 (New York: Frederick Ungar Publishing Co., 1969).

4. Justi, op. cit. 1, pp. 252–256, 365.

5. For a thorough discussion of Winckelmann's sensibility see Mario Praz, *On Neoclassicism*, tr. Angus Davidson (London: Thames and Hudson, 1969), pp. 40– 69.

6. Winckelmann, *Geschichte der Kunst des Altertums*, ed. cit. IV, p. 75.

7. About Heinse, see Waetzoldt, op. cit. pp. 117–131.

8. Georg Forster, *Die Kunst und das Zeitalter* (1790), quoted after Waetzoldt, op. cit. p. 203.

9. Wilhelm Heinse, *Ardinghello und die glückseligen Inseln* (1785) (Berlin: Propyläen-Verlag, 1921), p. 195.

10. Heinse, posthumous papers, quoted after Udo Kultermann, *Geschichte der Kunstgeschichte* (Vienna-Düsseldorf: Econ-Verlag, 1966), p. 84.

11. Heinse, *Ardinghello*, pp. 299–307.

12. Waetzoldt, op. cit. pp. 138–144, 155–179. Christian Beutler, *Einführung*, in Johann Wolfgang Goethe, *Schriften zur Kunst; Gedenkausgabe der Werke und Briefe*, ed. Ernst Beutler, vol. 13 (Zürich und Stuttgart: Artemis-Verlag, 2d ed. 1965), pp. 1105–1107, 1126–1129. John Gage, *Introduction*, in *Goethe on Art*, sel., ed. and tr. by John Gage (Berkeley and Los Angeles: University of California Press, 1980), pp. IX–XX.

13. Beutler, op. cit. p. 1106.

14. Gage, op. cit., p. 77.

15. Waetzoldt, op. cit. pp. 217–232. For a good, brief summary of Wackenroder's achievement see Elizabeth Gilmore Holt, *From the Classicists to the Expressionists, A Documentary History of Art and Architecture in the 19th Century* (New York: New York University Press, 1966), pp. 55, 56. The passage on Wackenroder is adapted from my essay "An Epoch of Longing," in *German Masters of the Nineteenth Century* (New York: The Metropolitan Museum of Art, distr. by Harry N. Abrams, Inc., Publishers, 1981), p. 10.

16. Friedrich Schlegel, *Ideen* (120), in *Kritische Friedrich-Schlegel-Ausgabe*, II, *Charakteristiken und Kritiken I*, ed. Hans Eichner (Munich-Paderborn-Vienna: Verlag Ferdinand Schöningh, Zurich: Thomas-Verlag, 1967), p. 268.

17. Waetzoldt, op. cit. pp. 252–272; Hans Eichner, *Einleitung*, in Schlegel, ed. cit. IV, 1959, *Ansichten und Ideen von der christlichen Kunst*.

18. Schlegel, ed. cit. IV, p. 241.

19. Ibid., pp. XXVIII–XXIX.

20. Waetzoldt, op. cit., pp. 293–318.

21. C. Fr. von Rumohr, *Italienische Forschungen* (1827–1831), ed. Julius Schlosser (Frankfurt am Main: Frankfurter Verlags-Anstalt A.G., 1920); includes Schlosser's important introduction, "Carl Friedrich von Rumohr als Begründer der neueren Kunstforschung."

22. Ibid., p. 60; Schlosser, p. XXIV.

23. Ibid., pp. 63, 64.

24. Waetzoldt, op. cit., p. 311.

25. *Italienische Forschungen,* p. 75; Schlosser, p. XXXI.

26. The following is a synopsis of all paintings by Giotto mentioned by Rumohr, with a sampling of their critical fortunes based on Roberto Salvini, *Giotto bibliografia* (Rome: Casa editrice Fratelli Palombi, 1938), and Giancarlo Vigorelli and Edi Baccheschi, *L'opera completa di Giotto, Classici dell'arte* (Milan: Rizzoli, 1966). The small paintings that formerly adorned the sacristy of the Minorite Church in Florence are considered by Longhi and Gnudi to be authentic, by others (Cavalcaselle, Toesca, Brandi, Salmi, Salvini) as works of Giotto's circle, reflecting his later style (see Vigorelli-Baccheschi, catalogue nos. 131–137). The murals in the Church of the Madonna Incoronata in Naples have been excluded from Giotto's oeuvre since the 1840s. Only Martin Gosebruch, *Giotto und die Entwicklung des neuzeitlichen Kunstbewusstseins* (Cologne: Verlag DuMont Schauberg, 1962), considers them authentic. The frescoes of the legend of St. Francis in the Upper Church at Assisi were first disattributed by Witte (1821), then by Rumohr, and, in the twentieth century, by Rintelen, Schlosser, Hetzer, Fisher, Meiss, and Smart. The Italian critics have always maintained their authenticity (e.g., Salvini, 1962). For an emphatic reaffirmation of their authenticity see Gosebruch, op. cit. The Franciscan allegories in the Lower Church at Assisi were disattributed by A. Venturi in 1905. Gnudi ascribes them to a pupil of Giotto's, the Master of the Veils. Gosebruch considers them as works by Giotto himself. The frescoes in the Scrovegni chapel at Padua are well documented and have never been contested. Rumohr's strange contention that their condition did not allow one to judge their merit was opposed instantly: by Selvatico in 1836 and by Foerster in 1837. The Stefaneschi polyptych is generally considered a work of Giotto's workshop; only Gosebruch and Supino claim it for Giotto himself. The bipartite painting with a flattened semicircular top in the Florentine Academy can no longer be identified. The Story of Job in the Campo Santo in Pisa was given to Taddeo Gaddi by Vasari in the *first* edition of his *Vite.* Rumohr follows Vasari in his *later* attribution to Giotto. Today there is agreement about T. Gaddi's authorship. The Last Supper from the Refectory of S. Croce (engraved by Ruscheweyh and Lasinio) is today also considered a work by Taddeo Gaddi.

It should be mentioned that Ghiberti's note about Giotto's father, Bondone, which Rumohr questions in his footnote 3, has been confirmed by documentary evidence.

27. The book referred to in Rumohr's footnote 28 is Johann David Passavant's *Ansichten über die bildende Kunst, und Darstellung des Ganges derselben in Toscana, von einem deutschen Künstler in Rom,* 1820. On Passavant, see Waetzoldt, op. cit. II, *Von Passavant bis Justi,* pp. 14–29.

28. Schlosser, op. cit., p. XXIV.

29. Waetzoldt, op. cit. II, *Von Passavant bis Justi,* pp. 95–129. Christian Tümpel, "Kolloffs Leben Bedeutung und Methode," in Eduard Kolloff, *Rembrandts Leben und Werke,* ed. Chr. Tümpel, *Deutsches Bibel-Archiv* 4 (Hamburg: Friedrich Wittig Verlag, 1971).

30. Ibid., p. 486.

31. Eduard Kolloff, "Die Entwicklung der modernen Kunst aus der antiken bis zur Epoche der Renaissance," in *Historisches Taschenbuch,* ed. Friedrich von Raumer, New Series I (Leipzig: F. A. Brockhaus, 1840), pp. 275–346.

32. Waetzoldt, op. cit., II, pp. 98, 99.

33. Kolloff, *Rembrandt,* ed. cit. (note 29), p. 424.

34. Ibid., p. 487.

35. Ibid., pp. 497–499.

36. See Gert Schiff, "Tissot's Illustrations to the Hebrew Bible," in *J. James Tissot, Biblical Paintings* (New York: The Jewish Museum, 1982), p. 25.

37. Waetzoldt, op. cit. II, pp. 172–209. Werner Kaegi, *Jacob Burckhardt, eine Biographie,* 7 vols. (Basel-Stuttgart: Verlag Benno Schwabe & Co., 1947–1982).

38. The essay was made available by Henning Ritter in his volume *Jacob Burckhardt, Die Kunst der Betrachtung, Aufsätze und Vorträge zur bildenden Kunst* (Cologne: Dumont Buchverlag, 1984), pp. 106–122.

39. Werner Kaegi, *Europäische Horizonte im Denken Jacob Burckhardts* (Basel-Stuttgart: Verlag Benno Schwabe & Co., 1962) maintains against the documentary evidence that Burckhardt's remarks were based on Murillo's famous *Immaculada Soult.*

40. *Die Kultur der Renaissance in Italien; ein Versuch* (1860). Jacob Burckhardt, *Gesammelte Werke* III (Basel: Verlag Benno Schwabe & Co., 1955). Trans. S. G. C. Middlemore as *The Civilization of the Renaissance* (Vienna: The Phaidon Press; New York: Oxford University Press, 1937).

41. *Erinnerungen aus Rubens* (published posthumously, Basel: Verlag von C. F. Lendorff, 1898). Tr. by Mary Hottinger as *Recollections of Rubens,* ed. H. Gerson (New York: Phaidon Publishers, distr. by Oxford University Press, 1950).

42. "Die Zeit Konstantins des Grossen" (1853), in *Werke* I (1955). Trans. Moses Hadas as *The Age of Constantine the Great* (New York: Pantheon Books, 1949).

43. "Der Cicerone, eine Anleitung zum Genuss der Kunstwerke Italiens" (1855), in *Werke* IX (1958) and X (1959).

44. "Geschichte der Renaissance in Italien" (1867), in *Werke* II (1955; as "Die Baukunst der Renaissance in Italien").

45. *Griechische Kulturgeschichte* (published posthumously, 1898–1902). *Werke* V, VI (1956), VII, VIII (1957). Tr. (abridged) by Palmer Hilty as *History of Greek Culture* (New York: Ungar, 1963).

46. *Weltgeschichtliche Betrachtungen. Ueber geschichtliches Studium* (published posthumously, 1905). *Werke* IV (1956).

47. For a penetrating interpretation by a disciple and admirer, see Fritz Strich, *Zu Heinrich Wölfflins Gedächtnis, Rede an der Basler Feier seines zehnten Todestages* (Bern: Francke Verlag, 1956).

48. *Renaissance und Barock; eine Untersuchung über Wesen und Entstehung des Barockstils in Italien* (1888; 4th ed. by Hans Rose, Munich: F. Bruckmann A. G., 1926).

49. Ibid., p. 83.

50. Michael Podro, *The Critical Historians of Art* (New Haven and London: Yale University Press, 1982), p. 110.

51. *Die klassische Kunst, eine Einführung in die italienische Renaissance* (1899); 7th ed. by Konrad Escher, Munich: F. Bruckmann A. G., 1926; trans. Peter and Linda Murray as *Classic Art,* New York: Phaidon Publishers, distr. by Garden City Books, 1952).

52. *Die klassische Kunst,* ed. cit., p. 166.

53. Ibid., p. 290.

54. *Die Kunst Albrecht Dürers* (1905; 5th ed., Munich: F. Bruckmann A. G., 1926, p. 10; trans. Alastair and Heide Grieve as *The Art of Albrecht Dürer,* New York: Phaidon, distr. in the U.S. by Praeger, 1971).

55. *Die Kunst Albrecht Dürers,* pp. 12, 122.

56. Heinrich Wölfflin, *Gedanken zur Kunstgeschichte* (Basel: Verlag Benno Schwabe & Co., 1941), p. 123; quoted by Strich, op. cit., p. 38.

57. *Kunstgeschichtliche Grundbegriffe. Das Problem der Stilentwicklung in der*

neueren Kunst (1915); trans. M. D. Hottinger as *Principles of Art History,* London: G. Bell and Sons, Ltd., 1932).

58. Wilhelm Waetzoldt, "Heinrich Wölfflin," in *Kunst und Künstler* 22, 1924, quoted after Kultermann, op. cit. (note 10), p. 318.

59. About Hetzer, see Gosebruch, op. cit. (note 26), pp. 61–66 and passim. The monograph by Friedrich Klingner, *Theodor Hetzer,* Frankfurt am Main, 1947, was not accessible to me.

60. I derive this summary largely from two books by Hetzer, *Giotto, seine Stellung in der europäischen Kunst,* 2d ed. (Frankfurt am Main: Vittorio Klostermann, 1960), and *Die Sixtinische Madonna* (Frankfurt am Main: Vittorio Klostermann, 1947).

61. "Paolo Veronese," in Theodor Hetzer, *Aufsätze und Vorträge* vol. I (Leipzig: VEB E. A. Seemann Verlag, 1957), p. 75.

62. "Rembrandt und Giotto," in *Aufsätze und Vorträge,* vol. II.

63. *Tizian, Geschichte seiner Farbe* (1935; 3d ed., Frankfurt am Main: Vittorio Klostermann, 1969).

64. "Goya und die Krise der Kunst um 1800" (published posthumously in 1950). This is the only work by Hetzer that hitherto has been translated into English, by Vivian Volbach in Fred Licht, ed., *Goya in Perspective* (Englewood Cliffs, N.J.: Prentice-Hall Inc., 1973), pp. 93–113.

65. Ibid., p. 102.

66. Ibid., p. 99.

67. "Giotto und die Elemente der abendländischen Malerei," in *Aufsätze und Vorträge,* vol. I, p. 175.

68. Julius von Schlosser, *Die Wiener Schule der Kunstgeschichte. Rückblick auf ein Säkulum deutscher Gelehrtenarbeit in Oesterreich,* in *Mitteilungen des oesterreichischen Instituts für Geschichtsforschung,* Ergänzungsband 13.2, Innsbruck, Universitätsverlag Wagner, 1934.

69. Max Dvořák, "Franz Wickhoff" (obituary), in his *Gesammelte Aufsätze zur Kunstgeschichte* (Munich: R. Piper & Co. Verlag, 1929), pp. 299–312.

70. "Ueber moderne Malerei," in Franz Wickhoff, *Abhandlungen, Vorträge und Anzeigen,* 2 (Berlin: Bei Meyer & Jessen, 1913), pp. 53, 54.

71. Ibid., p. 37.

72. See his "Römische Kunst (Die Wiener Genesis) (1895; ed. Max Dvořák in *Die Schriften Franz Wickhoffs,* 3 Berlin: Meyer & Jessen, 1912; trans. and ed. Mrs. S. Arthur Strong as *Roman Art; Some of Its Principles and Their Application to Early Christian Painting,* London: W. Heinemann; New York: The Macmillan Company, 1900).

73. "Römische Kunst," pp. 58–61.

74. Eva Strommenger, "Three 'Eye Idols,'" in Harvey Weiss ed., *Ebla to Damascus, Art and Archaeology of Ancient Syria, an exhibition from the Directorate-General of Antiquities and Museums, Syrian Arab Republic* (Washington, D.C.: Smithsonian Institute Traveling Exhibition Service, 1985), cat. nos. 41–43, pp. 118, 119. I owe this reference to Donald P. Hansen.

75. Emanuel Loewy, "Ursprünge der bildenden Kunst," in *Almanach der Akademie der Wissenschaften in Wien,* Wien: In Kommission bei Rudolf M. Rohrer, 1930; see the comments in E. H. Gombrich, *The Sense of Order, A Study in the Psychology of Decorative Art,* The Wrightsman Lectures delivered under the auspices of the New York University Institute of Fine Arts (London: Phaidon, 1979), pp. 257–262.

76. Max Dvořák, "Alois Riegl" (obituary), *Gesammelte Aufsätze,* pp. 279–298. Otto Pächt, "Alois Riegl," in *Methodisches zur kunsthistorischen Praxis, Ausge-*

wählte Schriften (Munich: Prestel Verlag, 1977; repr. from *Burlington Magazine* 105, London, 1963).

77. Dvořák, "Riegl," pp. 294–298.

78. *Altorientalische Teppiche* (Leipzig: O. Weigels Nachfolger, 1891).

79. *Stilfragen, Grundlegungen zu einer Geschichte der Ornamentik* (Berlin: R. C. Schmidt & Co., 1923). In my summary of these two books by Riegl, I am following Gombrich, op. cit. (note 75), pp. 294–298.

80. Gombrich, op. cit. (note 75), pp. 189, 190.

81. Alois Riegl, *Die spätrömische Kunstindustrie* (1901: Wien: Druck und Verlag der österreichischen Staatsdruckerei, 1927; trans. with foreword and annotations by Rolf Winkes as *Late Roman Art Industry,* Rome: Giorgio Bretschneider, 1985).

82. *Spätrömische Kunstindustrie,* pp. 251–254 and 184–188, 46–49 and 286.

83. E. H. Gombrich, *Art and Illusion, A Study in the Psychology of Pictorial Representation,* Bollingen Series XXXV, 5, Second Printing (Princeton, N.J.: Princeton University Press, 1972), pp. 17–21. Gombrich's critique is summarized by Pächt, "Riegl," pp. 149, 152. Compare, however, Gombrich's positive evaluation of Riegl in *The Sense of Order* (note 75), p. VIII and passim.

84. Pächt, "Riegl," pp. 146, 152.

85. Riegl, op. cit. (note 81), pp. 393–400.

86. Ludwig Münz, Nachwort, in Alois Riegl, *Das holländische Gruppenporträt* (1902; Vienna: Druck und Verlag der österreichischen Staatsdruckerei, 1931), pp. 287, 289.

87. For a good recent evaluation of Dvořák's work see Hans-Berthold Busse, *Kunst und Wissenschaft, Untersuchungen zur Aesthetik und Methodik der Kunstgeschichtswissenschaft* (Mittenwald: Mäander Kunstverlag, 1981), pp. 85–108.

88. Ibid., pp. 92–94.

89. About Morelli, see Edgar Wind, *Art and Anarchy* (New York: Vintage Books, 1969), pp. 34–44 and passim.

90. Max Dvořák, "Eine illustrierte Kriegschronik," in *Gesammelte Aufsätze* (note 69), pp. 242–249.

91. Max Dvořák, "Ueber Kunstbetrachtung" (unpublished lecture), quoted by Busse (note 87), p. 85.

92. *Kunstgeschichte als Geistesgeschichte,* ed. Karl M. Swoboda and Johannes Wilde (Munich: R. Piper Verlag, 1924), trans. by John Hardy as *The History of Art as History of Ideas* (London, Boston: Routledge and Kegan Paul, 1984).

93. "Idealismus und Naturalismus in der gotischen Skulptur und Malerei," in *Kunstgeschichte als Geistesgeschichte,* pp. 41–147.

94. Ibid., p. 56.

95. Heinrich Wölfflin, *Renaissance und Barock* (note 48), p. 62; quoted by Busse, p. 89.

96. *Kunstgeschichte als Geistesgeschichte,* p. 266; see below, p. 196.

97. Alois Riegl, *Die Entstehung der Barockkunst in Rom,* ed. Arthur Burda and Max Dvořák (Vienna: Verlag von Anton Schroll & Co., 1908), p. 153.

98. Carl Justi, *Diego Velázquez und sein Jahrhundert* (Zurich: Phaidon Verlag AG, 1933), pp. 84, 85, quoted by Kultermann, op. cit. (note 10), p. 355.

99. Otto Kurz, "Julius von Schlosser, Personalità, metodo, lavoro," in *Critica d'arte* 11/12, 1955, p. 419.

100. Julius Schlosser, *Die Kunstliteratur, ein Handbuch zur Quellenkunde der neueren Kunstgeschichte* (Vienna: Kunstverlag Anton Schroll & Co., 1924), pp. 401, 402.

101. See note 99. About Kurz, see E. H. Gombrich, "The Exploration of Cul-

ture Contacts, the Services to Scholarship of Otto Kurz" (1903–1975), in *Tributes,* op. cit. (note 1).

102. See note 100. For an updated edition, see Julius Schlosser Magnino, *La letteratura artistica; manuale delle fonti della storia dell' arte moderna,* trans. Filippo Rossi, updated by Otto Kurz, 3rd ed. (Florence: Nuova Italia, 1964).

103. "Schriftquellen zur karolingischen Kunst," Eitelberger-Ilg, *Quellenschriften zur Kunstgeschichte,* Neue Folge, IV (Vienna: C. Graeser, 1896).

104. *Lorenzo Ghibertis Denkwürdigkeiten (I Commentarii).* Zum ersten Male nach der Handschrift der Biblioteca Nazionale vollständig herausgegeben und erläutert, 2 vols. (Berlin W 15: Julius Bard Verlag, 1912); *Lorenzo Ghibertis Denkwürdigkeiten. Prolegomena zu einer künftigen Ausgabe.* Jahrbuch der Zentralkommission, 1910.

105. Julius von Schlosser, *"Stilgeschichte" und "Sprachgeschichte" der bildenden Kunst, Ein Rückblick. Sitzungsberichte der Bayerischen Akademie der Wissenschaften, Philosophisch-Historische Abteilung, Jahrgang 1935, Heft II,* p. 13.

106. Julius von Schlosser, *Die Kunst des Mittelalters* (Berlin-Neubabelsberg: Akademische Verlagsgesellschaft Athenaion m.b.H., n.d. [1923]), pp. 1, 2.

107. Otto Kurz, op. cit. (note 99), pp. 416–418.

108. *"Stilgeschichte"* (note 105), pp. 118–120.

109. Op. cit., pp. 418, 419.

110. Fritz Saxl, "Rinascimento dell'Antichità. Studien zu den Arbeiten A. Warburgs," *Repertorium für Kunstwissenschaft,* vol. 43, 1922. Gertrud Bing, "A. M. Warburg," *Journal of the Warburg and Courtauld Institutes,* vol. 28, 1965.

111. E. H. Gombrich, *Aby Warburg, an Intellectual Biography* (London: The Warburg Institute, University of London, 1970). See also: E. H. Gombrich: "The Ambivalence of the Classical Tradition, The Cultural Psychology of Aby Warburg," in *Tributes,* op. cit. (note 1).

112. "Sandro Botticellis *Geburt der Venus* und *Frühling* (1893) in A. Warburg, *Gesammelte Schriften,* I, ed. Fritz Rougemont and Gertrud Bing (Leipzig-Berlin: B. G. Teubner, 1932), pp. 1–59.

113. Jan Bialostocki, "Erwin Panofsky (1892–1968): Thinker, Historian, Human Being," in *Simiolus, Kunsthistorisch Tijdschrift* 4, 1970, 2, p. 79.

114. "Francesco Sassettis letztwillige Verfügung" (1907), Warburg, op. cit. (note 112), pp. 127–158.

115. For an account of the impact of Warburg's lecture see William S. Heckscher, "The Genesis of Iconology" (1967), in Heckscher, *Art and Literature, Studies in Relationship,* ed. Egon Verheyen, (Durham N.C.: Duke University Press; Baden-Baden: Verlag Valentin Koerner, 1985), pp. 253–280. Continued research on the frescoes in the Palazzo Schifanoja has corrected details of Warburg's analysis; see the Anhang to his *Gesammelte Schriften.* It was beyond the scope of this anthology to include this highly specialized material, yet two points should be mentioned. (1) One of Warburg's principal sources, the *De deorum imaginibus libellus,* is no longer considered the work of "Albericus" (around 1200), but an anonymous adaptation of c. 1400 of the two mythographies of Petrus Berchorius, a friend of Petrarch's (c. 1340, 1342). Throughout Warburg's text, his references to "Albericus" are therefore to be replaced by this much later adaptation of Berchorius. See Anhang, pp. 627, 628. (2) After Warburg, scholars discovered a further development of decan astrology beyond Abū Māʾsar, which also had an impact on the frescoes in the Palazzo Schifanoja; see Anhang, pp. 630–639.

116. Saxl, op. cit. (note 110), pp. 257–259, 264.

117. See Gombrich, *Warburg* (note 111), pp. 194, 260.

118. "Heidnisch-antike Weissagung in Wort und Bild zu Luther's Zeiten," *Gesammelte Schriften,* II, pp. 487–558.

119. Published in translation as A. Warburg, "A Lecture on Serpent Ritual," *Journal of the Warburg Institute,* II, 1939, pp. 277–292.

120. The literature on Panofsky is already vast. An excellent account of his mind and accomplishment is the essay by Bialostocki (note 113). For a more personal tribute, see William S. Heckscher, "Erwin Panofsky, A Curriculum Vitae" (1969), in Heckscher, op. cit. (note 115), pp. 339–362.

121. See Erwin Panofsky, *Vorwort,* in Wilhelm Vöge, *Bildhauer des Mittelalters, Gesammelte Studien* (Berlin: Verlag Gebrüder Mann, 1958).

122. *Die deutsche Plastik des elften bis dreizehnten Jahrhunderts* (Munich: Kurt Wolff, 1924).

123. *Idea, Ein Beitrag zur Begriffsgeschichte der älteren Kunsttheorie,* Studien der Bibliothek Warburg, ed. Fritz Saxl V, Leipzig, Berlin: B. G. Teubner, 1924; 2d improved ed. (Berlin: Verlag Bruno Hessling, 1960).

124. Erwin Panofsky/Fritz Saxl, *Dürers 'Melencolia I', eine quellen-und typengeschichtliche Untersuchung* (Leipzig, Berlin: B. G. Teubner, 1923).

125. Erwin Panofsky, *The Life and Art of Albrecht Dürer* (1943; 4th ed., I Princeton, N.J.: Princeton University Press, 1955), p. 171. I owe this quote and the comparison to Podro, op. cit. (note 50), p. 205.

126. Erwin Panofsky, "Zum Problem der Beschreibung und Inhaltsdeutung von Werken der bildenden Kunst," in *Logos* XXI, 1932, pp. 103–119; "The History of Art as a Humanistic Discipline; Iconography and Iconology: An Introduction to the Study of Renaissance Art," in Panofsky, *Meaning in the Visual Arts* (Chicago: The University of Chicago Press, 1955), Phoenix edition, 1982, pp. 1–25, 26–54.

127. Ibid., p. 30.

128. Ibid., p. 39. For a critique of Panofsky's concept of the structural unity of every given period of culture, see Gombrich, "In Search of Cultural History" (note 1).

Johann Joachim Winckelmann

On the Imitation of the Painting and Sculpture of the Greeks

I Nature

To the Greek climate we owe the production of taste, and from thence it spread at length over all the politer world. Every invention, communicated by foreigners to that nation, was but the seed of what it became afterwards, changing both its nature and size in a country, chosen, as Plato says,[1] by Minerva, to be inhabited by the Greeks, as productive of every kind of genius.

But this taste was not only original among the Greeks, but seemed also quite peculiar to their country: it seldom went abroad without loss, and was long ere it imparted its kind influences to more distant climes. It was, doubtless, a stranger to the northern zones, when painting and sculpture, those offsprings of Greece, were despised there to such a degree, that the most valuable pieces of Correggio served only for blinds to the windows of the royal stables at Stockholm.

There is but one way for the moderns to become great, and perhaps unequalled; I mean, by imitating the ancients. And what we are told of Homer, that whoever understands him well, admires him, we find no less true in matters concerning the ancient, especially the Greek arts. But then we must be as familiar with them as with a friend, to find *Laocoon* (Fig. 7) as inimitable as Homer. By such intimacy our judgment will be that of Nicomachus: Take these eyes, replied he to some paltry critic, censuring the Helen of Zeuxis, Take my eyes, and she will appear a goddess.

With such eyes Michelangelo, Raphael, and Poussin, considered the performances of the ancients. They imbibed taste at its source; and Raphael particularly in its native country. We know, that he sent young artists to Greece, to copy there, for his use, the remains of antiquity.

An ancient Roman statue, compared to a Greek one, will generally appear like Virgil's Diana amidst her Oreads, in comparison of the Nausicaa of Homer, whom he imitated.

Laocoon was the standard of the Roman artists, as well as ours; and the rules of Polycletus became the rules of art.

I need not put the reader in mind of the negligences to be met with in the most celebrated ancient performances: the Dolphin at the feet of the Medici *Venus*, with the children, being commonly known. The reverse of the best Egyptian and Syrian coins seldom equals the head, in point of workmanship. Great artists are wisely negligent, and even their errors instruct. Behold their works as Lucian bids you behold the Zeus of Phidias; Zeus himself, not his footstool.

It is not only nature which the votaries of the Greeks find in their works, but still more, something superior to nature; ideal beauties, brain-born images, as Proclus says.[2]

The most beautiful body of ours would perhaps be as much inferior to the most beautiful Greek one, as Iphicles was to his brother Hercules. The forms of the Greeks, prepared to beauty, by the influence of the mildest and purest sky, became perfectly elegant by their early exercises. Take a Spartan youth, sprung from heroes, undistorted by swaddling-cloths; whose bed, from his seventh year, was the earth, familiar with wrestling and swimming from his infancy; and compare him with one of our young Sybarites, and then decide which of the two would be deemed worthy, by an artist, to serve for the model of a Theseus, an Achilles, or even a Bacchus. The latter would produce a Theseus fed on roses, the former a Theseus fed on flesh, to borrow the expression of Euphranor.[3]

The grand games were always a very strong incentive for every Greek youth to exercise himself. Whoever aspired to the honours of these was obliged, by the laws, to submit to a trial of ten months at Elis, the general rendezvous; and there the first rewards were commonly won by youths as Pindar tells us.[4] To be like the God-like Diagoras, was the fondest wish of every youth.

Behold the swift Indian outstripping in pursuit the hart: how briskly his juices circulate! how flexible, how elastic his nerves and muscles! how easy his whole frame! Thus Homer draws his heroes, and his Achilles he eminently marks for being swift of foot.

By these exercises the bodies of the Greeks got the great and manly contour observed in their statues, without any bloated corpulency. The young Spartans were bound to appear every tenth day naked before the ephors,[5] who, when they perceived any inclinable to fatness, ordered them a scantier diet; nay, it was one of Pythagoras's precepts, to beware of growing too corpulent; and, perhaps for the same reason, youths aspiring to wrestling-games were, in the remoter ages of Greece, during their trial, confined to a milk diet.

They were particularly cautious in avoiding every deforming custom; and Alcibiades, when a boy, refusing to learn to play on the flute, for fear of its discomposing his features, was followed by all the youth of Athens.

In their dress they were professed followers of nature. No modern stiffening habit, no squeezing stays hindered nature from forming easy beauty; the fair knew no anxiety about their attire.

We know what pains they took to have handsome children, but want to be acquainted with their methods: for certainly Quillet, in his *Callipaedia*,[6] falls short of their numerous expedients. They even attempted changing blue eyes to black ones, and games of beauty were exhibited at Elis, the rewards consisting of arms consecrated to the temple of Minerva. How could they miss of competent and learned judges, when, as Aristotle tells us,[7] the Greek youths were taught drawing expressly for that purpose? From their fine complexion, which, though mingled with a vast deal of foreign blood, is still preserved in most of the Greek islands, and from the still enticing beauty of the fair sex, especially at Chios; we may easily form an idea of the beauty of the former inhabitants, who boasted of being aborigines, nay, more ancient than the moon.

And are not there several modern nations, among whom beauty is too common to give any title to pre-eminence? Such are unanimously accounted the Georgians and the Kabardines in the Crimea.

Those diseases which are destructive of beauty, were moreover unknown to the Greeks. There is not the least hint of the small-pox, in the writings of their physicians; and Homer, whose portraits are always so truly drawn, mentions not one pitted face. Venereal plagues, and their daughter the English malady[8] had not yet names.

And must we not then, considering every advantage which nature bestows, or art teaches, for forming, preserving, and improving beauty, enjoyed and applied by the Greeks; must we not then confess, there is the strongest probability that the beauty of their persons excelled all we can have an idea of?

Art claims liberty: in vain would nature produce her noblest offsprings, in a country where rigid laws would choke her progressive growth, as in Egypt, that pretended parent of sciences and arts: but in Greece, where, from their earliest youth, the happy inhabitants were devoted to mirth and pleasure, where narrow-spirited formality never restrained the liberty of manners, the artist enjoyed nature without a veil.

The gymnasia, where, sheltered by public modesty, the youths exercised themselves naked, were the schools of art. These the philosopher frequented, as well as the artist. Socrates for the instruction of a Charmides, Autolycus, Lysis; Phidias for the improvement of his art by their beauty. Here he studied the elasticity of the muscles, the ever varying motions of the frame, the outlines of fair forms, or the contour left by the young wrestler on the sand. Here beautiful nakedness appeared with such a liveliness of expression, such truth and variety of situations, such a noble air of the body, as it would be ridiculous to look for in any hired model of our academies.

Truth springs from the feelings of the heart. What shadow of it therefore can the modern artist hope for, by relying upon a vile model, whose soul is either too base to feel, or too stupid to express the passions, the sentiment his object claims? unhappy he! if experience and fancy fail him.

The beginning of many of Plato's dialogues, supposed to have been held in the gymnasia, cannot raise our admiration of the generous souls of the Athenian youth, without giving us, at the same time, a strong presumption of a suitable nobleness in their outward carriage and bodily exercises.

The fairest youths danced undressed on the theatre; and Sophocles, the great Sophocles, when young, was the first who dared to entertain his fellow-citizens in this manner. Phryne went to bathe at the Eleusinian games, exposed to the eyes of all Greece, and rising from the water became the model of Venus Anadyomene. During certain solemnities the young Spartan maidens danced naked before the young men: strange this may seem, but will appear more probable, when we consider that the christians of the primitive church, both men and women, were dipped together in the same font.

Then every solemnity, every festival, afforded the artist opportunity to familiarize himself with all the beauties of Nature.

In the most happy times of their freedom, the humanity of the Greeks abhorred bloody games, which even in the Ionic Asia had ceased long before, if, as some guess, they had once been usual there. Antiochus Epiphanes, by ordering shows of Roman gladiators, first presented them with such unhappy victims; and custom and time, weakening the pangs of sympathizing humanity, changed even these games into schools of art. There Ctesias studied his dying gladiator, in whom you might descry how much life was still left in him.[9]

These frequent occasions of observing nature, taught the Greeks to go on still farther. They began to form certain general ideas of beauty, with regard to the proportions of the inferior parts, as well as of the whole frame: these they raised above the reach of mortality, according to the superior model of some ideal nature.

Thus Raphael formed his *Galatea*, as we learn by his letter to Count Baldassare Castiglione, where he says, 'Beauty being so seldom found among the fair, I avail myself of a certain ideal image.'

According to those ideas, exalted above the pitch of material models, the Greeks formed their gods and heroes: the profile of the brow and nose of gods and goddesses is almost a straight line. The same they gave on their coins to queens, etc. but without indulging their fancy too much. Perhaps this profile was as peculiar to the ancient Greeks, as flat noses and little eyes to the Kalmyks and Chinese; a supposition which receives some strength from the large eyes of all the heads on Greek coins and gems.

From the same ideas the Romans formed their Empresses on their coins. Livia and Agrippina have the profile of Artemisia and Cleopatra.

We observe, nevertheless, that the Greek artists in general, submitted to the law prescribed by the Thebans: 'To do, under a penalty, their best in imitating nature.' For, where they could not possibly apply their easy profile, without endangering the resemblance, they followed nature, as we see instanced in the beauteous head of Julia, the daughter of Titus, done by Euodus.[10]

But to form a 'just resemblance, and, at the same time, a handsomer one', being always the chief rule they observed, and which Polygnotus constantly went by; they must, of necessity, be supposed to have had in view a more beauteous and more perfect nature. And when we are told, that some artists imitated Praxiteles, who took his concubine Cratina for the model of his Cnidian *Venus*; it is to be understood that they did so, without neglecting these great laws of the art. Sensual beauty furnished the painter with all that nature could give; ideal beauty with the awful and sublime; from that he took the Human, from this the Divine.

Let any one, sagacious enough to pierce into the depths of art, compare the whole system of the Greek figures with that of the moderns, by which, as they say, nature alone is imitated; good heaven! what a number of neglected beauties will he not discover!

For instance, in most of the modern figures, if the skin happens to be any where pressed, you see there several little smart wrinkles: when, on the contrary, the same parts, pressed in the same manner on Greek statues, by their soft undulations, form at last but one noble pressure. These masterpieces never show us the skin forcibly stretched, but softly embracing the firm flesh, which fills it up without any tumid expansion, and harmoniously follows its direction. There the skin never, as on modern bodies, appears in plaits distinct from the flesh.

Modern works are likewise distinguished from the ancient by parts; a crowd of small touches and dimples too sensibly drawn. In ancient works you find these distributed with sparing sagacity, and, as relative to a completer and more perfect nature, offered but as hints, nay, often perceived only by the learned.

The probability still increases, that the bodies of the Greeks, as well as the works of their artists, were framed with more unity of system, a nobler harmony of parts, and a completeness of the whole, above our lean tensions and hollow wrinkles.

Probability, it is true, is all we can pretend to: but it deserves the attention of our artists and connoisseurs the rather, as the veneration professed for the ancient monuments is commonly imputed to prejudice, and not to their excellence; as if the numerous ages, during which they have mouldered, were the only motive for bestowing on them exalted praises, and setting them up for the standards of imitation.

Such as would fain deny to the Greeks the advantages both of a more perfect nature and of ideal beauties, boast of the famous Bernini, as their great champion. He was of opinion, besides, that nature was possessed of every requisite beauty: the only skill being to discover that. He boasted of having got rid of a prejudice concerning the Medici *Venus*, whose charms he at first thought peculiar ones; but, after many careful researches, discovered them now and then in nature.[11]

He was taught then, by the *Venus*, to discover beauties in common nature, which he had formerly thought peculiar to that statue, and but for it, never would have searched for them. Follows it not from thence, that the beauties of the Greek statues being discovered with less difficulty than those of nature, are of course more affecting; not so diffused, but more harmoniously united? and if this be true, the pointing out of nature as chiefly imitable, is leading us into a more tedious and bewildered road to the knowledge of perfect beauty, than setting up the ancients for that purpose: consequently Bernini, by adhering too strictly to nature, acted against his own principles, as well as obstructed the progress of his disciples.

The imitation of beauty is either reduced to a single object, and is individual, or, gathering observations from single ones, composes of these one whole. The former we call copying, drawing a portrait; it is the straight way to Dutch forms and figures; whereas the other leads to general beauty, and its ideal images, and is the way the Greeks took. But there is still this difference between them and us: they enjoying daily occasions of seeing beauty (suppose even not superior to ours), acquired those ideal riches with less toil than we, confined as we are to a few and often fruitless opportunities, ever can hope for. It would be no easy matter, I fancy, for our nature, to produce a frame equal in beauty to that of *Antinous*;[12] and surely no idea can soar above the more than human proportions of a deity, in the *Apollo* of the Vatican, which is a compound of the united force of nature, genius, and art.

Their imitation discovering in the one every beauty diffused through nature, showing in the other the pitch to which the most perfect nature can elevate herself, when soaring above the senses, will quicken the genius of the artist, and shorten his discipleship: he will learn to think and draw with confidence, seeing here the fixed limits of human and divine beauty.

Building on this ground, his hand and senses directed by the Greek rule of beauty, the modern artist goes on the surest way to the imitation of nature. The ideas of unity and perfection, which he acquired in meditating on antiquity, will help him to combine, and to ennoble the more scattered and weaker beauties of our nature. Thus he will improve every beauty he discovers in it, and by comparing the beauties of nature with the ideal, form rules for himself.

Then, and not sooner, he, particularly the painter, may be allowed to commit himself to nature, especially in cases where his art is beyond the instruction of the old marbles, to wit, in drapery; then, like Poussin, he may proceed with more liberty. Minds favoured by nature have here a plain way to become originals.

Thus the account de Piles[13] gives, ought to be understood, that Raphael, a short time before he was carried off by death, intended to forsake the marbles, in order to addict himself wholly to nature. True ancient taste would most certainly have guided him through every maze of common nature; and whatever observations, whatever new ideas he might have reaped from that, they would all, by a kind of chemical transmutation, have been changed to his own essence and soul.

He, perhaps, might have indulged more variety; enlarged his draperies; improved his colours, his light and shadow: but none of these improvements would have raised his pictures to that high esteem they deserve, for that noble contour, and that sublimity of thoughts, which he acquired from the ancients.

Nothing would more decisively prove the advantages to be got by imitating the ancients, preferably to nature, than an essay made with two youths of equal talents, by devoting the one to antiquity, the other to nature: this would draw nature as he finds her; if Italian, perhaps he might paint like Caravaggio; if Flemish, and lucky, like Jordaens; if French, like Stella:[14] the other would draw her as she directs, and paint like Raphael.

II Contour

But even supposing that the imitation of nature could supply all the artist wants, she never could bestow the precision of contour, that characteristic distinction of the ancients.

The noblest contour unites or circumscribes every part of the most perfect nature, and the ideal beauties in the figures of the Greeks; or rather, contains them both. Euphranor, famous after the epoch of Zeuxis, is said to have first ennobled it.

Many of the moderns have attempted to imitate this contour, but very few with success. The great Rubens is far from having attained either its precision or elegance, especially in the performances which he finished before he went to Italy, and studied the antiques.

The line by which nature divides completeness from superfluity is but a small one, and, insensible as it often is, has been crossed even by the best moderns; while these, in shunning a meagre contour, became corpulent, those, in shunning that, grew lean.

Among them all, only Michelangelo, perhaps, may be said to have attained the antique; but only in strong muscular figures, heroic frames; not in those of tender youth; nor in female bodies, which, under his bold hand, grew Amazons.

The Greek artist, on the contrary, adjusted his contour, in every figure, to the breadth of a single hair, even in the nicest and most tiresome performances, as gems. Consider the *Diomedes* and *Perseus* of Dioscorides,[15] *Hercules* and *Iole* by Teucer,[16] and admire the inimitable Greeks.

Parrhasius, they say, was master of the correctest contour.

This contour reigns in Greek figures, even when covered with drapery, as the chief aim of the artist; the beautiful frame pierces the marble like a transparent racoon skin.

The high-styled *Agrippina*, and the three *Vestals* in the royal cabinet at Dresden, deserve to be mentioned as eminent proofs of this. This *Agrippina* seems not the mother of Nero, but an elder one, the spouse of Germanicus. She much resembles another pretended Agrippina, in the parlour of the library of San Marco, at Venice.[17] Ours is a sitting figure, above the size of nature, her head inclined on her right hand; her fine face speaks a soul pining in thought, absorbed in pensive sorrow, and senseless to every outward impression. The artist, I suppose, intended to draw his heroine in the mournful moment she received the news of her banishment.

The three *Vestals* deserve our esteem from a double title: as being the first important discoveries of Herculaneum, and models of the sublimest drapery.[18] All three, but particularly one above the natural size, would, with regard to that, be worthy companions of the Farnese *Flora*,[19] and all the other boasts of antiquity. The two others seem, by their resemblance to each other, productions of the same hand, only distinguished by their heads, which are not of equal goodness. On the best the curled hairs, running in furrows from the forehead, are tied on the neck: on the other the hair being smooth on the scalp, and curled on the front, is gathered behind, and tied with a riband: this head seems of a modern hand, but a good one.

There is no veil on these heads; but that makes not against their being vestals: for the priestesses of Vesta (I speak on proof) were not always veiled; or rather, as the drapery seems to betray, the veil, which was of one piece with the garments, being thrown backwards, mingles with the clothes on the neck.

It is to these three inimitable pieces that the world owes the first hints of the ensuing discovery of the subterranean treasures of Herculaneum.

Their discovery happened when the same ruins that overwhelmed the town had nearly extinguished the unhappy remembrance of it: when the tremendous fate that spoke its doom was only known by the account which Pliny gives of his uncle's death.

These great masterpieces of the Greek art were transplanted, and worshipped in Germany, long before Naples could boast of one single Herculanean monument.

They were discovered in the year 1706 at Portici near Naples, in a ruinous vault, on occasion of digging the foundations of a villa, for the Prince d'Elbeuf, and immediately, with other new discovered marble and metal statues, came into the possession of Prince Eugene, and were transported to Vienna.

Eugene, who well knew their value, provided a Sala Terrena to be built expressly for them, and a few others: and so highly were they esteemed, that even on the first rumour of their sale, the academy and the artists were in an uproar, and every body, when they were transported to Dresden, followed them with heavy eyes.

The famous Mattielli, to whom

His rule Polyclet, his chisel Phidias gave [Algarotti][20]

copied them in clay before their removal, and following them some years after, filled Dresden with everlasting monuments of his art: but even there he studied the drapery of his priestesses, (drapery his chief skill!) till he laid down his chisel, and thus gave the most striking proof of their excellence.

III Drapery

By drapery is to be understood all that the art teaches of covering the nudities, and folding the garments; and this is the third prerogative of the ancients.

The drapery of the vestals above, is grand and elegant. The smaller foldings spring gradually from the larger ones, and in them are lost again, with a noble freedom, and gentle harmony of the whole, without hiding the correct contour. How few of the moderns would stand the test here!

Justice, however, shall not be refused to some great modern artists, who, without impairing nature or truth, have left, in certain cases, the road which the ancients generally pursued. The Greek drapery, in order to help the contour, was, for the most part, taken from thin and wet garments, which of course clasped the body, and discovered the shape. The robe of the Greek ladies was extremely thin.

Nevertheless the reliefs, the pictures, and particularly the busts of the ancients, are instances that they did not always keep to this undulating drapery.

In modern times the artists were forced to heap garments, and sometimes heavy ones, on each other, which of course could not fall into the flowing folds of the ancients. Hence the large-folded drapery, by which the painter and sculptor may display as much skill as by the ancient manner, Carlo Maratta and Francesco Solimena may be called the chief masters of it:[21] but the garments of the new Venetian school, by passing the bounds of nature and propriety, became stiff as brass.

IV Expression

The last and most eminent characteristic of the Greek works is a noble simplicity and sedate grandeur in gesture and expression. As the bottom of the sea lies peaceful beneath a foaming surface, a great soul lies sedate beneath the strife of passions in Greek figures.

It is in the face of Laocoon [that] this soul shines with full lustre, not confined however to the face, amidst the most violent sufferings. Pangs piercing every muscle, every labouring nerve; pangs which we almost feel ourselves, while we consider—not the face, nor the most expressive parts—only the belly contracted by excruciating pains: these however, I say, exert not themselves with violence, either in the face or gesture. He pierces not heaven, like the Laocoon of Virgil; his mouth is rather opened to discharge an anxious overloaded groan, as Sadoleto says;[22] the struggling body and the supporting mind exert themselves with equal strength, nay balance all the frame.

Laocoon suffers, but suffers like the Philoctetes of Sophocles: we weeping feel his pains, but wish for the hero's strength to support his misery.

The expression of so great a soul is beyond the force of mere nature. It was in his own mind the artist was to search for the strength of spirit with which he marked his marble. Greece enjoyed artists and philosophers in the same persons; and the wisdom of more than one Metrodorus[23] directed art, and inspired its figures with more than common souls.

Had *Laocoon* been covered with a garb becoming an ancient sacrificer, his sufferings would have lost one half of their expression. Bernini pretended to perceive the first effects of the operating venom in the numbness of one of the thighs.

Every action or gesture in Greek figures, not stamped with this character of sage dignity, but too violent, too passionate, was called 'Parenthyrsos.'[24]

For, the more tranquillity reigns in a body, the fitter it is to draw the true character of the soul; which, in every excessive gesture, seems to rush from her proper centre, and being hurried away by extremes becomes unnatural. Wound up to the highest pitch of passion, she may force herself upon the duller eye; but the true sphere of her action is simplicity and calmness. In *Laocoon* sufferings alone had been 'parenthyrsos'; the artists therefore, in order to reconcile the significative and ennobling qualities of his soul, put him into a posture, allowing for the sufferings that were necessary, the next to a state of tranquillity: a tranquillity however that is characteristical: the soul will be herself—this individual—not the soul of mankind: sedate, but active; calm, but not indifferent or drowsy.

What a contrast! how diametrically opposite to this is the taste of our modern artists, especially the young ones! on nothing do they bestow their approbation, but contorsions and strange postures, inspired with boldness; this they pretend is done with spirit, with *franchezza*. Contrast is the darling of their ideas; in it they fancy every perfection. They fill their performances with comet-like eccentric souls, despising every thing but an Ajax or a Capaneus.

Arts have their infancy as well as men; they begin, as well as the artist, with froth and bombast: in such buskins the muse of Aeschylus stalks, and part of the diction in his Agamemnon is more loaded with hyberboles than all Heraclitus's nonsense. Perhaps the primitive Greek painters drew in the same manner that their first good tragedian thought in.

In all human actions flutter and rashness precede, sedateness and solidity follow: but time only can discover, and the judicious will admire these only: they are the characteristics of great masters; violent passions run away with their disciples.

The sages in the art know the difficulties hid under that air of easiness:

> ut sibi quivis
> Speret idem, sudet multum, frustraque laboret
> Ausus idem.   [Horace][25]

Lafage, though an eminent designer, was not able to attain the purity of ancient taste.[26] Every thing is animated in his works; they demand, and at the same time dissipate, your attention, like a company striving to talk all at once.

This noble simplicity and sedate grandeur is also the true characteristical mark of the best and maturest Greek writings, of the epoch and school of Socrates. Possessed of these qualities Raphael became eminently great, and he owed them to the ancients.

That great soul of his, lodged in a beauteous body, was requisite for the first discovery of the true character of the ancients: he first felt all their beauties, and (what he was peculiarly happy in!) at an age when vulgar, unfeeling, and half-moulded souls overlook every higher beauty.

Ye that approach his works, teach your eyes to be sensible of those beauties, refine your taste by the true antique, and then that solemn tranquillity of the chief figures in his Attila, deemed insipid by the vulgar, will appear to you equally significant and sublime. The Roman bishop, in order to divert the Hun from his design of assailing Rome, appears not with the air of a *rhetor*,[27] but as a venerable man, whose very presence softens uproar into peace; like him drawn by Virgil:

> Tum pietate gravem ac meritis, si forte virum quem
> Conspexere, silent, adrectisque auribus adstant:[28]

full of confidence in God, he faces down the barbarian: the two Apostles descend not with the air of slaughtering angels, but (if sacred may be compared with profane) like Jove, whose very nod shakes Olympus.

Algardi, in his celebrated representation of the same story, done in bas relief on an altar in St. Peter's at Rome,[29] was either too negligent, or too weak, to give this active tranquillity of his great predecessor to the figures of his Apostles. There they appear like messengers of the Lord of Hosts: here like human warriors with mortal arms.

How few of those we call connoisseurs have ever been able to understand, and sincerely to admire, the grandeur of expression in the *St. Michael* of Guido Reni, in the church of the Capuchins at Rome! they prefer commonly the *Archangel* of Conca,[30] whose face glows with indignation and revenge; whereas Guido's Angel, after having overthrown the fiend of God and man, hovers over him unruffled and undismayed.

Thus, to heighten the hero of The Campaign, victorious Marlborough, the British poet paints the avenging Angel hovering over Britannia with the like serenity and awful calmness.

The royal gallery at Dresden contains now, among its treasures, one of Raphael's best pictures, witness Vasari, etc. a Madonna with the Infant; St. Sixtus and St. Barbara kneeling, one on each side, and two Angels in the fore-part.[31]

It was the chief altar-piece in the cloister of St. Sixtus at Piacenza, which was crowded by connoisseurs, who came to see this Raphael, in the same manner as Thespiae was in the days of old, for the sake of the beautiful *Cupid* of Praxiteles.

Behold the Madonna, her face brightens with innocence; a form above the female size, and the calmness of her mien, make her appear as already beatified: she has that silent awfulness which the ancients spread over their deities. How grand, how noble is her contour!

The child in her arms is elevated above vulgar children, by a face darting the beams of divinity through every smiling feature of harmless childhood.

St. Barbara kneels, with adoring stillness, at her side: but being far beneath the majesty of the chief figure, the great artist compensated her humbler graces with soft enticing charms.

The Saint opposite to her is venerable with age. His features seem to bear witness of his sacred youth.

The veneration which St. Barbara declares for the Madonna, expressed in the most sensible and pathetic manner, by her fine hands clasped on her breast, helps to support the motion of one of St. Sixtus's hands, by which he utters his ecstasy, better becoming (as the artist judiciously thought and chose for variety's sake) manly strength, than female modesty.

Time, it is true, has withered the primitive splendour of this picture, and partly blown off its lively colours; but still the soul, with which the painter inspired his godlike work, breathes life through all its parts.

Let those that approach this, and the rest of Raphael's work, in hopes of finding there the trifling Dutch and Flemish beauties, the laboured nicety of Netscher, or Dou, flesh 'ivorified' by Van der Werff,[32] or even the 'licked' manner of some of Raphael's living countrymen; let those, I say, be told, that Raphael was not a great master for them.

Translated by Henry Fuseli

Notes

1. Plato, *Timaeus*, 23 D-24 A.
2. Proclus, Commentary on Plato's *Timaeus*, II, 122 B.
3. Euphranor, fourth century B.C. sculptor and painter, who called his own *Theseus* 'beef-fed' in contrast to the *Theseus* of Parrhasius, which he said was 'rose-fed'.
4. Pindar, *Olympic Odes*, VII.
5. Ephors were magistrates combining executive, judicial and disciplinary powers.
6. Claude Quillet, *Callipaedia* (Paris 1655), a treatise in Latin on how to have beautiful children.
7. Aristotle, *Politics*, Bk. V.
8. 'English malady' is an eighteenth-century term for nervous distempers, spleen.
9. Ctesias, first century, A.D. sculptor. Note in original text refers to Pliny, *Natural History*, XXXIV, 85.
10. Note in original text refers to engraving in Stosch, *Gemmae Antiquae*, engraved by Picart (Amsterdam 1724), Plate XXXIII.
11. The story is recorded in Baldinucci's *Life* of Bernini, first published 1682.
12. The *Antinous*, more probably *Hermes*, after a lost original by Praxiteles, one of the most famous of the antique statues in the Vatican Belvedere.
13. Roger de Piles, well-known seventeenth-century French theorist, whose principal works were *Dialogue sur le Coloris* (1673) and *Conversations sur la Peinture* (1677).
14. Jacques Stella (1596–1657), follower of Poussin.
15. Note in original text refers to engravings in Stosch, op. cit., Plates XXIX and XXX.
16. Note in original text refers to engraving in Antonio Francesco Gori, *Museum Florentinum* (Florence 1731–42), vol. II, Plate V.
17. Note in original text refers to engraving in Antonio Maria Zanetti, *Antiche Statue nell'Antisala della Libreria di San Marco* (Venice 1740–3), vol. 1, Plate IX.
18. Marble statues of a so-called *Matron* and a *Maiden* led directly to the discovery of Herculaneum. They are still in Dresden, as are the other works to which Winckelman refers.
19. *Flora*, now in the Museo Nazionale, Naples, one of the most famous statues in the Farnese collection, which in Winckelmann's lifetime was in Rome.
20. Count Francesco Algarotti (1712–64) was the leading Italian critic in the mid-eighteenth century, with a prolific output of essays and letters. The quotation is from a series of his poems on the theme of the influence of ancient Greece and Rome. This poem is dedicated to Winckelmann's patron, Augustus III, in *Opere Varie* (Venice 1757), vol. II, p. 428. A free rendering of '. . . Matiello: A lui/Lo scalpello diè Fidia, onde di Paro/Vinca gli antichi onor Ligure marmo.' Lorenzo Mattielli, sculptor, born in Vicenza (date unknown) and died in Dresden 1748.
21. Maratta (1625–1713) and Solimena (1657–1747) were both Baroque artists with strong classicizing tendencies. Solimena had a considerable contemporary reputation both as painter and teacher.
22. This argument is taken up by Lessing in his *Laocoon* (1766). Virgil's Laocoon in *Aeneid*, II, lines 199–231, when struggling with the snakes 'lifts to the stars his horrifying shrieks' (line 222). Jacopo Sadoleto (1477–1547) wrote a poem on the *Laocoon*; see the translation in the excellent study by Margarete Bieber, *Laocoon:*

The Influence of the Group since its Rediscovery (rev. edn, Detroit 1967), pp. 13–15.

23. Metrodorus of Lampsacus (about 330–277 B.C.) was the most important philosopher of Epicureanism, after Epicurus himself.

24. 'Parenthyrsos' means false sentiment or affectation of style. The word is used by Longinus in *On the Sublime* (3.5), who quotes Theorodus Epigrammaticus. Longinus was widely read in the eighteenth century, and in his passage, which Winckelmann knew, Longinus says of 'parenthyrsos': 'This is passion out of place and unmeaning, where there is no call for passion, or unrestrained where restraint is needed. Men are carried aside, as if under strong drink, into expressions of feeling which have nothing to do with the subject, but are personal to themselves and academic: then they play clumsy antics before an audience which has never been moved.'

25. *Ars Poetica*, lines 240–1, Latin extract from whole sentence which reads: 'My aim shall be poetry, so moulded from the familiar that anybody may hope for the same success, may sweat much and yet toil in vain when attempting the same.'

26. Raymond Lafage (1656–90), primarily an engraver of biblical and mythological subjects, including bacchanals.

27. At the school of the rhetor (fourth century A.D.) students were taught the art of rhetoric.

28. *Aeneid*, I, lines 151–2: 'Then should they chance to look upon a man by goodness and by service dignified, they hush, and stand around with ears attent.'

29. Alessandro Algardi's relief of *The Meeting of Leo and Attila* (1646–53), twenty-five feet high, is an important Baroque work, initiating the painterly relief.

30. Sebastiano Conca (1679–1764) was a pupil of Solimena, who emerged as a dominant late Baroque artist in Rome. His *St. Michael* is in Santa Maria in Campitelli, Rome.

31. Raphael's *Sistine Madonna* is still in Dresden, in the Gallery.

32. Winckelmann chooses three Dutch portrait and genre painters: Caspar Netscher (1639–84), Gerard Dou (1613–75), pupil of Rembrandt, and Adriaen Van der Werff (1659–1722).

Annotated by David Irwin

Wilhelm Heinse

Further Description of Several Paintings in the Düsseldorf Gallery

The Flight of the Amazons

This piece (Fig. 1) was the first star to rise on the firmament of our gallery. The Elector, who endowed our institution, was a man of great enthusiasm with the strength of will to persevere. He somehow obtained the painting in question and, little by little, after repeated scrutiny, grew so fond of it that he soon became a lover of art. In time he gathered the great collection which, with better guidance, would have become even more select than it is.

A terrifying battle of the sexes, it is a work in which one cannot take full pleasure until one has descended into the remotest precincts of nature.

The portrayal of a bloody combat at the point at which the die has finally been cast. The sad heroines must acknowledge defeat, they have been beaten, they are on the run, and the enemy flies after them in hot pursuit over a bridge. Of those who lingered, indeed the bravest, some are taken prisoner, some cut down with a vengeance, and some do not hesitate in turn to do their share of the killing. Here is war at its most vivid, to satisfy a hunger for heroics, a lust for blood and guts, and all this carried out by armed maidens who dare attack men—wild, terrible, and yet ravishing insurgents against the laws of nature. It is a terrible-beautiful display the like of which is rare.

Starting from the left, we see an already distant horde of women and horses in flight, and in their wake, some brown chargers (relieved of their riders) dashing over a bridge. The one in the lead is so frightened and wild that it is still tossing its mane in the air, baring its teeth and snorting steam from its nose; and the other is kicking out with its hind legs, still seething from the heat of battle. An Amazon follows, wielding a bloody axe in her left hand, and with both hands grasping a general's head, which she cut off at the bridge, where the decapitated trunk is left bleeding into the river. She sits on her steed, facing her pursuers, like the brave Roman who would hold off the enemy until the bridge collapsed. An enemy warrior is grabbing for her booty, which she refuses to relinquish. Two other Amazons beside her, though wounded and tumbling, horse and rider, into the river, continue to do battle—their fallen victims and their mounts give proof of the Amazons' prowess.

This is the most striking group in the overall scheme and, together with the river, it may well constitute the seminal idea for the whole painting, an idea that is perhaps the boldest ever conceived.

The first one to fall from the bridge, with her head bowed and bleeding from a blow to the forehead, is unconscious and yet still clasping her deadly weapon, with her knees still in the saddle. The arrows are falling out of her quiver, falling with her and the horse; the horse has an enemy arrow piercing its neck, its front legs forward, belly raised, and hind legs stretching backward. Below her, likewise falling headfirst, but very much alive, the other wounded Amazon, still mounted, is splashing about. With hers and the white stallion's back both underwater, she is fighting the current and, filtered through the foam, we witness the whole incredible feat. Her face is seething with blood lust and battle, yet resigned to all that she must suffer in the process. Farther to the right of her in the water, two other Amazons are trying to swim to safety. Of the two figures which I just described in some detail, the latter is tumbling from her horse directly in front of the two swimmers, while the former is falling on top of her, causing one of the swimmers to turn her face away in horror. And to the left, the head of an Amazon struck down and cast into the deep, rises sideward, with the desperate expression of drowning, and above her, another horse (whose rider lies cut down at the wall) tumbles down out of the dark. Up at the head of the bridge an Amazon is having her banner wrested from her; she refuses to let go of it and fights for it with all her might. She is being dragged by this banner off her rearing steed, with which she nonetheless remains joined (like a centaur) through the pressure of her legs; one enemy warrior and another are working on her. Both of them hold tight to the fringe of the banner, the one on foot, the other on horseback. The latter, yellow and white with rage and blood lust, with a sword in his right hand, goes at her with all the force that's in him. A little farther on to the right, the queen is most likely the first to be captured. She clasps her deadly axe firmly and tightly in her practiced fist, and yet is powerless against the horde that hold fast to her on all sides. In her face there is rage at the vain tyrants and her fate, rage and loathing in her eyes and lips, but also bitterness over her approaching death. One of the enemy has her by the arm, and one by the shoulders and throat, and is about to stab her; and another, behind her, has a dart aimed at her back. To the far right, beside the bridge, an Amazon comes bounding, like an Alcibiades, finally resolved to flee. She too, like the others, is still in full possession of her Amazonian freedom and self-determination, which, incidentally, can be read in all their faces; and the steed is just about to leap into the current, as an enemy on horseback, having caught up with her there, is about to split her head from behind. He has already raised his sword to strike, and she has turned herself about. And with the greatest presence of mind, burning with tears of shame and rage at the fact that she must flee, she is stabbing him with her double-edged sword deep in the armpit, where his tendons tear and bleed. Above her, a young knight is spearing another Amazon with her horse into the current. And beneath her, on the shore, a starving wretch is dragging a few of the fallen out of the water to despoil them; he has already finished with one corpse and tossed it aside, and is tearing the clothing from under the buttocks of another so as to thereby hoist her into the water. But the most awful spectacle of the entire painting is taking place under the bridge. The bridge has only a single arch, but it is wide and thick and built, so it seems, by some Michelangelo; it casts a very striking shadow, elevating and intensifying the light in the distance beneath it. In the river and upstream, there is a chaos of falling, swimming, rescuing, crossing the water, fighting and drowning, of friend and foe all in a jumble. Farther on up the shore, enemy forces are gathered in the distance, and beside them a city is in flames. Here and there the river washes the dead ashore.

I would rather not describe any more.

It is a piece full of heroic strength, from the age of Theseus, with nothing overdone about it, nothing but the best illusion that paint and brush can conjure up. Brute force bursts forth from manly shoulders, from arms and fists with deadly weapons, from chest and knees: and rearing, the war-horses display their ever-changing leap and stride. The fiery look and passionate glow of the chase, the loftiest feminine expression of rage and the desperate lust for vengeance over this forced retreat, the clobbering and stabbing and dragging down, the plunge of horse and rider into the deep, the blood and wounds, swimming and death, nakedness and torn garments and splendid armor: truest coloring and strength, courage and fear and death of man and woman: life at its highest pitch, in the thick of battle, lighted by the terrible torn shreds of the morning sky — all this the painting depicts.

The Amazons have nothing soft about them; they are tough and majestic, seething with fury and fire. And in accordance with both their Circassian climate and their ancient statues, they are lightly clad in an undergarment and a short red coat on top, strung from the left shoulder. This garment often falls off in their plunge into the water, after the shoulder strap is either torn or severed, baring the lively motion of their beautiful limbs. They ride on their bare bottoms, with both thighs hugging a thin saddle, their legs covered only by a leather binding from foot to calf. Rubens always managed somehow to have the right breast pushed to the side, or shaded in such a light, or concealed by a garment, so that we are hardly aware of it — presumably to avert the biased notion that the Amazons got their name from having burnt off their right breasts. We can, at any rate, still see that the breast is there.

These heroines doubtless once held sway over a mighty kingdom, if we are to lend credence to history and folk legends (and not to the skepticism of an old geographer, who, judging from his own experience with women, could not concede that females might be involved in such lofty business). There is no question that the Amazons derived their name not from the fact that their mothers were silly enough to burn off their right breasts, but rather because they just were not like other women. They had abandoned qualities commonly labeled as female: obedience to men, and the like. For that reason they were called Amazons, the breastless ones, for breasts are the most immediately apparent feature that distinguish women from men. Moreover, breastless (as the term is most often used) is too vague an expression to have been used by such sensuous naturefolk as the ancients were; and the Amazons would either have had to be known as the right-breastless or the single-breasted, for the desperate notion of a few grammarians to hold. Moreover, the ancient statues of Amazons invariably have one breast as large and ample as the other.

Sennacherib

This little piece (Fig. 2) could be called the triumph of the Netherlander over Giulio Romano and Le Brun.

First, the story:

"When the Children of Israel groaned under the bondage of Babylon, and only the tribe of Judah, under the rule of the good King Hezekiah, were still free, the King of the Assyrians sought to subjugate Judah, and demanded what he thought to be an impossible levy. But after Hezekiah, contrary to the expectations of the Assyrian, did indeed come up with the required three hundred talents of silver and thirty talents of gold, the King of Assyria nevertheless prepared to invade Jerusalem, reviled all the gods, including Him who created heaven and earth, and encamped before the city. But the Lord, heedful of the prayers of the righteous, protected his Children, and spoke to them through the mouth of Isaiah, saying that their enemies would become like grass on the housetops blighted before it is grown. And that night the angel of the Lord went forth, and slew a hundred and eighty-five thousand in the camp of the Assyrians. Then Sennacherib King of Assyria departed, and went home, and was slain by his sons as he was worshipping in the house of Nisroch his god."

How would ninety-nine others have depicted this story?

A wide field with corpses strewn about between tents and horses, with a small band of survivors who at daybreak prove very much surprised. And some sort of executioner with swan wings hovering in the distant dawn.

Not so Rubens.

A black thundercloud sky shot through with bolts of lightning — the angel descending in the darkness against the foe — the whole atmosphere aflame, and where the avenging fire burns, all is as bright as day.

A grand, lofty painting, infused with the rage of the Almighty, with fear and trembling, a work terribly vivid in the most palpable depiction of the moment.

The greatest mass of light emanating from the destructive flames falls toward the middle of the key figure and the key group, on Sennacherib, who is tumbling off his horse. The horse is frightened and, unwilling to run into the lightning, it rears backward in the air, while Sennacherib clasps its flying mane with his right hand, his left thigh still hanging in the saddle, his left side slipping off to the right over the small of the horse's back. Beside him a wounded man is taking a magnificent spill off his horse. The horse is kicking far back with its hind legs, and beneath it you can see a heap of bodies, still warm, but dead and already paled in the steady phosphorescence. They lie there among horses and trampled under, and one or two, consumed by a hellish terror, are trying to hide themselves under the crushing horses. What an awful sight! Some only have half their bodies crushed, so that the bottom half is struggling up.

On the left within the painting, the crowd is in flight, some naked, some dressed, blinded by the scorching light, some still looking back in terror lest it strike them.

To the right of the storm's path there are tents, and in front of them, mighty battle horses, rearing and raging, their muzzles and foreheads and eyes and nostrils raised in terror and amazement.

This is but an overview of the whole grand scheme. The life, the sheer, palpable nature in every aspect has to be seen; words alone cannot convey it.

But above all, let us speak of the head of Sennacherib:

The face of death incarnate, unconscious, like a drowning man. The horror in the wide-open eyes and the distended brow, the show of fear and trembling in all the muscles around the open mouth, the pride in every aspect of that cruel chap, crushed to mush against the wall—all this makes Sennacherib's head perhaps grander even than the famous head of Maxentius:* a lion's stroke of the imagination.

And then there is his noble steed, frightened by the storm: It turns away and, foaming at the mouth, rears up before a terrible lightning bolt that has just struck down horse and rider at its side. A masterpiece of striking stature, bold posture, animal nobility, and the most formidable sketching, indeed this is one of the most accomplished achievements that ever emanated from Rubens's or any other painter's brush. Both the falling horse and the king are to be counted among those depictions Rubens realized at the height of his vigor and fire.

The presence of each of the other figures in the scene, the passing of human life and the rearing and falling and horrible fright of the horses—in short, the presence and unity of the whole is such that one cannot ponder any aspect independently of the whole, nor can one in describing it single out any one part of the painting.

The coloring is powerful and true, and more diversified according to nature than in some of his other pieces. The brush stroke is so light and, in its intensity, so like the fire of the soul, that here and there he actually permitted the color of the wood to show through the glazes, since these had already defined the form unsurpassably.

Light and shadow are diffused throughout the painting, morning, night, and stormy darkness intermingled and divided and mixed together in one, perhaps as much so as art was ever able to imitate nature. This light and shadow play is there in the black and overcast sky, shot through with lightning, in the daylight rising around the tents, in the interplay between bright day and night over the Assyrian king and the dead, and on the backs of the fleeing multitude, who push on ever deeper into the darkness and disappear.

Rubens probably came up with the idea for this painting once while witnessing a terrible thunderstorm breaking over an army, with lightning bolts playing around with the muskets and cannons according to the tactics of electricity. Such scenes have been described to me by Prussian officers reminiscing about their campaigns in Silesia. Perhaps Rubens saw a soldier cut down, and

---

*In Heinse's time, the colossal head of Constantine was still considered a head of Maxentius (Roman Emperor 306–312) because it was found in the Basilica of Maxentius.—Ed.

another at his side, tumbling off a Spanish stallion. And when he came home, the whole impression may have been immediately transferred to canvas in the immortal form of Sennacherib.

With crescent moons embroidered in a banner, Rubens made the story more accessible to the common man.

The Rape of the Daughters of Leucippus by the Dioskuroi

No one at the gallery rightly knew until now what story this painting (Fig. 3) was supposed to represent, thus it was given all sorts of hypothetical titles. With my attention always taken up with other matters, I myself thought of it as a mere fantasy of the painter's. I supposed that he, like the Psalm singer of old on his balcony, must once have spotted another man's pride and joy in her bath, and scorning the monstrous notion of taking the liberties of a king, contented himself by raping them with his brush, under this exotic guise. And although convinced of this, I nonetheless felt that the painter hadn't raped enough. And so I allowed my own laxness to translate as goodness on the painter's part, since I make it a rule never to censor an otherwise outstanding individual until I have cause and am by dint of duty obliged to do so.

Thus I viewed the painting according to my own conception, as others had viewed it in accordance with their conception of the biblical story of Dina, as their conception of a fragment of the Rape of the Sabines, or of the story of God knows what Princess Armenia, and so on, thus doing great injustice to the painter.

This morning I went out for a walk in the fields and stuck a copy of Theocritus into my pocket. On a hill, by a stream, beneath a tall shady oak, where the wind whistled through, I sat down on the grass. Later I leafed through the book I'd brought along, and since my eyes didn't feel like reading, I scanned the titles at the top of the page and stumbled upon the Abduction of the Daughters of Leucippus by the Dioskuroi, and I discovered the lost painting.

It had already in fact been conjectured that the men on horseback in the painting might as well be Castor and Pollux, since there were but two of them. However, this did not prove any more helpful than the story of Dina, except that it made the presence of the cupids and the Greek dress of one of the riders more plausible. I always had some trouble accepting the identity of the figure of Pollux, as I shall further explain, for I was not thinking of Theocritus' idyll, and Homer had not touched upon this abduction.

But enough of all that.

The painting depicts the abduction of the brides of Lynkeus and the mighty Idas, although if we are to accept what Theocritus has sung to their praise, the sons of Leda ought to take more after their father, the swan—more so, indeed, than in our painting, in which they appear far less like demigods, and rather genial. Nowadays, one might add, now that the force of nature has been de-clawed and had its wings clipped, one dare not sing such praises (as Theocritus does of Castor) of princes who do such things—not to mention that, according to the Sicilian poet, his father Zeus sent a bolt of lightning to remove the last obstacle blocking Castor's heated desire, so as to permit him to fulfill it undisturbed in all its fury, despite the fact that bride and groom had amicably invited him to their wedding. Pindar, by the way, tells it altogether differently in the tenth of his Nemean Odes in praise of Zeus.

The key figure in our painting is Castor, decked out in Greek armor and mounted on a reddish brown steed whose reins are being held by a cupid; Pollux stands at his brother's side, dismounted from his white horse, whose reins are likewise being held by another cupid: Castor to the right, Pollux to the left.

In an open field Castor is hoisting a completely naked young lady onto his horse, with the aid of a red silken cloth wrapped around her back and drawn in under her bottom (upon which it casts a beautiful reflection); his right hand grasping her raised left thigh at the knee, her right arm in his left. Pollux is propping up the same woman with his right shoulder under her left arm, and with his left hand he holds her sister under her right armpit.

It is difficult to put into words even so much as an approximation of the sensual beauty of this group.

Castor's steed stands toward the right side of the painting, and the white horse rears up to the left. Bathed in light, the two virgins dominate the middle, in front of the horses.

The first one, facing left, has her head and breasts turned away from her abductor (who has already managed to raise her left thigh at the knee up to his saddle), while she lets the lower thigh of her right leg hang against the horse, with her left arm stretched out over his brother's shoulder, and her right hand on her abductor's arm, over her upraised knee.

The second young woman stands close to the first one, equally facing left, and struggling in amazement against her abductor. While her face is directed at Castor, she tries with her left hand lightly to hold off Pollux, who has seized her under her right shoulder. Her right leg (save for the upper thigh, which is turned diagonally) is still planted firmly on the ground, and her left thigh, which is completely visible, almost touches the ground at the knee.

Pollux is naked, for as much of him as we can see, since the girls cover his lower body and thighs.

Castor's face is the paragon of beautiful, manly youth, with a full brown curly beard. Passion oozes out of his every pore. His lofty brow, his eye voluptuously squinting with sweet desire, his lips all ablaze, and his blushing cheeks, his sinewy arm, and his hippodamian stance* all make for a dashing abductor. "I hate to have to hurt you," (he whispers) "but there was no way you wouldn't be mine!" The pleading, the tenderness is indescribable, and so is the boldness of the protruding brow and the flowering of his strength.

The virgins are both naked, with blond hair in loose open braids, a play to the winds, as though they'd both just stepped out of bed or bath; their youth is ripe for the picking. The look in the face of the first girl is indescribably exquisite: it speaks surrender, a powerlessness to resist, as well as modesty and the sweet stinging sensation that goes with it, and an absence of deliberation. Her breasts swell up under the pressure of her plight. She turns her face away from her abductor and yet squints back at him. "Hah, so now the game is up!" (she seems to sigh) "He's got you!" and she is full of fearful anticipation of future pleasures. Against her will, the young demigod who retrieved the golden fleece and liberated the archipelago from the bandits wields more power of love over her than her betrothed (how could it be otherwise with a girl?), and yet she feels compassion for this latter. Fear and love, a duel between morality and nature, alarm and sweetness emanate from her eyes, weeping and smiling compete for her lips. Only the imagination of a Rubens could have captured such an expression. Her body wafts in the air like a rose being plucked.

---

*From *hippodamos,* horse tamer, a Homeric epithet of heroes. — Ed.

The second girl we see in profile, all beauty and girlishness, yet seeming, however innocently, to know something of the nature of manhood. Only lightly resisting, she watches Castor and what he's doing to her sister, looking at him not unwillingly, preferring him in fact to the one whose prey she is to become. The portrayal of her twisting and the wresting of her back muscles, indeed, all the flesh of her back, can be counted among some of the best painting ever done.

In both girls we note the transition from one happiness to a greater one, from fear to hope, with the moon and the stars still shut up in their hearts, and the sunrise already before their eyes.

I have never wanted to consider Polydektes as a person of a class with Castor, since he seems more like an attendant and servant, and were it not otherwise, one could easily take him for a slave who loyally lends a hand, and though not lacking the sympathy for the girls, rejoices nonetheless in the success of their capture.

Yet Rubens vindicates himself and justifies his manner of execution. He focuses all attention on Castor, since it seems to him unlikely that both brothers should have simultaneously fallen so head over heels for two sisters, so much so that they would both feel compelled to abduct them violently from their brave and noble bridegrooms, who had after all invited them to their wedding. Thus Pollux abducts the other sister for Castor's sake (which indeed she seems to notice); thus the expression of his boxer's face is not altogether complimentary.

Castor has a Medusa's head set in his greenish breastplate. Pollux wears nothing, except on his legs, which are wrapped in a leather binding. One of the cupids is thinking: "Beware that nothing bad will happen to you both," and the other looks on mischievously, busy with the white horse in his charge. Neither cupid is superfluous here. The horses are proud and wild and full of fire; and yet they seem to sense what they are a party to.

As already mentioned, the light falls on the girls, and horse and man set off their delicate flesh incomparably. In regard to coloring, it is definitely one of the most beautiful pieces of painting that we possess by Rubens.

The artists chose the most picturesque moment in this tale of abduction, although it includes two more scenes which are also quite picturesque. The figures are almost life-size.

The Rainbow, a Landscape

Picture in your mind the loveliest and lushest Flemish countryside, over which on a summer's afternoon a warm, sultry storm has passed, filling the sky with thunder and lightning and rain (Fig. 4). In the storm's last electrically charged clouds a rainbow and its reflection in a secondary rainbow appear. The rainbow rises at one end out of a cheerful forest, over which the storm has passed; a grove of trees on a mossy height is visible on the left side of the painting. Behind the grove a clear river winds its way around. On its bank stands a shepherd, who, having waited for the sky to clear up, drives his cattle forth. The cattle stand around, wade, and drink to make up for the fear they have suffered, mirroring themselves in the water. On the river shore, at a bend farther up in the rush and reeds and berries and shrubbery, ducks are shaking the rain off their wings, quacking and making merry. And then there are two milk-maids, with empty pots, who brought food to the folks in the field. In their midst, a young fellow with a pitchfork just whispered some-thing to one of the beauties, over which she smiles in silence and, blushing, turns away. Beside them, a waggoner with a haycart sits cheerfully on one of his two workhorses and (rascal that he is) casts a glance at the lovers. A ripe crop stands in the field to his side. And farther up, on his other side, there are heaps of hay stacked around a slender alder tree with several stems. Two girls and a young fellow are loading the hay onto a wagon. And finally, the eye passes into the loveliest plain, scattered with brushwood, garden plots, and villages in the blue distance, losing itself by and by in the lingering fog.

The returning brightness, the freshness, the rising mist over grass and leaves, the dampness on the sagging branches, the Lord's bless-ing over crop and field, the fortifying spirit of ripening fertility, all speak to us; yea, to him who knows the world depicted here, it seems no less alive than nature itself.

Apart from the glorious feeling conveyed by the whole, which seems to envelop everything in a womblike warmth, and with which only a few Claudes, Salvator Rosas, Poussins, and Teniers, only very few of my heavenly joys can be compared, this landscape is also a masterpiece of brush stroke, even if the painter could hardly have spent more than a day on its execution: the color is applied as lightly and thinly as letters. Every painter worth his salt ought to stand in silence and study the magic, without being bothered by the unfinished rainbow, with whose colors Rubens had more than a schoolboy's exercise to tackle. The trees may not be like those by Pott,* their leaves are not defined, but they are still so recognizable in trunk and stems and foliage and motion, as alive in their verdure as Pott's ever could be. The crop is ripening by and by and stands in thick stalks, swelled by the rain; and if you look closely at the wooden panel, it is all a mass of green and yellow brush strokes, which is why even the most impassioned follower of Adriaen van der Werff may look with an envious eye at this feat of painting. The perspective here can be ranked among the best of its kind. In short, here is a place so fresh, warm, and fertile that any traveler would command his postilion to stop; for such a scene is not often witnessed in a lifetime, and embodies, as a matter of fact, all that I really ask of a painting: *pleasure* and *illusion*.

Rubens with His First Wife, Life-size in a Garden

He is indeed one of the finest looking men you've ever seen (Fig. 5). He is seated on a bench, leaning against the shady trellis of a blossoming woodbine, in all the youthful pride of his first manhood. His left hand is resting with the thumb on the crossbar of his diamond-studded sword, and his right hand is lying on his big left crossed leg. His lovely little wife (sweet and demure and altogether happy through him), seated next to and beneath him, softly rests the open palm of her own delicate right hand on his.

His lofty soul peers out from under that jaunty hat, and from that brave forehead arching over his proud brow, and from those light brown fiery eyes, looking down on the vanity of other mortals, capturing the essence of their manner and character. His nose climbs straight up his face like strength incarnate; his cheeks are flushed with a healthy color; and from his lips, perched in between the young oak branches of mustache and beard, an eagle's love is waiting on impulse to take flight. His little wife's face, on the other hand, expresses nothing but sweet affection and trust. The heart that sits in this man's breast seems to have been nurtured from

---

*Presumably Jan Both (Utrecht c. 1618–1652). — Ed.

childhood by a Chiron on lion's marrow. His whole being exudes the proud awareness of his own strength, and one can tell at a glance that he is more than the sum total of all his works, more than his God the Father, and God the Son, and God the Holy Ghost, more than his saints, angels, and heroes.

So it is written, that the blessed may one day behold the face of God. Oh, the unutterable bliss, if our heart were all at once to become a rapturous precipice fed by all the life-giving streams of the world, all tumbling in an instant like vast seas into its depths! Weighty, boundless idea, I yield to you. What mortal, what phenomenon, could endure it!

Rubens appears here a great man, full of life and wisdom, full of spunk and strength, a man free of any weakness, and perhaps also of any tender feelings. Everything about him bespeaks an extraordinary spirit in a rare state of virility and zest for life, yet harboring a secret inkling of the transitoriness of all pleasures and youth. She, his wife, is happy in his love and renown, she is all wrapped up in him and lives only through his soul. A charming picture of spiritual marital tenderness—to anyone who knows it when he sees it—of modesty and true grace, even if this latter is generally perceptible far more in movement than in form. He sits there like nature in all its fresh fecundity, and she like a rose in the early morning light of love. Both are dressed in chivalric fashion, she in jewels and luxury and yet with her dress falling into casual folds, and her Spanish straw hat (its pretty shadow falling down the right side of her forehead) perched more airily on her head than all the feathers on the hats of today's ladies.

The coloring is as true as life itself, particularly the flesh. In short: this painting is among those pieces that Rubens conceived with glee.

That's enough for now, dearest friend. I am as weary of describing as you, no doubt, are of reading. Some other time I will discuss Rubens's style and manner of painting, of which I've not yet spoken here, since in this hot weather I did not feel like talking about any of his larger works. In addition to those already described, we also possess forty pieces attributed to him, of which only about thirty are genuine, but most of those were indeed completed by the master himself. One would best be able to recognize the man in the life he lived, as distinct from that of his students and imitators, who but dreamed up a life in which, as it were, they put nothing but themselves on show. Rubens's life would indeed be his brightest hallmark were it not for the light, free, raw, decisive brush stroke, that touch that always hits the mark if viewed from the right standpoint.

Translated by Peter Wortsman

Johann Wolfgang von Goethe

On German Architecture [1772]

D. M.
Ervini a Steinbach[1]

As I wandered about your tomb, noble Erwin, looking for the stone which should have told me *Anno domini 1318 XVI Kal. Febr. obiit Magister Ervinus, Gubernator Fabricae Ecclesiae Argentinensis*, and could not find it, and none of your fellow-townsmen could show it to me, so that I could pour out my veneration at that holy place—then was I deeply grieved in my soul, and my heart, younger, warmer, more innocent, better than now, vowed to you a memorial of marble or sandstone (according to what I could afford) as soon as I should come into the quiet enjoyment of my inheritance.

Yet what need you a memorial! You have erected the most magnificent one for yourself, and although your name does not bother the ants who crawl about it, you have the same destiny as that Architect who piled up his mountains to the clouds.

It was given to few to create the idea of Babel in their souls, whole, great, and with the beauty of necessity in every smallest part, like trees of God. To even fewer has it been granted to encounter a thousand willing hands to carve out the rocky ground, to conjure up steeps on it, and when they die, to tell their sons, 'I am still with you in the creations of my spirit; complete what is begun, up to the clouds.'

What need have you of a memorial! And from me! When the rabble utters holy names, it is superstition or blasphemy. The feeble aesthete will forever be dizzied by your Colossus, and those whose spirits are whole will recognize you without need of an interpreter.

Now then, excellent man, before I risk my patched-up little ship on the ocean again, and am more likely to meet death than profit, look at this grove where all about the names of my loved ones are still green.[2] I cut yours on a beech tree, reaching upwards like one of your slender towers, and hang this handkerchief of gifts by its four corners on it. It is not unlike the cloth that was let down to the Holy Apostle out of the clouds, full of clean and unclean beasts;[3] also flowers, blossoms, leaves and dried grass and moss, and night-sprung toadstools—all of which I gathered, botanizing to pass the time, on a walk through some place or other, and now dedicate to your honour until they rot away.

'It is in a niggling taste,' says the Italian, and passes on. 'Puerilites,' babbles the Frenchman childishly after him, and triumphantly snaps open his snuffbox, *à la greque*.[4] What have you done, that you should dare to look down your noses?

Has not the genius of the Ancients risen from its grave to enslave yours, you dagoes? You scramble over the ruins to cadge a system of proportions, you cobble together your summer-houses out of the blessed rubble, and think yourselves the true guardians of the secrets of art if you can reckon the inches and minutest lines of past buildings. If you had rather felt than measured, if the spirit of the pile you so admire had come upon you, you would not simply have imitated it because *they* did it and it is beautiful; you would have made your plans because of truth and necessity, and a living, creative beauty would have flowed from them.

You have given your practical considerations a colour of truth and beauty. You were struck by the splendid effect of columns, you wanted to make use of them, and walled them in. You wanted colonnades, too, and ringed the forecourt of St Peter's with alleys of marble which lead nowhere, so that mother nature, who despises and hates the inappropriate and unnecessary, drove the rabble to convert your splendour into public cloaca, and men avert their eyes and hold their noses before the wonder of the world.[5]

That is the way it goes. The whim of the artist serves the obsession of the rich: the travel writer gapes, and our *bels esprits*, called philosophers, spin out of the raw stuff of fairy tales the history of art up to our times, and the evil genius murders true men in the forecourt of the sanctuary.

Rules are more damaging to the genius than examples. Before he arrives on the scene, some individuals may have worked out some parts, but he is the first from whose soul those parts emerge as an everlasting whole. But school and rule fetter all power of perceiving and acting. What does it matter to us, you new-fangled French philosophizing connoisseurs, that the first man — whose needs made him ingenious — hammered in four stakes, lashed four posts over them, and put branches and moss on the top?[6] From this you deduce the needs of today, and it is just as if you wanted to rule your new Babylon[7] according to the feelings of simple patriarchal societies.

It is also wrong to think that your hut was the first. Two stakes at each end, crossed at their apex, with another as ridgepole are, as you may daily see in the huts of field and vineyard, a far more basic invention, from which you could not even extract a principle for your pig-sty.

So none of your conclusions can rise to the sphere of truth. They all swim in the atmosphere of your system. You want to teach us what we should use, because what we do use cannot be justified according to your principles.

The column is close to your heart, and in another part of the world you would be a prophet. You say, 'The column is the first and most important component of the building, and the most beautiful. What sublime elegance of form, what pure and varied greatness, when they stand in rows!'[8] Only be careful not to use them out of turn: their nature is to stand free. Woe to those wretches who have wedded their slender growth to lumpish walls! And yet it seems to me, my dear Abbé, that the frequent repetition of this impropriety of walling columns in, by which the moderns even stuff the intercolumnia of ancient temples with masonry, might have given you pause. If your ear was not deaf to truth, these stones at least might have preached it to you.

The column is, on the contrary, no part of our dwellings; rather it contradicts the essence of all our buildings. Our houses do not arise from four columns in four corners, but from four walls as four sides, which are in place of columns, and exclude them, and where you tack them on, they are a tiresome excrescence. That goes, too, for our palaces and churches, except for a few instances which I need not notice. So your buildings present surfaces which, the more extensive they are, and the higher they soar, the more they oppress the soul with intolerable monotony. It would be a sad day for us if the genius of Erwin von Steinbach did not come to our rescue: 'Diversify the enormous walls; you should so build towards heaven that they rise like a sublimely towering, wide-spreading tree of God which, with its thousand branches, millions of twigs and leaves more numerous than the sands of the sea, proclaims to the surrounding country the glory of its master, the Lord.'

The first time I went to the Minster (Fig. 6), my head was full of the common notions of good taste. From hearsay I respected the harmony of mass, the purity of forms, and I was the sworn enemy of the confused caprices of Gothic ornament. Under the term Gothic, like the article in a dictionary,[9] I threw together all the synonymous misunderstandings, such as undefined, disorganized, unnatural, patched-together, tacked-on, overloaded, which had ever gone through my head. No less foolish than the people who call the whole of the foreign world barbaric, for me everything was Gothic that did not fit my system, from the lathe-turned gaudy dolls and paintings with which our *bourgeois gentilshommes* decorate their homes to the sober remains of early German architecture, on which, on the pretext of one or two daring curlicues, I joined in the general chorus: 'Quite smothered with ornament!' And so I shuddered as I went, as if at the prospect of some mis-shapen, curly-bristled monster.

How surprised I was when I was confronted by it! The impression which filled my soul was whole and large, and of a sort that (since it was composed of a thousand harmonizing details) I could relish and enjoy, but by no means identify and explain. They say it is thus with the joys of heaven, and how often have I gone back to enjoy this heavenly-earthly joy, and to embrace the gigantic spirit of our ancient brothers in their works. How often have I returned, from all sides, from all distances, in all lights, to contemplate its dignity and his magnificence. It is hard on the spirit of man when his brother's work is so sublime that he can only bow and worship. How often has the evening twilight soothed with its friendly quiet my eyes, tired-out with questing, by blending the scattered parts into masses which now stood simple and large before my soul, and at once my powers unfolded rapturously to enjoy and to understand. Then in hinted understatements the genius of the great Master of the Works revealed itself to me. 'Why are you so surprised?' he whispered to me. 'All these shapes were necessary ones, and don't you see them in all the old churches of my city? I have only elevated their arbitrary sizes to harmonious proportions. How the great circle of the window opens above the main door which dominates the two side ones: what was otherwise but a hole for the daylight now echoes the nave of the church! How, high above, the belfry demands the smaller windows! All this was necessary, and I made it beautiful. But ah! if I float through the dark and lofty openings at the side that seem to stand empty and useless, in their strong slender form I have hidden the secret powers which should lift those two towers high in the air—of which, alas! only one stands mournfully there, without its intended decoration of pinnacles, so that the surrounding country would pay homage to it and its regal brother.'

And so he left me, and I sank into a sympathetic melancholy until the dawn chorus of the birds who lived in the thousand openings rejoiced at the rising sun and woke me from my slumber. How freshly the Minster sparkled in the early morning mist, and how happily I could stretch out my arms towards it and gaze at the harmonious masses, alive with countless details. Just as in the eternal works of nature, everything is perfectly formed down to the meanest thread, and all contributing purposefully to the whole. How the vast building rose lightly into the air from its firm foundations; how everything was fretted, and yet fashioned for eternity! Genius, it is to your teaching that I owe it that I am no longer dazzled by your profundities, that a drop of the rapturous quiet of the spirit sinks into my soul, which can look down over such a creation and say, as God said, 'It is good.'

And now I ought not be angry, holy Erwin, if the German art expert, on the hearsay of envious neighbours, fails to recognize his advantage and belittles your work with that misunderstood word 'Gothic.' For he should thank God that he can proclaim that this is German architecture, our architecture. For the Italian has none he can call his own, still less the Frenchman. And if you do not wish to admit this advantage yourself, at least prove to us that the Goths already built like this: you will find it difficult. And if in the end you cannot demonstrate that there was a Homer before Homer, we will willingly leave you the story of lesser efforts that succeed or fail, and come to worship before the work of the master who first welded the scattered elements into a living whole. And you, my dear spiritual brother in the search for truth and beauty, shut your ears to all the blather about fine art; come, look, and enjoy. Take care that you do not profane the name of your noblest artist, and hasten here to see his excellent work. If it makes an unpleasant impression on you, or none at all, good luck to you, harness your horses and be off to Paris!

But it is to you, beloved youth, that I feel closest, for, standing there, you are moved and cannot reconcile the conflicting feelings in your soul. At one moment you feel the irresistible power of this vast whole, and the next chide me for being a dreamer since I see beauty where you see only rugged strength. Do not let us be divided by a misunderstanding. Do not let the effete doctrine of modern pretty-prettyness spoil you for roughness that is full of meaning, so that in the end your sickly sensibility can only tolerate meaningless polish. They would have us believe that the fine arts arise from our desire to beautify the objects around us.[10] This is not true! For not the philosopher, but the man in the street and the artisan use the word in the only way it could be true.

Art is formative long before it is beautiful, and it is still true and great art, indeed, often truer and greater than 'fine art' itself. For in man's nature there is a will to create form which becomes active the moment his survival is assured. As soon as he does not need to worry or to fear, like a demi-god, busy even in his relaxation, he casts around for a material into which he can breathe his spirit. And so the savage articulates his coconut shell, his feathers, his body with fantastical lines, hideous forms and gaudy colours. And even if this making visibly expressive is made up of the most arbitrary forms, they will still harmonize without any obvious relationship between them, for a single feeling has created a characteristic whole.

Now this characteristic art is the only true art. If it becomes active through inner, unified, particular and independent feeling, un-adorned by, indeed unaware of, all foreign elements, whether it be born of savagery or of a cultivated sensibility, it is a living whole. Hence among different nations and individuals you will see countless different degrees of it. The more the soul is raised to a feeling for those proportions which alone are beautiful and eternal, whose principal harmonies may be proved but whose secrets can only be felt, in which alone the life of godlike genius is whirled around to the music of the soul—the more, I say, this beauty penetrates the being of the mind, so that it seems to be born within that mind, so that nothing satisfies the mind but beauty, so that the mind creates nothing but beauty out of itself, so much the happier is the artist, and the more magnificent, and the lower we prostrate ourselves and worship the Lord's annointed.

And no one will remove Erwin from his high place. Here is his creation. Come up and acknowledge the deepest feeling for truth and beauty of proportion, brought about by the strong, rugged German soul on the narrow, gloomy, priest-ridden stage of the *medii aevi*.

And our *aevum*? That has renounced his genius, has driven its sons about after strange growths, to its ruin. The frivolous Frenchman who gleans far worse at least has the wit to pull his loot into a single whole; he does build a magic temple of a Madeleine for his Greek columns and German vaults. But I have seen one of our artists, when he was asked to devise a porch to an old German church, prepare a model with stately Antique columns.[11]

I do not wish to rehearse how much I hate our tarted-up doll-painters. With their stagey poses, false complexions and gaudy clothes they have caught the eye of the ladies. Your wood-carved face, O manly Dürer, whom these novices mock, is far more welcome to me.

And you yourselves, excellent people, to whom it was given to enjoy the highest beauty, and now step down to proclaim your happiness; even you harm genius, for it will be raised and moved on no other wings than its own, not even the wings of the morning.[12] It is our own power, unfolded in a childhood dream, and developed in youth until it is strong and agile like the mountain lion as he rushes on his prey.[13] Hence nature is the best teacher, for your pedagogues can never create the diversity of situations in which genius may exert and enjoy its present powers.

Hail to you, youth, with your sharp eye for proportion, born to adapt yourself easily to all sorts of form! When, little by little, joy in the life around you wakes and you feel a jubilant and human pleasure after the fears and hopes of toil: the delighted shout of the wine-harvester when the fulness of autumn swells his vats, the lively dance of the mower when he hangs his sickle, now idle, on the beam. If the strong nerve of desire and suffering becomes more manfully alive in your brush, then you have striven and lived enough, and enjoyed enough, and are sated with earthly beauty; you are worthy to rest in the arms of the goddess, worthy to feel at her breast that by which the deified Hercules was reborn. Receive him, heavenly Beauty, you mediatrix between gods and men, so that he may, more than Prometheus, bring down the bliss of the gods upon earth.

Notes

1. D.M. = *Divis Manibus*, an inscription to the blessed spirits on Roman tombs. Erwin von Steinbach was the architect of the first stage of Strasbourg Cathedral. The foundation stone (now in the Cathedral Museum) was inscribed: *A.D. 1277 in die Beati Urbani hoc opus gloriosum inchoavit Magister Ervinus de Steinbach*. Erwin's gravestone was not rediscovered until 1816, and Goethe took the inscription from an early guidebook.

2. In the woods at Sesenheim, near Strasbourg, Goethe had fixed a tablet with the names of himself and his friends on a tree.

3. *Acts*, X, II ff.

4. Goethe is alluding to the Abbé M. A. Laugier, *Essai sur l'architecture*, 1753, p. 3, where Gothic ornaments were described as *puérillement entassés*.

5. This example is also from Laugier (*Nouvelles Observations sur l'Architecture*, 1765, pp. 74, 76).

6. Cf. Laugier, *Essai*, p. 9. The source is Vitruvius, *Ten Books on Architecture*, II, i, 3–5.

7. i.e. Paris.

8. Cf. Laugier, *Essai*, p. II., 288.

9. i.e. J. G. Sulzer, *Allgemeine Theorie der Schönen Künste*, 1771, I, p. 489.

10. See Sulzer, p. 609.

11. La Madeleine in Paris (begun in 1764) was also criticized by Laugier (*Essai*, p. 178) although he was not against the possibility of combining elements of classic and Gothic architecture. The vaults of the Madeleine are hardly 'German'. Laugier also (*Observations*, p. 149) opposed the use of Classical porches on Gothic façades.

12. Cf. Psalm 139, 9.

13. Cf. Psalm 17, 12.

Translated and annotated by John Gage

Observations on the Laocoon[1]

A true work of art will always have something of infinity in it to our minds, as well as a work of nature. We contemplate it, we perceive and relish its beauties, it makes an impression, but it cannot be thoroughly understood, nor its essence nor its merit be clearly defined by words. In the observations we are about to make on the Laocoon (Fig. 7), we do not pretend to exhaust this fertile subject; what we have to say is rather on occasion of this excellent monument than upon it. May it soon be again exposed to the public eye,[2] so that every amateur may have an opportunity of satisfying himself concerning it, and of speaking of it according to his own ideas!

When we would treat of an excellent work of art, we are almost obliged as it were to speak of art in general, for the whole art is contained in it, and everyone may, as far as his abilities allow, by means of such a monument, develop whatever relates to art in general. For this reason we will begin here with some generalities.

All the beautiful monuments of art represent human nature; the arts of design have a particular relation to the body of man; it is only of these last that we are now speaking. Art has many degrees or steps, on each of which may appear artists of distinction; but a perfect work of art unites all the qualities which we only meet elsewhere dispersed.

The most beautiful monuments of art which we are acquainted with present to us:

Nature to the life and of an elevated organization. Above all things we expect to find in it a knowledge of the human body in all its parts, dimensions, interior and exterior, in its forms and its movements in general.

Characters. A knowledge of the difference of their parts as to form and effect. Qualities are separated and present themselves isolated; from thence arise characters and it is by this means that we can trace a significative reciprocal relation between the different monuments of art, just as the parts of a compound work may have a significant relation between themselves. The object is:

In repose or in motion. A work and its parts may be presented either subsisting of themselves, and only indicating their existence in a tranquil manner, or as very animated, acting, impassioned, and full of expression.

The Ideal. To attain this, a profound solid sense endowed with patience is required in the artist, to which should be joined an elevated sense to be able to embrace the subject in its whole extent, to find the highest degree of action which it means to represent, and consequently to make it exceed the bounds of its limited reality, and give it in an ideal world, measure, limits, reality and dignity.

Grace. But the subject and manner of representing it are submitted to the sensible laws of art, that is to say, to order, perspicuity, symmetry, opposition, &c. which renders it to the eye, beautiful, that is to say, graceful, agreeable.

Beauty. It is moreover submitted to the law of intellectual beauty, which results from the measure, to which man, formed to figure and produce the beautiful, knows how to submit everything, even extremes.

After having first indicated the conditions which we require in a work of art, elevated art, I may say much in a few words when I maintain that our groupe contains them almost all, and that we can even develop them by the observation of this group alone.

It will not be expected of me to prove that the artist has shown a *profound knowledge of the human body, that which characterizes it, together with the expression and the passion.* It will appear, from what I shall say in the sequel, how the subject is conceived in an *ideal* and *elevated* manner; no one will doubt that we ought to give the epithet of *beautiful* to this monument, who can conceive how the artist has been able to represent the extreme of physical and intellectual sufferings. But some may think it perhaps paradoxical, that I dare advance that this groupe is at the same time full of grace. I shall say a few words on this head.

Every work of art must announce itself as such, which can only be done by what we call *sensual beauty* or *grace.* The ancients, far enough in this respect from the modern opinion that a monument of art should become again to appearance, a monument of nature, would characterize their works of art as such, by a select order of the parts; they assist the eye to investigate the relations by symmetry, and thus an embarrassed work becomes easy to comprehend. From symmetry and oppositions resulted the possibility of striking out the greatest contrasts by differences hardly sensible. The care of the ancient artists to oppose varied masses to each other, to give especially a regular and reciprocal position to the extremities of bodies in groupe, is very happy and very well imagined, in order that each work of art may appear to the eye like an ornament, and abstraction made from the subject which it represents, and by seeing the most general contours only at a distance. The antique vases furnish us with a number of examples of similar groupe, very graceful; and it would be possible to propose a series of the most beautiful examples of a composition, symmetrical and agreeable, beginning with the groupe of the most tranquil vase to the extremely animated groupe of Laocoon. I think therefore, I must repeat that the groupe of Laocoon, besides its other acknowledged merits is moreover a model of *symmetry* and of *variety*, of *repose* and of *motion*, of *opposition* and of *graduation*, which present themselves together to him who contemplates it in a sensible or intellectual manner; that these qualities, notwithstanding the great pathetic diffused over the representation, excite an agreeable sensation, and moderate the violence of the passions, and of the sufferings, by *grace* and *beauty*.

It is a great advantage in a work of art, to submit by itself, to be absolutely terminated. A tranquil object only shows itself by its existence, it is terminated by and in itself. A Jupiter with a thunderbolt placed on his knees, a Juno who reposes with majesty, a Minerva absorbed in reflection, are subjects which have not, so to speak, any relation to what is out of them; they repose upon and in themselves, and they are the first and dearest objects of sculpture. But in the beautiful mythic circle of art in which these isolated and self-subsisting natures are placed and in repose there are smaller circles, where the different figures are conceived and executed in relation with others; each of the Muses, for example with their conductor Apollo, is conceived and executed separately, but it becomes yet much more interesting in the complete and varied choir of the nine sisters. When art passes to the impassioned significative, it may moreover act in the same manner, or it presents to us a circle of figures which passion puts into a mutual relation as Niobe with her children, persecuted by Apollo and Diana;[3] or it shows us the same work, the movement at the same time with its cause. We need only mention here the young man full of grace who is drawing a thorn from his foot,[4] the wrestlers,[5] two groups of fauns and nymphs at Dresden,[6] and the animated groups of Laocoon.

It is with reason that so great stress is laid on sculpture, because it strips man of everything which is not essential to him. It is thus that in this admirable groupe Laocoon is only a simple name; the artists have taken from him his priesthood, all that is national and Trojan in him, all the poetical and mythological accessories; all in fact that mythology has made of him is done away; he is only now a father with his two sons, menaced with death by the bite of two serpents. Neither are these animals sent by the gods, but only natural serpents, potent enough to be the destruction of many men; neither their form nor their action shows that they are extraordinary creatures sent by the gods, to exercize the divine vengeance. Conformably to their nature, they approach by sliding on the surface of the earth; they inlace and fold round their victims, and one of them only bites after having been irritated. If I had to explain this groupe and if I were unacquainted with every other explication, I should call it a tragic idyll. A father sleeps at the side of his two sons, they are inlaced by two serpents, and at the instant of waking, they strive to extricate themselves from this living cord.

This work of art is, above all, extremely important by the representation of the moment of the action. When in fact a work ought to move before the eyes, a fugitive moment should be pitched upon; no part of the whole ought to be found before in this position and, in a little time after, every part should be obliged to quit that position; it is by this means that the work be always animated for millions of spectators.

To seize well the attention of the Laocoon, let us place ourselves before the groupe with our eyes shut, and at the necessary distance; let us open and shut them alternately and we shall see all the marble in motion; we shall be afraid to find the groupe changed when we open our eyes again. I would readily say, as the groupe is now exposed, it is a flash of lightning fixed, a wave petrified at the instant when it is approaching the shore. We see the same effect when we see the groupe at night, by the light of flambeaux.[7]

The artist has very wisely represented the three figures in graduated situations, and which differ from each other. The eldest son is only interlaced at his extremities, the other is more so; it is especially the chest that the serpent has interlaced; he endeavours to deliver himself by the motion of his right arm; with his left hand, he softly removes the head of the serpent, to prevent it from clasping his breast once more; the serpent is on the point of sliding underneath his hand; *but it does not bite.* The father on the contrary, would employ force to deliver himself, as well as his two children, from the embraces; he grips one of the two serpents, who being now irritated, bites him in the haunch.

To explain the position of the father, both in general, and according to all the parts of the body, it appears to me reasonable to suppose that the momentaneous sensation of the wound is the principal cause of the whole movement: the serpent has not bit, but he bites, and he bites in the soft and delicate part of the body, above and a little behind the haunch. The position of the restored head has never well expressed the true bite; happily, the traces of the jaws have been preserved in the posterior part of the statue, if these very important traces have not been lost in the actual transportation of the monument.[8] The serpent inflicts a wound on the unhappy Laocoon, precisely in the part in which man is very sensible to every irritation, and even where the slightest tickling causes that motion which we see produced here by the wound; the body flies towards the opposite side, and retires; the shoulder presses downwards, the chest is thrust forward, and the head inclines on the side which has been touched. As afterwards in the feet, which are enfolded by the serpent, and in the arms which struggle, we yet see the remains of the situation or preceding action, there results combined action of efforts and of flight, of suffering and of activity, of tension and of relaxation, which perhaps would not be possible under any other condition. We are lost in admiration at the wisdom of the artist, when we try to apply the bite to any other place: the whole gesture, the whole movement would be changed and nevertheless we cannot imagine it more proper: it is therefore a principal merit in the artist to have presented us with a sensible effect, and also to have shown us the sensible cause of it. I repeat it—the point of the bite determines the actual movement of the members; the flight of the inferior part of the body, its contraction, the chest which advances, the shoulder which descends, the movement of the head, and even all the features of the countenance, are, in my opinion, decided by this momentaneous, painful, and unexpected irritation.

But, far be it from me to wish to *divide* the unity of human nature, to wish to deny the action of the intellectual force of this man of a form so excellent, to overlook the sufferings and the efforts of a great nature. Methinks I also see the inquietude, the fear, the terror, the paternal affection, moving in those veins, swelling in that heart, wrinkling that front. I readily admit that the artist has represented, at the same time, the most elevated degree, both of corporeal suffering and of intellectual sufferings: but I would not have us to be transported too feelingly at the monument itself, at the impressions which the monument makes upon us, especially as we do not see the effect of the poison in a body which has just been seized by the teeth of the serpent, as we do not see the agony in a sound, beautiful body, which makes efforts, and which is but just hurt. Let me be permitted to make an observation here, which is of considerable importance for the arts of design: the greatest pathetic expression which they can represent depends on the passage from one stage to another. Let us view a lively infant, who runs, leaps, and amuses himself, with all the pleasure and energy possible, who afterwards has been suddenly struck hard by one of his comrades, or who has been wounded either physically or morally: this new sensation is communicated to all his members like an electrical shock; and a similar, sudden, and pathetic passage in the most elevated sense, is an opposition of which we have no idea, if we have not seen it.

In this case, it is therefore evident that the intellectual man acts as well as the physical man. When in a like passage there still remain evident traces of the preceding state, there results a subject the most elegant for the arts of design: this is the case of the Laocoon, where the efforts and the sufferings are united at the same moment. It is thus that Eurydice, who is bitten in the heel by a serpent on which she has trod, at the instant when she is crossing a meadow, and is returning, satisfied with the flowers she has gathered, would be a very pathetic statue, if the artist could express the double state of satisfaction with which she walked, and of the pain which arrests her steps; not only by the flowers which are falling, but further by the direction of all her members, and the undulation of the folds.

When we have seized, in this sense, the principal figure, we may cast a free and sure glance on the proportions, the gradations, and the opposition of all the parts of the entire work.

The subject chosen is one of the happiest that can be imagined. Men struggling with dangerous animals, and moreover with animals which act, not as powerful masses, but as divided forces, which do not menace on one side alone, which do not require a concentrated resistance, but which, according to their extended organization, are capable of paralysing, joined to the great movement, already spreads over the *ensemble* a certain degree of repose and unity. The artist[9] has been able to indicate, by degrees, the efforts of the serpents: one only infolds; the other is irritated, and wounds his adversary. The three personages are also chosen with much wisdom: a robust and well-made man, who has already passed the age of the greatest energy, and who is less capable of supporting grief and suffering. Let us substitute for him, in imagination, a young man, lively and robust, and the groupe will lose all its value! With him suffer two young persons, who, in proportion to him, are very small. They are, moreover, two beings susceptible of the sentiment of pain. The youngest makes unavailing efforts, without, however being able to succeed; his efforts even produce a quite opposite effect. He irritates his adversary, and he is hurt by him. The eldest son is only slightly inlaced; he does not yet feel himself oppressed nor affected with pain; he is afraid at the wound and momentaneous movement of his father; he utters a cry, endeavours to extricate his foot from the serpent which has inlaced it; he is therefore here an observer, a witness who takes a part in the action, and the work is terminated.

What I have only hitherto touched on *en passant*, I shall here again notice particularly: and that is, that all the three figures have a double action, so that they are occupied in a very various manner. The youngest of the sons would extricate himself by raising his right arm; and he pushes back the head of the serpent with his left hand; he would alleviate the present evil, and prevent a greater one; this is the highest degree of activity which he can now exert in his constrained state. The father makes efforts to disembarrass himself from the serpents, and the body would, at the same time, avoid the bite which it has just received. The movement of the father inspires the eldest son with horror, and he endeavours to extricate himself from the serpent, which, as yet, has only infolded him slightly.

I have already said above, that one of the greatest merits of this monument, is the moment which the artist has represented, and it is on this point that I shall now add a few words.

We have supposed that the natural serpents have intwined a father sleeping by the side of his sons; that the different movements of the action might have a certain gradation. The first moments, during which the serpents infold the body then asleep, announce events; but it would be an insignificant moment for the art. We might, perhaps, imagine a young Hercules sleeping and infolded by serpents, and the artist might lead us to guess by his figure, and the tranquillity of his sleep, what might be expected from him when awake.

Let us go further and let us imagine the father and his sons feeling themselves interlaced by serpents; in whatever manner this may be, we shall see that there is only a single moment in which the interest is the greatest; it is that in which the body is so infolded that it can no longer defend itself; in which the second, although yet in a condition to defend itself, is nevertheless wounded; and in which the third has, lastly, some hope of saving itself. The youngest son is in the first state, the father in the second, the eldest son in the third. Let us endeavour to find yet another state: let us try to distribute the parts differently from what they are here!

In reflecting then on this action, from its commencement, and finding that it has arrived to its highest degree, we shall soon perceive, by representing to ourselves the moments which are to follow that which is figured by the monument, that the groupe must entirely change, and that we cannot find another moment of the action which is so precious for the art. The youngest son will be stifled by the serpent that infolds him; or if, in his situation, which deprives him of all succour, he irritates it further, the serpent will bite him. These two states are insupportable, because they are extremes which ought not to be represented. As to the father, the serpent may bite him again in other parts; but then all the situation of body would be changed, and the first bites would be lost for the spectator, or they would become disgusting, if the artist had a mind to indicate them. There is yet another case: the serpent may turn away, and attack the eldest son; this last is then brought back to himself; there is no longer any personage interesting himself in the action; the last appearance of hope disappears from the groupe, and the representation is no longer tragical, but cruel. The father, who reposes now upon himself, in his greatness and his sufferings, would turn round towards his son, and he would become an accessory figure, interesting himself with another figure.

In his own sufferings, and those of another, man has only three sensations, fear, terror, and compassion: he forsees with inquietude the evil which approaches him, he perceives on a sudden an evil which strikes him, and he takes part in the suffering which yet remains, or which has already passed; all the three are represented and excited by this monument, and even by the most suitable gradation.

The arts of design, which always labour for the moments when they choose a pathetic subject, will seize that which excites terror, poetry on the contrary, will choose those which excite fear and compassion. In the group of Laocoon, the sufferings of the father excite terror to the highest degree; sculpture has done in it all that it could do; but, either for the sake of running through the circle of all human sensations, or of moderating the violent impression of terror, it excites compassion for the situation of the youngest son, and fear for that of the eldest; leaving yet some hope for this last. It is thus that the ancients gave, by variety, a certain equilibrium to their works; that they then diminished or strengthened an effect by other effects, and were enabled to finish an intellectual and sensible whole.

In a word, we may boldly maintain, that this monument exhausts its subject and that it happily executes all the conditions of the art. It teaches us, that if the artist can communicate his sentiment of the beautiful to tranquil and simple objects, this same sentiment shows itself nevertheless, in its greatest energy and all its dignity, when it proves its force by figuring varied characters; and when in its imitation, it can moderate and retain the violent and impassioned expression of human nature.

The moderns have often been mistaken in the choice of subjects for pathetic representation in sculpture. Milo, whose two hands are locked in the rift of a tree, and who is attacked by a lion, is a subject which the artist will endeavour in vain to represent in such a manner as to excite a pure and true interest. A double grief, unavailing efforts, a situation which deprives him of all relief, can only excite horror, and cannot even touch.[10]

Lastly, I shall drop a word or two on the relation of this subject to poetry.

We are unjust towards Virgil and poetry, when we compare, be it only for an instant, the most finished chef d'oeuvre of sculpture, with the episodical manner in which this subject is treated in the

Aeneid.[11] As the unfortunate Aeneas is to relate himself that he and his compatriots have committed the unpardonable fault of suffering the horse to enter their city, the poet has only to contrive means to excuse this action; everything tends to this, and the history of Laocoon is only a rhetorical figure, in which we may very well allow of some exaggeration, provided that it answers the end which the poet designs it should. Immense serpents then proceed out of the sea; they have a crest on their head; they light on the children of the priest who had insulted the horse; they infold, bite, and pollute them with their venom; they afterwards infold the breast and the neck of the father, who runs to their succour, and they raise their heads to shew their victory, whilst the unfortunate one they oppress calls for succour in vain. The people, who are struck with terror at this spectacle, fly; no one dares any longer undertake the defence of his country; and the hearer and reader, affrighted at this marvellous and disgusting history, alike consent that the horse shall enter into the city.

The history of Laocoon, in Virgil, is only therefore a means to attain a more considerable end; and it is yet a great question whether this event be a proper subject for poetry.

Some observations on the Groupe of Laocoon and his two sons

The right leg of the eldest son is of a most agreeable elegance. The expression, and the turn of the members in general, and of the muscles, is admirable in the entire work. In the legs of the youngest son, which are not remarkably elegant, there is something so natural, that we find nothing like it under this relation; the legs of the father, especially the right leg, also possess great beauty.

Restorations[12]

A considerable part of the serpents, and probably the two heads, are of modern workmanship.

The left arm of the father, up to the juncture of the shoulder, and the five toes of the left foot, are restorations: the right foot, however, has suffered nothing.

In the *eldest son*, the end of the nose, the right hand, the three first toes of the left foot, the end of the great toe in the right foot have been restored; the belly having been somewhat damaged on the right side, this part has also been restored.

The end of the nose, the right arm, two fingers in the left hand, and the five toes in the right foot of the youngest son have been restored.

It is only the right arm of Laocoon which has been well restored in burnt earth, and as most say, by Bernini,[13] who, nevertheless, if it be really his work, has herein surpassed himself. The other restorations, which I have just mentioned, are in marble; they are carefully done, but with little art, and with convulsive contortions, in the taste of the school of Bernini. It is thought they were done by Cornachini.[14]

Notes

1. The translation given here is an anonymous one, printed in the *Monthly Magazine*, vii, 1799, pp. 349–52, 399–401. The original spelling and punctuation have been retained.

2. The group was taken from the Vatican to Paris as a result of Napoleon's Italian Campaign of 1796.

3. Goethe is thinking of the Roman copy after a fourth-century Greek group, attributed to Praxiteles or Skopas, of *Niobe and her Daughter* in the Uffizzi in Florence. The group originally included sons and other daughters killed by the arrows of Apollo and Diana.

4. The *Spinario*, a first-century A.D. Roman bronze in the Palazzo dei Conservatori in Rome.

5. A late Hellenistic marble group in the Uffizzi.

6. Probably two Hellenistic marbles of a satyr wrestling with a hermaphrodite.

7. Goethe planned for the *Propyläen* an essay on viewing statues by torchlight. On this important feature of the aesthetics of the period: J. J. I. Whiteley, 'Light and Shade in French Neo-Classicism,' *Burlington Magazine*, 117, 1975, pp. 768 ff.

8. There is no reference to this in the list of the major restorations given by M. Bieber, *Laocoon: The Influence of the Group*, 1967, p. 24, n. 15 (see below note 12).

9. Goethe has forgotten that he had earlier referred to the three artists Hagesandros, Polydoros, and Athenodoros of Rhodes, who, according to Pliny (*Natural History*, xxxvi, 37) carved the work.

10. But for the frequent treatment of this subject in painting and sculpture, especially in France: R. Rosenblum, 'On a Painting of Milo of Crotona,' *Essays in Honor of W. Friedlaender*, 1965.

11. Virgil, *Aeneid*, ii, 199 ff.

12. Goethe's information derives from Meyer, who published an essay on the restorations to the group in the *Propyläen* in 1799. Bieber (*loc. cit.*) lists the following major restorations:

Laocoon: whole of right arm, with shoulder and snake, part of the other snake near the left knee.

Elder Son: tip of nose, right hand and part of arm above snake, part and head of snake biting Laocoon's hip.

Younger son: tip of nose, right arm with uppermost coil of snake.

13. This supposition has now been abandoned.

14. Agostino Cornachini (1685–c. 1740).

Annotated by John Gage

Wilhelm Heinrich Wackenroder

Memorial to Our Worthy Ancestor Albrecht Dürer

Nürnberg! you once world-famous town! How I liked to wander through your crooked streets; with what childlike love I looked at your ancestral houses and churches which bear the firm trace of our old, paternal art! How deeply I love the forms of those times, that speak such a rough, strong, and true language! How they draw me back to that grey century, when you, Nürnberg, were the lively, swarming school of national art and a truly fruitful, exuberant spirit of art dwelt and stirred in your walls:

When the Master Hans Sachs and Adam Kraft, the sculptor, and above all Albrecht Dürer with his friend Wilibaldus Pirkheimer, and so many other highly praised and honoured men were still alive! How often have I wished myself back into that time! How often, born in my thoughts, did it again pass before me, Nürnberg, as I sat in a narrow corner, in the twilight from the small round windows, in your venerable library-halls, and brooded over the volumes of the gallant Hans Sachs, or over other old, yellow, worm-eaten papers; or when I wandered under the bold vaults of your dark churches, where through the colourful, painted windows all the sculpture and paintings of the olden times were wonderfully lighted by the day.

You are surprised again, and look at me, you narrow-minded and fainthearted people! Oh, indeed I know the myrtle forests of Italy; indeed I know the heavenly ardour of those enthusiastic men of the blessed South. Why am I called where the thoughts of my soul always dwell, where is the homeland of the most beautiful hours of my life! You, who see frontiers everywhere, where there are none; are Rome and Germany not on one earth? Has not the Heavenly Father laid roads from North to South, as well as from West to East

over the globe? Is one human life too short? Are the Alps insurmountable? And surely more than one love must live in the breast of
men.

But now my mournful spirit walks over the consecrated place
before your walls, Nürnberg; over the graveyard where rest the remains of Albrecht Dürer, once the pride of Germany—yes, of Europe. Visited by few, they rest beneath numberless gravestones, each
marked with a bronze sculpture the mark of the old art, and between them grow in profusion high sunflowers, which make the
graveyard into a lovely garden. Thus rest the forgotten bones of
Dürer, because of whom I am glad that I am a German.

Few, it must be allowed, are able to understand the spirit of your
pictures, and enjoy, with such fervour, the singular and the special
within them as it seems to be given me by Heaven more than to
many others; because I look around and I find few who stop before
you with such ardent love, such admiration, as I have.

Is it not as if the figures in your pictures were real men, who talk
together? Each is so characteristically marked that one would re-
cognise him in a large crowd; each one is taken so from the midst of
nature that he entirely fulfills his purpose. None, with half his soul
is there, as one would often say of the very delicate pictures of
modern artists; everyone is conceived in full life, and like that placed
in the picture. He, who is to mourn, mourns; he, who has to be
angry, is angry; and he who has to pray, prays. All the figures speak,
and speak loudly and distinctly. No arm moves uselessly, or just for
the play of the eyes, or for filling the space; all limbs, everything
speaks to us with force, so that we grasp the idea and the spirit of
the whole firmly. We believe everything that the artful man shows
us; and it is never erased from our memory.

How does it happen that today's artists in our country seem to me
so different from those praiseworthy men of the old times, and
especially you, my beloved Dürer? How is it that it seems to me as if
you have handled the art of painting much more seriously, more
earnestly, and more worthily than all the delicate artists of our
days? It seems to me that I see you as you stand thoughtfully before
the picture you have begun; how the conception that you want to
make visible, entirely complete, floats before your soul; how you
thoughtfully ponder what features and which positions would arrest the observer most strongly and surely, and as he viewed them

would most powerfully affect his soul; and how you then, with deep interest and friendly earnestness truly and slowly draw on the panel the beings befriended by your vivid imagination. But, the modern artists do not seem to wish that we should seriously take part in what they present to us; they work for noble gentlemen, who wish neither to be moved nor ennobled by the art, but wish only to be hoodwinked and tickled; they strive to make their painting into a sample of many lovely and deceiving colours; they try their cleverness in the scattering of lights and shadows; but the human figures often appear only to stand in the picture because of the colour and of the light — really, I would like to say — as a necessary evil.

I must cry "woe" over our times in that we practice art only as a light-minded plaything of the senses, when it really is something very serious and noble. Do people no longer respect mankind, that they neglect them in art and find pretty colours and all kinds of artificiality with light more worthy of their observation? . . .

If now art (I mean its main and most essential part) is really of such importance, then it is very unworthy and light-minded to turn away from the expressive and instructive human figures of our old Albrecht Dürer, because they are not furnished with the deceitful outward beauty that today's world holds as highest in art. It does not show an entirely healthy and pure soul, if somebody before a spiritual observation which in itself is weighty and impressive, stops his ears because the speaker does not arrange his words in delicate order or because he has a bad, strange pronunciation, or awkward gesturing with his hands. But would such thoughts hinder me from esteeming and admiring, according to merit, this external and, so to speak, corporeal beauty of art, where I find it?

You are also charged, my dear Albrecht Dürer, with the grave offense of placing your human figures, without entangling them artificially, comfortably beside each other, so that they form a homogeneous group. I love you for your ingenious simplicity, and fix my gaze involuntarily, first on the soul and the profound meaning of your beings without any censorious spirit ever coming into my mind. Many persons seem to be plagued by this, as an evil tormenting spirit, so much so that they are induced to despise and ridicule before they can observe quietly, and least of all, become able to go beyond the limits of the present and transfer themselves to former times. I will gladly admit, you eager newcomers, that a young student of today may speak more cleverly and learnedly about colours, light, and the arrangement of figures than would the venerable Dürer; but is it his own intelligence that speaks out of the youth, or is it not much more the knowledge and experience of art from former times? The true inner soul of art is only grasped, as a whole, by single chosen spirits, even if the handling of the brush is still very faulty; but all the aspects of art are brought, one after the other, to perfection, through invention, practice, and meditation. But it is a base and deplorable vanity, which sets the achievement of their times as crowns on their own weak heads, and hides their nothingness under borrowed splendour.

And also for that reason, today's teachers do not want to name Dürer, as well as many other good painters of his century, beautiful and noble, because they clothe the history of all nations, and even the sacred history of our religion, in the costume of their time. Here, I think that every artist who lets the spirit of former centuries pass through his heart has to give it life from the spirit and breath of his age; and it is fair and natural, that from love the creative power men have brings near to them all strange and distant things, as well as the heavenly beings, and envelopes them in the familiar and beloved forms of their world and their horizon.

At the time Albrecht Dürer was holding his brush, a German had still a special and excellent character of stability in the arena of nations in our part of the world; and his pictures bear truly and clearly, not only in their features and in the entire external appearance but also in their inner spirit, this serious, straight, and strong nature of the German character. In our times, this German character as well as German art has been lost. The young German learns the languages of all European nations, and by examining and judging, is supposed to draw nourishment from the spirits of all nations; and the student of art is taught how he is supposed to copy the expressions of Raphael, the colours of the Venetian school, the truth of the Netherlands, the magical light of Correggio, all at the same time, and in this way should obtain an unsurpassable perfection.

O sad sophistry! O blind belief of the time, that you can combine all kinds of beauty and every excellence of all the world's great artists and by observation of everything and by the begging of their manifold and great gifts, unite within yourselves all their spirits and conquer them all! The period of one's own power is gone; with poor imitation and clever arrangement they will try to force a missing talent, and cold, slick, characterless works are the fruit. German art was a pious youth reared among kinsmen, within the walls of a small town; now that he is older, he has become an ordinary man of the world, who has wiped from his soul, together with the provincial customs, his feeling and his special character.

I would not wish that the enchanting Correggio or the brilliant Paolo Veronese, or even the mighty Buonarotti had painted as Raphael. And I also do not join in the empty phrases of those who say: "If Albrecht Dürer had only lived for a while in Rome, and had learned the true Beauty and the Ideal from Raphael, then he would have become a great painter; one must feel sorry for him, and only wonder how in his place he still could have come so far." I find nothing to feel sorry for here; on the contrary, I am glad that with this man fate has bestowed to German soil a truly national painter. He would not have remained himself; his blood was not Italian blood. He was not born for the Ideal and the exalted majesty of a Raphael; he had his pleasure in showing us how the people around him really were, and in this he succeeded excellently.

But in spite of this, it occurred to me, when, in my younger years, I saw in a magnificent gallery the first pictures of Raphael as well as of you, my beloved Dürer, how of all the painters I know, these two had a very special, close kinship to my heart (Fig. 8). In both, what pleased me so much was that they placed, so clearly and distinctly, mankind full of spirit before our eyes, simple and straightforward, without the ornamental digressions of other painters. At that time I did not dare to disclose my opinion to anybody, because I believed that everybody would laugh at me, and I knew quite well that most people saw in the old German painter something stiff and dry. Comparison is a dangerous enemy of enjoyment; even the purest beauty in art only impresses us as it should with its full power, when our eye does not at the same time glance sidewards to other beauty. Heaven has so distributed her gifts among the great artists of the world that we need to stand still in front of each one and offer to each his share of our admiration.

Not only under the Italian sky, under majestic domes and Corinthian columns, but also under pointed arches, intricately decorated buildings, and gothic towers true art grows.

Peace be with your remains, my Albrecht Dürer! and may you know how I love you, and hear how I am the herald of your name in this, to you, modern, strange world! Blessed be your golden time for me. Nürnberg! the only time that Germany could boast of a true national art. But the beautiful times pass away over the world and disappear, as splendid clouds move over the arch of the sky. They are gone and not thought of any more; only a few from an intimate love in their soul summon them back out of dusty books and remaining works of art.

Translated by Elizabeth Gilmore Holt

Friedrich Schlegel

From *Descriptions of Paintings from Paris and the Netherlands in the Years 1802 to 1804*

From Second Supplement of Old Paintings, Spring 1804

Art itself cannot deviate from its original function, universal in ancient times, of glorifying religion and revealing its mysteries in a manner still more beautiful and lucid than can possibly be achieved with the written word, without running the risk of losing itself in all sorts of vanity and, finally, wavering between misunderstood ideals and an empty display of effects, sinking into mere vulgarity. So too can the theory of art never be separated from observation without slipping inevitably into arbitrary figments of the mind, or empty generalities. Hence we will proceed as we have done before: Instead of merely outlining, in so many words, the fine concept of painting, we shall expound it thoroughly through a wealth of observations made on old pictures. Let observation always come first; later, when the eye takes a short rest, the results of our observation will by necessity be absorbed into universal principles whose coherence, as well as the inner unity of our view, will readily become apparent to the thoughtful reader.

However, the study of painting by way of scrutiny of individual works can, especially now, never aim at completeness, but is bound to remain fragmentary. And yet this fragmentary knowledge does not in any way prevent the attainment of a unified view for anyone who has really grasped the idea of the art of painting; and it is even good that in this way we are ever reminded of something which must by no means be forgotten. Our perception of art must now indeed be fragmentary, since art itself is nothing but a fragment, a ruin of bygone days. Even the corpus of Italian art is today torn and scattered; and seldom, so seldom, do we find much attention paid to the oldest artists and the oldest works of this school, which do after all exemplify the original sense and purpose of art in a much purer and truer manner than do the later works. And much worse still is the state of the old German school, which is indeed at least as important as the Italian; perhaps even more so, in that it held the unchallenged lead in the thoroughness of its technical mastery, and in that it stayed truer to its religious purpose and always remained painting, never straying into the realm of other arts. The old German School is still almost completely unknown. The bulk of this art no longer exists, it has been destroyed; only a few scattered remains are left, which can at any rate inspire with a vision of the future anyone who has grasped the spirit of the past. But in yet another way does this fragmentation accord with the direction and overview of recent art. The entire body of the existing works is scattered among distant lands and the most diverse collections, of which not a single one is altogether satisfactory and complete, so that works that belong together and ought to stand side by side are often far removed from one another. The fact is, moreover, that Christian art itself has remained fragmentary, and has never really been completed; and even if this is not as visible in painting as it is in the unfinished towers and churches of Gothic architecture (which remained incomplete for a millennium, some having fallen into ruin before they were even built up), it holds likewise for both schools of Christian art, the Italian as well as the old German. In the archaic paintings of the earlier style we find the true artistic ideas and the beautiful symbols of Christian painting quite often very deeply felt, in part also already rightly conceived and altogether clearly developed; the Christian message is sometimes most beautifully conveyed where art in the practical aspects of its execution still languished in its infancy. What a plenitude and what a wealth of truly heavenly pictorial appearances and lovely artistic ideas are evident in the pious paintings of Angelico da Fiesole, even though in a technical sense they still belong to the infancy of art and in that sense lag far behind the contemporary masterpieces of the old German School!

But no sooner had art attained technical perfection, no sooner had it become possible, through this certainty of execution, to render not only the inner, spiritual beauty, but also every charm of the palpable external appearance—when the idea became obscured by secondary intentions, and finally completely succumbed to them. Artists wanted their art and rare knowledge to be visible so as to bedazzle the public; they strove above all after sensual stimulation and even sought to produce voluptuous effects, or else they lost themselves in all sorts of other vain pursuits. They chose pagan subjects, and even treated the Christian subjects in an altogether flat, manifestly sensual, almost pagan, manner, a manner which for that very reason was essentially senseless. The Italian School degenerated more and more into an art at first strained and artificial, then completely superficial and characterless, a flat and vapid ideality. German painting, however, had, if possible, even less of a chance to ripen to maturity, and remained one step less accomplished than even the Italian. The Reformation acted here also as a political force by creating a brutal caesura, drawing the artistic focus away from the traditional subjects of Christian devotion. This resulted in the more recent Netherlandish School in that state of elemental dissolution of the art that allowed, as soon as the destructive principles had been assembled into a system, to tear any conceivable parts of a complete painting out of their organic context. Thus, not only landscape and portrait, but also kitchen and pantry scenes, hunting and hounding pictures, fruit, flower, and animal pieces, still lifes and church perspectives, domestic scenes and comic caricatures, battle scenes and half-comic depictions of low life—all were treated individually in vivid alternation, in a manner ever more technically refined, until finally in this chaotic confusion of slavish replication of the crudest subjects from nature, art degenerated into mere technique and completely lost sight of its original idea.

And yet the fortuitous meeting of the beautiful idea with technical proficiency and a comely richness of sensual form occurs for only a few moments during the flowering of the old style, or in those rare, as yet untainted, beginnings of the first great period of the newer school. Almost everywhere, this harmonious perfection that we seek out above all in our examination of aesthetic beauty is but a beautiful exception; and therefore, as easy as it may be to outline the course of artistic development in general terms, we must not imagine this development as tied by necessity to a stringent regularity, and forcibly filled into such a chain of development. For an individual work often outshines the other products of the same master, or even stands out from among the works of its time and artistic period. We must keep this in mind in returning to the thread of our observations, and we will, where the opportunity affords itself, not refrain from drawing attention to it.

Among those paintings displayed on June 27, 1803, in the round hall of the Louvre, there were only a few new additions of great importance; most had already previously been exhibited. . . .

Here is a work that is completely classical, not through an affected imitation of the ancient statues, but through the truly Roman grandeur, freedom, and strength of its conception. Yet the subject is a genuinely Christian one: the *Martyrdom of Saint Agatha,* by Sebastiano del Piombo (Fig. 9). In terms of treatment and interpretation, this is one of the most instructive pictures that one could hope to see—a classical painting, if there ever was one deserving of the name. By this I do not mean to imply that the picture corresponds in every particular to the requirements that theoreticians are wont to put into their textbooks, but rather that this rare work is altogether inspired and governed by that relentless force, that thoroughgoing intellectual penetration, that dignity and magnanimity that are characteristics of classical antiquity.

But how—I hear our readers ask—how can such a cruel incident furnish the subject matter for such a beautiful painting? Indeed, I have observed many viewers who, after a quick glance, turned away from the picture in revulsion, and censured the artist for his choice. Yet these were the same people who with complacent admiration lingered in front of Domenichino's *Martyrdom of Saint Agnes,* or Guido's *Murder of the Innocents,* without being in the least terrified or put out by that medley of corpses and bodies writhing in agony, those streams of gore, those gesticulations. Yet of all this there is nothing to be seen in Sebastiano del Piombo's *Saint Agatha.* No blood, no convulsions of pain, no wound, for as yet the threatening instruments have not actually touched the saint's body; not even an expression of revolting wickedness can be found here. It is therefore probably due above all to the deeply serious and moving veracity of the depiction that most viewers are at first blush so thoroughly repelled and shocked by this painting; for it is as completely lacking in any nauseating or ignoble features as other depictions of martyrdom are full of them. The artist has chosen the moment immediately preceding the execution. Already the red-hot iron is closing in on the breasts and the gorgeous bare body of this superb woman, and the violently aroused expectation that this entails may indeed give rise to painful sensations. Yet these might perhaps be experienced as *too* painful only by those who perceive and feel this pain merely as pain; who are totally unaware of its higher, divine significance and totally insensitive to the majesty of its form.

The composition is quite simple. The figures are life-size, yet the picture is small because the figures are tightly grouped together. The saint stands in the center. She is stripped to the waist; her tunic lies at her feet; her undergarment, girded around her hips and loins, is slung into a knot in front of her body. She is leaning backward against a column. Her arms, too, are bent around this column and firmly tied to it. They are, however, concealed by the heads of the two executioners who are standing at her side, and by a green curtain trailing down from above. All in all, the painful impression of violent constriction has been avoided. The sufferer seems to be standing almost free, and of her free will, amid her executioners. To the left, the tyrant faces her, with a strangely foreshortened arm leaning on a table, which on this side forms the foreground. Behind him one notices an attendant, with his eyes ominously cast down. On the opposite side, in the foremost zone in front of the executioner to the right, a big knife lies on a gray base. The executioners hold the tongs with both hands. To the right of the column dividing the background one notices a fiery forge and small figures preparing the instruments of torture. To the left the backdrop gives way, and one sees behind the drawn curtain a quiet landscape and still waters in the serene distance. In front of the landscape, and closest to the attendant with the downcast eyes, there stand two Roman soldiers in shining helmets, with the visors raised, compassionate witnesses of the incident.

The saint's body possesses heroic virginal beauty and strength. Its pure, solid limbs glow, hit by the raw sunlight, not with the colors of lilies and roses, but with the flush of ruddy good health. Her face radiates not transcendental spirituality but earthly heroic virtue and vigor. In her dark eyes one senses all the ardor of the passionate woman, but with an expression of steadfastness, grandeur of soul, inner dignity, and self-possession. The negligent fall of the black curls still leaves her noble forehead and her lovely, strong neck quite bare. While she exposes her body to the torture without shrinking or trembling, she turns her head with a moving grandeur and with a generous indignation upbraids the tyrant: "A woman's body has carried thee, her breasts have fed thee—art thou not ashamed to deliver them to the torturers?" Only her pallor betrays the fear of her earthly nature at this hideous moment. Her bearing and sublime features express more anger and scorn of the tyrant than concern for herself. In the midst of her suffering she triumphs over him, who confronts her with visible uneasiness and gazes at her, as if the sight of her torment could fortify him against his doubts. His strikingly constrained pose, the all but unnatural attitude of his arms pressing against the table, intensify the tyrant's expression of insecurity. He seems to force himself to persevere in his anger, as if his stubborn toughness resisted and finally repressed a better feeling.

His head is, incidentally, of noble shape and very forceful. Even more forceful in their own way are the two executioners, as they prepare to tear off the breasts of the saint with their tongs. They are what they are meant to be: mean, ugly, and completely insensitive, merely tending to their business as if it were any other. However, the tremendous force that informs the articulation of their faces and the indescribable thoroughness and objectivity of execution mitigate the effect without weakening it—for those qualities direct the viewer's attention so forcibly to their character and form that the natural and inevitable emotions become muted.

The grandest and most remarkable conception of the entire work may well be found in the two soldiers with their cuirasses and open helmets, who, behind the tyrant, watch the incident with the sincerest compassion. Their faces evince a tender feeling and the most honest sorrow. They betray no wild indignation against the tyrant, nor do they fruitlessly demonstrate their willingness to help. Silent witnesses of what they cannot, and must not, prevent, they can only gaze at the saint. She is all they can think of or perceive. They seem to listen to her words. Their sublime and tender pity seems to appease her suffering like a calming music, like the chorus in Greek tragedy. In their thoughts the highest grief seems wedded to the concept of Necessity and the unalterable rule of nature. As both resemble each other to the point of identical sameness, they seem to represent the same personality in two persons. Hence, they are even more reminiscent of the function of the ancient chorus. Otherwise they are in their bodily frame and bearing quite plain and martial, not wild and vehement, but possessed of the most masculine firmness and an all but iron character. The emotion in such manly heroes is all the more moving. The view of the distant landscape calms the beholder's soul like faith in a future happiness. No effulgence of heavenly light, no angels are descending to offer the martyr the palm of heaven. Her steadfast soul, unswerving in her confidence in her own strength, rushes toward her union with nature in eternal freedom. This, too, distinguishes our painting from most other depictions of Christian martyrdom.

How could it happen that all the *martyria* came to be branded, unconditionally, as subjects unfavorable, or even unworthy of pictorial representation? Is not the painting under discussion (which can never be praised enough) alone sufficient to refute such an opinion and to proffer evidence as to how such a subject can be treated in a beautiful and dignified manner? It is true, the great question concerning appropriate and suitable subjects for the arts in general and painting in particular has been decided, blindly and haphazardly, in accordance with an arbitrary and biased theory, concocted of this and that half-understood philosophical concept. A preliminary orientation on the historical plane would have led to a different answer. It may well be that the Mother of God with the infant Jesus is not only the oldest subject of Christian art, but also the one that can neither be exhausted nor ever be perfectly rendered. Scarcely less ancient, and perhaps even coeval, is that other subject depicted as many times, but even less adequately: the image of the dolorous head, crowned with thorns, the blood-stained Redeemer, the *Ecce Homo,* and the Crucifixion itself. The legend of Saint Veronica offers hardly less evidence for the extreme age of this symbol than does the legend of Saint Luke for the image of the Mother of God. If, moreover, the Annunciation, the Holy Family, the Adoration of the Magi, the Sacred Conversation, are all more or less reminiscent of the simplest and purest expression of infinite loveliness ever conceived by the loving mind of man, then one has to recognize, by the same token, that every humble martyrdom reflects the Passion of Christ. Art, however, as well as religion (from which art can never be separated without losing its identity), ought to point out to man not only the Divine as he might imagine and intuit it, abstracted from all relationships, in a state of serene peace; but art and religion must likewise demonstrate how the Divine breaks through the confines of our earthly existence and manifests itself in a glorious epiphany; that is, they shall and must show us the deep sorrows of the Savior, as He was imprisoned in His mortal body and, on His journey back to heaven, exposed Himself voluntarily, in His supreme love, to all the torments of His Passion. The image of Mary and the suffering on the cross—these are the basic subjects and primary concepts, inexhaustible in their infinitely varied expressions, variations, and combinations. They are, as it were, the eternal poles of higher, and true, painting.

Depictions of hermitages, as they are suggested by so many delightful legends, are indeed more pleasing and agreeable than any ever-so-edifying martyrdom. But would not an exclusive search for whatever is agreeable and enjoyable soon lead into the most mannered one-sidedness? Quite apart from the fact that enchantment seems to shun precisely those who most anxiously court it—since it prefers to appear voluntarily—one should receive and recognize it gratefully wherever it presents itself. Yet in the last analysis it is not enchantment and beauty that one should request from a work of art, but only supreme, even divine, significance, for without this latter the work of art is not even worthy of its name, and with it, enchantment as the blossom and reward of divine love will appear quite of itself. *Martyria,* however, are certainly eminently capable of conveying that high and profound significance. If only the painter knows how to avoid whatever is revolting, he will find it easy—by focusing upon the commingling of pure and loving characters (the sufferers) with mean, degenerate, or manifestly evil ones (their persecutors), and by depicting their struggle in all its various stages and entanglements—to draw a painfully truthful picture of the tragedy of real life, and of the terrible fate that the more innocent may expect on this earth. But even in so doing, the artist will still find enough opportunities to remind us, if he is so inclined, of the most sublime beauty and love. There is, however, one difference between such depictions and common reality: In actual fact, the martyrdom of the righteous and pious in their struggle with the evil ones extends rather over the entire course of their lives, and does not appear in such concrete, tangible terms. But does this put art at a disadvantage? Art requires tangibility, especially in painting. The concentration in a tremendous focal point of all that which in actuality is widely scattered may well be the principal difference separating art in its treatment of individual destinies from the laws of reality. Hence *martyria,* appropriately rendered, may even belong to the advantageous subjects of painting—at least they are much more useful for painting than for poetry. We may disregard cases where the martyrdom is connected with a whole wealth of other incidents, so that it forms no more than one point, or even the climactic point, of a much broader context. Otherwise, poetry will hardly succeed in evoking the martyrdom as an isolated fact. The poem might turn icy and monotonous in the attempt or, at the very best, exhaust itself in an anxious striving after an unattainable concreteness of representation. Miracles, of which so many have been painted whenever a cyclical representation of the entire legend was requested, seem nonetheless rather an exclusive property of the poet, since only he can sufficiently prepare the reader for their complete revelation, however enigmatic and rich in mysteries they still may remain. Yet it is precisely in mysteries and enigmas that poetry is wont to excel and shine in all its splendor. Only the very generally known miracles, such as the Ascension and the Transfiguration, have the advantage of carrying conviction and moving the viewer, even when painted.

From Third Supplement of Old Paintings, Summer 1804

(There is hardly a picture that can) compare to the excellence of a little painting by *Altdorfer* (Fig. 10), with figures one or two inches high. Shall I call it a landscape, a historical painting, or a battle scene? None of these designations really suffices. It is all that together and much more; it is a completely new and unique kind of painting, a genre unto itself, a term that we have yet to invent. How shall I describe my amazement at first sight of this wondrous work? Like someone who, heretofore familiar only with the pleasant light verse of the Italians and having taken that for true poetry, suddenly experiences the unfolding of the magical world of Shakespearean characters—this is exactly how I felt. And yet this describes only the splendor, the richness and depth of Altdorfer's painting or poem, not the chivalric spirit that prevails over it, prevails to such an extent that one could call this work a *chivalrous* painting. It depicts the victory of Alexander the Great over Darius, and yet not in mere imitation of the antique manner, but rather as in medieval poetry, as a depiction of the highest adventure of knighthood in its flower. The costume is altogether German and noble; horse and rider are bedecked with armor, in gilded and embroidered doublets, the spikes on the forehead of the stallions, the glittering lances and stirrups, the plenitude of weapons—the combined effect of all this makes for an indescribable splendor and richness. Nowhere is there a graphic depiction of blood and guts, or severed limbs or injuries; and only in the immediate foreground, if we look very closely do we notice beneath the feet of the armies charging at each other from both sides, and under the hooves of their chargers, rows of corpses lying closely side by side as though woven together into a fabric that serves as the carpet of this world of war and weapons, of sparkling iron and even brighter glory and chivalry. It is the depiction of an entire world, a little world spread out over a few square feet; innumerable and immeasurable are the hosts streaming from all directions at one another, and even the vista in the background leads into infinity. It is the seven seas all in one, with a historical inaccuracy, if you will, that does, however, create a very significant and true allegory. A depiction of the seven seas then, high cliffs with a craggy island in between, distant warships and whole flotillas to the left, the setting moon, the sun rising to the right—a symbol of the depicted history, as clear as it is big. The warring hosts are, by the way, all carefully arranged in closed ranks, without any of the ponderous stances and bodily distortions that one otherwise expects to find in the so-called battle scenes. How, at any rate, would such posing be possible in this immeasurable multitude of figures? The painting embodies the straightness, the sternness, or, if you will, the stiffness of the old style. Character and execution are, on the other hand, so wonderfully accomplished in these tiny figures that even a Dürer would not have cause to be ashamed of such work. Let it be said once and for all that the thoroughness of the workmanship in this painting, as much as it seems to have suffered the ravages of time, is of a level of perfection the like of which never manifests itself in the otherwise accomplished paintings of the old Italian

School, a workmanship that one can find only in the paintings of the early period of the old German School. And what plenitude, what vivid expression, not merely in the character of each individual warrior, each knight, but also in the evocation of the entire host! Here a row of black archers gushes down from the mountain with the fury of a swelling stream, and always others and still others keep pushing from the back. On the other side of the painting, high up on the cliff, we already see a scattered force of knights fleeing through a narrow pass; we see nothing of them but their helmets reflecting the sunlight; and even at such a distance, everything is crystal clear. The decisive action and the pivotal moment of this whole scene stand out resplendent in the middle of the painting. Alexander and Darius are both gleaming in their golden armor; Alexander on Bucephalus, with his lance extended, charging out in front of his forces, chasing after the fleeing Darius, whose charioteer has already fallen onto his white horses, and who, with the dejected air of a vanquished sovereign, turns around to regard the victor. Even if we step so far back from the painting that all the rest is no longer recognizable, this group still stands out clearly and moves us, evoking the deepest emotion. To the thinking painter who strives after new and grandiose subjects, who wishes to abandon for once the sacred sphere of Catholic symbology and seeks to create a truly romantic painting, this little Iliad in colors could teach the essence of chivalry in the language of painting. Another painting, the siege of a city, by Martin Fezele,* is executed in an hardly inferior style, although it is clearly not infused with the same lofty poetic spirit. I particularly liked a group of knights in the outermost background in the outer courtyard of the fortress, who, decked out in armor with plumed helmets, all shake hands, swearing an oath of loyalty. Thus the old German artist invests feeling into such subjects which for others represent merely an opportunity for the display of triflings and contrasts, or for the effortless execution of insignificant conceptions.

Both paintings were, as indicated, carried off [by Napoleon] from Munich. If there are in that city more paintings of such a high quality, then German painters ought to make pilgrimages there, as

---

*Schlegel refers to the painting *The Siege of Alesia by Julius Caesar,* 1533, by Melchior Feselen (Munich, Alte Pinakothek). — Ed.

they do to Rome or Paris. We may not — let it be said on this occasion — raise any new hopes for the state of art in Germany, until an art-loving and German-oriented prince attempts to bring together into one collection of old German paintings as many as possible of the still extant, though in part already widely scattered, documents of the German artistic spirit. The rays of German culture, which hitherto had been scattered even in its painterly manifestations, would in such a collection be united in one single focal point and shine forth, immeasurably strengthened and doubly fortified; and surely the result would strike us as equally astounding and fruitful as the unified treasures of Italian or Greek art would do. For surely the old Germans were no less great and innovative in the art of painting, and we shall have occasion to offer further evidence of this. It is only that the public in its ignorance remains unaware of this fact, and the shallow imitation mania of the Germans refuses to admit it, as they curiously put their pride in their own self-denigration. But what good and praiseworthy work has resulted from this imitation mania? Nothing, absolutely nothing but altogether perverse and insipid, useless things. We can sooner tolerate that poetry should let her imagination wander to distant regions; and yet poetry must always, enriched by these foreign treasures, return, as to her native haunts, to that which forms for her time, for her nation, the highest focal point of feeling and of poesy, lest she grow cold and impotent. Sense, however, and sensual art will, through this apparent cultivation of diversity (in truth, of aimless rambling in all directions), inevitably become completely dulled and diluted. Sense, and what it is meant to achieve, can only flourish mightily and take on its own unique form within definite limitations. Intellectual truths are universal; the imagination tends to soar into the hazy distance; sense, however, aims far more to penetrate the particular and the familiar down to its very depths, its actual roots, and to bring it into renewed existence in the picture. Thus, in this reborn and transfigured image of the inscrutable essence of nature, we reencounter simultaneously the riddle of our own emotions shining forth unexpectedly and erupting in inexpressible language. Purely sensual art can do no more than this. Art focuses on the particular and the familiar; that means that it must be local and national. Whether we consider generalized form more in terms of symbolic depth and meaning or more in terms of idealized shape and external aspect, the fact remains that the relationship of generalized form to the particular characteristic and national features of fact and expression is of paramount importance for the visual arts. As long as art remains in the service of the church and is confined within the circle of its symbols and mysteries, their spiritual beauty and sacred significance (which are the same throughout all the Christian nations) remain indeed art's first and foremost concern, which ought everywhere to prevail over ethnic and national characteristics. However, the national element must not be excluded or altogether expunged; it must rather be intermingled with and assimilated by that higher religious purpose, according it then its unique spark and its lively appeal. In the Italian School, in the works of the old masters, the Italian character of the facial structure and expression stood out, often in the strongest, most glaring and strident way, whereas later on this characteristic quality dissolved more and more into an idealized generality that in the end became flat and characterless. In the German School, the very opposite development seems, by and large, to have predominated. In the oldest paintings, still executed in the Greek style, symbolic sanctity according to a strict idea of, and respect for, the devotional meaning was the rule; it is in the later German School that the lively expression of the true national character first emerges in physiognomy and costume, often to a crude degree, bordering on caricature. This tendency is manifest in the work of Lucas van Leyden and other Netherlandish painters of his day. Dürer is closely akin to these artists in the liveliness with which he expressed his understanding of the many facets of the German national character; and this kinship is all the more evident since, in the Upper German School, where it was always prevalent, the national strain took on a less flexible character and a more ponderous and broader expression. We must not however forget that in the heyday of the older Netherlandish School both the general and the particular existed harmoniously side by side; as in the work of van Eyck and Hemmelink, the deeply symbolic quality of devotion and sacred beauty and the emotional German strain are united. As early in fact as in the paintings of Wilhelm von Köln (whose work still borders on the Greek style), we find first the quiet divinity that constitutes the dominant character of his paintings (particularly in the depiction of the Mother of God, or in other transfigured saints). In addition there is an evocation of that merry German life very clearly depicted according to the contemporary manner and custom, in the varied expressions of the other faces and secondary figures as well as in the fantastic splendor and daintiness of the colorful costumes. But today we must take even greater pains not to neglect this same element of lively characterization and uniquely national specificity, since it constitutes, particularly in painting, an essential, indispensable ingredient of every lively artistic representation. And our contemporary art still runs the risk of losing itself in abstract generality and characterless, idealistic shallowness, rather than stumbling into the opposite mistake. Up until the most recent days of devastation and confusion, every ancient nation had its own distinct physiognomy in customs and life-style, sensibility and appearance, as well as its own music, architecture, and sculpture—and how indeed should things have been any different? There has been much talk in recent times about a general beauty in art, without any local aspects; but until now nobody seems to have a clear idea of what will come out of it; nor do the present attempts in this direction bode well for the further results of this new faith. In the narrow constraints of national particularity, the Greeks and Egyptians, Italians and Germans all achieved a greatness in art, a freshness that was lost as soon as imitation replaced independence. Pictorial beauty can only suggest the outline of bodily form; yet it can grasp, and magically wake through color, the spiritual essence contained in the sensual appearance; hence it ought to remain individual within the idealized form; however individual in a grander dimension, objectively individual as this is the case in every true representation of national and local facts. May the painters of today heed and adopt the well-considered creed of the old Dürer, who said: "No, I don't want to paint in the antique manner, or the Italian manner, what I want is to paint like a German!"

Translated by Peter Wortsman and Gert Schiff

Carl Friedrich von Rumohr

On Giotto

Ille ego sum per quem pictura extincta revixit.
Cui quam recta manus, tam fuit et facilis.
    Naturae deerat nostrae, quod defuit arti.
Plus licuit nulli pingere nec melius.
    Miraris turrem egregiam sacro aere sonantem.
Haec quoque de modulo crevit ad astra meo.
    Denique sum Jottus. Quid opus fuit illa referre.
Hoc nomen longi carminis instar erit.

                    Obiit an. MCCCXXXVI. cives pos.
                    b.m. MCCCXC.[1]

This tribute is, as it were, the official manifesto of an established opinion, already generally accepted in Florence by the middle of the fourteenth century. It confirms the truth of the old remark that whoever sets the tone in one field, by discovering heretofore unknown or long-forgotten artistic techniques, as a rule wins greater posthumous renown than one who achieves uncommon and abundant results on already trodden ground. The celebration of the innovations that Giotto introduced into painting lived on among his students and imitators for an entire century after his death; the veneration of those painters for whom he set the tone and direction coincided with the most beautiful epoch of Tuscan literature, whose best and most articulate authors lent their pens to this conviction. The more time carries Giotto's achievements beyond close scrutiny, allowing the imagination of his commentators a freer hand to develop their necessarily very general encomia into statements of greater appeal, the more his posthumous fame will necessarily grow and flourish. Meanwhile it may still be in time and not in itself fruitless to establish his historical position, his cast of mind and artistic direction, and finally also to place the quality of his artistic achievements in a historical context. Let us first examine the extant and accessible sources for such passages that transcend the general and dwell more on the specific and singular aspects of his story.

To what extent Giotto exerted an influence on the artistic practice of his contemporaries we may surmise above all from the comments of those artist-writers upon whom I already drew in no small way in my examination of the development of the Byzantine influence, and of the period in which this latter influence made its mark. Ghiberti, one of these artist-writers, begins his compendium on the more recent art history with an anecdote which Vasari repeats. It seems too beautiful to be true; and since there are also extraneous reasons to doubt that Giotto was in fact the student of Cimabue,[2] the son of a certain Bondone,[3] I will be permitted to skip over this story, which is more charming than informative. The essence of what Ghiberti has to say about the life and works of Giotto can be summed up, after the elimination of repetitions and awkwardnesses, in the following sentences: "Giotto developed into a great master in the art of painting; he pioneered the new art and left behind the crude manner of the Greeks—many of his students were skilled in accordance with the style of the *ancient* Greeks. Giotto saw in art that which remained inaccessible to others. He introduced natural-ness and grace, without going too far." Ghiberti's contemporary or near predecessor, Cennino, who concurs with Ghiberti's state-ments and judgments, likewise reports that Giotto broke with the Greeks and thus thoroughly reformed the artistic prac-tice of the Italians. These writers may well be more dependable in this regard than some more recent commentators will admit. For Cennino studied with Agnolo Gaddi, the great student of Giotto; Ghiberti was born less than fifty years after Giotto's death; both Cennino and Ghiberti had sharpened their sense of artistic matters. Moreover, as I will later show, the existence of that artistic upheaval of which they speak is confirmed by all dependable artistic monuments of the period. And yet we are bound to ask here, how and in what way exactly did Giotto deviate from the Byzantines, and in what respect is he in fact to be viewed as an innovator? Both aforementioned writers point, in complete agreement, first of all to Giotto's renewal of the manner, or the technique, of painting; and in fact we can confirm, in examining those paintings that are definitely by Giotto and his Florentine contemporaries, that he completely abandoned the more viscous binding medium of the Greek painters and returned to that more fluid and less darkening medium, which the older Italian painters had long used before going over to the Greek manner. However, Giotto was able to derive incomparably more advantage than those crude painters of the Middle Ages from this binding medium, in which the purified sap of young sprouts and green fruit of the fig tree served as the base. Cennino, however, who devotes all his attention to the technical aspects of painting, has apparently only this return to the native practices in mind, when he says that Giotto retrieved painting from the Greek manner and brought it back to its native Italian roots. Ghiberti, on the other hand, states clearly enough that Giotto also introduced the most successful innovations in the more encompassing aspect of meaning, in the choice as well as the treatment of his subjects. As we may recall from my former explorations, the Greek painters preserved the typology of many conceptions and characters (albeit stripped of their own true essence), which earlier and more accomplished stages of Christian art had developed. The dignity and the intense beauty of these forms had not completely eluded the brush of Cimabue, and especially, Duccio; they showed a free hand in copying them, in retrieving these motifs, and by comparing them with reality, they succeeded in lending them a new life; they also often succeeded in stripping off the mummylike husk with which the mechanical imitators of the Middle Ages had gradually surrounded them. But Giotto broke through the barriers that these painters had still respected; while casting off the rust of antiquated manners, he discarded at the same time that lofty, truly Christian, and truly artistic spirit which still shone forth out of those so manifoldly stunted depictions—the possibility of any innovation is based on strength; the mentality, however, from which the innovator arises, is generally unholy and sacrilegious. Whereas we must admire in Giotto the talent, the courage, the mental force, that empowered him to map out an altogether new direction for the majority of his contemporaries, we should not overlook the fact that his direction was the very opposite of what some more recent writers have ascribed to him.

If these writers unequivocally attribute to him a certain religious austerity in his handling of the predominant artistic tasks of his day, thus asserting that his artistic merit rests exclusively in the depth and substantiation of his conception, they will be proven wrong, as long as we grant any validity to the testimony of his closer contemporaries. Wherever the contemporaries delve more closely into the character of our painter, they point, with notable unanimity, at his lightheartedness, newness, prolific output, and versatility, even, as I will show, at a certain degree of frivolity and disregard for the symbols of sanctity: just as we would expect from an innovator.

The devotion to such an artistic stance had necessarily to lead to objectivity; and whereas Giotto, considering the rather lowly state of artistic technique of his day, could neither wholly grasp nor depict the appearance of things or their character, he was at any rate able to accord his depictions enough consistency, enough movement, variety, and expression in the reciprocal relations of his figures as would suffice to confirm his tendency to observe life around him, and to explain that his contemporaries, in their youthful imagination and in the absence of objects of comparison, believed they saw in his paintings a convincing appearance of true being and happening.

Just as Ghiberti, in a passage cited above, praised Giotto for having introduced naturalness into art (presumably alluding here not to form, but rather to action), so too did Giovanni Villani write of "Giotto, our fellow Florentine, who was the greatest master of his day in the art of painting, and the one who was able to depict figure and action most naturally."[4] In the same vein, Boccaccio asserts, although not without rhetorical exaggeration, that nature could not create anything that Giotto had not copied to the point of deception.[5] The references of Dante and Petrarch (who did however equate him with his Simon of Siena) are, like the encomia of many Florentine historians,[6] too general to offer a more definite characterization. On the other hand, several stories by Boccaccio and Sacchetti portray Giotto as a clever man of bright and sober intelligence, who had a clear sense of his time.

"Messer Forese da Rabatta," Boccaccio tells, "had a small, deformed body, a flat and doglike face, but an altogether uncommon knowledge of the law. Equally ugly, Giotto possessed such an outstanding ability that nature created nothing which he could not copy so faithfully with his pencil, or with his pen, or with his brush, that the result was not so much similar to nature, as it seemed to be the thing itself. And often it happened that, standing before his works, the viewer was convinced that the subject of the painting really existed.[7] Since, moreover, after having suffered for so many centuries from the blunders of those who painted only for the satisfaction of ignorant people, this art lay as though buried and forgotten,[8] and was restored by Giotto to the light of day, we may rightfully count him among those who brought renown to the Florentines; all the more so since he humbly rejected the title of Master,[9] although he was himself the master of others who greedily angled after this title.

"Messer Forese and Giotto both resided in Mugello (a countryside intersected by the road from Florence to Bologna). Once during the court recess, when Messer Forese had visited his lands, and by chance was riding back on a poor hired horse, he met Giotto, who had likewise visited his lands and was riding back to Florence. The latter was neither better mounted nor of finer appearance than the former, and slowly riding, they continued on together. They were, as chance would have it, overtaken by a heavy summer shower, which forced them to seek shelter with a farmer of their acquaintance. Since the rain continued and they were in a hurry to get to Florence, they borrowed a pair of pilgrim's cloaks from the farmer and two altogether worn-out hats, and set out on their way. After they had ridden on a while, and were soaked through and through, and besplattered with mud from the horses' trot, all of which did not help to grant them a more stately appearance, the sky grew gradually clear, which, after a protracted silence, loosened their tongues again. And as Messer Forese rode up close the better to hear Giotto, who was renowned as an excellent speaker, he could not refrain from looking him over from all sides and from head to toe, and unaware of his own looks, he had to laugh at his friend's foul and unseemly appearance, saying: 'Oh, Giotto, if a stranger were to meet us now who didn't know you, would he be able to believe that you are the greatest painter in the world?' To which Giotto immediately replied: 'Indeed, Messere, that is, if looking you over, he were to believe that you know your ABC!' Messer Forese acknowledged his blunder and felt he had been repaid in kind."

In this tale, whose ending, it seems to me, was rather predictable, and which displays on Giotto's part more presence of mind and healthy common sense than uncommon intelligence, our painter appears as a clever and practical man who acquired lands with his savings, paid the necessary attention to his business, and knew how to get along with and retain the respect of people of all sorts. A look at the novellas of Franco Sacchetti will permit us to add to this picture of the artist.

"Who didn't know," says Sacchetii,[10] "how superior Giotto was to all others in the art of painting? And so it came to pass that an unschooled artisan who was probably about to take on an office,[11] and had the idea of commissioning the painting of his coat of arms, entered Giotto's atelier together with another fellow who carried the empty escutcheon. 'Good day to you, Master,' he said to Giotto, whom he met at home. 'I would like you to paint my coat of arms.' Giotto, who observed the man and his manners, answered plainly: 'By when should the work be done?' and said, once he'd been informed of the allotted time: 'I'll take care of it,' and the artisan went away.

Giotto then thought to himself: Did they send me this fellow to play a joke on me? I've never in my life been commissioned to paint a coat of arms! Whereupon he painted the escutcheon with all sorts of heraldic figures, helmet, cuirass, sword and lance, got into an argument with his client, went to trial and won, because he was more skillful with words."

This humorous anecdote, based on the double meaning of the word "arms" (*arme*) portrays a Giotto more protective of his artistic honor than Boccaccio had imagined him. In the latter, as well as in the former instance, moreover, he appears quick-witted and worldly, deft of tongue and quick to collect his thoughts and take action. These personality traits are heightened to frivolity and impudence in a second novella.

"Whoever knows the ways of Florence," the same author tells,[12] "knows that on the first Sunday of each month, everyone makes custom of going to San Gallo; and men and women go more for pleasure than for the absolution. On one of these days, Giotto decided to go there with his friends; and, just when he had stopped a while on the Cocomero Road to tell some story, a herd of pigs came charging by, one of which ran so heftily against Giotto that he fell to the ground. After his friends helped him to his feet and dusted him off, he neither cursed the pigs, nor did he complain, but rather, turned to his friends with a chuckle and said: 'Well, aren't they right, after all? Haven't I earned thousands with their bristles and not even offered them a bowl of soup in return?'

"His companions laughed and said: 'What's the use, Giotto is master of all things. You never painted any story as well as this one with the pigs.' And so they continued on their way to San Gallo, and stopped on the way back, as was customary, to look at the paintings in San Marco and in the church of the Servites. And since they saw there a picture of the Virgin with Saint Joseph at her side, they said: 'Tell us, Giotto, why is it that they always paint this saint with such a downcast expression?' To which Giotto replied: 'Doesn't he have good reason?' Then everyone turned to each other and agreed that Giotto was not only a great painter, but also a master in the free arts."

These anecdotes, the last of which displays far more frivolity than wisdom, and in any case, a down-to-earth mind, give evidence of far too much individuality and general agreement to have been altogether imagined; they do no doubt at least show us what Giotto's contemporaries and close followers thought him capable of. Fortunately, he also expressed his healthy, unbribed, and independent good common sense in the form of a Canzone.[13] This poem contains many lucid and clearly expressed ideas, the gist of which merits our attention in various regards. We find here, first of all, that healthy, manifestly practical common sense which we encountered in all the aforementioned references—a consistency that cannot be altogether coincidental. However, especially remarkable is the choice of subject and the direction of the criticism. Giotto labored hard and long and executed some curious and monastic works for a number of the monasteries of the Franciscan Order; therefore he did not miss opportunities to discover several weaknesses in the rules of that order, or to realize the failings which such rules had evolved in the course of their day-to-day application. Giotto makes use of these failings (dissimulation, untruth, hidden ambition, and clandestine world-liness) to strengthen his attacks on the principle of monasticism which, as it was understood by the fanatics of his day, seemed to him to go against any nobler dispositions of the human soul.

Thus, far from lending his enthusiastic support to the views and notions of his contemporaries, Giotto rather regarded them with a sober awareness and a critical eye. However, cold reasoning and clarity of thought go against the grain of that enthusiastic and unreserved surrender without which at least the more poetic artists could not succeed in grasping the lofty and the noble. This may perhaps explain why, even when the opportunity suggested itself, Giotto refrained from pursuing the undoubtedly nobler path of his predecessors and perfecting their artistic creations, so needy of further elaboration. Yet we must not overlook the fact that at that time the monastic religiosity had completely vanquished the evangelical and archaic Christianity. The result was that the artists of that period were everywhere diverted more and more from repeating or further developing the oldest types of Christian art. The representation of incidents from the lives of modern saints, the allusions to the foundations of their orders and to their beneficial activities, while banishing those older concepts from artistic practice, claimed more and more space and swallowed up more and more labor, especially since the tiniest details of their lives were still vividly remembered, and there was no end to the enthusi-astic evocation of their manifold merits. Thus, since Giotto had been distracted from the older direction (whether as a result of indifference, or external pressure, or even through an accidental coincidence of both) he was almost exclusively restricted to the depiction of actions and allegories that hardly enthused him and which were of value to him only inasmuch as they implied human relations and activities, which he could indeed imbue with much truth and strength, in accordance with the peculiar brand of his imagination.

Hence the artistic revolution ascribed to Giotto by his con-temporaries must have consisted, technical innovations apart, in the fact that he neglected, although not altogether abandoned, his predecessors' aiming at noble representation of holy and divine characters, and instead directed Italian painting toward the representation of actions and effects in which, in accordance with the character of monasticism, the burlesque coexisted, side by side, with the pathetic.[14] The naturalness that the contemporaries admired and lauded in Giotto's works, is, in view of the artistic level of the time and several surviving samples of his artistry, in fact nothing else but that liveliness of movement and action which did indeed lend charm and interest to the aforementioned subjects, yet by the same token pushed away the high seriousness of the preceding artistic endeavors—endeavors whose value we today can more freely assess than could those ancients, caught up as they were in their admiration and imitation of Giotto.

Let us now consider whether a close examination of Giotto's artistic works will result in the same or an altogether different conclusion. Unfortunately, we have only a single painting which, through an inscription, can be confirmed as the work of his hand. As to the remaining paintings ascribed to Giotto, since Vasari and more recent commentators are altogether unreliable in matters of such antiquity, we must depend largely on Ghiberti's statements, even though these too are often vague and imprecise, and cannot be accepted without careful consideration.

The aforementioned painting (Fig. 11) hangs in the Baroncelli Chapel in the Church of Santa Croce in Florence; it consists of five sections of Italian-Gothic configuration. These sections were, however, reset in a newer frame, probably in the fifteenth century; yet this renovation did not affect as much of the socle of the painting as to give us reason to doubt age and authenticity of the inscription it bears, which, judging from the lettering and its setting (the same in each case), is definitely older. It reads, in separate letters which are in every instance ringed by a Gothic hexagon: OPUS MAGISTRI IOCTI. This painting, which depicts the crowning of the Virgin, has clearly been ravaged at an early stage by acids and, more recently, in part through pealing. Nonetheless, since it has neither been washed out nor was it altogether painted over, this painting preserved the mark of his originality, and it can thus be considered an authentic instance of Giotto's manner and training.

In the central panel, Mary and Christ are seated on a shared raised throne of Gothic design. With both hands, Christ places the crown on the Virgin's head, a motif often repeated by a host of later Italian and German painters. Like the motif itself, so too do the character of the Savior and his garment definitely belong to the modern period, and are probably of Giotto's own invention. The antique, or Christian-Roman type, which we still find in the works of Duccio and Cimabue, has been altogether effaced here. Particularly striking are the short, bordered sleeves of the Savior's garment, the oldest example I know of this predilection for strange garments and frivolous tailoring and embroidery, in which some painters of the fourteenth and fifteenth centuries took such pleasure; and which more recently have been taken as typical by some unschooled, albeit well-meaning artists, whereas in actual fact they were hardly more than the passing whims of some painters.

Although this and other similar deviations from the tradition earned Giotto much fame and acclaim among his contemporaries and his followers, we less-enthralled observers cannot help but recognize that these innovations of Giotto's, like artistic transformations in general, do not all represent changes for the better; and that many of these changes derived in fact from an unapprovable disregard for the dignity of his subjects. He could most certainly not have failed to realize that clothing in a painting is by no means lacking in significance, that it indeed designates the character of the work, and can on occasion change and even distort that character. The simple, unassumingly dignified dress, with which the artists of old had for so many centuries adorned the Savior and the Apostles, underlined the gravity which one likes to perceive in these characters, and even accorded their actions a certain solemnity. Perhaps it was this very consideration that prompted the Sienese to preserve the typical attire a century longer than the Florentines, prompting the Umbrian painters, and Raphael in particular, to restore it again in all its purity.

Giotto was more in his element in the execution of the four side panels of this painting, in which he accorded especially to the exaltant angels a great deal of diversity and grace of motion.[15] This notwithstanding, the painting fails, in both its entirety and its parts, to afford the satisfaction which one would expect of a master who was for so long preferred by his followers to painters like Taddeo Gaddi, Giottino, Arcagnuolo, Giovanni di Milano, and other masters, whose still extant works continue to arouse much admiration and delight to this day. Even if we wished to ascribe the unanimous praises of the older commentators in part, at least, to prejudice in the artist's favor, we will all the same have to assume that Giotto achieved greater and better results in other works whose subjects more suited his talent.

Let us therefore, in our examination of this one authentic example, concentrate exclusively upon his manner and technical peculiarity, and try to delimit these as sharply as possible.

If we look at the coloring, or rather the mixture and treatment of the ingredients of his colors, then we see from this painting that Giotto had already abandoned that binding agent which Cimabue and Duccio had used, and which (according to the studies Morrona commissioned Pisan chemists to undertake) consisted of some sort of solution of wax. Giotto obviously made use of a more fluid and less viscous binding agent; for this painting was executed with a light and delicate hand, and certain aspects, as, for instance, the edges of the folds, dissolve in the lit masses in a manner without precedent in the older sharply and angularly executed paintings. His binding agent also had much less of a darkening and yellowing effect than did the one commonly used before him; hence the bright and rosy appearance of this painting and of other Florentine paintings of the period that followed. The Sienese painters, on the other hand, seem from all appearances to have held, with few modifications, to the older, originally Neo-Greek binding agent; for their paintings are without exception more leaden than those of the Florentines in their shadowy parts, more yellowish in the light areas. This I would moreover suggest as new proof of the independent evolution of both schools, which, even in later times, always preserved, in pure and unadulterated form, the distinctive character of their respective city-states.

If, however, we consider the forms, then I cannot deny that they seem in my view to be far more imperfect here than in the aforementioned works of Cimabue and Duccio. The heads of the angels and of the Christ child, and several smaller heads in the decorative borders of the painting in Santa Maria Novella, do indeed manifest more delicacy and inner refinement than one would expect of a painter of the thirteenth century; the same can be said of Duccio, at least of his smaller figures. But here, in the more than a hundred figures, we find everywhere the same generalized head,[16] which, despite the great diversity of age and celestial rank, always reappears and is not even in itself appealing. The eyes have not the slightest trace of foreshortening and roundness, they are long and narrow, are circumscribed by two parallel and completely straight outlines, and pressed up far too close to the roof of the nose. The noses, although of very considerable length, are nevertheless stunted in profile and lacking sufficient width; the jawbone is narrow and square, the chin protruding. The remaining forms of the human figure remain predictably invisible; whereas, on the other hand, the clothing here, as always in a comparative study of the oldest masters, is of particular importance.

In their drawing and modeling of the folds, the older painters followed good, originally classical examples; they sharpened their sense of the beauty and accuracy of the folds sufficiently so that even those parts that they added from their own invention were executed with intelligence and assurance. But Giotto, who had completely abandoned the imitation of those old prototypes, was, on the other hand, too unskilled in his perception and imitation of natural appearances to accord each fold its proper course and direction, and to define their ends sharply enough. And yet, with a general artistic intuition, he avoids cutting through light masses. The accuracy and sharp delineation of the folds were of little concern to him; he therefore blurred and blunted the ends of the folds, wherever they are hit by the light, in an indistinct and washed-out manner. Since in this regard, even Taddeo Gaddi (who, of all Giotto's followers, otherwise remained closest to him) deviated from his master and strove after a greater clarity in his depiction of the narrow folds, I am inclined to believe that this treatment of the folds was in fact a definite characteristic of Giotto's manner. And in cases where this feature is combined with the snubbed profile and the abovementioned elongated, sharply converging eyes, I do not hesitate to accept the authenticity of works ascribed to Giotto by early authors, notably Ghiberti.

Here we must include that long series of small paintings that formerly adorned the sacristy of the Minorite Church in Florence. Some of them are now on display in the Gallery of the Accademia, while others were sold and are dispersed throughout the world.[17] The subject of these representations, whose treatment is very light and sketchy, consists in that naive yet somewhat presumptuous comparison between the life of Saint Francis and the life of the Savior, a subject formerly so favored by the Franciscans. Ghiberti remarks very generally that Giotto painted four chapels and four altarpieces in Santa Croce, of which only the one described above has survived; I therefore have no earlier authority than Vasari for the provenance of this series of small paintings. This notwithstanding, I consider them to be authentic works of the master, because the characteristic features of his manner that we have cited are all clearly in evidence; and because they are imaginatively inventive, full of motion, and varied. This latter attainment, combined with the facility of Giotto's production and treatment, most likely contributed a great deal to the limitless acclaim he enjoyed among his contemporaries. In his portrayal of the life of Saint Francis, he tends here and there to the humorous; whereas in his depiction of the life of the Savior, he returned several times to the traditional compositional order, particularly in the Transfiguration, which follows older depictions by Greek painters. Raphael gave the very same arrangement to the upper half of his famous altarpiece; perhaps he borrowed his order from this series, with which he must have been familiar; he did at any rate show here, as in other instances, that one could borrow general artistic traits from one's predecessors, without falling into the futile and wearisome effort of aping their personal, local, and temporal characteristics.

According to Ghiberti, Giotto also painted in Naples, and Vasari, who (on what grounds I don't know) goes into greater detail here, maintains that the murals in the Church of the Madonna Incoronata are likewise the work of Giotto's hand. About twenty years ago, a portion of these paintings, partly damaged, partly quite well preserved, was still in situ above the choir; they covered the fields of a Gothic vault and comprised representations of the seven sacraments. The two best-preserved of these, facing the church, satisfied me in their arrangement, which seemed commodious and harmonious. In the ordination scene, several initiates sing and pray with great fervor, while another, who is led before the Pope, displays the shyness that one would expect of an individual on such an occasion. In the opposite representation of the sacrament of marriage, we must admire the diversity of gesture and facial expression that the artist was able to give to the women in the scene. If these paintings are indeed by Giotto (which I don't doubt, for they reveal all those characteristics that I have enumerated above), then they truly bring honor to his name and reveal the naturalness that his contemporaries admired in his paintings. In such an early time, there could be no question of truth to nature, neither in the illusionistic, nor in the physiognomic sense; only in motion and gesture, and in the interaction of the figures, could a resemblance to nature be desired and achieved. These virtues are equally evident in these as in several other paintings that Giotto executed in the Church of Saint Francis in Assisi.

Ghiberti says, apparently merely from memory, that "Giotto painted almost the entire lower church of the Minorites in Assisi."[18] Vasari limits this obviously untenable claim to the cross vaulting over the tomb of the saint, with which, for reasons already cited above, I concur. On the other hand, in the upper church, whose main nave was almost exclusively painted by one single hand, Vasari finds an open field for speculation, since the master who painted these things is completely unknown. He ascribed these frescoes to Giotto, and more recent historians have followed him;[19] it may be that Ghiberti's untenable contention led Vasari to surmise that the copyist had distorted that passage, that consequently, we ought to read "di sopra" instead of "di sotto." In any case, he, too, is here heeding altogether imprecise memories, since he cannot even name the precise number of those paintings that appear along both walls of the main nave under the windows. For there are not thirty-two of these, as Vasari says, but only twenty-eight. He may very well then have cast just as cursory and superficial a glance at the frescoes themselves.

In fact, these frescoes in the upper church in Assisi do not conform with any of the characteristics which I drew earlier from the one painting that is most definitely by Giotto. The proportion, whose correct observation Ghiberti counts among Giotto's achievements, and which in fact is never seriously violated in any of the aforementioned pictures, reaches such a degree of excess in these frescos that many figures may indeed stretch to thirteen heads tall, while their arms are as short as the kangaroo's; even the truly lively and pathetic grouping of certain compositions does not suffice to reconcile the viewer to such inconsistencies. However, in mannerisms such as modeling, openings of the eyes, and the like, as well as in buildings and costumes, one notices frequent traces of customs and taste of the first half of the fifteenth century. In the picture in which Christ appears to Saint Francis in his sleep, the architecture of the palace displays, in addition to its Gothic parts, traces of the incipient manner of Brunelleschi. Many of the depicted legends may also belong to the later period, and convince those for whom artistic evidence does not suffice, of the falsity of Vasari's contention. As far as I am concerned, I am satisfied that in no instance do these paintings accord with that first painting of Giotto's, but contain incontrovertible traces of more recent origin. In several of the paintings to the right of the entrance, I clearly recognize the hand of Spinello Aretino, and I therefore believe that the remaining works were painted by his son or pupil, Parri di Spinello.

On the other hand, the paintings in the sections of the cross vaulting above the tomb of the saint conform both with the Florentine picture and with the wall paintings in the Church of the Incoronata in Naples; they are of a rosy tint, the figures are uniform in size, the profiles somewhat blunted, the grouping crowded. The underlying allegory is monastically childlike, and, as was usually the case,[20] was definitely assigned by the patron, and not conceived by Giotto, to whose own sensibility and tendency it must surely have been repugnant. I may omit them, since Vasari expounded upon them at length, and more recently, a German traveler,[21] seems to have taken great delight in observing how the angels draw all sorts of poor sinful monks up to heaven on the beneficent cord of Saint Francis's frock—an aesthetic amusement which may be enjoyed by a viewer who feels that he himself is out of the woods. It will suffice for us to commend that fresco as a diligently executed and well-preserved instance of Giotto's brushwork to those who, dissatisfied with an empty swell of praise, want to see Giotto as he is. Even in this somewhat peculiar allegory, the artist will not altogether disappoint them, for he took advantage of every opportunity here to reveal his sense of grouping and his unrestricted eye for the things around him, either in a hidden way or openly, depending on the circumstances. The artist may also have found an open field for the depiction of, or allusion to, the embezzlement of public funds by corrupt officials in those frescoes, which, according to Ghiberti and Vasari, he painted in the Palace of the Podestà in Florence, and repeated in Rimini and Ravenna. These works have since been covered with whitewash, or have been altogether destroyed.

Of the remaining works by our artist mentioned by Ghiberti, only the frescoes in the chapel by the former amphitheater in Padua are still in existence, although in a sad state of disrepair, since they were washed over by an unskilled hand and newly painted over with distemper. Della Valle assures us that they are among Giotto's finest works; perhaps he still saw them in an undamaged state. Their current condition does not allow us to pass any judgment on their artistic merit or lack thereof. Other remnants, fragments, so it seems, of a multipaneled painting[22] currently in the sacristy of Saint Peter's in Rome, are likewise ascribed to Giotto.[23] Although we have no old and dependable testimony for this, still, considering the fact that Giotto did work for this church,[24] and that these fragments, although more beautiful, do not contradict Giotto's manner as we have described it above, they may well be the work of his hand. The Apostles, in particular, in the cross bands are superb and definitely better suited than any of the aforementioned works to arouse respect for the master. In these works (if indeed they are, as I believe, to be ascribed to him) and also in a bipartite painting with a flattened semicircular top in the Florentine Academy, which is said to have formerly belonged to the sacristy of Santa Croce, Giotto approaches, more than in any other instance, the strivings of the oldest Christian artists, without altogether forsaking the peculiarities of his manner; perhaps he had been moved by the mosaic works of the Roman basilicas. In the depiction of the story of Job, in the Campo Santo in Pisa, which at least Vasari ascribes to him, he appears, on the other hand, to have completely followed his own imagination and observation from life. These paintings have suffered greatly over time; yet one can still recognize the composition and action, which are lively and forceful and seem to accord with Giotto's tendencies and temperament.

I will skip over another painting that Ghiberti leaves unmentioned, which Vasari, however, either from hearsay or based on his own judgment, ascribes to Giotto, that *Last Supper* of which Ruscheweyh executed an engraving of exemplary accuracy.[25] And I will pass on to those accomplishments of our master in the fields of architecture and sculpture.

The older chroniclers are unanimous in ascribing the design of the freestanding tower of the Cathedral of Florence to Giotto, and in fact, we still have the record of his appointment as the chief architect of this building,[26] whose construction he did indeed supervise in the last years of his life. Is Giotto himself to be credited with the concept, which is definitely praiseworthy, and for an Italian building, of rather pure Gothic design, or was this concept discussed, altered, and revised during one of those conferences, the protocols of which are still to be found in the archives of Italian cathedrals? I would not hazard to decide this question, since I have not been able to examine either the as yet uncatalogued parchment scrolls in the archive of the Florentine Duomo, or the Archive of the Riformagioni of that same city, where the oldest sources of the history of this building are to be found. The known documents do however reveal the fact that Giotto in any case possessed many of the additional skills required for architecture, so that he was not only an adroit and prolific but also a many-sided artist. If we are to believe Ghiberti, then Giotto was even versed in the art of sculpture. "The first representations," says Ghiberti, "among those which are inserted in his building, the tower of the cathedral, Giotto chiseled and sketched with his own hand."[27] Yet it seems that the latter "sketching" was a rectification of, rather than a supplement to, the foregoing "chiseling"; and it is rather doubtful that he would have shifted his attention so late in life to a task the technical aspects of which entailed all the greater difficulties, since its entire mechanism was still at a very primitive stage. We must, on the other hand, believe Ghiberti, when in the course of his statement, he tells us that he saw drawings and models[28] for these half-embossed works, which latter were indeed of ingenious design and excellent style. His unique qualities may in fact have developed more splendidly in sculpture than in the arts of painting; for wherever in the paintings actually done by him, or those merely ascribed to him, we find compositional beauties, they are often really pleasing only in a sculptural sense, and viewed as a relief; but where the nature of the task precluded the arrangement of figures on a common plane, as for instance, in his ceiling frescoes in Assisi, the result is definitely not nearly as admirable. Some would contend that Giotto took after the sculptors of the Pisan School. Since such a contention is historically absolutely ungrounded, it is probably based on a fleeting observation of his sculptural abilities, which could only have been innate, and which in any case, he would not have had to ape from anyone—who then of the Pisan sculptors, one might ask, would he have taken as his model, the classicizing Niccolo? or the livelier Arnolfo? or the Italian-Gothic Giovanni?

In Giotto, then, we have encountered an artist who acquired and, in a certain sense, truly earned the applause and the admiration of his contemporaries, especially the Florentines, because of his facility, prolificity, and versatility as well as because of that fresh and clear observation of life that endowed the movements and groupings of his figures with a greater truth to nature than one had been wont to find in paintings before him. But since the distance of time accords us a certain overview, which those closer to him lacked, we are able to recognize a fact that must have eluded his contemporaries. By turning art toward liveliness and agility, at least in his own school, Giotto also aided that gradually advancing and steadily increasing alienation from the ideas of early Christian times, a tendency that characterizes and distinguishes the Florentine School and all the artists who associated themselves with it, up until Leonardo and Raphael, with the possible exception of Mino da Fiesole and Masaccio. He introduced effect and action into art, and would also perhaps have added character, were the time already at hand to delve into physiognomic distinctions. Yet, by spreading his attentions over the most diverse conditions of life, he succeeded in directing his school toward the depiction of life in motion, a direction that would be its hallmark for centuries to come.

Under these circumstances, I am frankly baffled by those who devote all their energies to parading Giotto's direction and achievement as the sublimest contribution to modern art. Were they merely to maintain that he was a lively, imaginative, observant, thoughtful artist, we might agree. Yet I am afraid they fancy that he grasped with particular depth and purity those ideas that constitute the soul of Christian artistic aspirations. This is where they err, provided that what I summarized above should appear more deserving of credence than arbitrary delusions.

"He appears altogether different from his teacher, and as a mighty towering spirit, surrounded by his friends and his students," one recent writer says of him.[29] "As the greatest Italian poet has to be viewed with regard to the poetry of his country (?), so Giotto, who was a friend of Dante's (?), ought to be seen as the father of the great, lofty style in the painting of that period. Never was he surpassed in the greatness and truth of his concept (?), in the serious, all-encompassing coherence of a single depiction, or a series of paintings, etc."

If the clear-headed, sober-minded, practical master could only listen for a moment to what is being said of him almost five hundred years after his death with an emphasis and exaggeration that were alien to him as well as to his time, he would surely have an uneasy feeling. For no one likes to perceive the truth of his own being, even if it is beautiful and magnified, in the mirror of a mere fever dream.

How did posterity gradually work itself up to such heights of delusion? The Florentines of the fourteenth century were caught up in a certain idolatry vis-à-vis Giotto's talent and achievement, of which I have cited several examples. They were as though blinded to the advances of the artists who followed him, which probably helped to keep art as a whole for such a long time on that still rather lowly level that Giotto had achieved. Thus, in light of the praises of Boccaccio, Ghiberti, and others, even Vasari forgot that these earlier commentators perceived and praised Giotto from a different standpoint than was or could be his own; he joined in with their tune, without applying his own power of judgment. What Vasari had already in his words expressed overlavishly and profusely, Lanzi, who favored bold similes and highflown phrases, reasserted anew in still more glowing terms. However, we must grant this much to the author of the passage quoted above that he surpassed by far both Lanzi and Vasari and thus reached the limit of exaggeration. In accordance with the ordinary course of human events one might hope that, exhausted by this surfeit of exaggeration, public opinion will gradually return to the truth.

Notes (abridged)

1. I am the man through whom the extinct art of painting came back to life.
   Whose hand was as controlled as it was fluent,
   My art was deficient in nothing that lies within nature.

None was permitted to paint more or better.
You may marvel at the superb tower, resounding with sacred music,
Which, based on my module, rose right up to the stars.
In a word, I am Giotto. To tell what has to be told,
My name alone will deserve a lengthy panegyric.

Died 1336. The citizens erected this monument in 1390.

From a well-known monument in the cathedral of Florence. The inscription is attributed to Angelo Poliziano, the bust to Benedetto da Maiano.

2. Cennino Cennini, *Il libro dell'arte, o trattato della pittura,* goes all the way up to Giotto without mentioning his teacher.

3. Ghiberti had spent a considerable period of time in Siena (to which fact I will return), where he completed works, which, like the related records of negotiations and payments to the artist, are still in existence. He might there have heard of a certain Giotto, son of Bondone, who, contemporaneously with our artist, served the Sienese state as a diplomatic agent, and was most certainly not a painter and not a Florentine citizen (here Rumohr cites various archival references). This Giotto first appears in this archive *B. To. 99 anno 1301. fo. 250. a tergo,* as: *offitiale del commune di Siena;* he is sent out on a mission because of certain *secreta. Eod. To. fo. 259. — a Giotto buondoni Ugieri;* herewith the name of his grandfather is also given. *B. To. 104 anno 1310,* he also appears on several pages. Since such an active servant of the community must after a hundred years still have been remembered by his countrymen, Ghiberti may have heard of him and confused him with our artist. Both names are so rare that their simultaneous coincidence in the names of two different persons cannot be accepted without documentary proof.

4. Giovanni Villani, *Storia Fiorentina,* Book XI, ch. XII; *E quegli, che più trasse ogni figura ed atti al naturale,* which means: Who copied the appearance of things with the greatest fidelity and the most fortuitous success.

5. *Decamerone, Sixth Day, Nov. V.*

6. (Here Rumohr includes a quote from Buoninsegni, Historia Fiorentina, 1581, which exemplifies the laudatory tenor of all mentionings of Giotto in Florentine historiography. Rumohr adds:) Praise of Giotto continued since Villani to be a permanent fixture of Florentine historical writings.

7. *Decamerone, op. cit.* Perhaps the classically trained Boccaccio is recalling in this passage some classical painter's myth. As much as Giotto may have aroused the imagination of his contemporaries, he could hardly have engendered delusions in perception.

8. This passage obviously influenced Vasari in the composition of his vita of Giotto, at the beginning of which he says: "Although born amidst incapable artists, and at a time when all good methods in art had long been buried, he alone resuscitated the art, which had taken a bad direction, and brought it back to a form which could be called a good one, etc." We will not here fail to recognize that the learned Boccaccio did not, like Ghiberti, perceive in the Middle Ages a complete cessation of artistic practice, but rather only a profound decline. We will, by the way, have to make allowances here for the master of the word, since he did not have an in-depth knowledge of the artistic tendencies that preceded Giotto, never himself having seen their products, but accepted completely the tone and the opinion of the artists of his day.

9. This assertion is, as Della Valle already reminded us, inconsistent with an inscription that I shall publish at a later date.

10. *Novelle To. 1. Fir. 1724, novella LXIII.*

11. Ibid. *per andar in Castellaneria.* Some bitterness is contained in this allusion. Sacchetti hated the participation in public affairs, which, in many cities of Italy, was at that time allotted to the lower, less-educated classes.

12. *Nov. LXXV.*

13. (Rumohr inserts here a lengthy poem, attributed to Giotto, which he copied from a medieval manuscript. The poem represents the involuntary poverty of the monks of Giotto's time as motivated by sheer hypocrisy, and conducive to every possible vice.)

14. In recalling here the amusing and gently ridiculous quality ascribable to the worldly awkwardness of genuine, naively pious monks, I do not intend to chime in with the familiar declamations against a historically memorable, influential institution for the sole purpose of defining its relation to more recent painting. This same naively burlesque strain has been amply used in Italian painting, not to speak of the Spaniards, whose dramatic poets also employed it often enough to great advantage, although the greatest among them were themselves monks. The above allusion is at least as harmless as the elaborate depictions of those painters and poets.

15. In these figures too, which Vasari found so particularly appealing, Giotto demonstrated little respect for the tradition. Up until Giotto's time and ever since late antiquity, angels were generally painted dressed in a tunic with folds and a flowing cloak and carrying at most a stick in their hand. But Giotto gave them tight-fitting garments and a great variety of musical instruments with which they seem, to all appearances, to make more noise than music. This new feature, which became very popular thereafter in modern painting, adds, however, a bit of the burlesque. The possibility of representing supernatural beings in human form is based on the expression of the spiritual element in the most perfect creation of nature; such musical instruments obviously have nothing whatsoever of this spiritual element, and therefore, as much as we may have grown accustomed to their presence, necessarily detract from the impression that these figures are otherwise able to give.

16. See *Jen. Lit. Zeitg.* 1813. Col. 135., where in a review that reveals the hand of a connoisseur, the same remark is elaborated upon in greater depth.

17. Some of these paintings can be found in the Royal Bavarian Collection of Paintings; some others I myself own. (About these paintings see *Introduction,* Note 26.)

18. Cod. cit.—Dipinse nella chiesa d'Asciesi nell'ordine de'frati Minori *quasi tutta la parte di sotto.*

19. Lanzi and others. Della Valle questions Vasari's statement, but without giving any reasons for his objection.

20. Anyone who has ever had cause to read through several hundred artists' contracts of the fourteenth and fifteenth centuries knows that the artistic assignment in the earlier periods was generally very sharply defined.

21. See *Kunstblatt* 1821, May and June.

22. They are supposedly the leaves of a door and ornamental work from the former *confessione, dove è il corpo di s. Pietro.* They could well, however, also be the remains of the altar that Vasari cites as the artist's greatest church painting.

23. Lanzi, op. cit. calls them: *graziosissime miniature ed estremamente finite* — using an inaccurate expression which, not so very long ago, made its way into the Italian artistic parlance. They were however painted *a tempera.*

24. *Lor. Ghiberti Cod. cit.* — *Di sua mano dipinse la tavola di san Pietro in Roma* — the subjects of the aforementioned fragments are Christ, the Madonna, apostles, the beheading of Saint Paul.

25. Ruscheweyh as well as Lasinio brought out their version of this *Last Supper* under Giotto's name, both following Vasari's claim. I however am convinced that this

work is much more recent. The refectory in which this *Last Supper* was painted was, according to Richa (*della Chiese di Firenze*) only built toward the end of the thirteenth century; this notwithstanding, there is another fresco underneath the *Last Supper;* however, it is not likely that one would have instantly covered that older painting by a newer work. Still, it might have happened; but the manner in which it was painted corresponds to the manner of the painters from 1350 to 1400, but by no means to the giottesque manner, which is less bold and accomplished, softer and more washed-out in appearance. Moreover, the invention cannot, in any case, be attributed to Giotto or to the unknown artist who painted this picture; for the same arrangement of the figures, which is originally sculpturesque, can already be found in the half-raised relief works of the twelfth century.

26. Richa, *delle Chiese di Fir. To. VI, P. 62.*

27. Cod. cit fo. 8 — "*Le prime storie (che) sono nello edificio, il quale fu da lui edificato del campanile di sta Reparata, furono di sua mano scolpite e disegnate* — Ibid. *fo. 9. a.t.* concerning the same sculpted works: "*Giotto, si dice, sculpi le prime due storie.*" Thus Ghiberti was not quite so sure here.

28. Ibid. "*Vidi provedimenti di sua mano di dette storie egregissimamente disegnati.*"

29. See Introduction, Note 27 (Ed.).

Translated by Peter Wortsman

Eduard Kolloff

Rembrandt's Coloring and His Color Technique

Like the moral interpretation of the subjects in Rembrandt's historical paintings, so too has their technical execution been called altogether odd and peculiar, and even from a technical standpoint it is
said that there is something about his genius that likens it to the
kabala, or the philosopher's stone. Very discerning cognoscenti and
lovers of art who scrutinize everything with a magnifying glass are
baffled and perplexed by his painting. They are unable to say how it
is done, and can find no other way out of their dilemma than to
resort to the spurious explanation that the entire hermetically sealed
execution of his paintings is a work of magic and that the painter
himself had no clear idea of what he was doing.

I confess that I have no sympathy for this kind of explanation.
One might just as well assert that Beethoven did not understand his
symphonies as he composed them, and that it was left to later
dilettantes and performers to empathize with the mood swings of
the master and to stroke out the beauties of his works with the bow
of the violin.

Rembrandt shall not be so grossly offended by me. What so often
engrossed and amazed me about his works was the coherence of his
technique, a clearly discernible, harsh, and yet purposeful command and control of all the means of artistic representation.

Rembrandt combines all the best qualities of color: opulence and
clarity, power and delicacy, glow and depth. And meanwhile, his
work remains a consummate play of illusions, and his rightfully
celebrated coloring, the delight of connoisseurs as well as amateurs,
is essentially based on convenience. Even his extraordinarily lively
flesh color is on close examination the result of a deceptive play

with colors. Yet Rembrandt, we might add, took no greater liberties with truth and nature than did other great masters such as Rubens and Titian. Rubens, who mixed vermilion in with his flesh tones, paints flesh that shimmers like satin and burns as with persons who are all flushed. In Rembrandt's work, as in Titian's, a sometimes bright, sometimes dark yellowish tint stands out, not feverishly and biliously, but rather as though amber and gold instead of blood were mixed in with the bodily fluids and had spread an even warmth all over the body. The secret of Rembrandt's coloring is thus not to be sought by way of a strict comparison with the true color of his subjects as they exist outside his paintings. One only has to approach his pictures with a certain general idea of those colors that differentiate the objects in nature, to convince ourselves, by contrast, of the truth of the color of each object in his paintings. If, for instance, we consider a single cheek of a figure in Rembrandt's paintings and cover the rest of the canvas, then this cheek may not appear truly fleshlike; if however we see it beside the other parts of the face, or even beside hair and clothing, it does indeed give the impression of living flesh. What sets him in this regard as well above all those other painters who try to delight and dazzle with a vivid play of color is the fact that he really does enchant the viewer, that the brilliance of his coloring is combined with strength and harmony. At the same time his chiaroscuro has an indescribable appeal and a truly magical attraction.

According to the clever and apt remark of one expert,[1] Rembrandt is, with respect to his chiaroscuro, the *Dutch Correggio*. His work stands, however, in inverse relation to that of the Italian master: In the case of the latter, light and a general brightness, in which everything is bathed, predominate; whereas, in Rembrandt's work, shadows and a general darkness, from which only a few individual complexes spring forth, constitute the dominant elements. Among the natural phenomena it was, above all, light that concerned the two masters; but for Rembrandt it was not the clear purity of light, but rather the striking mixture of light and shadow, by which the external world revealed itself to his perception. The way light cuts through the dark with lightning bolts, vanquishing the darkness, smashing it with its force and subduing it with its penetrating power: This is the material problem with which for almost thirty years, brush in hand, Rembrandt tirelessly tested his talents; this is the problem that he resolved in the most wondrous way. In his paintings it is therefore generally nighttime or dusk, a darkness into which he lets fall a glowing ray of the setting sun or a pale ray of moonlight, the glimmer of burning candles or torches, often also the poetic light of his imagination, which wrestles with the celestial and earthly lights for dominance. This is our master's hallmark; with such altogether new, highly extraordinary, piquant lighting effects he always startles and takes his viewer by surprise. He has dark lanterns, so to speak, under his coat, which he suddenly pulls out and flashes in our face, so that at first we are almost blinded by the glare. It is as if we had stepped into a deep, dark room, sparingly illuminated by a flickering flame, and in which we cannot immediately make out all the different objects. The eye first has to grow accustomed to the meager quantity of light, until little by little it can make out objects with a definite outline and presence amidst that dark mass in which at first the whole room was drowned. Reynolds claims to have noticed that the Venetian painters generally conceded but a quarter of their paintings to the light, another quarter to the darkest shadow and the rest to halftones; that Rubens sought to bathe more than a quarter of his paintings in light, but Rembrandt, on the other hand, much less, namely an eighth of his paintings at most. This explains why Rembrandt so much liked to set the scene of his depicted actions in the interior of churches, grottoes, vaulted, cellarlike rooms, where the darkness as the dominant element only permits the light to hold sway in scattered spots.

For Rembrandt, the effect of his chiaroscuro is the main tool for the realization of his painterly purposes, and the key factor after which the other elements of painting have more or less to fall in line. He seeks above all to give depth to the surfaces on which he paints, and to make his subject stand out against this depth. We do not, however, mean by this that feature which so many art critics single out as of prime importance, the setting apart of objects and the placement of figures in striking relief. This was not the effect for which Rembrandt so resolutely strove. Far more insignificant painters achieved better results with this effect, so highly prized by the old masters and still favored by some art lovers today, who take particular delight when they encounter a figure around which they can, so to speak, stroll. This sort of illusion does not accord with the basic disposition of Rembrandt's works, which is achieved by letting the shadows dissolve in a background that is even darker than they are. In contrast, the relief effect is achieved by brusquely cutting off the outlines and inserting the figure in the ground, as it were. Rembrandt's approach consists above all in letting the contours blend in with the background, and letting the background recede far back. He then tries to hold the light together, so that the eye is affected by the contrast of this mass of light with the darkness as by the effect of sunlight in nature. In this regard, Rembrandt approaches, to a certain extent, the method of Caravaggio, in that, like the Italian, he accords the objects in his painting the effect of partial illumination. Unlike Caravaggio, however, Rembrandt does not place his objects beneath a light falling through a narrow opening from above, and it is a great error to presume that he first began by restricting all light except for that which comes through a crack in the window. By this means, the artist would indeed achieve the effect of dark shadow, but not much else; what is missing is the bright light that also makes the shadows clear and luminous. Nothing is so adverse to the light, that is supposed to constitute a mass and to spread throughout an entire painting, as those sparks that are forcibly elicited through the contrast of tones and which only dazzle us for an instant, leaving us thereafter to the darkness. Such tricks only glitter because of the contradiction of a single corner of an object, the remaining sides of which all disappear in the darkness. Rembrandt presupposes for his paintings the kind of light which a fortuitous coincidence of nature occasionally casts on objects if certain related phenomena focus and strengthen it effectively; if, for instance, sunlight falls through clouds, or candlelight breaks on dark bodies, so that an array of bright and dark spots form. In a similar way, just as Rembrandt's method diverges from that of Caravaggio, so too is the coloring of the head of the Dutch school different from that of the coryphaeus of the naturalistic school. In both cases, a deep darkness is the dominant tone of their paintings, from which strong lights and powerful colors emerge. But here Rembrandt has a decisive advantage over Caravaggio in that he is able to bring the bright and dark spots into a beautiful harmony, keep the shadows transparent, direct the light in a purposeful manner, and combine extensive groups, indeed extensive compositions consisting of several groups, into a cohesive whole, held together by consistent illumination. Caravaggio's chiaroscuro consists of a strong and powerful coloration and is often exquisitely executed, but it is not really that which the Italians call "chiaro nel scuro." Rembrandt achieves the true chiaroscuro: His paintings are characterized by a most subtle gradation of tones from the brightest lights to the darkest shadows, so that they seem to glow with their own light, and we are able to discern in them not the objects set in the spotlight, so to speak, but also those which without damage could be removed from light and put in the shadow. A painting by Caravaggio is striking in that the piercing divergence of the lit masses from the dark ones strongly stirs our optical nerves; but this sensation has something painful about it, for the impression is too harsh. Rembrandt's paintings, on the other hand, soothe the optic nerves. Light and shadow here do not merely create black and white spots, but rather evoke alternately dark, dusky, bright, brighter, and luminous areas, which hang together harmoniously and with natural transitions from one to the other. We forget that the objects are depicted on a flat surface, so deeply is the canvas hollowed out and the whole depth is broken down into a mass of smaller planes. These planes and all parts of the objects we find in them are lit proportionately, and the reflections and clash of all the lights upon one another combine to create a most pleasing effect on the eye, whose glance is attracted and fastened everywhere as it rests, proceeds forward, and turns back again to take up anew its painterly perusal of the whole. The figures have roundness and motion; the groups, in their opposition and contrast, their halftones, their glazes, their reflexes, and their shading, create the wonderful effects of stasis and stress. Light and shadow absorb and support each other, and united by these transfers of effect they build a single mass. All this produces a concert of striking color effects, which, as a whole, builds to a harmonious crescendo and displays its own bravura and beauty in isolated spots.

The resultant combined effect of variety and unity is enhanced extraordinarily by the choir of colors that support the thrust of the work. Rembrandt clothes the objects with colors that come as close to nature as the pleasant effect of his chiaroscuro permits. Thus, if a particular color that can actually be found in nature should impede and refract the light in any one spot in the painting, and thereby hinder that spot from blending in with the rest, then that color is altered as much as the harmony of light and dark demands, without, however, resulting in a complete distortion of the truth. For the sake of this harmony, some parts are kept darker and others, lighter, creating greater contrasts than nature actually presents. In this regard, however, Rembrandt did not permit himself to take greater liberties than, say, Paolo Veronese, who once, in answer to the question of why he kept certain figures in shadow for no apparent reason that the painting might suggest, merely replied: "una nuevola che passa," (a passing cloud). Colorists above all else, these masters believed that in such cases all other considerations were subservient to the satisfaction of the eye; they could surely have painted truer to nature, but at the cost of that which they held to be more essential and more true to art, namely, the harmony that arises out of the contrast and interplay of colors.

It was in this aspect of the painter's craft that Rembrandt developed the most energetic virtuosity. What strikes us at first glance in his paintings is the impact of their masses and their thorough harmony. You can hang any one of his paintings among twenty others of the most diverse schools, and you will immediately be able to pick it out by the richness and vitality of its coloring, and even more so by the mighty harmony of its dominant key. This is what makes him so truly original and masterful, and it is with this that he made such a great sensation in his day, all the more so in that the then current concept of coloring consisted of a conscientious application of bright tints, and no one had any real sense of chiaroscuro in large compositions, or of the cohesion and distribution of light and dark in well-defined masses. Rembrandt's principal strength lay in his very powerful coloring, in the blending of colors via halftints into the most pleasing harmonies, the painstaking subordination of all shades to one main tone, the true gradation of light so that it dissolves in the most delicate transitions, the astounding vitality and striking emergence of his main figures. All this must have given him a high eminence in the eyes of the experts when he appeared on the scene; and it must be above all these qualities that preoccupied his fellow artists when they saw his paintings. This side of his talent was indeed cited with unanimous praise by the older commentators. Sandrart celebrates in Rembrandt's paintings "the overall harmony, in which he excelled, and with which he opened the eyes of all those who, by common custom, were more dyers than painters, those artists who impertinently and insensitively put hard and coarse colors side by side, so that the result had nothing in common with nature, resembling rather those color boxes filled in grocery shops, or the cloth brought back from the dyers." In much the same way, Samuel Hoogstraten speaks of the piece at the "Guardhouse in Amsterdam," the famous *Nightwatch*: "This work, although not without fault, ought nonetheless in my opinion to outshine all its rivals, for it is so pictorially conceived, so superbly arranged and so powerfully colored that, in the view of many, it makes all other paintings look like mere playing cards. Still, I would have wished that he had let more light in."

In view of the then prevalent concern for harmony and balance, we understand the answer with which Rembrandt allegedly once defended himself against the accusation of an all too uneven execution: "A piece is finished once the artist has achieved his desired effect." It is for this very reason that in his depiction of armor and other glittering objects he sometimes slipped back into that old mistake of which Houbraken accused him in the anecdote of the pearl, for the sake of which Rembrandt drowned a beautiful Cleopatra in abysmal shadows. For even if the artist employs the purest white to evoke the brightest light of glittering metal or mother-of-pearl, it does not stand out so vividly against the flesh in the painting as it would in nature unless you tone down the flesh color. According to this principle, Rembrandt sometimes painted his armored warriors with the flesh tone of their heads dully colored so as in this way to achieve a commensurate gradation of color between the armor and the face, thus maintaining an overall harmony. His paintings of this sort therefore generally turned out too black, and one must admit that Rembrandt forfeited a bit too much of nature here for the sake of achieving his main purpose, whereas in other cases he sometimes held almost too strictly to nature, as for instance, in several of his etched night pieces, in which, for the sake of reproducing the natural effect of candlelight, he left everything around the candle so dark that if we cover up these sources of light, the rest almost goes dark, and at a distance we see nothing more than a light speck. In these pieces Rembrandt perpetrates the opposite mistake of a Rubens, who not only scatters more light over his moonlight paintings than fidelity to nature permits, but also employs in such works his usual warm and brilliant colors, so that one could very easily be deluded, and had he not added stars and a lantern, would think that he had wished to paint a weak sunset. Even if we must admit that Rubens's manner of treatment has its faults, it is still not so faulty as the opposite manner of keeping night scenes so dark that the objects in the depiction are only visible under a certain light, and even then, are barely recognizable. Nevertheless, this kind of lighting is an exception for Rembrandt, who, as a rule, makes a most adroit use of his light-and-shadow play for the clarification of his subject. He does indeed generally permit but little light into his works, and only at those key places that he wants the viewer's eye to focus on, and around which he artificially keeps light and shadow together, including appropriate reflexes, so that the light melts very plausibly into the shadow. At the same time, however, he manages to direct the eye first to the key figures, effectively emphasized by means of the stronger light, then to the less brightly lit figures and finally into the mysterious darkness of the background. This painterliness, which distinguishes Rembrandt's talent to such a high degree, could also be called the musical element in his paintings, for it works upon the eye in a similar fashion as tones work on the ear. This similarity is already evident in the language. Painters speak of muffled and noisy, shrill and dissonant tones, of a harmony of colors, of their scale; musicians for their part speak of a chromatic scale. These are metaphors; but the metaphors of common usage, if not always those of the poets, are all true. Color tones are thus in an actual and immediate sense able to produce melody and harmony. One can make them resonate in all sorts of ways and elicit chords from them. All the great colorists, Titian, Rembrandt, Rubens, Murillo, Velasquez, and so on, play in a particular key, and every one of these masters has a prevalent keynote out of which the harmony of his paintings evolves. If one wished to extend the parallel even farther, one could divide the colorists into melodists and harmonists, as one sometimes does with the composers. Rembrandt would be more of a harmonist. Let us not meanwhile forget to take note of the fact that the musical characteristics of color and its effects are not mere meaningless optical illusions; nor are they mere amusement or amazement to the eyes, as is the flicker of a kaleidoscope.

In painting, as in nature, we see color only as it appertains to physical objects whose essence and characteristics, contour and relief it expresses in its own way. Color envelops forms and holds to lines that are the words of this music, as it were. It clarifies in its way the subject of the painting, just as the orchestra involves itself in the dramatic action of a piece of music and makes it comprehensible by bathing it in symphony. Color is thus suited to more or less precise expressions, and it is one of the legitimate means of artistic representation. This is the source of its truth, its beauty, it poetry, its ideal. And not every painter is necessarily a colorist. This talent appears above all to be innate, and even constitutes a kind of genius if it comes to the fore in combination with the inventiveness, the powerful effects, and the originality of a Rubens, a Murillo, or a Rembrandt. Perhaps no other artist was so much a colorist as Rembrandt: Before his eyes everything explodes in brilliant fireworks or shines like a peacock's tail; all the nuances of the prism shimmer between his eyelashes, and all the colored lights that shoot through nature are snatched up in his paintings. One can very well compare the effect of his paintings with the effect of a heap of jewels: His colors sparkle and gleam like precious stones but do not have that opalescent and flickering quality that one would have expected of such brilliant hues.

In regard to treatment, as with all great masters, several distinct manners can be differentiated in Rembrandt's work. His first manner is a painstakingly clean form of painting which his pupil Gerrit Dou took as a pattern for his own work. In many of the books about art it is falsely asserted that this manner of Rembrandt's is related to the delicate painting of Mieris, with which it has not the least bit in common. A careful application, delicate execution, refined shading, precise modeling, are the characteristics and merits of the paintings from the master's first period. Nowhere do we find heavy impasto, bold heapings of color, robust brush strokes. All is soft, blended, smooth; silver tones are present in abundance; and yet what a certainty of workmanship do we find here already, what a thoroughness of artistic knowledge, what a power of restraint! Gerrit Dou held firm to this first manner of his master, which greatly enchanted the Dutchmen of the day, so passionately fond as they were of artistic "special effects." But with increasing practice and growing insight, Rembrandt altered his technique. The clean, smooth work of his first paintings gave way to a thicker, less-blended application of paint. His second manner of painting is pasty, mellow, full of juice and lust, and was, in contrast to his first blended manner (manière fondue), accorded by the French art dealers of the day the not very elevated, albeit telling label of buttery manner (manière beurrée). The softness is common to both manners; but the latter has something about it that does indeed distinguish it from the delicate blend and flow of the first manner, like churned butter. Amber tones dominate in the paintings of the second manner; his white tints, although sometimes altogether pure when used for his main light, are more often, in the titianesque manner, dipped in the golden glow of the late afternoon sun, and the whole is infused with a warm, shadowy hue of brown and gold. A strict and thorough elaboration of all the parts is combined with a freer and broader execution, which gradually passes over into a greater lightness and virtuosity of workmanship characteristic of Rembrandt's third and last period. The manner of this last period is marked by such a boldness and coarseness of brush stroke and color application that it almost seems to border on vulgarity and impudence, but is in fact infused with a truthfulness and energy of execution and effect that are downright magical. The effect here is not merely one of striking characterization, but rather, there are real instances of a kind of optical illusion, and on first impression his art makes you gasp in amazement. This impression is increased still more if you step up close to one of these paintings to examine it in order to discover the means employed and the manner of its execution. How intense are these deep and yet not black shadows, how sharply do these bright and yet not blinding lights glitter, and how lightly and playfully are all these brush strokes applied! It is often difficult to take these brush strokes as anything but chance effects, but take just two steps back and you will find that they all have their precise representational function, and you will at the same time convince yourself that all these effects are precisely calculated. It is also by no means the first sketchy design that makes these figures, possessed of such a consummate roundness and posture, emerge and recede from the viewer. No, from one plane to the next, we become conscious of a fine gradation. All in all, the artist's striving after the greatest possible effect was his primary concern; to this end Rembrandt required contrasts everywhere, of light and shadow as well as of colors and tones among themselves; indeed, here and there, certain parts were intentionally sacrificed so as to achieve an all the more striking plasticity elsewhere in the painting. Foreshort-ened fingers are rendered with one single stroke of the brush, gold embroidery is modeled in relieflike fashion, and so are precious stones and jewels, whereby the colors are applied pastily and palpa-bly; some colors stand out like small, irregular crystals and hit the eye, sparkling with the full lustre of a smooth, granular, and faceted substance. Both extraordinary and characteristic of Rembrandt's genius, this manner of execution is at the same time incredibly brutal and delicately refined; it is a delicacy that consists of kicks and punches, yet one which the most punctilious of miniature painters could never have achieved: out of this chaos of hacking and slashing strokes, out of this turmoil of shadow and light, out of this heap of seemingly random and disorderly placed colors, there arises the highest and most beautiful harmony.

Rembrandt therefore differs from so many other great masters in the singular course of his artistic development. His first paintings are marked by a quiet, sober, thorough execution, by bright colors and a soft effect; with increasing age, he gets more fiery instead of cooler, more exuberant instead of restrained. In total control of all representational means, he gives free rein to his imagination; his originality reveals itself all the more boldly and richly, and his bold-ness finally almost borders on impertinence, his bravura on wild-ness. Fiercely he strikes about with the lion's paws in asphalt and ochre; his mane gets caught up in the act and glows redder and redder, and finally sets itself on fire, as it were. No cavern, though it may be as dark as it will, can frighten him now; boldly he charges in, knowing that he need only dab here and there with his brush to convert the blackness of the darkest night into a broad daylight that illuminates everything.

Rembrandt most certainly never made cartoons. The main issue to him was not form and drawing, but color and light; to approxi-mate these to their natural appearance, and to work with them according to the laws of chiaroscuro, such were his principal aims. Based on the premise that isolated parts of the painting are to be sacrificed to the whole for the sake of harmony and balanced com-position, there was no longer a need for cartoons: Rembrandt paint-ed according to color sketches, for which he collected detailed stud-ies. A number of his pupils told Houbraken that he often drew a head in ten different ways before painting it on the canvas or the board. This is why there are, not only so many individual studies, but also so many complete compositional sketches by Rembrandt. Even Houbraken admits that he knew of no other artist who had composed so many different sketches of one and the same subject, for Rembrandt was rich in ideas and paid much attention to the variety of costume and affects. Other sources likewise confirm how conscientiously Rembrandt pursued his art, that he did not pick up the palette until he had gathered all he needed; he had a clear and complete image of his subject before painting it on his panel or canvas.

It appears that, like the Venetians, Rembrandt painted on white ground. Before starting to paint, he applied a warm ochre tone to his white primed panel or canvas and shaded in the whole image with this color.[2] In this manner, he established from the very beginning the composition of his painting; only thereafter did he brush in all the local colors with transparent colors, set up the highlights in body color, and finish the shadows in tonal gradation. Buchanan[3] claims that Rembrandt often mixed his local colors and his first glazes with fine residues of painter's gold, which created the great transparency or the glowing depth and richness of tone in his shadows; small particles of this gold should have become visible in strong light, or after the removal of an old varnish. However, this view is not tenable. The alleged gold particles that are supposed to shine forth in the shaded parts of Rembrandt's paintings seem to all appearances to derive from the warm ochre ground, which he often left bare and which he purposely used to make his tints bright and diaphanous. His tints do indeed have something indescribably juicy, transparent, and fresh about them, and his colors look as though they had just been put on the canvas and were still wet. This effect is partly due to the beautiful durable pigments which in those days were imported from the East Indies, or which in Rembrandt's time[4] were more expertly and carefully manufactured than today. But the principal reason lies in Rembrandt's excellent handling. Through years of extensive practice he had achieved such an assurance of mind and hand that he hardly ever, or never, wiped paint away once it had been applied, but rather let it stand in its pure state on the canvas. His highlights were always evoked by masses of different colors that harmonized well and which he applied in a pure and unmixed form. Once the first coat was finished, he never softened the effect, but rather continued to add color, brush stroke by brush stroke. In his last period, his impasto was often so thick that the colors, particularly in bright light, resemble specks and even look like blotches of mortar splattered at random on a wall. But since he knew how to put these unmixed and unsoftened tints well measured and appropriately at precisely those spots where they mediate, and establish the proper gradation, between the adjacent hues, his colors appear to blend perfectly, even in works of his boldest manner, when viewed at the proper distance. In his last period, Titian also painted very roughly and thickly; this did not work from close up, but from a distance very well indeed. In essence, Titian and Rembrandt shared one and the same method, but with one difference: In the transition from one color to another, Titian employed the entire range of tints, whereas Rembrandt applied only a few, the essential, most striking ones. Therefore, Titian's paintings ought to be viewed at short distance, whereas Rembrandt's appear in close-up view almost like a wild chaos of color specks which seem to have been applied, not with a brush, but rather with a scraper or God knows what other tool. It is claimed that Rembrandt often impastoed with his fingers, or scooped the color by the handful out of a bucket, flung it at the canvas and only thereafter smoothed it out with a palette knife. It does appear at any rate that Rembrandt, if he wished to employ chance effects, did not use a brush, but rather a palette knife or some other tool to put on and spread his paint. Whether he in fact used a palette knife or comb or some other tool, it seems to have been something whose use he had not altogether under control. But by this means he often brought forth bold and extraordinary effects that astonish the viewer through their facility, and which most certainly could not be the calculated result of steady brush strokes. Such effects could, however, only be achieved in the depiction of objects that demanded no exactitude, like tree trunks, rocks, columns, or certain forms of soil. As a result of this indiscriminate and rough treatment, the furrowed, fluted, raked, or combed impasto of these objects brings forth those free and easy effects that one notices on their counterparts in reality; therefore, the paint creates a lively, organic impression, especially when, as in Rembrandt's case, the effect is heightened by the contrast of delicate and spirited brush strokes. Rembrandt's technique is always of the most varied and purposeful kind. Each object is modeled with a feeling all its own. His garments are not painted with the same brush stroke that is used on his naked bodies. In putting on highlights, his manner is bold, vigorous, and pasty; but the deeper his coloring darkens into shadow, the more cautiously and sparingly he applied his paint, so that the deepest shadows consist almost exclusively of the first coat and show the same transparency as in nature.

The broad, bold manner with which Rembrandt brought forth such magical effects has often been scorned as cheeky bravura painting, and if we may admit here that the artist did thereby go to the very limit of the permissible, we will surely not likewise fail to acknowledge that he always remained within the perimeters of reason. It is true that Rembrandt first breaks all the rules with the vitality of his conception and the bravura of his execution, but he makes more than adequate amends through the lively truth that emanates from every feature of his boldest virtuoso pieces, and through an emotion as compelling as one finds with only a few artists. The fire that burns in the execution of his artistic ideas spreads to the soul of the viewer and draws him into the heart of the depicted action. Everything is alive in these pictures, which seem to be magically conjured up, rather than painted. Through his peculiar emphasis on the accessories, even in the least significant objects, through the depth of the pathological expression of his figures, even of his ugliest faces, Rembrandt succeeds in evoking a bizarre beauty that can better be felt than described. A powerful character dominates all his paintings, raising them to an equal rank with all masterpieces. The magical and masterful manner in which he distributes shadow and light, his magnificent effects of chiaroscuro, make him as poetic an artist as there ever was. To move us and make us spend the whole day in meditation,[5] he needs only make an old man rise from a chair, or make a single star glimmer in the darkness.

Rembrandt has rightly been lauded as the father of chiaroscuro; he enriched it with a plenitude of painterly finesse and magical effects, and added to it a luminosity and variety the like of which no one before him had ever conceived, let alone imagined. The middle-, half-, and shadow tones flow from his brush in wondrous richness. Yet, all these exceptional qualities notwithstanding, some of which are rooted in the very nature of Netherlandish art, Rembrandt, like so many other artists, could have aged and fallen out of fashion had he not in his own unique way of painting represented *himself*, had not everything that poured forth from his brush evinced the expression of his character, his physiognomy, so to speak. What we love in Rembrandt's work is Rembrandt himself. His style, or, if you prefer, his manner, is, so it seems, merely the interpreter and mirror of his soul. This naive, well-intended, and honorable manner mirrors the goodness of the man's heart and the wealth of poetic attitudes that were part of Rembrandt's own temperament. Could he have painted his masterpieces and given them so much geniality, so much that is gripping, without himself feeling the moods and sensations that he sought to evoke?

And if the argument which I here propound appears idiosyncratic, is it not derived from the study of Rembrandt himself? What else are his works but his best, his innermost, self?

Furthermore, if that special emphasis and mood that Rembrandt could bring even to still lifes and lifeless objects were merely the function of a material process, an acquired artifice, why then does he distinguish himself from all his students (who benefited to such a high degree from his teaching, and in some cases, enjoyed his particular favor) most of all in the fact that he alone could give his figures a soul and an expression? How is it then that he stands out among many of the greatest masters of all schools, in that his paintings, with all that is incorrect, objectionable, and displeasing in their form and style, still move us so deeply? Because, for one, he possessed a painter's genius, the originality of talent that can exist side by side with many faults, which cannot, however, be replaced by any acquired faculty; and secondly, because he held unremittingly to that lively and personal originality that the strict art critics scorn as whimsicality, insufferable audacity, deliberate demagogery, or worse. Rembrandt held firm to that free, proud, and naive independence which is to the mind what salt is to matter, and which alone can keep the mind fresh, powerful, and alive. With no thought to the academic rules and dogma of his day, he penetrated into the untrodden regions of the free working of nature and brought home from these artistic forays the secret of a mode of painting that for its colors employed heart and soul rather than ochre and asphalt. His art is no invocation of fantastic dream phantoms, no conjuring up of a supernatural world, nor is it mere slavish imitation of nature; it is rather the free creation of a different nature, as it were, a realm in its manifestations every bit as wondrous as the nature that it imitates, and which in magical moments it grasps in its essence, and reflects.

I shall leave off here. I haven't the space and even less the time to elaborate on my views on Rembrandt's etchings. I will say only this much: Whoever goes by what he reads on this subject in art books and specialized writings is getting a false picture of the engraver, upon whom tradition and mindless repetition have heaped as much posthumous scorn as on the painter. Perhaps at some future time I shall, here or elsewhere, have the opportunity to say more about this subject, and to place our master in both a more human and a more artistic light, even in this respect, which, after all, did constitute the other half of his self.

Paris, June 30, 1853   *Translated by Peter Wortsman*

<h2 style="text-align:center">Notes</h2>

1. Gustav Friedrich Waagen, *Kunstwerke und Künstler in Deutschland.* Leipzig, F. W. Brockhaus, I, 1843, II, 1845, p. 582.
2. Occasionally he would also paint on a gray ground and brush in the entire composition in brighter or darker shades of this gray color. Rembrandt's paintings of this kind, e.g., the celebrated *Sermon of the Baptist,* formerly in the collection of Cardinal Fesch, have a stone-colored tonality and are called graeuwties, *grisailles,* in the old Dutch sales catalogues. Yet one should certainly not take this to mean what we understand by this term.
3. William Buchanan, *Memoirs of Painting,* vol. 1, p. 197. Printed for R. Ackermann (London 1824).
4. Sandart praises first "the genuine, durable cuttlebone white, prepared with English pewter or lead, and called by the Amsterdam color mongers 'Schulpwitt,' because it remains durable and does not die away. They have there also a lot of beautiful yellow ochres, one of the most-needed colors, whose brightest shades may also be intermingled with shadows, and cannot be found in the same glowing quality in Germany. Next follows a brown-red, especially that shade which does not look as dark and near-black; this is likewise imported from England to Amsterdam, like *Terra verda.* They have furthermore brown ochre, 'culsche' earth color of good substance, etc."
5. Winckelmann who, carried away by overflowing emotion, shed tears of rapture and admiration at the sight of the Apollo Belvedere, once spent an entire day lost in musing and contemplation, in front of the thoughtful head of an old man by Rembrandt.

Jacob Burckhardt

On Murillo

Paris, beginning of August 1843

Time and again, I feel carried off by an irresistible force to the halls of the *Musée espagnol*. There, I meet her every day, my sun, Murillo's *Maria* (Fig. 12). Then I say to myself: Such a girl lived, two centuries ago, in Seville! And right now, perhaps, this city goes up in flames because of that regent whom the *Urmau** always defended.

Murillo is still one of the greatest who ever lived. Here hangs his portrait (by his own hand)†. It is the key to all his works. Compare it with all the beautiful cavalieros from the court of Don Philip IV, which, by no means badly painted by Velazquez, shine forth here from every wall, and you will comprehend what it was that elevated Murillo above his own time — it is the physical and intellectual power still wielded by this force of nature, while around him his magnificent fatherland and its noble people sank lower and lower.

Look at these splendid, slightly pouting, lips! Do they not reveal the man of action! These slightly retracted nostrils, these flashing eyes under the splendid, wrathfully arching eyebrows, this whole face, is it not an arsenal of passions? Yet above it there reigns

---

*Gottfried Kinkel (1815–1882), art historian and revolutionary, pioneer of adult education. "Urmau" was Kinkel's nickname in the so-called Maikäferbund (May Bug Association), an intellectual students' union in Bonn, of which Burckhardt was a member from its foundation in 1841 to its dissolution in 1847. — Trans.

†B. E. Murillo, *Self-portrait,* 1618. Private collection, U.S.A. D. Angulo Iñiquez, *Murillo: Catalogo Critico,* 413. — Trans.

supreme an imperious forehead, which ennobles, controls, spiritualizes everything; and by its sides, the most beautiful jet-black locks flow down. Happy the woman who has been loved by this man! His mouth has kissed a lot, I believe.

Bartolomé Esteban Murillo was born in Seville in the year of grace 1617; he became a pupil of Juan del Castillo and Velázquez, lived continually after 1645 in Seville and died there in 1682. These are (by God!) all the documented facts I know about him. Yet in his pictures, the history of this great soul lives for all to see, and with it the history of his time.

We know well enough what a time this was. In the wake of Don Philip II's reign, grave economic ills preyed upon the pith and marrow of Spain's existence. Under his second successor, the first flagrant defeats occurred. Spaniards were forced to recognize the autonomy of Portugal, and to admit themselves beaten by Cromwell. Among the completely impoverished masses, a brooding fear spread that worse times were at hand. Nonetheless, the nation's intellectual movement was as fresh and alive as ever. The heyday of Calderon coincides with the youth of Murillo. And yet, the nation was bound by heavy chains. It choked with its very health, since a fatal impulse from above systematically checked or misguided its external activities. Add to this the tributary pressures that favored those close to the government, and the foreign fabrications — pressures more preposterous and terrible than those that any other country has ever had to endure. According to the historian Ranke, entire families were seen to set out for a life of begging, since it was no longer possible to make an honest living. Hence, this was no time for action, which is why Murillo was unable to evolve a historical style. Residues of his genre painting crept even into his most sublime creations, and this holds as well for his slightly older contemporary, Zurbarán. By the same token, composition is his weakest point; he puts his figures in the picture as the case may be, and in this respect even the daubers of the Roman school from Vasari's epoch are superior to him, as it is possible anyway to acquire a certain compositional facility like a mere handicraft.

But then, Murillo's beggar boys, his groups of children, which are among the foremost credits to the Munich Gallery, betray a feeling heart for the profoundly oppressed common people. These are his mute laments, which defied all Dominican censorship, and which we understand only now, as we feel more compassionate toward

Spain than ever. These splendid, robust children clad in rags, leaning on an overgrown hedgerow or a dilapidated wall—are they not an image of the very nation, still unaware of the whole extent of its strength and, for the time being, merely looking around among the dusty ruins of its past? Whoever wants to grasp entirely the heavenly poetry of these pictures should read the adventures of Guzman de Alfarache. He, too, was such a begging brat, yet capable of renouncing all the wonders of Italy out of longing for the beauties of his native Seville.

But before I begin to ramble I shall dispose of Murillo's external characteristics. There one has to applaud first and foremost a coloring that often achieves the transparency of fire, and which is supported by a chiaroscuro that puts him in the direct lineage of Rembrandt and Correggio. Add to this a capacity indigenous to several Spanish painters, and to a high degree, namely, the altogether masterly indication of the atmospheric layer (*l'ambiente*) between the figures in the painting and the viewer. Those who have seen many paintings know that this comprises a good deal of poetry, and that the Düsseldorf school could be one of the best schools in the world, if its artists had the secret of this effect, and if their colors were not so hard. On the other hand, one only has to look at any Rembrandt in order to know how much spirit can be infused into even the most vulgar figures through lighting and air. Murillo's drawing is by no means faultless, especially in his ideal figures, and that brings me to the core of his artistic character.

He is a thorough realist, and does not want to be anything else, with the exception of only a few cases. His *Saint Anthony of Padua* is a true and right mendicant friar, not the mere abstraction of such; his *Jacob at the Well* is a Spanish shepherd, as good as they come— but think what an advantage the artist had! He didn't have crippled factory workers for compatriots, but one of the most beautiful peoples on earth, a people who did not become haggard through begging nor wretched through poverty, but attained, through thoughtful idleness, an awareness of their own beauty! This is, after all, what explains the often so striking beauty of the people of the South; they simply make it a point to be beautiful without any northern affectation; their movements are, in spite of all their liveliness, simple and grand, like the lion's and eagle's.

And in precisely the same manner beauty, with Murillo, is still a piece of nature and not a reflection that has passed through so and so many mirrors. Ordinarily I am not prone to making comparisons, but here I cannot help speaking of Raphael. In Raphael's Madonnas, especially in the Sistine, you sense a (howsoever *unconscious*) *reflection*. It is true, he doesn't say more about this in his well-known letter than that he "followed a certain idea"; but who can deny that the *Madonna di San Sisto*, the *Madonna di Foligno*, and *La Belle Jardinière* (this latter in the Louvre) transcend already all the possibilities of even the most beautiful model? It is the same case as with Luther's theory of miracles: *miracula non fiunt praeter naturam, sed supra naturam* (Miracles are wrought, not *outside* of nature, but *above* nature).

Murillo instead seeks out in Seville the most beautiful, pious, and intelligent girl and, from looking up at her, derives the enthusiasm necessary for the creation of his Madonna. She would be pious enough to give birth to the Messiah, but she can *never* become queen to the saints and angels, no matter how purely Spanish the blood that pulses under this white, clear skin. Therefore, wondrous woman, step down from the canvas and just look at me; that will make me happy for the rest of my life!

Well, you may laugh! I wouldn't exact such a favor from the *Sistine Madonna*, since in front of her I have to cast down my eyes, so earnestly does she stare into the viewer's face! The girl from Seville, however, modestly crosses her hands above her throbbing heart and gazes continually into the high heaven, where in golden clouds myriads of angels' heads kiss one another; she isn't even aware that she stands on the globe and crushes the serpent's head—she isn't aware of it, for it is streaming down into her eyes, the divine light, and now she knows that she will give birth to the Savior. But for all that, she is still no more than a girl from Seville, and I wished she had flesh and blood.

Well, you may laugh, I say; one can lose one's mind in front of this picture, just because it is an ideal image.

It is a different matter with his images of Christ. Here, unfortunately, he is an idealist, in the sense that he is trying to approximate, as far as possible, the long-known *Vera Icon*, the age-old effigy of Christ, spread over the entire Occident. I have no words to describe the effect of such a piece of archaic typology amidst a realistic painting, brim-full of chiaroscuro and aerial perspective. That the result is quite unfavorable, namely, a fearful and insignificant physiognomy, goes without saying. (Mind you, there are still only very few painters who can realize such a head; I am only measuring Murillo by his own standards.) If one sees next to this his *Infant Christ on Saint Joseph's Lap,* one cannot understand how this beautiful, strong, and frolicsome boy could grow into such an insignificant man.

For all that, this is a very curious phenomenon. Murillo did have the courage to paint the Mother of God in accordance with his principle. Yet with Christ, his heart failed him and he relied, exhausted, upon the tradition. I think this can be explained, in part at least, in the following way: Murillo had a precious overview of the past history of the Italian and Spanish schools of painting; he knew how many painters had risked the leap and had a great fall; how many had at least run for it, yet stopped just short of the ditch. However, I cannot think of any painter who should have renounced the artistic, unfettered representation of Christ so flatly. He has depicted him a hundred times as a child, and with what heavenly beauty! I believe his beautiful wife must have given him a very beautiful, lively boy; otherwise he couldn't have created it.

9 August 1843

What a queer fish this Murillo is! His figures are aglow with the most beautiful and cheerful sensuality; time and again, a roguish laughter breaks forth from even his most sacred scenes, and yet all this takes place in front of the most sombre, gloomy backgrounds! The loveliest Christ child, for example, stands in front of a Capuchin friar; full of simple piety and monastically humble devotion, he opens his traveling sack and the young god slips a loaf of bread into it. This all could be bathed, with no damage to the effect, in a beautiful evening light, or in the afterglow of a serene sunset; yet Master Murillo situates his scene before dark, with gray clouds, in a wilderness—one could not ask for gloomier surroundings in Norway. The heavenly *S. Antonius of Padua* in the Berlin Museum, and most of his larger compositions, are treated quite similarly, except when he puts on an ordinary, gray-brown background.

First I thought: the painter needs a contrast to those glorioles of angels that one finds in the above-mentioned pictures. But these works are surrounded by different, historical paintings by his own hand, which display the same kind of background, the same murky, thundery skies, without angels and glorioles. I was even more astounded when I found two *landscapes* by Murillo, which were gloomier than anything else. Not for him the pitch-black shadows, the furiously glaring lights of Salvator Rosa or (in history painting) Ribera and other Neapolitans—no, he uses a melancholy, rather uniform gray; he displays not fury and despair, but gloom. To quote an example:* A turned-up path leads through craggy hills covered with miserable little trees and shrubs, and overhung by the same sultry, wicked clouds. He has painted this rather carelessly and more or less as a study; for the depiction lacks the determination and individualization necessary to create a truly *sinister* impression.

What I want to prove by these observations is the following: He has envisioned nature in human beings with entirely different eyes than nature in landscapes, or man-made architecture. Do I draw theory too far when I say: he viewed his country with a sorrowful eye, but his people with a joyful and hopeful one?

The matter becomes all the more remarkable, the longer one contemplates it. This landscape has perhaps been painted during the same decade when Claude Lorrain painted his beautiful, glowing sunsets over Genoa, his shimmering palaces on the sea shore! It belongs to a country that we are wont to consider as a favorite child of the southern sun, which in the richness of its vegetation, in the azure of its sky, is inferior not even to Hellas. And mind you! the picture is not even a product of the school of Madrid, for which there were no better subjects at hand than the desolate New Castilian heaths; no, Murillo the Andalusian, the son of Seville, has painted it.

But let me go on with my speculations. I think I have come across a similar phenomenon in the works of several great painters, namely Michelangelo (provided his *Venus* was really painted, after his cartoon, and under his supervision, by Pontormo) and with Rubens. Figural painters of this rank develop occasionally a total disdain for landscape and background, and treat these parts of their pictures *en bagatelle,* with arbitrary diffusion of light and shade, to the sole

*Perhaps *Landscape with Sheep,* London Cooper coll. Iñiquez 3019 (disattributed; none of the landscapes attributed to Murillo is accepted by present scholarship). —Trans.

end of letting the figures stand out in strong relief. But no other artist tramples so obviously and deliberately upon the pictorial beauty of his fatherland as does Murillo; and this happened not even in the sixteenth century, when our sensibility for the landscape was not yet truly awakened, but during the lifetime of Claude Lorrain, Gasparo Poussin, and Albert van Everdingen. The comparison with this last, who is known as a northern landscapist of the most serious kind, seems to me particularly striking. Everdingen still includes in all his paintings a piece of blue sky, glorious fir trees, and romantic castles and waterfalls. Even Jacob Ruysdael, this "grand and sombre mind" (as Eichendorff says of his Count Victor) paints a mighty vegetation of oaks even into his gloomiest ravines and swamps. *Only* Murillo makes do with the most wretched underbrush—he who had every day the lemon groves of the Carthusian monastery of Seville, the palm trees and aloes, right before his eyes.

But it is perhaps indigenous to a great mind that he creates from time to time an opposite pole to his own inner joy—a gloomy solitude, conducive to concentration. This is the *divine sadness of genius,* which we find in some of the great characters of history. Numa went to the source of Egeria, Mohammed withdrew into the cave, Christ retreated into the desert. There the mind may create for itself a solitude even more desolate, a night even darker than it actually is; for then, the joyfully centered self emits all the more splendidly its mightiest, innermost light. "Und die Fülle des eigenen Wohllauts."*

12 August 1843

I cannot get rid of this Murillo; he has transfixed me in his magic circle. Today again, I have looked very carefully into his character and his curious idealism, and I have come up with the following:

His figures of Christ include, apart from the clearly recognizable reminiscence of the *Vera Icon,* still a strong Spanish element. It is true, there is no trace in these figures of the inner strength and fire that glows, for instance, in some of Murillo's Madonnas and beggars' children; timid and undecided, his otherwise so powerful hand

---

*"And the fulness of its own harmony": apparently a quote from Burckhardt's own poetry. — Trans.

has here strayed across the canvas. But if he was unable to make his Christ a god, he made him at least the most pure-blooded Spaniard. It is impossible to paint a finer, whiter epidermis; his glance has all that noble fixedness that one notices in some of the cavaliers of Velázquez, and which occurs nowhere else in the works of Murillo.

At this point, the following scale of characterization can be established: Next after Murillo's figures of Christ, there follows his *John the Baptist,* a no less insignificant, idealized figure who, probably out of a dogmatic whim, bears an unmistakable family likeness to his Christ. He is followed by a kneeling Magdalen, who is however not idealized in the sense of the Roman school, yet lies nonetheless outside Murillo's ordinary circles inasmuch as she is modeled more or less upon the ideal of Titian (who himself can be called, in his own way, a realist). Then I could only name a *Head of St. Peter* which, albeit more generalized than other figures by Murillo, yet represents a rather coarse Spanish type. The collection of independent, completely realistic characters is led by the wondrous *St. John the Evangelist;* a gulf separates him from the *Baptist.* Then follow the *Immaculate Conception* and all the other miraculous pictures, right down to the *Repentance of the Prodigal Son* and the beggar boys.

Is, then, Murillo a religious painter? Is Rubens in his sacred subjects a religious painter? The question touches upon one of the most profound chapters in the philosophy of art. Overbeck* would say no, for he does not even accept the late works of Raphael as religious paintings.

If one approaches the question from a historical angle, it all becomes very simple, and it is not even necessary to agree with Heine, that extreme leftist, who thinks it is much easier to paint angels than, s.v., a puking peasant *[sic]*.

Was not the seventeenth century, the epoch of the Counter-Reformation, as pious as, perhaps even more pious than, the time of Fra Angelico da Fiesole and Stephan Lochner? Did not Rubens devote his life to Flanders and Brabant, the combatant outposts against Holland, and to the true *ecclesia militans?* Did not Murillo belong

*Johann Friedrich Overbeck (1789–1869), head of the Nazarenes, a school of German painters in Rome who, through deliberate imitation of Dürer and the Italian artists before Raphael, endeavored to reform painting in the sense of pious simplicity, in the vein of Wackenroder. — Trans.

to that nation that all but perished in its relentless defense of Catholicism? Florence, on the other hand, has never known a more frivolous epoch than that of Fra Angelico da Fiesole, which, moreover, was the epoch of the great Schism. Besides, we know at least this much about Rubens, that he was a very good Christian, and there cannot be any doubt about Murillo, either. Hence, if Overbeck in his silly fanaticism speaks about an *apostasy of the art,* he doesn't really know what he is saying, especially if he makes Raphael the scapegoat.

This alleged apostasy was a quite natural development, upon which the convictions of the painters had not the slightest influence. I distinguish two elements in this evolution: the sudden improvement and increase of the artistic means at the end of the fifteenth century and, in connection with it, the material expansion of the arts as well as the suddenly added competition of secular subjects.

Here lies the secret—in the miraculous development of the arts that preceded the Reformation, and not in a so-called apostasy of the poor painters. Leonardo da Vinci marks the high point of this evolution, not Raphael; for the school of Perugino was still chained and fettered when Leonardo had already created his great cartoons, and Raphael, as is well known, made big eyes when he saw Florence for the first time.

It is, however, a proven fact that only as long as the artistic means are imperfect, a primary idealism can unfold; only a child can cherish hopes that some day he will reach the goal of all his wishes, be it a coach box or a royal throne. In the beginning, the painter has only a very general knowledge of the human figure, hence all his figures look more or less alike; he is not yet able to fill his form with flesh and blood and reality, and it is precisely because of this limitation that he collects, whatever poesy and piety he might possess, in that one point, the human face. But that does not make early art and artists more pious, and better, than those of fully developed epochs. For to the occidental nations, idealism is a natural and necessary form, as long as their eyes have not yet been opened to reality. Yes, even the oriental nations, Mongols and Jews, and to the same (or even a higher) degree, the Mexicans, are possessed by an imperfect idealism, and if Brahma has four to twelve arms, this is an idealistic symbol of power. If the peoples of the Occident are more resourceful in such matters, this proves only that they form the intellectual aristocracy of the world.

Yet among all the evidence produced by cultural history in favor of the human spirit, one observation will always stand out for its beauty: the fact that art in its infancy is also possessed by the sweet dreams, the healthy, naive idealism of childhood; that with the imperfection of its means it displays, at the same time, the greatest depth and beauty of intention, and this all the more clearly and openly just because it is not yet distracted and confused by the universality of the artistic means.

Most peculiar is the manner in which art groped its way toward realism. The development was different in the South, and it occurred there almost an entire century later than in the North.

In the Germanic North, a new trend in the history of culture engendered, toward the end of the fourteenth century, the replacement by realism of the idealism which so far had been prevalent in the Flemish school. Suddenly the Van Eycks opened the eyes of their contemporaries for reality and its assertion in painting. Not only do they refashion the human figure, they also give it a background—landscape, street, or room—that accords with reality. They forget neither the dog in the narrow lane nor the cat on the windowsill, the plum, or the vial on the chimney. However austere and dry in its formulation, this realism still holds an immense appeal as immediate testimony to a long-past way of life.

However, in the South the awakening of realism at the end of the fifteenth century went hand in hand, most fortunately, with its diametrical opposite, the newly undertaken study of antiquity. Thereby it should not be forgotten that the craving for works of art was, as a consequence of the Italian orientation toward externals, much stronger, and the battlefield much broader than in the North, where everything was preparing for the highest spiritual conflicts. Italy was the seat of the Church, and politics was already bogged down in that kind of depravity that is quite conducive to the blossoming of the plastic arts. Germany, on the other hand, was drunk with the future, and its art would from now on take second place behind Italy's.

Around the year 1500, Italy lived and enjoyed life up to the hilt. The really great time of its art lasted hardly more than forty years;

this is the lifetime of Raphael. How dearly has Italy paid for this time!

During this Medicean epoch idealism and realism interpenetrated the art of the South. The summit may well be marked by the *Sistine Madonna* (1517?). After Raphael it is only Venice that maintains a kind of union of the two principles, and even there, realism begins to prevail in the later works of Titian. The Roman-Florentine school degenerates into a hopelessly insipid, one-sided idealism, whereas with the more forceful characters, Caravaggio and the Neapolitans, realism runs away in large leaps. Whatever was welded together again after this disintegration *through reflection* by the Bolognese school belongs — just because it was the work of a conscious, and no longer naive, idealism — to the new chapter of modern art. Murillo and the school of Seville are an offshoot of the realistic Neapolitan school, or at least this latter decisively influenced Murillo.

After all, what I have traced here are altogether natural processes, such as have determined the course of art in all eternity; and it takes an Overbeck to say one school had apostatized from the other. But that means to measure the spirit and its works by a policeman's yardstick. No *artist* will ever be able to bind himself to go never and under no condition beyond his teacher. But no more words! Every reasonable person knows today that the foremost quality of the spirit is its movement and infinite capacity of development.

Now it is notorious that the epoch of the Counter-Reformation was a very devout one. Massive destruction was countered by an enormous effort of reconstruction. No matter how many paintings had been burnt in Germany, Italy produced as many or even more. During the second half of the sixteenth and the first half of the seventeenth centuries, the Catholics even managed to recapture countless churches from the Protestants; they were instantly redecorated with a pomp that often astounds us.

This brings us back to the principal phenomenon, namely, the all but complete disappearance of that *pious idealism*[1] from the art of the Counter-Reformation. This is a fact, and we don't want to deny it. But that the art was amply as pious at the time of Fra Angelico is also a fact; the piety had only found a different outlet.

Now the Madonna is far removed from her erstwhile divinity, her full purity and virginity; already Giulio Romano paints no more than a beautiful woman, and Titian does the same. Christ in the

Italian paintings becomes ever more insignificant, trite, even repulsive. Of these two great subjects, one had exhausted itself through too frequent representation; as far as the other is concerned, it may well be that it is hardly capable at all of worthy representation by a human hand, except in a few blessed moments, and even then, only intuitively. Art, however, as long as it is really alive, always wants to create something really *new,* and if the artists produce new, unprecedented things, they do not do so out of hubris, but out of inner necessity.

Hence, the renunciation of the idealized rendition of the divine persons was inevitable, until some true forces of nature, such as Guido Reni and Murillo, succeeded in recapturing their ideal significance by way of realistic depiction. Yet their achievement was still a far cry from the archaic mystery of a Fra Angelico.

What made up for the loss is perhaps the following:

The less the artists succeeded in rendering the *adorable* figures, the more did they succeed in depicting the *adoring* ones. The art of the Counter-Reformation has graced us with a number of representations of human piety and Christian love, which together constitute perhaps the most moving body of works in all art. Hence, counter-reformatory art is not the opposite of the older idealistic art, but its complement. Angelico was strongest in painting the *ecclesia triumphans,* Christ, his Mother, and the saints; Murillo, on the other hand, depicted the *ecclesia militans,* the martyrs, the *orantes,* the sufferers. It was no longer the time for the heavenly glory; now, earthly suffering, the whole earthly pilgrimage, had its day. However, it took as pious a mind to conceive a *St. Francis in Prayer,* such as Annibale Carracci and Zurbarán succeeded in creating, as it took to produce a Madonna by Giotto. I remember the most striking example: it is the so-called *Christ à la paille* by Rubens, in the Academy in Antwerp. The dead Christ, leaning on a stone bench, is supported by his kin. Here, the Madonna is hardly more than an ordinary, pale woman, as Rubens painted her, hence hardly divine; but the deep, infinite sorrow that is spread over her features lends her nonetheless the sanctity of a devotional image. The like occurs even much more frequently in the works of Van Dyck, but I quote here advisedly the ill-famed Rubens.

Ranke speaks very well apropos this century about its *"ecstatic"* art. No other epoch has represented religious *devotion* as profoundly and extensively. And in this respect, Murillo is again the master of masters. His *Immaculate Conception* and his *Saint John on Patmos* embody perhaps the greatest and purest expression of devotion ever produced by painting. Here, Fra Angelico would not prove sufficient, nor would even Raphael.

Let us grant every epoch its worth! None is devoid of the works of the divine spirit; only, one should not ask for grapes from a fig tree.

Our epoch, as counted since Winckelmann, represents as important an age of development as the era of the Medici, inasmuch as, as if by magic, the *historical* study of art gained influence on the artists. Several independent schools have already emerged out of an eclecticism that was at first tedious and confused, and a beautiful future is at hand.

The suddenly recognized greatness of Murillo will not fail to act as a ferment in the near future. His works are already studied eagerly; six painters are engaged at the same time in copying his *Immaculate Conception*. Let us hope that all the beauty and greatness of this heavenly genius may strike and inspire the youthful minds of struggling talents!

I should love to have one more word with Overbeck about the apostasy! I would tell him what I consider an apostasy, namely, not the honest and inspired efforts of the schools of Bologna and Antwerp, but his very own artistic peitism, in the name of which he dares to malign Raphael; he who is not ashamed to abstract, lazily and cowardly, from those artistic means that have been acquired honestly and safely established by the gigantic efforts of a Rubens, Van Dyck, Murillo, David; as if he could make do, without all that ballast of general artistic education, firm drawing, real and truthful coloring, and with nothing but mere "simplicity and godliness." An artist who nowadays imitates a Fra Angelico appears to me like someone who would endeavor to describe the French Revolution in the style of a medieval chronicle. Why, then, did our Lord invest our time with that universality that swells its every vein?

Translated by Gert Schiff

Notes

1. It might seem as if I confounded holiness of expression and idealism of representation, but in the period under discussion, they go hand in hand with astonishing punctuality.

1. Peter Paul Rubens: *The Battle of the Amazons* (c. 1615; Munich, Alte
Pinakothek).

2. Peter Paul Rubens: *The Defeat of Sennacherib* (c. 1614–1615; Munich, Alte Pinakothek).

3. Peter Paul Rubens: *The Rape of the Daughters of Leucippus* (1619–1620; Munich, Alte Pinakothek).

4. Peter Paul Rubens: *A Landscape with a Rainbow* (c. 1636; Munich, Alte Pinakothek).

5. Peter Paul Rubens: *Rubens and Isabella Brant* (1609–1610; Munich, Alte Pinakothek).

6. Strasbourg Minster.

7. Hagesander, Polydorus, Athenodorus: *Laocoon* (Marble, late hellenistic; Vatican Museum).

8. G. C. Hoff: *Dürer and Raphael Kneeling before the Throne of Art* (Etching after a lost drawing by Franz Pforr of 1810; Frankfurt, Städelsches Kunstinstitut).

9. Sebastiano del Piombo: *The Martyrdom of St. Agatha* (1520; Florence, Palazzo Pitti).

10. Albrecht Altdorfer: *The Victory of Alexander the Great over Darius* (1529; Munich, Alte Pinakothek).

11. Giotto: *Baroncelli Polyptych* (Before 1329? After 1332?; Florence, Sta. Croce).

12. School of B. E. Murillo: *The Immaculate Conception* (London, National Gallery, on loan to the Bradford Art Gallery).

13. The Arch of Aosta (25 B.C.).

14. The Arch of Titus in Rome (82 A.D.).

15. The Arch of Ancona (115 A.D.).

16. The Arch of Septimius Severus in Rome (203 A.D.).

17. Younger Son from
the *Laocoon* Group.

18. Michelangelo: *Dying Slave*
(Marble, c. 1513;
Paris, Louvre).

19. Mourning St. John
(Wood, c. 1470(?),
with many modern additions,
Frankfurt,
Liebighaus).

20. *The Three Graces*
(Classical Group in Marble,
Siena, Library
of the Cathedral).

21. *The Zodiacal Man*
(Miniature from the
*Très Riches Heures du
Duc de Berry*, c. 1410;
Chantilly, Musée Condé).

22. Raphael, *The Three
Graces* (1505–1506;
Chantilly, Musée Condé).

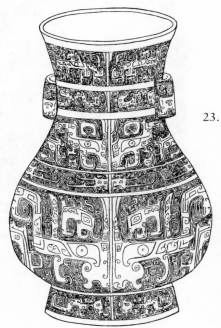

23. Sacrificial Vessel
(Chou Dynasty, 1045–256 B.C.),
after an illustration in
the *Si-ts'ing-ku-kien*, c. 1749).

24. Cup of Exekias (c. 525–500 B.C.; Munich, Glyptothek).

25. El Greco: *Entombment of Count Orgaz* (1586–1588; Toledo, Santo Tomé).

26. Michelangelo: *Christ on the Cross with Two Figures* (c. 1545–1557; Oxford, Ashmolean Museum).

27. Tintoretto: *The Ascension of Christ* (1577/8; Venice,
Scuola di S. Rocco).

28. Jacques Bellange: *The Three Maries at the Tomb* (Etching).

29. El Greco: *Christ at the Mount of Olives* (1605–1610; Budapest, Szépművés-zeti Muzeum).

Prima facies arietz ē mar
lis ⁊ ē facies audacie:forti-
tudinis:altitudinis:⁊ inue-
recundie.

Secunda facies est solis ⁊
est nobilitatz:altitudinis:
regni ⁊ magni dominij.

Tercia facies est veneris
est subtilitatis in ope:⁊ m
suetudinis:ludoꝛ:gaudi
⁊ limpidationum.

In primo gradu arietis
Ascedit vir dextera tenes falcē:
⁊ sinistra manu balistam.

Homo aliquādo laboꝛat:ali-
quando vero bella exercet.

Homo cum capite canino de
tera sua extensa:⁊ in sinistra b
culum habentem.

Homo litigiosus erit et in
dus vt canis.

Aries

1—2

30. *Aries Decans*, from *Astrolabium Magnum* (ed. Engel, Augsburg 1488).

31. Francesco del Cossa: *April Fresco* (1467–1470; Ferrara, Palazzo Schifanoja).

32. Francesco del Cossa: *March Fresco* (1467–1470; Ferrara, Palazzo Schifano-ja).

33. Francesco del Cossa: *First Decan of Aries*
(March Fresco).

34. Unknown Artist: *July Fresco* (1467–1470; Ferrara, Palazzo Schifanoja).

35. *Eros and Anteros*
(after Andrea Alciati,
Emblemata, Paris 1583).

36. Rembrandt: *Danae* (1636; Leningrad, Hermitage).

37. Titian: *Danae* (c. 1545; Naples, Museo Nazionale).

38. Annibale Carracci (or Francesco Albani?): *Danae* (c. 1605; Formerly London, Bridgewater House).

Inclusam Danaen risit Venus alma Iouemaq, Conuersum in pretium, gremiuq, implere puellę, Cunctaq, ęrulens penetrare sub orbiß Aurum Jero W. inu. et fi.
Gode van haele ex.

39. Hieronymus Wiericx: *Danae* (Engraving).

Heinrich Wölfflin

The Classical Triumphal Arches in Italy:
A Study of the Evolution of Roman Architecture
and Its Relation to the Renaissance

The architecture of the Renaissance offers the extraordinary spectacle that, whereas generations were enthralled by antiquity, applying
all their energies to the task of resurrecting it in the present, the
works conceived in this spirit are, to our critical eye, so little like the
originals that we may indeed doubt whether these people were really serious about their intention of reawakening "the good old architecture." And yet there is nothing more unwarranted than this
doubt. We may rest assured that the Florentine early Renaissance
seemed as Roman in its own eyes as did, say, the neoclassicism of
the eighteenth century. They may not, as in the neoclassical period,
have reconstructed classical temples and arches exactly according to
pattern, but if they refrained from direct reproduction they limited
their efforts to the exploitation of the other possibilities left open by
antiquity: a fundamental desire for deviation must be absolutely
discounted. The fifteenth century stood in relation to antiquity in
somewhat the same way as the fourteenth century stood in relation
to nature. At that time, everything was *one* voice: Giotto achieved
unheard-of advances in truth to nature, and things painted by him
were all but undistinguishable from their counterparts in reality; it
would be a long time before the talent for seeing became so developed that this illusion was dispelled. In very much the same way, the
Quattrocento could harbor the blessed delusion that no marked
difference existed between its buildings and those of ancient Rome.
The gulf immediately apparent to us simply did not exist in the

perception of the time. Here too the ability to differentiate was sharpened little by little, but it took a long time. At the risk of some exaggeration, one could say that the Renaissance—I emphasize the conventional meaning of the word—that the Renaissance only truly recognized antiquity at that moment when it stopped being a "renaissance" and the Baroque knocked at the door. Then, at the end of the epoch, a few arched structures were built which are indeed comparable to their classical forbears, whereas the earlier Renaissance attempts hardly bear comparison. Thus Vignola in 1562 repeated in the Porta del Popolo the design of the arch of Marcus Aurelius that stood on the Corso and was torn down exactly a hundred years later in 1662. Of course, the classical models did not suit the popular taste for very long: this was the period in which one could openly say that one had surpassed the ancients at their art, the period in which a desire for the massive and for powerful motion sought to satisfy itself.

I have in the following discussion attempted a historical examination of the classical arches. My work would not be worth the effort if all I sought to establish was what classical motifs were evident in the arches of the Renaissance. There is as yet another question that bears upon the relationship between the Renaissance and antiquity. We speak of an early and a High Renaissance and a late, painterly style (Baroque). Are these same terms likewise applicable to the evolution of classical art? Did the Renaissance repeat the path of classical artistic evolution? Did the same phenomenon appear twice in the history of art? In order to answer this question it is essential to gain a clear idea of the artistic evolution in antiquity. For this purpose I have decided to focus on the example of the triumphal arch.

The interpreters of Roman architecture for the most part contented themselves with a mere classification of the various structural types, without offering anything more than a few very general remarks concerning the evolution of style. And yet we cannot say that this reticence is the result of the lack or the poor condition of surviving monuments. So much is after all still standing everywhere that an in-depth study of the material would indeed provide the evidence upon which to base a history of style. As to the triumphal arches, we are here dealing with a class of monuments that virtually demands an examination of its evolution, insofar as the surviving buildings not only constitute an almost unbroken chain, but also are for the most part astonishingly well preserved.[1]

One's notions as to the origin of the triumphal arch are of no account in a study of the history of its stylistic evolution. Let us begin with the finished type that we find in the Augustan buildings. The given features of this type are threefold in nature: a lower mass of masonry with a system of supports and an entablature, which is pierced by the archway; then an attic, which generally bears the inscription; and finally, the crowning feature of the entire building, the actual triumphal statue with the quadriga or something similar. Here in a small space, a plenitude of motifs capable of development are crowded together. I am not speaking of the possibilities of doubling or tripling the archway, of adorning the building more or less with sculptural ornament, coffering the vaults and such; these are features that have but little to do with the stylistic evolution of the arch itself. It is essential to ascertain how the arch is connected with the columnated part of the building, how the support system and the opening of the arch are shaped, how the closed plane is related to the pierced one; which is the proportional relationship between the crowning features of the attic and the triumphal statue, and the actual structure of the archway itself. (As to the next to the last point, there is unfortunately nothing that can be said, since in no one instance is the triumphal statue still standing in its original place.)

We see here an almost typically pure instance of a process that repeats itself in all architectural development: In place of homogeneous forms, differentiated forms appear; instead of coordination, we find subordination; in place of loose agglomeration, a structure in which each part is integral to the whole.

According to these criteria, the Augustan period, which is often viewed as the golden age of architecture as well, appears merely as a preparatory period, as an early art, like that of the Italian Quattrocento, whereas the true classicality seems to set in only with the Flavians and can hardly be reckoned to have lasted an entire century. By the second half of the second century we already see the signs of a dulling of the sense of form, which in some aspects corresponds clearly enough to the Baroque style of the seventeenth century. The Septimius Severus Arch of A.D. 203 already shows the high art in a state of total disintegration.

It is not my intention to run through the twenty-five or thirty triumphal arches of conceivable consequence in Italy. The interest of clarity demands the greatest possible limitation of our selection; mere variants or even repetitions of the same form cannot be included in our discussion.

One additional point must be established. We require as a basis for our study a homogeneous substratum. There are from the very beginning various kinds of triumphal arches, various systems out of which we shall have to chose one. If we exclude exceptional forms, we are left with three distinct designs: 1) the arch with one archway and two columns; 2) the arch with one archway and four columns; and 3) the arch with three archways (with four columns). These different designs, as we have already said, appear side by side. The three-archway structure, in the manner of the arches of Septimius Severus and Constantine, is not in essence a form of the late period; if we discount the (early) arch of Orange as an extra-Italic example, we might well select the two Augustan arches beside the Temple of Julius Caesar in the Forum. On the other hand, whereas the simple design of an arch with only two columns (or pilasters) appears with marked frequency in the beginning (Spoleto, Susa, Rimini, Trieste, and others), there are other solutions to the problem that indicate that the system could also have been designed to suit the later taste. In any event the taste for such humble monuments seems soon to have grown scarce. What remains is the one-archway building with four columns. The monuments of this type more or less constitute the "normal" arch in that a compromise is established here between the system of simplicity and control and the system of pomp. For this reason alone, this type would seem to suggest itself as the essential starting point of our inquiry. But there are additional circumstances that simply leave us no choice but to begin here. For only here may we observe a longer development in all its conceivable intermediary stages. Moreover, all surviving buildings in the classical style were fashioned according to this type: the Arch of Titus in Rome, the arches of Beneventum, of Ancona, and the Arch of Marcus Aurelius in Rome, stylistically already very different from the others.

Where shall we look for a precedent of the Arch of Titus? Among the surviving monuments on Italian soil, there is only one that anticipates the system of the Arch of Titus: that is the Arch of

Aosta,[2] from the year 25 B.C., one of the very oldest Italian arches (Fig. 13). The attic is missing, but the building is otherwise moderately well preserved. The essential aspect above all, the order of the columns with the entablature, is very distinctly visible. Thus we have here a system of four columns, so disposed as to give rise to three fields: a wide middle field with the actual archway and two narrow lateral fields with closed masonry surfaces. The columns are three-quarter columns. They support an entablature the mass of which is not however equally distributed over the four columns, but rather juts out over the corner columns, then slips back into the wall surface only to reemerge again as a continuous connecting piece over the two middle columns.

Thus the archaic aspect of the Arch of Aosta consists not only in its individual forms and their connection, but—more striking at first glance—in the proportioning of the principal parts. The older buildings tend to favor a wide and relatively low archway (compare with Rimini,[3] 27 B.C., and Susa,[4] A.D. 8), and the closed lateral planes are kept so narrow that they cannot rightly compete with the main section. In addition, we have here a very curious treatment of the arch supports. They stand together with the entablature supports on a common high pedestal; the wall surface left between this pedestal, and the springer height of arch and vault are so negligible that only dwarfish forms still fit, and so we find here a series of dwarfed pilasters; not only the corners, but also the middle of the walls (in the archway) are beset with such miniature support forms.[5]

The archivolt, very wide according to archaic taste, presses trenchantly upon the overlying entablature. The keystone is missing and an unpleasant hardness is evident in that the entablature juts far out, whereas the archivolt is a mere planar shape.[6]

If the circular molds of the archivolt are partially overlapped by the big three-quarter columns, this then is a similar archaically hard motif. A more developed style permits each form to stand out and never permits the covering of springer points.

The spandrels beside the arch remained unadorned, whereas the Arch of Rimini inserts here heads in round medallions,[7] and in later buildings this space is commonly reserved for winged victories. The intercolumnar surfaces on the other hand are bedecked with a filler motif, at least on the side facing the city: nichelike small hollows attest to the fact that a kind of trophy adornment was displayed here. In other places, as for instance in Saint-Rémy, statues were also attached to the flat wall. The stylistically significant aspect here is that in all older instances the filling of these surfaces is applied vertically, whereas later a horizontal partitional form was preferred.

The attic, as we have already said, is missing. It is likely that it shared the articulation of the understructure (a wide middle field, narrow lateral fields); at least there are no instances that would contradict this supposition. In particularly rich monuments of the older style, on the other hand, the attic is dissolved into many individual pedestals (for statues). On a small scale, the Arch of the Sergii in Pola[8] is an example of this type;[9] on a larger scale, we have the pompous Arch of Orange. In the next arch treated here, we will speak of the motif of a projecting pediment, which can also be surmised to have existed in Aosta.

More than a hundred years separate the Arch of Aosta from the Arch of Titus (Fig. 14). It must seem eminently desirable to fill this long period with an intermediary link. Gräf's compilation does not provide this; such a link does however exist and is in fact to be found in the structure of the Arch of the Gavii in Verona, which is not Trajanic—as Gräf assumed—but belongs rather to the Augustan, or at least the Julian period. This is definitely confirmed by our stylistic analysis. If this arch was accorded less attention to date, this may have resulted from the fact that it can only still be studied in drawings and old publications, since it was demolished in 1805. Rossini illustrates an unpublished drawing by Palladio, which the latter had prepared for a publication of a collection of triumphal arches.[10] We can compare it with the woodcut in the third book of Serlio's *Architettura*.[11]

The Arch of the Gavii is already much more refined than the one in Aosta. Even if old drawings may not be relied upon as accurate evidence, particularly in regard to proportions, it can nonetheless be clearly surmised that the Arch of the Gavii had a more attenuate design and that its side parts were conceived in a more harmonious relation to the middle part, since they were accorded more importance. The slenderness of the arch thus permits a greater height of the arch supports, they are now full-fledged pilasters, not dwarfed forms anymore. They also share the same pedestal height with the supports of the entablature. Although there is no longer a common pedestal on which the two support systems rest, the columns have

instead each been accorded their own pedestals, and still the foot-
ings of both support systems lie on the same level. We might also
mention that the columns are fluted here, as they shall be henceforth. The entablature juts out in the same way as in Aosta.

When a drawing was made of the arch in the sixteenth century, an
attic was here, too, no longer present; nonetheless Serlio assures us
that the traces of the springer line of a pediment are clearly recognizable. The pediment in front of the attic can only be found in
early examples of triumphal arches in Italy. It can be found on the
Arch of Rimini,[12] it has been documented to have existed on the
Porta Tiburtina and on the Arch of Drusus in Rome, and we may
also point to its presence on the Arch of Orange in neighboring
southern Gaul. If these parts were not particularly prone to destruction, we would surely have more instances. Pediments are still to be
found in illustrations of Trajanic arches on coins. Yet I do not wish
to grant any documentary weight to this fact: we know that in the
architectural relief in the Lateran[13] even the Arch of Titus is given a
pediment! We may lend more credence to the presence of a pediment on the coin representing an Arch of Claudius (Fig. 1972 in
Baumeister, after Donaldson, architectura numismatica), or on the
Vinicius coin (Fig. 1975, ibid.) whose illustration we now hold to
be an Augustan arch to the side of the Temple of Julius Caesar in the
Forum.[14]

What is certain is that in all the later arches in which the attic has
been preserved, a pediment is no longer present — for the simple
reason that the space was needed for the inscription. That there are
instances in which both exist side by side, a pediment and above it
an attic with an inscription, as for instance in the Arch of Rimini, is
a case of a surfeit of features, which the later, grander art rejected.

The archivolt of the Arch of the Gavii presses as trenchantly upon
the entablature as in Aosta;[15] here too is missing a keystone or any
other kind of mediating key piece. A coin that depicts a Nero gate,
shows, as far as I know, the first keystone (Fig. 1973 in Baumeister,
after Donaldson). From this we may deduce an approximate *terminus
ante quem* for our arch. Later the keystone is never missing, except in
such very late examples as the Gallienus arches in Rome and Verona,
where old and new features are haphazardly crowded together.

The supports of the arch are joined to the archivolt by a foliated
capital. This creates a dissonance. The foliated capital with its verti-

cals was by its very nature designed to carry a horizontal load; here, without any mediating form, the verticals encounter the sideward-descending curving line of the archivolt. In the capital the middle is emphasized, whereas the archivolt with its three semicircles has no defined middle, and places the emphasis rather on its outer edge. There are two ways out of this dilemma: either to do completely without a foliated capital and to make do with a purely horizontal impost cornice, or to insert a piece of entablature between the archivolt and the capital. Both solutions were applied; the former became the common practice in later buildings. Wherever we find genuine capitals we can safely assume that the building belongs to an earlier period. Consider, in addition to the Arch of the Gavii, those of Susa, Spoleto, and Aosta.[16] Among these, only Aosta has the inserted piece of entablature or cornice. Perhaps we might also restore (as Rossini does) the Arch of Drusus in Rome to its original form in this manner.

The spandrels are still empty on the Arch of the Gavii, as in Aosta. On the other hand, the filler of the side surfaces between the columns offers new motifs: a rectangular niche with pilasters crowned by a gable, on top of which is an oblong tablet, and finally, not to be overlooked, a demarkation of the capital zone in that the springer lines of the capitals are connected. In the same way, at the bottom, the base profiles of the columns are extended over the surface of the wall. The niche, which to a certain extent repeats the middle and main motif, still belongs to the older mode of filling the interstices; it is no longer to be found on the Arch of Titus. The little tablet on top, on the other hand, appears again later; I remind the reader of the Trajanic Arch in Ancona.[17] The connection of the base profiles of the columns and the demarkation of the capital zone will become a lasting feature of the arch structure until a cruder taste, that takes pleasure in the dissolution of forms, bursts the despised fetters.[18]

It doesn't seem as though a great distance separates the Arch of the Gavii from the Arch of Titus (A.D. 82).[19] If we set front views of both these monuments side by side, we notice hardly any differences at first glance. And yet it is at this very point that the architectural style took some decisive steps. To begin with the most important aspect: the final differentiation between arch- and entablature supports has set in. We no longer find two analogous forms that compete with each other, rather, an attempt has been made by all possible means to distinguish between the two members. First of all, the foliated capital is reserved for the columns with a straight entablature, and the archivolt is set upon an impost cornice. This is a very simple device, and one that was already prepared elsewhere (Rimini). In addition, however, an energetic twofold division is effected. First, the bases of the two support systems are set at different heights: the arch supports now reach all the way down to the ground, whereas the wall columns start only at half their height; this is even more strikingly emphasized by the common pedestal placed under them.[20] Secondly, the orientation has been changed: the arch supports make a quarter turn, they turn their faces inward, toward the passageway. The resulting effect in the articulation of the forms is that only the inward-turned surface of the supports is decorated, whereas the other surface remains bare, and in frontal view, becomes one with the wall.

The columns—now semidetached, no longer three-quarter columns—have here moved so close to the gateway that they touch the very point at which the archivolt meets the impost cornice with its outermost ring. Up at the apex of the arch an intermediary space remains in between archivolt and entablature: the hard collision is avoided, the connection is effected by a henceforth never absent keystone.[21] In the spandrels, the hovering victories (later also reclining figures) establish themselves—the first Italic instance of this we find apparently in the Arch of Pola—and in this regard, we must assert once and for all that the filling of a given space with a figure is effected all the more massively the later the monument was erected; the style of the Arch of Titus is still partial to wide and unconfined space. The same holds for the filling of the coffers on the vaults: On the Arch of Titus, which is the very first building in Italy to display such a decoration, the flower is still surrounded by a lot of space; a crowded opulence is the mark of a later period.

The new treatment of the arch supports also has direct consequences for the archivolt: The barrel-vault does not run evenly throughout, but rather its fringes are turned into (inner) archivolts, which in their shape correspond precisely to the supports, and also differ similarly in the treatment of their surfaces from the outer archivolts.

We have just spoken of the cofferwork of the vault. Underneath the impost cornice, and framed laterally by the (decorated) arch supports, we now find space for reliefs. The wall can here be hollowed out without damage, since we are dealing with soft parts, not essential structural members. Brunn has coined the fitting expression "Romanized metopes" to describe these reliefs.[22]

In its outer surfaces, the Arch of Titus, as opposed to later monuments, still maintains a greater restraint. Though the spandrels above the arch and the frieze are sculpturally adorned, and even the undersurface of the projecting entablature is not left bare, the decoration on the wide intercolumnar fields is still reduced to the essentials. As a result, the concentrated wealth of decoration in the interior appears all the more striking. In half the height of the field, a tablet reaching from one column to the other overlays a lower, doorlike, and flat niche.[23] The original solution is, as we have mentioned, the filling of such a space in a vertical manner. Yet in recognition of the fact that in a place already replete with vertical lines a horizontal would be better suited, this bandlike stripe was inserted, without altogether displacing the older vertical shape. (The same, incidentally, had been done, according to the coin, on the above-mentioned Arch of Claudius.) Yet comparison with the older examples teaches us that the vertical shape is here already in a state of definite retrogression. It is remarkably reduced in size and had to suffer its degeneration into a mere planar shape. Later, the architects put up with the tablet alone.[24]

From the very beginning, by the way, the tablet's shape was continued in the stripe that ran sideways around the building, whereby in a new way the whole and the parts appear tied together.

The preservation of the attic gives us here for the first time an opportunity to judge the important role that this member was designed to play in the economy of the whole. At the same time, we ought not to envision earlier arches restored according to this model, since the attic clearly grew only gradually to this size and stature. We need only compare the attic of the Arch of Titus with the almost paltry attic on the Arch of Susa. The Arch of Titus itself constitutes only an intermediary stage; the growth process is not yet complete. The organization of this mighty mass is effected in accordance with the protruding entablature: The corners are drawn out and shaped in a pillarlike fashion; a projecting section of the wall with a framed inscription in mightly letters sits in the middle.

A powerful cornice crowns the whole structure. A pediment would no longer have any place in this context.

It is possible that the resulting simplification of the lines—except for the arch, there are only horizontals and verticals—is one of the causes for the altogether unique effect of the building in its completely closed and unified aspect. Such effects, however, are always only partially based on the lines; the real secret lies in the interrelation of the proportions as they reveal themselves, in the whole or in the individual parts, to the eye. Since it is impossible here to deal with these questions in any detail I would like to refer the reader to the interesting results that August Thiersch published in the *Handbuch der Architektur* (edited by Durm et al., vol. IV, 1).

The Arch of Titus affords us the opportunity to refer back to a group of monuments that I have so far mentioned only in passing, but which have been connected with the Italic arches: the monuments of southern Gaul. They have their own unique characteristics and cannot merely be placed within the Italic development. Nevertheless, it has been maintained that without them the forms of the Arch of Titus could not be explained.

The monument in southern Gaul that can be compared to the Arch of Titus is the Arch of Saint-Rémy. It is more closely related to the former than is the Arch of the Gavii in Verona. Here already a differentiation between the two support systems has been attempted, albeit in inconclusive form—the springer lines are different; however, the columns still have individual pedestals instead of a common one.[25] The treatment of the arch supports and of the vault is already the same except for the inward-turning of the corner posts. The cofferwork, however, is executed in the complex hexagonal form, whereas the otherwise more developed Arch of Titus makes do with square coffers. The design of the archivolts in the form of fruit garlands is a similar, freely painterly motif, surpassing anything in Italic sculpture. A keystone is still missing. The wall surfaces are filled according to the old system (with statues), without any horizontal division. The whole conception is still lacking unity. The wall columns have no contact with the arch opening, a fatal intermediary space remains, and the spandrels, where the victories soar, are wide open at the bottom.

The Arch of Saint-Rémy would surely have a decisive place in the evolutionary history of the triumphal arch, if it was indeed built in the year 52 B.C., as Gräf (with reference to Gilles) is inclined to presume. It would then not only be the oldest of all known buildings of this kind, but would also constitute such a mighty advance over Italy that one could hardly contest the notion that the architecture of the Italic arch must have evolved after the model of southern Gaul. For the present, however, we are not obliged to accept this supposition, since what Gilles presents in support of this dating in his *Précis des monuments triomphaux des Gaules,* is mere assumptions that cannot possibly be credited with any stringency. If one has to arrive at a date, I would suggest setting it a good half century forward, so that the Arch of Saint-Rémy would not remain too distantly removed from the Arch of Orange, which is after all very closely related to it. Its significance for Italy would then be markedly diminished. Ignoring for the moment the question of dating, if we were to ask ourselves whether the Arch at Saint-Rémy was essential to the Italic development, the answer would have to be "no." No architectonic motifs are offered here, whose germ is not also present in Italy. The actual uniqueness of the monuments in southern Gaul, that which lends them their innovative distinction, is their decorative forms; however, none of these very striking details was adopted in Italy. Without wishing to say the final word about the connection between the arches of southern Gaul and Italy, I must nonetheless say that no proof has as yet been presented for the thesis of the genesis of the triumphal arches in southern Gaul.

How much the solution of the archway problem as achieved in the Arch of Titus was valued, can be surmised from the fact that this same type, almost unchanged, was maintained for decades. In the Arch at Beneventum[26] (A.D. 114), which was constructed one generation later, we do not as yet find any deviations in the architectonic framework. The only noteworthy exception is the aversion of later generations to bare spaces. They felt compelled to enliven every empty space with some sort of decoration. Here, where means were available, they put up reliefs. The risk thereby, however, is that the feeling for the importance of the individual surfaces in a higher architectonic sense is soon lost. It is already questionable to find deep unframed reliefs cut out of the block of the attic beside the protruding inscription tablet. There, of all places, the eye demands a solid ground on which the protruding parts can rest. In the lower building, the reliefs are placed in the same way without any real frame between the rounded bodies of the semiengaged columns, which makes the columns appear almost wholly detached from the wall. In any case, the undercutting clearly paved the way for the actual detachment of the columns, which followed later.

The Arch of Ancona[27] (A.D. 115, Fig. 15), erected at almost the same time as the Arch at Beneventum, is a low-budget affair, a building of such small proportions that for that reason, too, it has a special place in the development. The outer schema is still the same as that of the Arch of Titus, whereas the narrowness of the intercolumnia on the other hand calls for a different filling: two tablets divide the vertical fields into three almost-square planes, the upper two of which one has to imagine adorned with bronze festoons (see Fig. 15). Here too we sense clearly the desire for a more incisive and lively effect of the forms. So as to cast stronger shadows, the aforementioned tablets have been fitted with far protruding roofing and richly profiled frames. The corner posts of the attic and the column plinths are similarly wrapped with framing profiles, and here again the columns project from the common pedestal, each fitted with its own additional socle: the flat surface seemed too monotonous.

The most important innovation in the Arch of Ancona, however, concerns the design of the archway. For the first time, there are no individually shaped supports on the corners. The barrel vault, devoid of coffering, sits on top of the impost cornice that runs all the way through, and the wall rises directly out of the floor, without any socle profile. Naturally the inner archivolts are also missing. We cannot establish for certain whether all this was due to the lesser depth of the arch, or to a singular insistence upon simplicity; what is certain is that henceforth even more lavish and deeper arch structures leave out arch supports (and the inner archivolts) for the sake of a more massive effect.[28]

This is the case, first, at the (demolished) Arch of Marcus Aurelius in Rome[29] (circa A.D. 165), which for this reason alone would not rightfully belong in the series of historically important monuments. Its legitimization lies above all in its detached columns. If Gräf presents the Arch of Timgad in Africa as an earlier instance, this must give us cause to doubt. Based on the evidence of an inscription found "nearby," the Arch of Timgad is taken to be a Trajanic building. Its forms attest, however, all in all, to a later period. Precisely the motif of the freestanding columns occurs here in a more developed form than on the Arch of Marcus Aurelius, with corresponding pilasters at the back of the columns, the like of which are still missing in the Roman example.

The introduction of detached columns engendered the need to separate the outer columns from the corners, whereas until then the incorporated supports had enclosed the massive lower structure just by its corners.

Put in that place, the detached column would appear weak and fragile; it demands a back wall that extends all the way through. This arrangement became, of course, also valid for the corner posts of the attic, and soon architects far and wide would seize upon this motif because they liked the massive effect achieved in this way. Durm[30] is mistaken when he restores the Arch of Titus in such a way that its corners remain bare. He let himself be led astray by older illustrations, possibly by the plate in Bellori's collection of triumphal arches. Following the taste of his time, Bellori had to accept this resolution of the corner problem as most suitable. The encasement of the wall through engaged columns is, however, everywhere a characteristic of the stern and high style.

The craving for variety also led to the introduction of an important new form in the entablature. I don't mean the bulging formation of the frieze, but rather the new way in which the entablature is wrapped around the protruding parts. It is the direct inversion of the kind that was common until then. Rather than jut out over the actual archway and recede above the lateral fields, it now returns back to the wall in the middle, and juts out over the sides, thereby joining the paired columns beneath it. I do not wish to suggest the Arch of Pola as a precursor of this formation, since there the entablature projects merely over the coupled columns at the corners. At the Arch of Marcus Aurelius, the architect permits himself an altogether different liberty, and the later architects also gladly made use of this new-found freedom.

Where nothing could be gained by a reversal of the forms, a multiplication was attempted. Here the treatment of the socle is particularly instructive. The innovation arrived at in the Arch of Ancona (the protrusion of the socles of the columns from their common pedestal) is adopted here; in addition, however, another pedestal is added on, without any apparent objection to the reduplication, the repetition of like elements.

Finally, a new spirit is also noticeable in the manner in which the interstices between the columns are filled. These spaces are now decorated so that a decisive accent falls upward: A single relief tablet is placed, not in the center, but sharply shifted upward. The capital zones seem not to have been spared in the process.[31]

The Arch of Septimius Severus[32] (A.D. 203, Fig. 16) is separated from the Arch of Marcus Aurelius by a span of some forty years. As a three-gate structure, the former falls outside our examination. We do not, however, have any surviving monument of the one-gate, four-column system in Italy that would exemplify the important shift of the architecture toward painterliness, which occurred in the third century.[33] I do not wish to suggest that this system was abandoned; the fact cannot, however, be denied that it was no longer suited to the highest purposes. If Titus had triumphed at this time, he would probably have been honored with a three-gated arch.

The three gates of the Arch of Septimius Severus (large middle gate, smaller side gates) are enclosed by four mighty detached columns, over each of which the entablature juts out. Without any regard for this arrangement, an attic is placed on top as an enormous, undivided block, on which the lines of the inscription run uninterrupted from end to end. It is an unheard-of brutalization of that taste, which had trained itself on the works of the preceding century![34]

The columns are of the developed kind already referred to before — they are accompanied by corresponding pilasters on the rear wall, the like of which were not yet present in the Arch of Marcus Aurelius.[35]

Their plinths stand on very high pedestals, beneath which yet another three-tiered base is set, a characteristic multiplication of forms. Meanwhile, the pedestals have already received figurative reliefs!

What, however, makes the arch appear rich is not the protruding columns with their rear pilasters, nor the ubiquitous reliefs, but rather the actual arches of which there are five in all, in three different sizes. Not satisfied with the three straight archways, the architects also cut transverse gateways inside, through the middle pillars, as a completely senseless innovation, which can only be explained as the result of a desire to include arches of a third order. One counts on the painterly effect of the semilateral view in which the diversely oriented arches and vaults do indeed make for an attractive picture. The viewer is treated to a further striking effect in the contrast that arises from the meeting of the various forms of different scales—the columns on the outside are so large that the side gates (of the second order) with their impost cornices do not reach very far above their pedestals, and the arches of the third order remain below them. So as to make the effect all the more vivid, the impost cornice of these smallest (albeit still rather large) lateral arches is likewise carried over onto the wall of the facade where it cuts at a completely arbitrary point into the flank of the pedestal of the column, a crudeness the like of which one does not find even on the Arch of Constantine with its partially barbaric detail.

Dissonance seems to have been made a principle. Focusing on the narrow strip of relief that extends over the side gates, we see that it is a vestige of that form already present in the lateral fields of the Arch of Titus; we expect to find this band extended all the way around the outer facades; this has purposely been avoided, and the viewer is not spared the dissonant clash of the two (originally related) forms.

The capital zones are completely negated. A square (chaotic) relief reaches all the way up to the edge of the entablature. And as to bring the monstrous nature of this transgression to full consciousness, the base lines of the capitals are extended to one side (toward the corners of the buildings).

One thing, however, must be borne in mind here. We must not judge these dissonances according to the impression that they produce in geometric elevation on paper. In reality, they are overpowered by the great masses of light and shadow, which determine the entire structure of this building. Those instances of formlessness only engender a little motion and restlessness as long as the eye attempts to find its way through the profusion of details; however, the emphasis here is not at all on the forms, but on the masses.[36] And the value of this wild arch lies in its distribution of mass. What has been achieved here is an overall conception, and the impression of the whole will forever be powerful and striking, despite the objectionable nature of individual features. The Arch of Orange offers the best comparison. It is a building which with all its richness of detail and all its superb workmanship does not engender a similar effect. The indeterminate stature of its three arches—there is no coordination and no real subordination—is already enough of a reason to prevent a resounding effect.

And something else. Whereas the Arch of Septimius Severus relies so much upon the overall effect, we must assume that the lack of the crowning sculptural elements effected here a more sensible mutilation than elsewhere. It seems likely that the statues on top were correlated to the columns and that the most injurious dissonance was thereby resolved.

We have come to the end. The Italic triumphal arch has run its course. We can at any rate speak of the end of a unified development. It is striking to what extent the arches of Gallienus, erected sixty years later, already deviate from the tradition. Outside influences clearly gained the upper hand. The result is a composite style, for which one can show only a limited interest. Old motifs, long since discarded in Italy, are once again employed and blended with all sorts of senseless combinations of forms, lacking even the one justification possible in such a case: the compelling painterly effect of the whole. Henceforth grandeur was sought in a multiplication of smallness, and we must deem it almost a miracle that Constantine still found the man who could build him an arch—in the old style—which, although not the "crown" of Italic triumphal arches, did nonetheless round out the tradition with dignity.

The triumphal arches naturally constitute only a small part of Roman architectural achievements; we may, however, conclude from the part at the whole: The periods that we have delimited here will also apply to the overall development of Roman architecture. And if it was already worthwhile to come up with even more definite divisions in this area that is still so lacking in order, then the reward of our efforts shall be twofold if, as a counterproof, a parallel development can be discovered in more modern times. But why wait for the proof? Anyone with an even superficial knowledge of the Renaissance must have been reminded at any turn of our argument of parallel developments. Can one analyze the Arch of Aosta without being reminded of Brunelleschi? The ancient motifs that we have presented here—can they not all be found again in the earliest buildings of the Renaissance? The archivolt, for instance, which is not fully visible, but overlapped at its ends by pilasters, can be found again in the Capella Pazzi and in many other places. The Quattrocento likewise offers pendants for the dwarf pilasters. The unequal construction of the archivolt bands (the outer one being particularly decorated) is here and there a symptom of the early period. The difficulties experienced in setting an archivolt upon a foliated capital were as common to the fifteenth century as to the first; The artists wavered and finally arrived at exactly the same solution. Things were no different with the treatment of the arch supports. The problem of bringing a wide middle field into a harmonious proportion with narrower lateral fields was only solved in modern times by Bramante (the "rhythmic travée" in the Cancelleria*); in antiquity, it was the classical style of the Arch of Titus that first provided a perfect solution. The filling of coffers and other framed surfaces underwent the same process: In the beginning the planes seem rather too empty; later they are bursting at the borders. A related development can be noted in the increase of the mass that needs to be supported (the growth of the attic). And finally, as to other signs of the ripe or overripe taste: the reduplication of the forms, their exaggeration, the transformation of the semiengaged column into the detached one, the uncovering of the corners of the building for the sake of a massive effect, and so on—these are all features whose appearance in the architecture of the sixteenth and seventeenth centuries likewise requires no substantiation. Let us only still note that the Arch of Septimius Severus corresponds in its profile formation to the style of Michelangelo—the base profiles are repeated in the Palace of the Conservators—whereas the Arch of Titus accords altogether with the Cancelleria.

A playful early period; a period of classicality in which the loosely aligned elements are more tightly interlocked, the diverse becomes simplified and developed into a great and immutable order; finally, a period of dissolution in which forms lose their definition and become distorted until an open dissonance results, in which the forms lose all sense and significance and only continue to exist as elements in a calculus according to masses—I maintain that a rise

---

*In the facade of the Cancelleria, the pilasters divide the wall in such a way that there is always one big interval flanked by two small ones. The width of the lateral intervals in relation to the central one is determined by the Golden Section. This motif was called, by the architectural historian H. A. Geymüller, the "rhythmic travée of Bramante." Bramante's authorship of the Cancelleria has been variously contested. The facade is, according to Bruschi (1977) "possibly associated with Bramante."—Ed.

and fall in just about this same sense can be traced in every style in the history of art. What makes the parallelism between Roman antiquity and the Italian Renaissance so instructive and interesting is that here, in both cases, we find the same apparatus of forms. I shall refrain here from a systematic exposition; perhaps someone at some point in the future will follow through on the comparison on an all-encompassing basis. We might then also arrive at a complete answer to the question, to what extent the Renaissance *recognized*, in its various phases of development, stylistic affinities in the multitude of classical buildings of earlier and later origin.

It is very interesting to note how assuredly the architects in general were able to select what in each case happened to suit their purposes; and it is even more interesting to see just how they attempted to come to terms with these strange fragments in such instances in which they made wrong choices.

Translated by Peter Wortsman

Notes

1. The subject was last treated in Paul Gräf, "Triumph-und Ehrenbogen" (in August Baumeister, *Denkmäler des klassischen Altertums*, Munich and Leipzig, R. Oldenbourg, 1889, 3 vols. pp. 1865–1900). The older literature is also cited there. The major reference work for Italic arches is Luigi Rossini's folio publication, *Gli archi trionfali onorarii e funebri degli antichi Romani sparsi per tutta Italia*, Rome, The Author, 1836.

2. Illustration in Rossini, op. cit., tav. 4–6. A view likewise appears in Baumeister, op. cit., Illus. 1967.

3. Rossini, tav. 12, 13; Baumeister, Illus. 1981.

4. Rossini, tav. 2–3; Baumeister, pl. LXXXI, 4.

5. We may well recall here the similar small supports in older Italic buildings, as for instance, in the two gates of Perugia. Later they disappear completely.

6. Of the old monuments, only the Arch of Rimini gives evidence of the attempt to show a keystone formation. By the same token, the archivolt does not there press upon the entablature. But the bull's head, which is set in place of the keystone, sits *above* the archivolt, half encased in the architrave.

7. On the still older gates of Perugia, there are heads without any medallion setting.

8. Rossini, tav. 7, 8; Baumeister, Illus. 308.

9. It is a mistake to date this building back in the Trajanic period, as Gräf does. The inscription confirms unquestionably that it was erected in the Augustan epoch.

10. Rossini, tav. 19.

11. Sebastiano Serlio, *Trattato di Architettura*, Edition in 4°, Venice, 1566, fol. 112.

12. Here a particularly curious instance, in that the pediment with its sides does not touch the columns, around which the entablature is wrapped, but reaches only as far as the entablature.

13. *Annali dell'Istituto di Corrispondenza Archeologica* (precursor of the inst. mentioned in note 14), Rome, XXI (1850).

14. Cp. O. Richter, *Die Augustusbauten auf dem Forum Romanum*, in *Jahrbuch des kaiserlich deutschen archäologischen Instituts*, 1889.

15. If one should want to add yet more reasons for the earlier dating of this arch, then we would also have to go into the unique formation of the archivolt: the third, outermost ring has received a particular trimming with fluting. In later arches, the three rings are always treated equally.

16. It is only in the composite style of the Arch of Gallienus that a similar phenomenon occurs again in Italy.

17. In this context it is instructive to take note of the diverse forms of framing in the earlier and the later monuments. The simple profile of the frame at the Arch of the Gavii can hardly still be compared with that of the Arch of Trajan, which aims at a strong interplay of shadows. We might sooner find its analogue in the little tablet of the Bibulus sepulchre in Rome, which as we know, dates back to the Republican period.

18. The Arch of Pola also shows the latter motif, though here the merit is lesser since we are dealing with coupled columns that hence are placed very close to one another.

19. Rossini, tav. 31–37; Baumeister, Illus. 1966 and 1969.

20. Cp. the Arch of Susa, in which a similar differentiation has been attempted with a two-columned structure (A.D. 8).

21. It is not until the buildings of Gallienus, which do not acknowledge any rules, that the past is once again rediscovered in this respect, and we find arches without consoles.

22. The Arch of Titus is, by the way, not the first instance of this. (See the Arch of Claudius.)

23. It does indeed on one side serve the function of a door.

24. In instances in which a series of intercolumnia are present, the tabernacle with its pediment naturally maintains its rightful place. The horizontal then comes vividly enough to the fore in the outline of the entire building. A. L. J. comte de Laborde, *Les Monuments de la France, classés chronologiquement . . .* 2 vols. Fol. Paris, 1816–1836.

25. The drawing in Laborde, *Voyage pittoresque en France*, which Gräf reproduces (Baumeister, Illus. 1987), is faulty in one detail: the cornice line that joins the upper edges of the column socles among themselves ought not to be extended all the way to the gateway. Cp. the better rendering in Auguste Nicolas Caristie, *Monuments d'Orange; Arc de Triomphe et théatre*, Paris, Firmin Didot frères, fils et cie., 1856.

26. Rossini, tav. 38–43; Baumeister, pl. LXXXI, 9.

27. Rossini, tav. 44–46; Baumeister, Illus. 1982.

28. The similar arrangement on the otherwise early Arch of Fano (A.D. 9) may indeed derive from a later restoration. The very form of the architrave and the presence of a keystone would already be strange at that time.

29. Rossini, tav. 47–49.

30. Josef Wilhelm Durm, *Die Baukunst der Etrusker. Die Baukunst der Römer*, in *Handbuch der Architektur* II, Darmstadt 1885.

31. Rossini's drawing is unreliable in this respect. It contradicts the photographs he himself published of the Chigiana in Rome, which were taken at the time the arch was demolished. Even in other respects his reproduction is untenable. The columns were in any case fluted. The attica has to be assumed higher up.

32. Rossini, tav. 50–59; Baumeister, Illus. 1985.

33. The Arch of the Argentarii at the Foro boario, erected in 204, is not only an exception because of its smallness; what makes it completely useless for our purposes is the absence of a real arch. It is a gate with a *straight* (entablature) top, without an attica. Here too, of course, some aspects are instructive: above all, the treatment of the entablature with its two tablets stacked one on top of the other, which completely cover up the frieze and the architrave. Compare it to the modest little tablet set in the frieze (*only* in the frieze) of the Arch of Pola.

34. The attica with the inscription running throughout its length was in any case overlapped by statues on the entablature, where this latter is wrapped around the columns. This seems to be a liberty, founded on the painterly style.

35. A still more detailed study would here have to show how these pilasters in turn affected the formation of the springer endings. Since the (markedly protruding) springer cornice can no longer press upon a wall column, but rather meets a flat form, the pilaster, a mediating solution had to be found. The Arch of Constantine circumvents this problem; in the Arch of Septimius Severus, on the other hand, a solution has been attempted. One should notice how, in this context, the exact attachment of the archivolt to the pilaster becomes impossible, and how then immediately this wider formation is adopted even in places where a need for it did not exist.

36. All forms are now treated more and more summarily; the architrave, for instance, still has two members instead of three. In a similar manner, large, all-encompassing, flowing lines are sought for the profile. Compare the socle profiling here with the corresponding forms on the Arch of Titus.

Theodor Hetzer

The Creative Union of Classical and Northern Elements in the High Renaissance

The art of the Renaissance emerged as an Italian response to the Gothic, a period in which the northern medieval spirit attained perfection and dominance over western Christendom. The Italian masters of the fifteenth century were conscious all the while that, in reaching back to classical antiquity, they were tapping the wellspring of their own great past; the early sixteenth century, the period of the High Renaissance, established a new ideal of beauty in opposition to "Gothic barbarism," an ideal which, largely determined by its relation to antiquity, wielded such power that it continued to prevail for centuries over all European art. It was not until the great upheavals of the late eighteenth century that its authority was called into question; there followed a rediscovery of the northern Middle Ages and a reawakened sense of their particular value and unique beauty. But the original opposition continued to dominate the views of the nineteenth century and found its expression in the doctrine of the styles. The Gothic style and the style of the Renaissance were sharply distinguished from each other; they were studied by scholars and artists as one studies the grammar of two distinct languages that have nothing to do with each other.

This alleged antithesis between the Gothic North and the classical Renaissance is in its exclusiveness an abstraction discounted by historical fact, a figment that arrogantly asserted itself while life continued on its quiet, conciliatory, and twisting and turning path. The fact is that Gothic forms survived throughout the fifteenth century, especially in northern Italy, and were often combined in a most attractive way with the new classicizing motifs. Let me remind you of the hospital in Milan, of the Doge's palace and numerous patrician palaces in Venice, and of the multipaneled altarpiece, the so-called Ancona. But even in Florence, where the new movement took so decisively its beginning, recent research offers convincing evidence that Gothicizing undercurrents survived. This is of course not overly surprising, for new trends take a while to catch on. But how do matters stand by the early sixteenth century, at the beginning of the High Renaissance? The Gothic world of forms may well have been shaken off, but not so the northern spirit itself, of which the Gothic was but one, time-bound manifestation. What happened rather was again a lively and important confrontation with the art from north of the Alps, a facing-off that kept repeating itself again and again during the entire period that lasted until the end of the eighteenth century. The Italians had already admired Old Netherlandish painting; they even copied it in its noble technique and in its careful depiction of its multifarious microcosm. Later on, ties were never broken off between Italy and the Netherlandish Mannerists, as well as with the later Flemish and the Dutch. We have yet to study in depth the influence in Italy of Rubens and Rembrandt, of Dutch genre painting and landscape. At the beginning of the sixteenth century, however, in the most agitated and eventful, the most important years of the new European artistic era, it was not the Dutch with their extraordinary painterly culture who heralded the northern influence in Italy, but rather the Germans. The turbulent and rousing, heaven- and earth-encompassing imagination of the last strains of the late Gothic, and the young Dürer; the bold spatial concepts of Altdorfer; the controlled and wonderfully rich inventiveness of the mature Dürer—this all had a remarkable presence and made a deep impression on the Italians. The young Michelangelo is supposed to have painted a copy of an engraving by Schongauer, Raphael is said to have hung woodcuts and engravings by Dürer in his studio, and Veronese is supposed to have sketched copies of these very same works. The connections between the great Italian and the German art of the early sixteenth century are manifold and by no means inconsequential. We may assume that in the studios of the Mannerist and Baroque masters, German graphic works hung side by side with casts of classical sculptures and drawing and etchings after the founders of the High Renaissance. Zanetti, the biographer of Tiepolo, the last great Venetian master, relates how this latter liked to study the works of Dürer.

We are thus faced with the fact that, although, since the fifteenth century, the classical ideal had replaced the Gothic in Italy, yet it did not hinder the continued influx of the northern spirit; and we are faced with the question of how and in what way antiquity and the North met in the Italian Renaissance. The answer that I propose is the leading idea of this lecture: Whereas the Early Renaissance had not yet obtained an overview nor a true understanding of the situation that resulted from this confrontation of cultures, such a clarification was achieved in the High Renaissance, and moreover, in such a way that the two formerly opposed positions of antiquity and the North fused into one. But this fusion, which would become so essential to the further development of European art, and which alone made possible the lively development of northern art in the spirit of classical ideals and classical forms (think of Rubens and Rembrandt, of the splendors of the German Baroque), this fusion did not come about as a conscious process, nor as a compromise, nor as an arithmetic model; it happened rather as a creative act in the deepest recesses of the artistic conception. In the unified vision of Michelangelo and Raphael, Titian and Dürer, classical and northern imagination were, in each case, inseparably fused. The works of these great masters—not their opinions, thinking, and theorizing—inaugurated the new era and pointed the way to its future. The High Renaissance is not, in its very special scope and sense, merely the result, but, indeed, the expression of that creative impulse. Rembrandt and Rubens are no doubt comparable in their genius to the masters of the early sixteenth century, but with their mighty personalities, they stand within the unfolding of a grandiose development, as Tiepolo and Watteau stand at its end; and in the case of these artists we will always be inclined also to draw attention to the imperviousness of their personalities. The great masters of the Renaissance, on the other hand, allowed their particularities to harmonize in a wondrous way; this enabled them to derive an objective, universally valid vision—a vision upon which a whole system of representation could be based—from their own creative strength, from their own idiosyncratic conduct. In this way, as we shall see, a fundamentally northern element was mixed in with the Italian.

II

The meeting of the freshly and passionately experienced antiquity with the manifold forces of the North, the resultant and pathetically proclaimed awareness of the opposition between the two, the fruitful union that finally was effected through the grace and wisdom of the creative spirit — all this was preceded by many centuries, during which the surviving late antiquity came into contact with northern art, which was gradually ascending, and more and more evolving its own unique character. As in the political, so in the artistic realm: Italy slipped into that sphere of influence whose center lay on the other side of the Alps. Italy participated in all the events of the early and late Middle Ages; yet until the fourteenth century, she received more than she gave. In these early times, whose great beauty exudes something very quiet, devout, and even dreamlike and remote (how very different is the light enchantment of the Cathedral of Pisa from the forcefully animated rhythms of the northern Romanesque!) Italian art came into being. But there is something imperceptible about this process of individuation; it is self-sufficient and does not reach out beyond itself. The Florentine Duomo, though indeed a true emblem of Florence, is by no means as encompassing and universal as Speyer or the Cathedral of Amiens. St. Peter's is the first cathedral that can be considered both Italian and universal, the temple of Christendom and prototype of baroque European architecture.

The classical tradition naturally played a major role in the evolution of the Italian identity. For the Italians carried the heritage in their blood; it spoke to them in its monumental presence. How often do we find real classical columns and capitals in early Italian churches! The classical ideal of physical beauty, balance, and static tranquillity had an everlasting influence, and no less so, the classical sense of measure. What we do not find here is the impassioned outbursts of the Germanic world, the clash of the creative imagination with the self-consistency of pregnant, dark matter, the struggle for form and the superhuman quality of its expression. Thus what was created in Italy in the Middle Ages will, to the Italians, always appear less barbaric. By the same token, it was also less new, less grand, and less capable of inciting progress.

And so, in my view, the rediscovery of classical antiquity as a national patrimony would never have occurred in Italy had not the powerful Gothic influence disrupted that early medieval adherence to the classical tradition. In the Gothic, the northern spirit (now evolved into a highly developed system) came head to head with antiquity. The result was that the Italians became conscious of the difference, and henceforth, for their part, no longer perceived antiquity as a somehow enduring, dark, and magical element, but rather, as a dispossessed and threatened heritage that, as an integral and absolute entity, ought to be pitted against the Gothic. Of course, Brunelleschi's early Renaissance buildings were influenced by the medieval-classical quality of the Baptistery and San Miniato, but not in such a way that the fifteenth century master merely adopted the tradition here so notably enlivened and so artfully mastered. He rather reverted back to these buildings as though they belonged to the Golden Age of Rome — so markedly had the Gothic current already disrupted the continuity.

The position of the Gothic was therefore necessary in order to give rise to the contrary position of the Renaissance. Tuscany, a region that had come to terms with the Gothic in the most inward way, became also the matrix of the Renaissance. But Rome stood apart until the sixteenth century and affected the development more through its majestic eternal presence than through its activity. Upper Italy, meanwhile, in contrast to Florence, seemed rather nonchalant. However, this was a nonchalance based on the liveliness of a serenely tranquil, sensuously powerful existence, devoted to the pleasures of the here and now. But the Gothic was not merely important to Italian art because of the fruitful opposition, which it encouraged. Precisely during the time of its spread, and we may say *because* of its spread in the late thirteenth and fourteenth centuries, Italian art reached its first clarification, the first and in many respects most important solidification of its *structure*. Only in this way could it happen that shortly thereafter the classical world was incorporated in Italian art as a truly formative and intellectually mastered element.

It was Giovanni Pisano and Giotto who at the turn of the thirteenth to the fourteenth centuries contributed the most to the evolution and structural solidification of Italian art. We know that the eldest of the Pisani, Niccolo, held very closely to the influence of classical prototypes in his pulpit reliefs. Giovanni Pisano turned just as markedly in his statues and reliefs toward the Gothic. Niccolo was hitherto considered the founder of modern Italian sculpture, precisely because of his dependence on classical antiquity. Yet his classicizing has still much more the character of the medieval Italian—heavy, with dreamily constrained adherence to the tradition—than that of a determined and conscious new departure. Missing here is the very hallmark of the Renaissance, the mastery of the naked human body through the medium of classical art. We may in fact go so far as to assert that French sculpture, which did after all also come into contact with classical works, has done more to pave the way for the future perception of antiquity, than did Niccolo Pisano. In addition, it cannot be overlooked that Giovanni Pisano did just not carry on the classicizing of his father. In place of that classical heaviness and imposing tranquillity, we find in his work a very personal and at times wildly passionate response to the all-pervading Gothic motion; he stands closer in this respect to the German Gothic, that is, to the reliefs of the Naumburg rood screen, than to the always restrained and lucid works of the French Gothic. In this redirection, however, in this comprehension of the unifying Gothic motion and its reinterpretation in the *personal expression* of an *inspired individual*, Giovanni became the founder of modern Italian sculpture; from him, not from his father, the path leads via Donatello to Michelangelo and all the way on to Bernini. We observe a similar, and from a cultural-historical standpoint, an even more important phenomenon if we compare the exploit of Giotto with the conduct of his Roman contemporary, Cavallini. In his frescoes and mosaics (Rome, Santa Cecilia and Santa Maria in Trastevere) Cavallini never rises above an accomplished, albeit merely general concept of Roman dignity and majesty; he too stands thus within the context of the Roman tradition. Just as Giovanni Pisano learned from his father, so did Giotto learn from Cavallini; and as the former did for Italian sculpture, so the latter paved the way for the future of Italian painting. In Giotto's case, it is also the Gothic motion, the inner tension of its linear abstraction, transformed into something personal and reshaped by the monumentality of his personality, that made possible this epoch-making achievement. It was Giotto's greatest exploit to have bequeathed the *image* to Italian, and in a broader sense, to European painting: the image as a coherent—and in its coherence clearly organized, and richly referential—linear and colored unity. It is thanks to Giotto that unity and beauty of the image (prefigured already in the Italian Middle Ages) took on a solid form, a form which, through the interaction of linear structuring of the picture plane, energy-irradiating figures, corporeal weight, and space, became capable of a rich development.

III

The medieval development of Italian art, as compared to that of the North, has known only little motion. It has happened that scholars disagreed as to whether the Cathedral of Pisa belonged to the eleventh, or to the thirteenth century, an uncertainty that would have been unthinkable in the case of French and German buildings. However, the close of the thirteenth century saw an increase in activity in all the Italian arts. This activity lasted until the end of the eighteenth century and gave rise to those constant and, in spite of the basic unity, so lively changes, that we are used to sum up in fixed stylistic terms. At the beginning of the fifteenth century Italy turned away from the Gothic. There ensued that memorable and new recognition of classical art, which by now meant something entirely different from the mere placid spinning away on the thread of tradition, something different also from the occasional shock caused by the sight of an isolated antique fragment. Antiquity was perceived like a distant, transfigured image, a totality that appeared, radiant and flawless, beyond the gulf of the damnable Middle Ages. But such a perception would never have come about had not the European spirit once again succeeded in creating an artistic totality in the system of the Gothic, and had this totality not become incarnate, precisely in Italy, in the new pictorial unity created by Giotto. It is, however, also noteworthy that this new perception of antiquity as an image, which was simultaneously distant, and directly related to the present, emerged at the same moment when the continuity of space, and the relation of "far" to "near," were perceived in the appearance of nature. Moreover, I think it is significant that the very artist in whose mind antiquity flared hottest and became most palpably transfigured, that Andrea Mantegna had also the greatest mastery of the imaginative interplay of near and far.

This image then that the fifteenth century developed of classical antiquity was combined in the most diversified manner with all the dictates of the day, with an art that started to include all earthly matters within its sphere, even if it did not yet, as has falsely been asserted, cast off the religious context. The perception of the classical world in the fifteenth century went hand in hand with the perception of the individual, of the unique qualities of the Italian character, of the city-states, of the Italian landscape. It also went hand in hand with the beginning of the consciously mathematical, technical, scientific ordering of the world. Thus the affinity for the classical world takes on the character of discovery, topicality, freshness, and open-mindedness. The classical forms of the medieval Florentine Baptistery have something enchanted about them, they are like an intuition of ineffable secrets; the form is inseparably bound up with the massiveness. The architects fitted classical fragments into their buildings, thus incorporating the real existence of antiquity in their art. To the Renaissance, on the contrary, the art of antiquity represented beauty, transfiguration, but no longer magic and mysterious substance. Classical art—and this is now of fundamental significance—functioned as a standard of beauty and order, as a purely spiritual element that entered the sovereign spirit of the creative artist. After San Lorenzo or Santo Spirito, classical columns and capitals themselves seemed no longer fitting; only their form, their image, could easily and without resistance be assimilated into Brunelleschi's overall concept. This liberation from the real presence of surviving antiquity would likewise have been impossible without the de-substantiating (*substanzüberwindenden*) and ordering energies of the Gothic.

It was a particularity of the fifteenth century that it rather set things side by side than let them interlock. So antiquity still stands beside the Gothic, as beside the immediately realistic elements; and the universal and ideal continue to exist side by side with the individual, and with period costume. So the classical models, though considered exemplary and comprehended as *form,* were still not yet moved into the center of the creative process. Quite often it is merely the decorative and antiquarian elements, or masquerade—and pageantlike features—that prevail. Fifteenth-century Italians were very interested, very enthusiastic, very open to classical antiquity, but not fundamentally moved by it. Or else things had not yet gotten to the point at which antiquity and life were considered synonymous. Even if the great Donatello (the master of both the characteristically ugly and the most sensitive, passionate beauty) lets us understand to what extent his sense of beauty is moved by a classical profile, a classical pose, by the body of a classical youth, we nonetheless feel rather affected by a wondrous fragrance, than persuaded that the classical spirit had had its share in shaping the natural and ethical foundation of this demonic existence. It is precisely this that constitutes the essential difference between Donatello and Michelangelo. It is likewise instructive to consider the small sculpture of the Quattrocento, as, for instance, the bronzes of Riccio. They display a simultaneity of classicizing and naturalistic forms; on the whole, however, they epitomize the crisp agitation characteristic of the century, which as an expression of the spiritual makes use of the body, though it does not manifest itself through the body.

IV

I shall now turn my attention to a consideration of the sixteenth century, to that creative union of antiquity and the North which, as I believe, was realized in the work of the great masters of the High Renaissance. I mentioned earlier that by 1500 the stylistic phenomenon of the Gothic had once and for all been vanquished in Italy. The classical orders (transmitted theoretically by Vitruvius) and classical ornament dominated architecture, the decoration of interiors, and the applied arts. At the same time, daintiness, angularity, and precious linearity (features by which the figures of Botticelli and Verrocchio show themselves as coeval with those by Schongauer and Riemenschneider) disappeared from sculpture and painting. Also in the depiction of the human body, the classical model became more and more canonical. Think of Michelangelo's early works and Raphael's *Stanze*, Giorgione's *Venus* and Titian's *Sacred and Profane Love*! But as we further asserted, though the Gothic itself had been done away with, not so the northern spirit. The early sixteenth century reshaped the world from top to bottom, everywhere breaking through to the elemental, to the roots, to the very essence of things: just as the Reformation reverted back to the Bible as the source of all revealed knowledge, so did Machiavelli revert back to the fundamental conditions of all statal existence. Italian art fathomed the problem of antiquity in much greater depths than it had one hundred years before, and in German art, the northern imagination freed itself from the outdated forms and rules of the Gothic and propelled its indigenous energies in ways both grandiose and violent. For we must realize that, as in Italy, so too in the North, the Gothic, inasmuch as it had crystallized into specific forms, was cast off internally, not, as has often been contended, through the pernicious intrusion of the Italian influence. Suffice it to mention the name of Grünewald! In place of northern Gothicism, the northern spirit burst forth as a raging movement, as the ecstatic vision and free-playing force of the great artist. Proliferating growth, multilayered ambiguity, mysteriousness, indefiniteness in transitions, the super-individual—all that we hold to be particularly northern-Germanic was infused with new life, appropriating the visible world with an astonishing immediacy, and according it a new significance—a significance in which the experience of organic nature was combined in a devout and intuitive way with the splendor of God and his incarnation in Christ. But the freeing of the imagination also gave rise to a different conduct on the part of the artist, and a different estimation of the artistic pursuit. This is what is so overwhelmingly new about Dürer, that we perceive his creative act as an event, as the transition from the creator to the created; and that we find his essential means of expression, the line, not determined by the objects of representation, but conversely: The line is the element in which and through which the objects take on their shape. Consequently, then, the line becomes as essential and primary as it was in the most ancient ornamentation, albeit now under completely different conditions.

If we now turn our attention to Italy, we see there, too, in the land of the classical tradition, of strictness of form and restraint, that the remodeling of the world bursts forth from the most elemental layers in the minds of the early sixteenth-century artists. In the frescoes of the Sistine ceiling, Michelangelo depicted the creation of the world as a process of power, motion, and will, in such a way as it had never before, nor would it ever afterward, be done in the visual arts. What he created is not a symbolic order, not a symbolic diagram, as in the Middle Ages, nor is it a narrative of the sort common in the fourteenth and fifteenth centuries: It is an immediate spiritual and physical representation of the creative act itself. Here too, the artistic activity is different from what it had been in the past. We feel his work being born, we feel the form being wrested out of the chaos of inspiration and matter, and in this subjective process we experience the objective act, the creation of the world. And if Raphael is impelled by his genius to assimilate all his depictions to the simple shapes of the circle and the sphere, this elemental tendency bespeaks with him, too, a harmony with the cosmic forces.

This disclosure of the forces at work in the artist, and their oneness with the cosmic-divine, links Italian art with the art of the North in a heretofore unknown and unclassical way. For it was through the Germanic peoples that the creative unrest, the tension between spirit and matter, between formative act and form, was first introduced into European art. However this change may have occurred in Italy, it explains the interest in the passionate and fantastic German art of the late fifteenth and early sixteenth centuries and the inner readiness of the Italians to assimilate it into their own creative work. All the theoretical detraction of northern barbarism (spurred on by national touchiness) and all the insistence upon the classical ideal could not alter the fact that the northern element took root in Italy. But how did the unclassical northern character of agitated, multilayered representation fuse with the ultimate crystallization of classic-antique form which, as I stated already, was received by the Italians with especial vigor at the *same* historical moment, at the beginning of the sixteenth century?

To answer this question, we must consider how the High Renaissance understood the authority of antiquity. The early Renaissance recognized in the classical form, in contrast to the Gothic, a possibility of creating self-contained, individualized shapes of firm and steadfast corporeality. In this sense Brunelleschi's Pazzi Chapel is different from the surrounding walls and arcades of the monastery courtyard of Santa Croce. In this sense also, Masaccio reverts back to Roman reliefs in the conception of his figures, while the figures of his contemporary Lorenzo Monaco still fill the picture with their bodiless hovering, their flowing folds and dazzling color. Furthermore, the artists of the early Renaissance attached some importance to classical decoration and, when copying figural motives, to the decorative flow of their outlines and their generalized attitudes. Now the High Renaissance no longer held to that immediate, generationally conditioned opposition to the Gothic, even if the anti-Gothic theory still gained ground; hence, the artists needed no longer to seek out in antiquity whatever ran counter to the Gothic. Thus, the High Renaissance could become attentive to the spring-like qualities of classical art, to its suggestions of growth and exuberance, hence to those elements that antiquity shared in a certain way with the northern spirit (the root of the Gothic), and which just now asserted themselves in the North. In a certain sense, then, the High Renaissance had more in common with the Trecento than with the Quattrocento. What the early Renaissance perceived in classical statuary was its *firm* corporeality; what the High Renaissance discovered was its *organic* corporeality. In the same way it was the sixteenth century that first seized upon the great motifs of figures in motion in classical art, and on the possibilities for dynamic expression; the fifteenth century had emphasized the static. This again has something to do with the fact that since High Renaissance and Baroque it was more and more the connection of figures in the *group* that was influenced by classical models, and this in its turn facilitated an approximation to the northern imagination and its supra-individual mode of composing. In fact, the impact of the Laocoön group—a work which, as we know, came to light in 1506 and caused an enormous sensation—is not so very far removed from that of Dürer's *Riders of the Apocalypse*.

But the High Renaissance, in its study of the antique, also reverted back to the elemental, specifically plastic forces. Just as the northern imagination of the early sixteenth century no longer relied upon the finished forms of the Gothic, so did the classicizing of the High Renaissance no longer rely upon the outward features of specific classical models. Of course, in the sixteenth century, faithful copies of classical works were also made, indeed that period was the very heyday of such copying. Yet the artists learned to copy well, with more empathy than had been the case with the fifteenth-century artists. They began to comprehend the structure of their classical models, and these pointed the way toward an understanding of build and functioning of the human body. In regard to the sixteenth century, one must now be far more particular than in past centuries to distinguish between the copy intended as such, and the artwork which, although suffused with the study of ancient art, yet has transformed its classical model into something wholly unique and

German Essays on Art History

new. Particularly in the case of Michelangelo, it is truly astounding how greatly in his sculpture as well as in his architecture he is indebted to antiquity, and how little of this emulation is actually visible in individual works. But with Raphael, also, the classical influence—which permeates his mature and late works much more strongly than may be at first sight apparent—is completely absorbed in his own creative conception; nowhere are we confronted, as sometimes in Mannerism, or later with Poussin and in Neoclassicism, with the classical statue itself in its stony finish. What we see and sense is living nature, heightened and transfigured by the artist's awareness of a high, distant, and poetic realm of existence, which governs his imagination.

V

If until now we have attempted to understand how a union of antiquity and the North in the High Renaissance became possible, we now ask how it occurred and what it resulted in. How did Michelangelo, the greatest and historically most important sculptor of the postclassical period, respond to antiquity, and what aspects of his work, on the other hand, are related to the North? The *Dying Slave* in the Louvre (Fig. 18) can be compared with the younger boy in the Laocoön group (Fig. 17), a work which, as we know, preoccupied Michelangelo very much. The motif is similar. It is readily apparent what Michelangelo owes to the late-Hellenistic model: the beauty and the rich development of the nude body, the free and natural motion of the limbs. In this regard, the northern world of forms has nothing comparable to offer. And yet I should like to join to these two figures, the classical one and that of Michelangelo, a German wood carving, a lamenting Saint John, dated ca. 1470,* now in the Liebighaus in Frankfurt (Fig. 19). Why the comparison? Because, like the dying slave, the late Gothic figure is also an expressive figure. But the boy in the Laocoön group, too, has an expression:

---

*According to recent investigation and stripping, the figure is no longer considered an authentic work of ca. 1470. At the very best, the inner core is medieval; otherwise, the figure received its present shape through substantial additions during the nineteenth or early twentieth century. See Michael Maek-Gérard, *Nachantike grossplastische Bildwerke/Die deutschsprachigen Länder*, vol. III (c. 1380–1430/40), Liebighaus-Frankfurt am Main, Verlag Gutenberg Melsungen 1985, pp. 114–15.—Ed.

the movement of his body and his face is caused by his mortal pain. And yet there is a difference! The classical figure displays the *body* and the *face*, as they are moved and altered by the pain; Michelangelo, on the other hand, represents the *pain* as it takes shape through the body, This, however, links his work to the Saint John, in the making of which the artist likewise took his departure from the concept of pain, which he expressed through the generalized mimic content of folds and facial features. For the classical artist, the body was the given, the pain the additional element; to the northern sensibility, the pain, something incorporeal, a behavior, was the representational problem. The northern imagination tends to render this behavior likewise through incorporeal, or corporeally indeterminate, means: through lines, through dynamic distribution and displacement of weight and volume, through the plastic activity in itself. Although it needs the bodily substratum, it has no scruples about treating it arbitrarily, or even contrary to its nature. Michelangelo, and all European sculpture that came after him, respected the natural, and, in the classical sense, the beautiful appearance of the nude human body; even in the rich interplay of ornamentation one finds no longer that part weirdly menacing, part merrily coarse medley of spooky masks, which thrived so carefree in the Middle Ages. Antiquity acted as a control and as a norm and sometimes also as a constraint on the freewheeling imagination. However, the point of departure is not the body in its relaxed naturalness but the expression incarnate in the human form. It is thereby remarkable how the northern, abstract element of the generalized, humanly indefinite expressive figure embodies itself in the humanly specific classical model. The Saint John appears as a triangle set on its point, and this outline repeats itself again in the design of the head. According to what Lomazzo wrote in his *Trattato*, it was said that Michelangelo likewise requested that his figures formed triangles, which either rest on their points or on their bases. Similarly, Lomazzo traces the derivation of the well-known ideal of the Mannerists and the followers of Michelangelo, the "linea serpentina," back to the master himself.

Another example! In one of the drawings done by Michelangelo for Tommaso Cavalieri, depicting the fall of Phaeton, we notice a river god at the bottom; this figure was very clearly derived from the *Nile*, that famous, and at that time already well-known statue in the Vatican collection. Even the reclining allegorical figures of the Me-

dici tombs may, in my view, be connected with this classical work.
The classical river god is in the truest sense of the word a *personification* of the Nile; the flowing, wide, calmly majestic, beneficial
quality of the river is expressed in the repose, the relaxation, the
mildness and grace of posture — thus through purely and exclusively
human features. There is nothing about the figure that is inconsistent with the standards of human physical appearance. Michelangelo, on the other hand, permits the flowing motion to enter into the
human form; hair and beard are visually related to the sedge that
adheres to it, the soft modeling of the body is flowing like the water
that pours out of the vessel on which the god rests his arm. So, once
again, something that is general, intangible, and all-pervading at-
tains definite and beautiful shape by way of the human figure. In the
case of the *Dying Slave*, it was a psychological process; here it is a
physical-dynamic one within the realm of organic nature.

One might indeed be tempted to say that though all this may very
well apply to Michelangelo, he is in this very regard different from
other Italians: has he not already been called the "last Gothic artist,"
and is he not for that very reason particularly close to the German
mentality? Let us then examine the works of a few other masters of
the High Renaissance. How do matters stand with Raphael, the
epitome of Italian classicism? The small painting of the *Three
Graces* in the Musée Condé in Chantilly (Fig. 22) is a copy of a
group often depicted in classical painting and sculpture (Fig 20).
The most famous example is the marble group in the Libreria of the
Cathedral in Siena, which Raphael might have seen. Although there
can be no question as to the derivation of this painting from the
classical model, it seems to me nonetheless possible to feel reminded
here, too, of a northern forbear, a miniature from the "Très riches
heures" of the Duc de Berry, hence a very delicate, precious work of
the late Gothic (Fig. 21). No doubt Raphael himself would have
bristled at such a comparison, for it was this very feature, the ugly
arbitrariness of the northern body distorted by fashionable dress,
that the study of classical art had helped to transcend. And yet in
some respects, Raphael's little painting bears a relation to the miniature, and not because it included *still* some Gothic residues, but just
because it appropriates creatively some features of northern art in a
new interpretation. For we sense in Raphael's figures the working of
an absolute and suprapersonal element, the like of which is un-

known to antiquity; a play of pure curves that culminates in the three balls held by the Graces. Never would shape and outline of a classical figure have been related to a spherical form, which itself is an attribute of this figure. It is evident that here Raphael touches upon a fundamental aspect of the northern experience. But this use of curves is not limited to the figures of the Graces, it also affects their environment. Figures and landscape, body and space, are united by a suprapersonal element. And this too is something unknown to antiquity, yet characteristic of the northern sensibility. I could demonstrate to you how already in the Romanesque, the representation of space, that is, of the noncorporeal, appears strangely substantial; how then, in the Gothic, the spatial element movingly and dramatically penetrates the seemingly closed plastic forms; and how finally, in the fifteenth century, in part through the texture of light and color, in part through the energy of radiant motion, body and space begin to come together. It was, however, the Italian masters of the High Renaissance who achieved the union between the newly revived corporeality of classical antiquity and the northern sense of infinite space. The bodies become spatial, and the space takes on a corporeal quality. Thus we see the genesis of what I choose to call the global sense (Globusgefühl) of the new era, which lasted until the end of the eighteenth century: the mighty conception of an infinity, which nonetheless, as a structured, comprehensible, self-contained entity, palpitates and rests in itself.

If in the works of the central Italians Michelangelo and Raphael the union of body and space is still largely realized within the human figure, we find in the work of the great Venetian, Titian, to whom the Alps were home, a greater emphasis on the nonhuman element, that is, nature. In Titian's art, the incorporeity of color, of light and shadow, of the shimmering, rushing atmosphere that reaches out to infinity—plays a much greater role than with the artists of central Italy. If we compare the *Madonna of Ancona* with Raphael's *Madonna di Foligno*, a painting that has certainly served as a model for Titian's altarpiece, this difference becomes very apparent. Titian's Madonna in the clouds appears like a condensation of the atmosphere. It is therefore not surprising that the northern element acted as a particularly important ferment in Titian's work, and that his art in turn found favor and, in part, even congenial understanding among northern masters like Rubens, van Dyck, and

Rembrandt, and also among the French and English painters of the
eighteenth century. It has been assumed that Titian had little use for
classical antiquity, less than the artists of central Italy. This is not
the case. In his depictions of figures in motion, he follows his classical prototypes often quite closely, and no artist had a livelier appreciation for the substantial fullness and splendor of classical physicality. Thus he contributed the most to that happy and, for future
developments, so very important union of the richly animated landscape with the beauty of classical man. In Titian's work, classical
plasticity is fully absorbed in the unifying texture of his painterly
surfaces; conversely, the panic forces of northern landscape, which
break forth explosively in the works of Grünewald, Altdorfer, and
Wolf Huber, are with him subdued and softened as they are integrat-
ed into the ripe fullness of classical form. Consider the splendidly
stormy painting *Bacchus and Ariadne*, now in the National Gallery
in London! Almost all figurative motifs can be traced back to classical motifs, but the rhythm of the whole and the harmony between
figures and surroundings call to mind two woodcuts by Dürer: *The
Four Riders of the Apocalypse* and the *Arrest of Christ* from his
Large Passion.

VI

The fusion of classical form with northern fantasy, as it evolved in
the High Renaissance, gave rise to a development that continued
until the last decades of the eighteenth century and only came to an
end in Neoclassicism, a new confrontation of the European spirit
with classical antiquity. The new style developed by Italian artists
on Italian soil spread over the sixteenth and seventeenth centuries
and into the eighteenth, all over Europe, and notwithstanding the
national character of each country, attained a universal currency
comparable to that of the Gothic. But this fusion with antiquity
would never have borne such a genuine and vital fruit in the northern countries if at the moment of the conception of this new universal movement, antiquity and the North had not met. In this way
alone could it happen that the great Italian ecclesiastical architecture of the Baroque was able to gain a foothold and be truly assimilated in the North; that in the most faraway corner of southern

Germany, on a meadow in the midst of an evergreen forest in the Bavarian highlands, an echo of classical corporeality and form can be found, and that such a building by Dominicus Zimmermann appears nonetheless very German, and deeply rooted in the German soil. Here is a building which, though different from the medieval Gothic, is at the same time not foreign and inimical to it, but rather, in its transformation, related. And in this way alone was it furthermore possible that in the full-blooded genius of a Rubens, the whole richness of the figural cosmos of antiquity could blend so organically with the streams of movement, the bursts of light, the glorious color play and the northern experience of landscape. But consider also the interior of St. Peter's in Rome, compare it to the interior of Santa Maria degli Angeli (classical thermae transformed into a Christian church), and you will feel how the transcendental-incorporeal northern sensibility lives and breathes everywhere in the classically derived orders of the Baroque building, how the throngs of people passing through St. Peter's harmonize with the totality of the space, whereas in the wide, farflung halls of Santa Maria degli Angeli every visitor appears as a plastically defined earthbound being. Consider Bernini's *Ludovica Albertoni* (Rome, San Francesco a Ripa). Observe how this marble figure is permeated by the interplay of the lights and shades, and how thereby the life beyond as a rapturously ecstatic experience has suffused her fully developed, classically inspired corporeality. Such a sculpture would never have come into being were it not for the creation, centuries past, of a figure like the dying Maria in the tympanum of Strasbourg Cathedral. Or look at Bernini's *Saint Theresa*, in its motif so similar to the Barberini faun, and yet in the treatment of the marble as unclassical as possible, a negation of all dense matter and its heaviness. At the end of this series I should like to cite a *Pietà* by Franz Ignaz Günther, a Bavarian sculptor of the eighteenth century. The theme of the "Vesperbild" (Pietà) was particularly dear to German art, and no one will doubt the German character of this group. Nevertheless, the body of Christ is clearly derived from the Patroclos of the well-known Pasquino group, indeed its dependence from the classical motif is strikingly close. This Pietà may mark for us the end of the great era in which antiquity and Christendom, southern and northern spirit, met in a fruitful, rich, and expansible union in the visual arts. It would not be long before that union would break apart. Just as the Renaissance turned against the Gothic, so did Neoclassicism turn against the late Baroque, the last phase of the artistic movement that began in the sixteenth century. And Neoclassicism also refuted the older style on the authority of the classical ideal. Yet Neoclassicism was not destined to see its own ideal establish itself as a living presence in the visual arts of the nineteenth century. For the rise of Neoclassicism was not effected by the forces of great creative masters. The transformation of late eighteenth-century art had its roots not in a creative, but in an ethical, impulse: in the striving after truth and knowledge. And it is for this reason that in the nineteenth century classical art lived on above all in the domain of scholarship. It became a subject of research and study. The heavy loss of creative inspiration is counterbalanced by a gain of deeper insight into the nature of classical antiquity. Winckelmann in whose memory we have once again gathered here today,* was the great pioneer of this all-encompassing and penetrating insight. And art history, which in this festive hour was allowed to be the guest of archeology, in like fashion owes deep gratitude to Winckelmann.

Translated by Peter Wortsman

*This is the text of a lecture, delivered by Hetzer on the occasion of the traditional Winckelmann celebration on his birthday, December 9 (probably in Rome, at the German Archaeological Institute, in 1934). — Ed.

Franz Wickhoff

On the Historical Unity
in the Universal Evolution of Art

The reception of Japanese art, whose works had in previous centuries been regarded as mere exotic curiosities, was perhaps the single most consequential event, among many, to affect nineteenth-century painting. It was the Japanese influence, with its heretofore unknown power of expression, that helped make the nineteenth century stand out above all previous artistic periods, and through an evocation of the impression of the natural appearances and the mood of air and light, established landscape painting as the central artistic imperative. None of this would have been possible were it not for Japanese artists, who, at the end of the previous century, familiar with the European tradition, attempted to bring this influence to bear on their native style, so that the new Japanese works would be accessible and acceptable in Europe. The essential point here was the adoption by the Japanese of the European representation of the horizon, which of all artistic norms, would of course prove to be most important to landscape painting.

As we know, it was not the most celebrated painters of the day in Japan who took this step of universal historical importance, as a result of which the great artistic tradition would once again come full circle, and Far Eastern art, originally an offshoot of the European, would return to establish a strong new bond. Instead, these great Japanese reformers were humble draughtsmen who prepared the original compositions for the popular woodcuts.If today the names Hokusai and Hiroshige are mentioned in the same breath with the great names of all time (the one as the model master draughtsman, the other as the imaginative master of the landscape), with all due respect to the former, whose fame rests upon a truly prodigious talent, it is in fact the latter who played the more important role in the aforementioned artistic transformation, and as a paragon for the West. When Hiroshige died in 1853 (the poor fireman of Yedo who, in his spare time between fire watches, labored to become an artist), the world lost a spirit who, like Giovanni Pisano, like Giotto or Jan van Eyck, pioneered new directions in art. Together with Constable and Turner, Hiroshige was one of the three ingenious forerunners of the modern landscape. Just as Constable first managed to evoke in his sketches a sense of reality bathed in light, and Turner's creative ingenuity paved the way for the representation of all atmospheric moods, the Japanese master, through his simplification and effective limitation of motifs, forcing the eye to focus only on the essential, had a formative influence on the composition of the modern landscape.

Yet, no sooner have we begun to appreciate the historical significance of these Japanese artists when that carping tendency, so prevalent among us Germans, starts tugging and tearing at their reputation. Now all at once the older woodcuts are held up for praise, those works in which the Japanese spirit, as yet untouched by other influences, supposedly reigns supreme, and the great draughtsmen of this (the nineteenth) century are defamed. We forget meanwhile that before Hokusai, the woodcut trailed subserviently in the tracks of the painters, that it never would have achieved its own independent artistic significance had not these Europeanizing artists granted it a new style.[1] The evolution of the Japanese woodcut is just like that of the German engraving of the fifteenth century. The older engravers did their historically insignificant work, each in the style of his local school; it was not until Master E. S. and Martin Schongauer had assimilated the principles of the highly sophisticated Netherlandish art that they became influential masters in their own right, thus according German art an importance far beyond the borders of the Fatherland. Nothing in our art would have changed, Japanese works would, as before, have continued to be relegated to curio cabinets, had it not been for those practitioners of the woodcut who succeeded in evolving a new style readily accessible to Western art. Hiroshige, the man of the moment, who is credited with the creation of the new form, was of course only the brilliant crucial link in an artistic chain initiated before him, who would in turn point the way for his own Japanese contemporaries to follow.[2] We might mention here the students of Toyokuni, all of whom had an effect on European art, but among whom Kuniyoshi surely merits particular recognition for the formative influence some of his compositions had on our art.

Yet even if no one would now deny the coming together in the nineteenth century of the Western and the Far Eastern styles, a process initiated in Japan and completed in Europe, I shall still have to prove the contention I made earlier that both styles derived originally from a common source. If the view generally held today were correct, namely, that Far Eastern art, and in particular, its oldest branch, Chinese art, had evolved independently, then we could no longer speak of a historical unity in the universal evolution of art, and it would indeed be amazing how two artistic realms so far removed from each other from the start could nonetheless come together in the end.

It has certainly not passed unnoticed that the oldest Chinese artworks, the originals or copies of which have been preserved, are covered with the so-called *meander*, that ornamental band which for centuries was of such paramount importance for Greek art. But an independent origin was supposed. Friedrich Lippman has pointed out that the Chinese meander is not, like the Greek, always composed of an unbroken, often twisting line, but rather consists frequently of separate meanderlike formal elements. He showed furthermore that the ornamental bands composed of these separate parts are arranged in stripes, one on top of the other, to cover a surface.[3] This quite accurate observation in fact comprises two: first, that the ancient Chinese meander is formed differently from the Greek one; and, second, that it was applied on the ancient Chinese vessels in a different manner than it was on the Greek vases. Only the first observation can be relevant to the question of origin. Szombathy has published clay pots from the Wies in Styria that in like manner display a broken meander line.[4] In this case, the connection with the Greek meander can by no means be mistaken. The pots clearly display the influence of Greek art, and no one can maintain that the meander was independently invented in the Alps. Instead we see clearly on a single vase fragment from the Wies how the Greek meander was first rendered accurately, and how, next to it, another version falls into separate parts, which are again combined to make a band, and how finally these bands, arranged one on top of the other, form a complete surface decoration. This is exactly the same principle as that employed on the ancient Chinese bronze vases. We may, I believe, permit ourselves the analogous conclusion that the Chinese meander evolved in the same way. The fact that, as Friedrich Hirth relates, in the eleventh-century A.D., the Chinese author of the Meng-ch'i-pi-t'an explains the motifs in the meander band as abbreviations of the Chinese character for cloud,[5] is of course irrelevant to the question of their derivation. This is a later, secondary, explanation.

The meander first appears on the Greek urns as a geometric decoration, the style of which we call the Dipylon style, after one of the richest archeological sites of its discovery. After the decline of Mycenean culture, which evolved the acanthus out of the connecting spiral bands of Egyptian art,[6] geometric decoration burst forth once again in Greece. Here, as everywhere else, before a consistently developing art had crystallized its own style, the urns were decorated with a few motifs derived from the basic rhythms of everyday life and from the most rudimentary technology. In the Dipylon style, the great art that came out of Egypt clearly left its imprint: Based on reminiscences of the spiral band and the acanthus, the simple geometric form was arranged into a regular unbroken band. This band is the meander, the great mark of order and measure in the art of the Greeks, which attests, wherever it is found—in Italy, in Panonia, or in the Alps—to the dissemination of Greek forms, as well as to the inevitability of their influence.[7] The meander is a peculiar product of historical and ethnic conditions, of the temporary rule by the representatives of a highly developed culture over a people predestined for art who, after the expulsion of these foreign rulers, preserved the meander as a residue of the art of these aliens, and kept it for centuries to come as the master mark, as it were, of their own artistic production. No one can maintain that an art form that developed under such unique circumstances could have evolved elsewhere in the same way, and the very genesis of the meander itself vouches for Greek influence wherever it appears, in China as well as in Italy and in the Alps. One could very well conjecture that just as the meander slowly traveled to the West, so too did it make its way through the civilized countries of the East until finally it landed in China. But that is not the way it happened. The Near East and

Central Asia had a highly developed culture, from which the Greeks still had several centuries to learn. If the transmission did not first take place in the Hellenistic period, when Greek art gradually pervaded the East, a spontaneous transmission must have taken place. The conditions under which this transmission took place and the period during which it took place can be established.

In his book, *On Foreign Influences in Chinese Art* (Über fremde Einflüsse in der chinesischen Kunst), Friedrich Hirth published the drawing of an ancient Chinese bronze pot,[8] which we reproduce here (Fig. 23). It comes from the *Si-ts'ing-ku-kien*, a work produced by the court scholars to Emperor Kien-lung, by order of a court decree of December 1749, as a richly illustrated catalog of the emperor's collection.[9] Hirth provides an extensive account of the more ancient and later Chinese published reproductions of old pots, from which, as an example, he had this drawing copied. "What we learn from all these works," says Hirth, "is the fact that from its earliest documented beginnings until the 3rd Century B.C., Chinese visual art has always displayed a pronounced national character. On certain forms of pots developed in accordance with the purposes of the ancient sacrificial service, we find certain reappearing ornaments, *of which it can by no means be claimed that they were borrowed from an earlier foreign culture, ornaments which for that very reason must be considered genuinely Chinese.* One such ornament that appears on the larger faces of all these pots in the form of a stylized, cat-like grimacing mask is a representation of the monster T'au-t'ie, the symbol of gluttony, whose appearance is intended to remind the owner of the holy vessel to keep to a simple life, by warning him of what he might otherwise face."[10]

We too would like to emphasize the distinctive character of this decorative art, and to admit that it is indeed national, if national means nothing more than that ornaments transmitted from elsewhere convey a different impression in their new surroundings than they did in their place of origin, as a direct function of their new application. Nations of a different ethnic background than that of the original creators of the form, who live in another kind of climate, under social conditions that evolved differently, must of necessity use the borrowed artistic forms differently than they were used in their place of origin. For these are in fact *borrowed forms, derived from a foreign culture, ornaments, not a single one of*

*which can be considered Chinese; they are all Greek ornaments,
which only because of their new combination give the impression of
being Chinese.* A glance at the illustration showing a black-figured
cup (Fig. 24) immediately reveals the fact that the major motif of the
decoration was taken from the Greek eye vases, the slanted eyes of
which, similar to those of the Oriental facial type, may well have
been very appealing to the Chinese. So the Chinese included the
pair of eyes in every stripe, filling in the surface with the meander,
and added a Greek palmetto in several empty spots in the wide
section of the central stripe. The homogeneous application of three
Greek decorative elements, beside which no elements of any other
shape appear, precludes any coincidental congruency. The eye vases
likewise suggest the epoch during which this cultural transmission
took place: they date back to the second half of the sixth century, a
period when the Athenian export of clay pottery experienced such a
marked upsurge. Just as the meander and other Greek ornaments
made their way to the peoples of the Hallstätter period, eleventh to
seventh century B.C., who derived them from a few scattered pieces
of metalwork, so the export en masse of Greek ware effected a style
change in the Etrurian art of the West and gave rise in the East to
Chinese art. It would not surprise me if now, in the course of a
complete exploration of China, we were to find, there as in Italy,
fragments of black-figured vases.And so it is Attic art that pushed
its way victoriously all the way to China, and that gave this distant
nation its style.

In his informative book, Friedrich Hirth showed us how, in the
Hellenistic period, Greek art penetrated again into the Far East
through Bactria (Afghanistan), and that consecutive waves of this
influx continued to occur for the duration of the reign of classical
culture.[11] Indeed, one cannot but conclude that the Chinese also
learned painting (that is, the depiction of rounded bodies with light
and shadow on a flat surface) from Greek painters, for painting is
likewise an Attic invention. And this invention may very well be the
greatest cultural achievement of the Greeks, considering the fact
that an artistically astute people like the Egyptians, with their great
talent for drawing, labored for centuries without ever achieving this
level of invention.

Friedrich Hirth has promised us studies of the history of Chinese
painting that will readily shed light on certain dark points that still

elude us. But there is one thing, I believe, that we can already assert today. Far Eastern painting differs from the painting of the West in that it never went through a Middle Ages. In the Louvre there is a Japanese painting in which fish dashing through the waves are rendered in an absolutely illusionistic or impressionistic manner. The piece is ascribed to Hasengam Nounèbjn, and it is thought to be a seventeenth-century copy of a Chinese painting by Han-an-Yin (Yuan dynasty) of the thirteenth century.* If this is true, then there can never have been an interruption in the artistic tradition. This painting is on a par with the paintings of Velázquez or Rembrandt, at a level of artistic accomplishment which the Romans had already achieved in the third century.[12] The degree of artistic expertise thus remained constant in China, entered Japanese art, and has been maintained down to the present day, so that one could say that it is classical illusionism which is instrumental in shaping the artistic achievements of today. It truly is a single tradition that came full circle, and all art of the modern civilized nations can be traced back directly to the Greeks, whose influence spread in all directions. And this also explains one of the most extraordinary phenomena in the history of art, namely, the ever- and ever-recurring periods of renascences. Since all art derives from one common source, so much of the original must have been preserved in each of its branches that a lost thread could be found everywhere by means of which the rediscovered remains of past periods could be tied into the artistry of the present.

Translated by Peter Wortsman

---

*According to Prof. John Hay, these garbled names refer presumably to Hasegawa Tohaku (also known as Hasegawa Nobuharu (1533–1610), and Fan An-jen (mid-thirteenth century; he was, however, more of a Southern Sung painter). — Ed.

Notes

1. In his book on the Japanese woodcut, Woldemar von Seidlitz gave short shrift to his predecessors, who had rightfully appreciated the value of the modern Japanese woodcut artists. With the yardstick of a pawnbroker, who values only what

is old, rare, and expensive, he set the historical significance of the Japanese woodcut on its head.

2. In China, at the beginning of the eighteenth century, [Chiao] Ping-chen had already made an attempt to institute the European conception of the horizon, without however making any inroads among his countrymen. Cp. Friedrich Hirth, *Ueber die fremden Einflüsse in der chinesischen Kunst*, Munich and Leipzig, G. Hirth, 1896, p. 55 et seq.

3. Friedrich Lippmann, *Studien über chinesische Email-Vasen*, Vienna, 1870, p. 15.

4. Szombathy, *Urgeschichtliche Forschungen in der Umgebung von Wies in Mittel-Steiermark* (IV) in *Mitteilungen der Anthropologischen Gesellschaft*, vol. XX, Vienna, 1890, p. 182 et seq., fig. 100 and 101, repeated in Moritz Hoernes, *Urgeschichte der bildenden Kunst in Europa*, Vienna, A. Holzhausen, 1898, p. 572. Unfortunately, I was not yet able to make use of this excellent work, so rich in content, which has only just recently appeared in print.

5. Friedrich Hirth, *Chinesische Studien*, Munich and Leipzig, 1890, p. 234 et seq.

6. Cp. Alois Riegl, *Stilfragen*, Berlin, G. Siemens, 1893, p. 111 et seq.

7. Cp. Alexander Conze, "Ueber den Ursprung der bildenden Kunst," *Sitzungsberichte der k. preuss. Akad. der Wissensch.*, Berlin, 1897, VII; J. Boehlau, "Zur Ornamentik der Villanovaperiode," *Festschrift der XXVI. Jahrvers. der D. Anthr. Gesellsch.* Th. G. Fisher Verlag in Cassel, 1895; S. Wide, "Nachleben mykenischer Ornamente," *Athenische Mitt.* XXII, Athens, 1897, p. 233, and now, above all, the great work by Moritz Hoernes, *Urgeschichte*, etc.

8. F. Hirth, *Fremde Einflüsse*, p. 4.

9. Op. cit., p. 6

10. Op cit., p. 7

11. Op. cit., p. 10. Cp. also Friedrich Hirth, *China and the Romain Orient*, Leipzig and Munich, G. Hirth, 1885, and H. Nissen, "Der Verkehr zwischen China und dem römischen Reiche," *Rheinisches Jahrbuch*, 1894.

12. Cp. my remarks at the end of the introduction to the Vienna Genesis (*Die Schriften Franz Wickhoffs*, vol. III, Berlin, Meyer & Jessen, 1911).

Alois Riegl

Late Roman or Oriental?

In an essay entitled "Hellas in the Embrace of the Orient," which recently appeared, Professor Joseph Strzygowski, of Graz, expounded his views on the nature of the art of late antiquity. According to his own admission, however, his intention at that time was not so much to propagate his own ideas as to hinder the dissemination of mine as I last presented them in my book, *Late Roman Art Industry*. In this he was not successful, and surely silence would have better served his purpose, for Strzygowski hereby rather introduced to public discussion the results of my research to date, for which I am most grateful.He did however lash out in the process, directing a sharp polemic at me, which naturally calls for a defense. And so I put myself in the en-garde position—at which, however, I immediately admit to being a little perplexed. I search for a point of mine that he concretely chose to attack, and I find none. This confession may indeed come as a surprise, if we recall the temperamental and somewhat nervous manner in which the attack was perpetrated on the part of my opponent, a man known for his combative and cutting manner. As seriously as the attack was no doubt intended, it nevertheless rather called to mind a theatrical clamor. The issue itself, however, around which this whole controversy revolves, merits our attention, and it is for that reason that I chose to present my views in these pages.

The problem of late antiquity is to my mind the most important and most trenchant one in the entire history of mankind to date. We see here an art which, according to our modern view, achieved a wondrous blossoming (and indeed in certain areas reached a level of mastery that has never since been matched), to sink apparently in the course of a few centuries to a low point that at first glance we must label as barbarism. We see the free citizen of the classical Greek and the republican Roman era bow willingly to a kind of sultanic regime with a servile bureaucratic state. In place of the free reign of the rights of the strongest, in the noblest sense of the word, in place of the love of victory, beauty, splendor, we witness the appearance of a veritable cult of the weak, the lowly, the ignominious, the ugly, a cult that climaxed typically in the crucifix. And all this took place in the course of a largely peaceful process, without any violent overthrow of a ruling and pace-setting race, without any earthshaking political or economic catastrophes!

To the nineteenth century, which, despite romantic interludes, was generally given to a cool and sharp grasp of perceptible and tangible reality, such phenomena must have presented an unresolvable riddle, in the face of which the question suggested itself: What ghastly figments of the imagination so terrified and confused the spirits of late antique humanity that they could willingly give up all the splendid riches amassed over many centuries? And this is supposed to have happened to the Hellenes, the people that first taught mankind scientific thinking, and to the sober, practical Romans? This just didn't seem possible, and so the nineteenth century came to the conclusion that in late antiquity, the carriers of culture on the Mediterranean were not Greeks or Romans any longer, but rather members of a barbarized and mixed race, corrupted in the West by the Teutons and the Celts, in the East by the Orientals. However, in this way the enigmatic knot was not unraveled, but simply cut through. The question was answered one-sidedly from the standpoint of the materialist critique of reason of the nineteenth century, and thus the importance of feeling as a culturally motivating factor was completely ignored.

Since then a change has set in in the predominant attitudes of European thought, a change that, since the beginning of the twentieth century, can no longer be mistaken, and reveals itself essentially as an emancipation of the faculty of feeling in modern man. Thus a fundamental breach had been established which allowed us moderns an understanding of the decisive causes of the transformation that took place in late antiquity. Whereas before, we merely shrugged our shoulders with passing regret at the "barbaric" works of the classical "period of decline," we now begin gradually to study these works, recognizing in them certain positive, deliberate, stylistic features. Thus it is slowly dawning on us that we are here faced with a problem, the resolution of which can be attempted via the natural path of research, and not by the mere hypostatizing of a pathological condition. Thus the problem of late antiquity has been accorded a place on the agenda of scholarly research, and I believe I may hazard the prophecy that it will not be dropped until a universally satisfactory solution has been found.

In my *Late Roman Art Industry*, I attempted such a solution, based on fifteen years of research; I had already presented preliminary results ten years before in my *Questions of Style (Stilfragen)*. Yet Strzygowski rejects my solution offhand by calling it a "preconceived notion." But the reader of his critique is never enlightened as to the essence of my hypothesis; he is only repeatedly assured that I erroneously regard late antique art as a continuation of Roman antiquity, and that I remain blind to the true oriental character of late antiquity. In support of his contention, he quotes several altogether general remarks of mine, which are taken almost exclusively from my earliest writings and from a review I wrote ten years ago. Reference is indeed made to my *Questions of Style* and *Late Roman Art Industry*, so that one would expect on Strzygowski's part a knowledge of their contents. His polemic against my work is, however, essentially limited to a passionate attack on the term used in my title, "Late Roman," which in his view ought to read "Oriental." Thus at best the reader learns that there are two catchwords wrestling for validity here; but what the actual heart of the controversy is remains a mystery. In the following remarks I will attempt to reveal the heart of the matter, and I hope thereby to approach the more general concerns of the reader interested in this cardinal question of cultural history. The fact that my remarks appear in part in the form of a polemic will, I hope, not only not detract from my intended purpose, but will also direct further access to the controversial character of this question.

It seems advisable to begin with a presentation of the Strzygowskian position, for it is apparently the more simple of the two. According to Strzygowski, late antique art is nothing but an outright oriental art. Is this "solution" of his, in fact, a new one? We have already alluded to the fact that the materialistic conception of history in the nineteenth century viewed late antiquity as the product of a barbarization of the classical peoples by the Orientals and the Celto-Germanic tribes. This is how I too learned it from my teacher, Thausing, and if Strzygowski wishes to enlighten himself as to what the Viennese School thought about this matter fifteen years ago, he might seek out and read the highly informative, albeit small work by the short-lived Friedrich Portheim, *On The Decorative Style in Early Christian Art,* wherein he will find a fair account of the significance of the Orient as an influence on the art of the Roman Empire and the early Middle Ages. But this was all of course mere "orientalized antiquity," and Strzygowski "does not want to beat around the bush." In his view, the Indogermanic and Greco-Roman antiquity was already long dead by the Early Christian period, and the entire art of that period was already completely oriental, for the Orient enjoys the privilege of eternal life. The new aspect of Strzygowski's attempt at a solution to the problem of late antiquity thus consists in an absolute denial of the presence of an Indogermanic element in late antique art; he would have us view the art of that period as strictly oriental. It is the old hypothesis of the barbarization of antiquity, only one-sidedly carried to the extreme, in that the Mediterranean peoples are here stripped of even that minuscule remnant of Indogermanic culture that earlier scholarship still accorded them. It is only then a natural consequence that Strzygowski, like all his predecessors, appraises late antique art as an art of decay. As contrasted to the virgin of Hellenistic-classical art, he compares late antiquity to a harlot, an allusion that we probably have to excuse as a result of desk fever. I fail to perceive herein a real "solution" to the problem. All that Strzygowski has essentially done is cut through the knot again, and in an even more brusque and ruthless manner than any of his predecessors; and it is only in this ruthlessness that we find the novelty of his view.

Strzygowski's hypothesis would merit discussion if the Mediterranean peoples of Indogermanic origin had been completely wiped out at the beginning of the Roman empire, and supplanted by oriental invaders. Since this, however, was not the case, and the series of events so often brought up and exaggerated in support of this contention—the influx of foreigners into the Roman empire in the form of mercenaries—first began at a time when the process of spiritual transformation was already far advanced, every attempt at a genuine solution will have to present the transformation, which becomes clearly recognizable since the time of Constantine the Great, as a necessary product of the immediately preceding developmental phases, indirectly, of all the oriental and Indogermanic precedents of late antique art. It is a process of evolution, not revolution. In the life of art there is no death, but only an eternal interpenetration of all that once was, in an endlessly advancing waving line, which sometimes approaches the extremely materialistic oriental pole and at other times veers toward the psychophile Indogermanic pole, without ever reaching all the way to either side, for that would indeed be the death of art.

I have thus understood my purpose as the elucidation of a developmental problem; this, however, has been declared by Strzygowski my "preconceived idea." What led me to this conclusion was the realization that late antique art (and its culture in general) in a decisive manner paved the way for all future advances over antiquity. As to the fine arts, I only wish to indicate in passing how all the art of antiquity—oriental as well as Greek—systematically aimed at presenting the artistically recreated things in their objective entity, as undisturbed as possible by the inevitable admixtures of subjective vision; how conversely all later art since the Middle Ages aimed at representing the subjective aspects of the appearances; how, finally, it was precisely late antique art that broke free of the objectivism of the classical conception and paved the way for modern subjectivism.

Thus I was impelled by necessity not to envision late antiquity from the point of view of modern subjective taste as an art of decline, but rather, from the standpoint of the universal evolution, as a progressive art, progressive indeed in the most eminent sense of the word. This evaluation, however, seemed at first sight to be contradicted by the unmistakable oriental elements in late antique art, because these represented, as it were, a relapse into the most ancient antiquity. I could not withdraw from these impressions, all the less so since I had published books about oriental artworks at a time when Strzygowski was still searching for the origin of late antique art in Greek Byzantium, claiming the same infallibility then as he now does for his oriental hypothesis. Thus I had not merely to prove late antique art in all its essential features to be the necessary product of the preceding development, I had also to demonstrate how its seemingly oriental features, on the one hand, do indeed

touch upon ancient oriental art, yet how, on the other, thanks to the
preceding classical development, they fundamentally differ from it.
It is this problem that I have tried to resolve in my *Late Roman Art
Industry,* and as uniformly as possible for all four areas of the fine
arts. I would like then to present here a summation of my essential
findings.

Architecture must by rights come first. Its development originates
in the ancient Egyptian temple. The Egyptian temple is a single
edifice and presents the viewer with an undivided uniform wall; it
appears thus delimited in height and width, not, however, in depth,
and it remains without any division into parts. The Greek temple is
likewise a *single* edifice, and also still as a whole presents a uniform
wall, which is, however, already divided into a series of forms
(peripteros). As a whole, therefore, it is still delimited in height and
width, like the Egyptian temple, but in its parts (columns) it is also
already delimited in depth. The monumental architectural form of
the Hellenistic period is the simple rotunda: it too remains a single
edifice, but it is also as a whole delimited in its depth, and is in this
regard altogether unoriental; whereas, on the other hand, the rotunda remains again without any division into articulated parts,
and in this regard, it harks back to the oriental. Late antique art
finally breaks free of the common classical objectivism, which desired to envision the building externally as an altogether isolated
formal unit, and introduces the *Massenbau* (building composed of
masses) (according to G. Semper's definition, as a higher unity
composed of several individual forms). Leaning against a rotunda
we now find a number of smaller, halved circular buildings (apses);
against all four sides of the oblong temple hall lean halved lower
structures (a basilica with narthex, aisles, and apsis). The flat,
uniform wall of the basilica and the suppression of any external
articulation of the wall gives this building a decidedly ancient oriental appearance; but the distribution of masses and the coloristic
interaction of the facade and its perforation, anathema to ancient
oriental art, came into being in the course of the occidental, Indogermanic development.

Architecture is not, however, solely external structure, but also
interior: it must create interior space. To an objectivistic conception
of architecture, which strives after clearly delineated appearances,
the very idea of empty spatial depth must be disconcerting, and in

fact, "space fright" is one of the most important features of classical architecture. The ancient Egyptian temple hall is sliced up by a forest of columns into numerous narrow corridors; even the Greek temple does not yet comprise a monumental interior space. Only the hellenistic rotunda admits this kind of interior space, however in such a way that the tactile, isolated exterior of the rotunda still remains clearly sensible even within the intangible, empty interior. Once again it is late Roman art that makes the decisive break here by opening up vistas from a principal room to side rooms, and once again we are reminded here of the ancient Egyptian temple, which had even anticipated the influx of light through clerestory windows. But here too we are actually faced with two extremes that are only externally related. The ancient Egyptian temple had no naves with lateral development, but only corridors with mere longitudinal development; its windows were indeed meant to let in a subdued light, but were not themselves supposed to be visible from either the outside or the inside, whereas in the early Christian basilicas the windows constituted the most effective aesthetic element and were thus multiplied to such an extent that they had in the Baroque period, for cogent artistic reasons, to be largely walled up. The window as a means of communication between the inside and the outside is the truly modern element in architecture; it was despised by the monumental art of the ancient Orient, came little by little to be tolerated by the Greeks, and achieved total acceptance only in late antiquity.

In this overview the reader will perhaps miss any mention of Mesopotamian art, on which Strzygowski believed he had to lay so much store, as he took it for the earliest instance of "spatial art." I, however, understand awareness of space as a soothing awareness of spatial expanse in all directions, thus especially also in width, even if height or depth may prevail. But the Mesopotamian vaulted spaces are never true spaces, that is, spaces also developed in width, but rather mere corridors surrounding courtyards; their depth prevails so much over their width that, not unlike the Egyptian columned halls, the viewer is more aware of the delimiting flat walls than of the empty space between them. No one will of course deny that herein lies a certain advance over Egyptian architecture; but this does not mean that Mesopotamian architecture is a veritable *Raumkunst* (art of space). One will seek in vain among the Babylonians and Assyrians for the exterior composed of masses, even if they seem to have taken lesser pains than the Egyptians to see to it that their exterior walls conformed to a mathematically exact vanishing line. The coloring of their buildings was polychromic, not coloristic: a confusion that nowadays one should still encounter only among laymen. Finally, columns and vaulting, architectural features that play such an important role in late antique art, were indeed already employed by the Mesopotamians, and moreover, not only for utilitarian purposes (as the Egyptians and later the archaic Greeks had done), but rather for monumental buildings. However, we do not see clearly enough concerning this aspect of Mesopotamian architecture, since such buildings have not been preserved intact, and for this reason, I have refrained from any detailed discussion of these phenomena in my *Late Roman Art Industry*. So much seems already certain, that the Mesopotamian monumental buildings encompassed for the most part merely barrel-vaulted, corridorlike spaces, and not the mighty, round, domed buildings and cross-vaulted halls of the Romans, and one will seek in vain in Mesopotamian art after an arch over a column.

So much for late antique architecture and its relation to its ancient oriental and classical precursors. Sculpture ought to come next in line, but I feel impelled first to insert here a brief digression on a particular perceptional principle of art history.

The modern art reformers all believe they should begin the artistic education of the public by encouraging them to learn how to "see." We modern men have gradually grown accustomed to such an extent to operating with countless mental images that the colored impression of a thing suffices to awaken our conception of that thing in our consciousness, the depot of our experience, and we don't even feel an urge to explore its limitations and qualities. The sensual act of *seeing* appears thus to have been reduced in us moderns to a bare minimum, pushed back, as it were, by the intellectual act of conceptual completion from the realm of our actual experience; this, however, constitutes an obvious threat to the fine arts, which could not exist were it not for sensual perception, and it is for this reason that the aforementioned reformers are convinced that people need once again to be stimulated to resume *seeing* as a sensual act. Is seeing however really the sole sense function that reveals to us the nature of things, that is, above all, their extent and delimitation in relation to each other? The eye merely conveys colored appearances, which may well conform to the actual contours of the thing itself, but do not necessarily do so. It is only finally the sense of touch that can inform us about these limitations, that is, about the relative impenetrability of things. And all our impressions of solid things, which we have absorbed via the detour of our visual faculty, will finally revert us back to the primitive experience of our tactile faculty. It is thus in any case essentially through the sense of touch that we experience the true quality, the depth and delimitation of objects in nature and works of art. I have therefore called these qualities of things the tactile (from *tangere* = to touch),[1] as opposed to the optical (visible) qualities, like color and light. Whereas the optical qualities disappear in the dark, the tactile qualities remain: extent and delimitation are thus the more objective qualities, color and light the more subjective ones, for the latter depend to a greater degree on those chance circumstances in which the perceiving subject finds itself.

The art of all of antiquity can be characterized as a fundamental objectivism, for it has aimed at the clearest possible delineation of the individual figure in all dimensions. From its very inception, the art of antiquity could not of course do without certain residues of subjectivism, for every work of art does after all presuppose the existence of a perceiving subject, but the contingencies of subjective vision were still as much as possible to be eliminated from the appearance of the work of art. The fundamental goal of all the art of antiquity was then the creation of a distinct demarcation of the individual figure.

Since objects extend in three dimensions, they are likewise limited in height, width, and depth. The extension of height and width, which together form a single surface, is inevitably demarcated by outlines; the outline immediately reminds our sense of touch, that it is here confronted with an impenetrable boundary. But how can the delimitation according to depth be indicated? If the surface remains completely flat, delimited only in height and width, then no depth at all is revealed, nor can it be delimited. Only by means of shadow (and only secondarily through foreshortening and overlapping) does the presence of depth become recognizable; however, shadow is an optical element, which as such stimulates the visual faculty and thereby detracts from the utilization of the tactile sense. The art of antiquity, which sought as much as possible to enclose the figures in objective, tactile borders, accordingly was bound from the very beginning to include a subjective, optical element; this, however, gave rise to a contradiction, the resolution of which was to pose a problem. Every attempt to solve this problem led in turn to a new problem, which was handed down to the next period, and one might well say that the entire art history of the ancient world consists of a developmental chain made up of such problems and their solutions.

The oldest documented art of antiquity, the ancient Egyptian—and here I begin my survey of the development of sculpture—consequently placed the sharpest possible emphasis on the outline within the plane (height and width); it accorded access, however, in the most limited way to depth-designating shadow, admitting just enough of it to allow recognition of depth in the modeling of the surface. We are often stunned when, while letting our fingertips glide over the ancient Egyptian relief figures, we perceive the most delicate modeling, whereas from a distance, the eye appears only to take in an undifferentiated lifeless surface. The strictest objectivism demanded furthermore the avoidance of any foreshortening or overlapping as a subjective and vague effect, dependent on chance. Thus came into being the well-known striding figure types of ancient Egyptian reliefs and paintings with their profile positioning of head and legs and their frontal view of eyes and shoulders. No human being ever saw a fellow man in such a projection; yet it was the most objective one, for it showed as much as possible and did so with the least possible foreshortening. It was of course not possible to do entirely without subjective residues. It is true, the rear view was missing, yet every reminder of it was carefully eliminated; neither the temple wall nor the figure should remind the viewer of something which behind them extended in depth. Furthermore, certain foreshortenings and overlappings had unavoidably to be admitted, as, for instance, in the belly and on the upper thighs—all problems for which the art of later periods had to provide equalizing solutions. Finally, as far as coloring is concerned, ancient Egypt stuck to the strictest polychromy: As far as the tactile limits of an object extended, a single, unbroken color was applied.

I have devoted so much time to a consideration of the ancient Egyptian relief, for it is here that one recognizes most clearly the fundamental artistic precepts of antiquity, and at the same time sees the future problems that these precepts portend. Greek art was resolved to achieve a thorough delimitation according to depth, and hence to tolerate as much as necessary the prerequisite, a significant increase in the subjective elements of the visual appearance. The relief figures grow in bulk, which results, in particular, in an increase of shadows. However, an attempt was made, by way of symmetrical distribution and regular outlining of the shadows, to let this vague optical element as far as possible attain a clear-cut effect and an objective appearance within the surface of the relief. In this way, the classical art of the Greeks brought about the sought-after balance; the art of the Diadochi went one step farther and raised the height of the relief to the highest permissible level. The entire surface thus dissolved into convex protrusions, but each one was clearly delimited in its height and width. These Hellenistic figures produce, as we are wont to say, the greatest plastic effect, that is to say, the sight of them provokes the tactile organs of the viewer to reach out and touch them, to a greater degree than any earlier and later sculpture of antiquity. This is the result of the clear delimitation of the frontal surface, where the figure's extension into depth is facing the viewer. We must not, however, overlook the fact that this effect came about because of the far-ranging inclusion and utilization of a means essentially opposed to the tactile sense, namely the optical shadow; the next consequence is also immediately evident in the fact that the delimitations in height and width henceforth no longer stand out as sharply and clearly as in ancient Egyptian art.

The actual goal of the artistic development of antiquity was, however, the complete closure of the individual figure in every dimension, and thus also in its depth on the side turned away from the viewer. The Egyptian relief figure had no reverse side, it receded deliberately into the ground. The Greek relief figure endeavored more and more to free itself from the ground; if however it wished to go beyond the relative independence achieved in Hellenistic art, the mere application of the shadow in its modeling function, that is, as body shadow (Körperschatten), no longer sufficed. The shadow had rather to appear as something enclosing the body from the outside, something that separated the body on all sides from its surroundings, and thus also at the rear: the body shadow had to become a spatial shadow (Raumschatten). The moment in which this transformation took place was one of the most important and epoch-making moments in the history of all art, not only the art of antiquity. Had Strzygowski taken account of it, he would never have thrown together the oriental art of the post-Christian era with ancient oriental art, he would never have been able to overlook the occidental element in all the more recent oriental art. The limitations of the present context permit me only to point out a single, albeit particularly striking symptom of that transformation. From the late Hellenistic period onward, the relief figures appear often set off against the ground by a sharply engraved outline, which, analogous to the shadows marking the fringes of the figures in seventeenth-century paintings, separate the figures completely and manifestly from the ground and place them in a free spatial sphere. But even this did not suffice in the long run: little by little, the ground was completely hollowed out around the figures, so that, as for instance on the reliefs of the Arch of Constantine, they step boldly out of the relief, almost like the wall groups of the seventeenth century. Here for the first time the essentially objectivistic development of antiquity achieved its ultimate goal, the complete delimitation of the individual figure in all its dimension. Yet from the fourth century A.D. onward, we encounter apparently altogether different reliefs that once again rest rather flatly against the smooth, not hollowed-out ground, like those of ancient Egypt. This seems to be the same relapse into ancient oriental modes as in the architecture of the period; in actual fact, it is here, too, merely the external meeting of two extremes. For whereas the ancient Egyptian figures receded with their rear sides into the ground, as it were, they now spring forth from it, aiming at perspectival roundness, and casting shadows; and whereas in the older works only the most delicate, planar half-shadows were admissible, now deeply engraved spatial shadows determine the character. One need hardly ponder such details. Even a cursory glance must already reveal to the art historian that he is here dealing with two, despite apparent relatedness, fundamentally different phenomena. Strzygowski needs only compare these orientalizing reliefs, such as those on the sarcophagus of Constantine in Rome, with ancient Egyptian reliefs, and he too will recognize the gulf that separates them as it was torn open by the Greek development. I likewise refer his attention to the frontal gaze of the late antique relief figures as opposed to the rendition in profile of the ancient oriental ones, and I further point at the background buildings in late antique reliefs and paintings, which are always placed at an angle to the ground, as opposed to the flat facades in ancient oriental works: all extreme differences in the most elementary points of artistic conception, which, without the interference of Greek art, would not be comprehensible at all.

Yet as if by necessity, a parallel development occurred. In Roman art of the imperial time, the relief turned back away from the height of projection achieved during the Hellenistic period; the figures retreated ever farther into optical distance from the viewer; their outlines according to height and width, on the other hand, became all the more marked again; the folds were more and more indicated by deep shadowy clefts instead of the former, planar shadows that effected a shallow modeling of the bodies; the colorism of the surface appearance increased continually from Marcus Aurelius to Decius, and from this latter to Diocletian. However, I can here barely hint at all this; the whole development can be followed, step by step, on the grounds of the monuments, in my *Late Roman Art Industry*.

The attentive consideration of the development of the relief is of such inestimable value for the solution of the problem of late antique art for the very reason that it clearly reveals the decisive shift from the striving after objectivity in the tactile appearance (haptic objectivism) to the objectivity of the visual appearance (optical objectivism). Had Strzygowski considered this distinction, he would surely never have been able to say that classical art followed exactly the same course as that of the modern development and then died a natural death. For all of the more recent art is essentially subjective; classical art is, however, completely lacking in the subjective qualities of aerial perspective, and of linear perspective, too, insofar as it extends beyond the individual figure. And even in the most accomplished individual figure of antiquity an observant viewer will be able to detect things that an observing subject could never have perceived simultaneously side by side in a human being; this is generally less apparent in human figures in motion, but it is clearly evident in stationary and delimited buildings, and I would like to hazard the contention that antiquity left us not one single depiction of a perspectivally (that is, subjectively) correctly drawn building. Thus, even in the case of the individual figure, the subjectivism of optical perception had to be suppressed if it threatened to stand in the way of the objectivism elicited by the observed object.

This art-historical approach, which endeavors to look beneath the surface appearance of things, and thereby uncovers essentially new areas, must of necessity first create its own dialectical terminology, which will not immediately be comprehensible to every reader. It appears that this holds for Strzygowski as well, for he finds the language in the first chapters of my work, in which I present the essentials of my case, mysterious and incomprehensible. However, I can also report opposite experiences. Not only sculptors like Zumbusch, who never designated his art to his students as anything but a tactile art, or art historians, who like me aim at a deeper understanding of the connections between artistic phenomena, even rank amateurs have, to my own surprise, completely understood me if only they took the trouble to read the book from beginning to end. But that seems to have been too wearisome a chore to Strzygowski: for from the title alone he already concluded that the entire book was only intended to express a "preconceived notion."

The chapter devoted to painting had for extraneous reasons to come out somewhat scanty. Strzygowski will hold that very much against me; even though he does not speak of it in his critique, I must come to this conclusion, for he faulted Wickhoff, in that the latter neglected to begin his discussion of Roman art of the early imperial time with the encaustic portraits discovered in Egypt. I maintain, however, that whoever is capable of accurately perceiving a marble head of Marcus Aurelius is very well able to imagine on his own what the contemporaneous painted portraits must have looked like, even if he had never laid eyes on one of those encaustic paintings.

The chapter on the art industry was, according to the specifications of my publisher, supposed to have constituted the entire book. But ever since I began to concern myself with the history of the art industry, I always asked myself, even in regard to the most inconsequential piece of applied art: How does this work reflect the character of the contemporaneous architecture, sculpture, and painting? And thus I was able to demonstrate even in late antique art industry the determinant role of those forces which I already alluded to above and, no less so, the same relationship of the externally related extremes to the ancient oriental art industry. Where in ancient oriental antiquity would Strzygowski be able to name works, which, like the fret- and wedgework of the fourth and fifth centuries A.D., were conceived solely on the basis of the indefinite coloristic interplay of light and shadow? In one passage indeed he does refer to the well-known drill technics of the Roman marble works as being of ancient oriental derivation, but this I must once again ascribe to a bad case of desk fever. There is no greater contrast imaginable than between the slashed optical appearance of the late antique marble sculptures and the palpably cohesive surface appearance of the ancient oriental stone figures. On the other hand, those inlays of colored stone in gold, which one has likewise already heard referred to as Gothic workmanship, can in fact be traced back to ancient Egyptian times, where they always appear in eminently polychrome application, so that the motifs and the ground are clearly and sharply delimited one against the other, whereas the late antique garnet inlays in gold aimed systematically at a coloristic confusion between pattern and ground.

Thus we find everywhere the same phenomenon: a regression, so it would appear, back to most ancient forms, to the haptic objectivism of the ancient Orientals, in fact, however, an extreme contrast, a radical optical objectivism. The screw of time has seemingly turned all the way back to its old position, yet in reality it has ended up one full turn higher, and it is now removed by a deep furrow from that point at which it seemed once again to have arrived.

Strzygowski hopes to achieve a particularly baffling effect with the report that Greek paintings were recently discovered in the Nile delta beneath a layer of Egyptian ones; this means indeed, beyond any doubt, that the Egyptian works must have been executed later than the Greek. And is this not the most crystal-clear proof of a reorientalization of Greek art? However, we have always known of the existence in Egypt, for at least three centuries before the birth of Christ, of a Greek art of the conquerors and settlers side by side with native Egyptian art. We likewise know that for at least another three centuries after the birth of Christ, Greco-Roman antiquity and the ancient Egyptian artistic tradition continued to develop essentially independently side by side. Ancient Egyptians and Indo-Germans just stood to each other like fire and water, and the Egyptians proved absolutely unable and unwilling to develop an appreciation of the Greek manner. The presence of the Egyptian element in the

post-Christian time does not then signify a reaction, as Strzygowski
would have it, but rather, as we have always known, the confirmation of a never-interrupted tradition. Incidentally, even the Egyptian
spirit was not all that impermeable to change, as soon as the impetus came from a culture less odious to them than that of the Greeks.
For Strzygowski's claim that the fellahs of today are in every respect
like the Pharaonic Egyptians is at best a gross exaggeration; in their
language, faith, dress, and art, they have long since become Arabs,
and what then is left of their old ways? There may indeed not have
been any possibility for the Egyptians to mix with the Indo-Germanic peoples, but little by little they have well assimilated the
optical objectivism of the semitic Arabs.

   This often overly scrupulous weighing of the oriental and the
Indo-Germanic shares in late antique art forms indeed the red
thread of my book, *Late Roman Art Industry*. Now some reader
may ask in amazement: How could Strzygowski ever have accused
me of not taking the oriental element into consideration? He cloaks
this accusation in the contention that I am not sufficiently familiar
with the Orient and its artistic monuments. There are however
readers of my writings who know me exclusively as a student of
oriental artifacts, and who for a time regarded me (whether rightly
or wrongly) as a kind of authority in the older history of the art of
textiles. Such readers will have responded with no little shaking of
their heads to Strzygowski's doubts as to whether I had ever seen
Sassanian and purely Arabic silks. Since the fact cannot have eluded
even Strzygowski that for twelve years I have been the conservator of
one of the biggest collections of textiles of the aforementioned sort,
and repeatedly have written about that subject, one might well
presume that Strzygowski does not so much fault me for not having
seen such textiles, as for not having seen them with his eyes. He
does however call into account his numerous voyages in the Orient,
and the works of art that he was privileged to see there and which
have remained unknown to me. Here he touches upon a point
which in my view is of more general importance, and this fact, not a
desire for further polemic, induces me to comment upon this point.
The issue here is nothing less than the ever more topical question:
Of what essential worth is the familiarity with a monument as a
historical fact?

   I readily admit that of the Eastern Mediterranean countries I have to date only visited Egypt, up the Nile as far as Luxor, and the area of Greece around Athens. There can be no doubt but that it would have been beneficial to me had I been able to travel beyond that to the extent that Strzygowski did. Yet I would ask, was this deficiency not to a certain extent compensated by the publication, and appearance in European collections, of oriental works of art, which thus were accessible to me and allowed me to join in the debate over the solution of the problem of late antiquity? The answer to this question might be most conclusive if it were known exactly how much more Strzygowski has seen than I have. He claims to have a lot still hidden among his papers; nevertheless he did after all publish some examples, and one must assume that the most important and most remarkable of these were included in his polemic against Wickhoff, *Orient and Rome.* The first and main chapter of this work presents the instance of an extraordinary group of sarcophagi, characterized by the far-reaching use of the drill; these were discovered near Constantinople and in Asia Minor, and therefore, in all likelihood, derive from that region. I was not familiar with any of these sarcophagi, and since my own book appeared earlier than his, I could not very well have made use of this knowledge. This was, however, not at all necessary, for the genre to which these sarcophagi belong was not unknown to me. I had, it is true, come upon only one instance of this kind of sarcophagus before, but that example sufficed for me to recognize first of all its oriental, or, more accurately, Eastern Roman origin, and secondly, and more importantly, I believe, to establish its place in the development. I would like to note in passing that the sarcophagus of which I am speaking is still to be found in an easily accessible spot in Rome, and nevertheless, it appears to have eluded Strzygowski, since he would surely otherwise have mentioned it in his so loudly boasted scrupulous exactitude. How easy it would have been in this case, and how much more justified—as we are here dealing with a monument that has long been well known—were I to charge him in this regard with ignorance of the monuments. But I refrain from leveling such a charge, for I do not share the view that a knowledge of monuments alone already constitutes the alpha and omega of art-historical knowledge. The well-known, dubious, and loud-mouthed argument, "What, you don't know that? Then you don't know anything at all!" may have had a certain validity in the period of materialistic reaction to Hegelian overestimation of conceptual categories. In the future we will have to ask ourselves in regard to every single reported fact, what the knowledge of this fact is actually worth. Even the historical is not an absolute category, and for the scholar, not only knowing per se, but also the knowing-how-to-ignore certain facts at the right moment may well have its advantage. The fact, however, that Strzygowski still holds fast to the overestimation of isolated data, indeed excessively so, does not, I would once again contend, mark him as an innovator, a builder of new inroads, but rather as a ruthless and radical defender of the old. Such a function does no doubt also have its beneficial side as seen within the greater purview of scientific inquiry, for it keeps awake the conscience of those who take more than one factor at a time into consideration, and who aspire to dig a little deeper beneath the surface. A fruitful, defensible solution to the problem of late antiquity, however, is rather to be anticipated from the latter more open-minded scholarly faction.

Translated by Peter Wortsman

Notes

1. It has been objected that this designation could lead to misunderstandings, since one could be inclined to comprehend it as a borrowed word from the Greek, quite like the word "optical" which is used as its opposite; and my attention has been drawn to the fact that physiology has long since introduced the more fitting designation "haptic" (from *haptein-fasten*). This observation seems to me justified and I intend henceforth to use this proposed term.

Max Dvořák

On El Greco and Mannerism

El Greco's fame among his Spanish contemporaries was established by a single painting. It hangs in the church of Santo Tomé in Toledo and depicts the entombment of the Count of Orgaz (Fig. 25).

A stone plaque beneath the painting explains what it represents: Don Gonzalo Ruiz of Toledo, Count of Orgaz, protonotary of Castile had been a benefactor of this church which was now to be his final resting place. But, just as the priests were about to step forward and inter the count, an astonishing and wonderful thing happened — St. Stephen and St. Augustine appeared and buried him with their own hands.

This legend is portrayed by El Greco in a most remarkable way. His painting is composed of two parts: in the lower half, he portrays the actual entombment, while above, he depicts the count's reception into heaven. In fact, the lower section of the picture also consists of two parts: a ceremony and a miracle. The ceremony reflects a dignity that is eminently Spanish but is, at the same time, painted so realistically that one might well be reminded of works by contemporary Dutch masters. To the right of the bier, on which the armour-clad knight had lain, a priest is reading the prayers for the dead in an attitude of profound meditation; counterbalancing him, on the left, is an unbroken line of mourners. Dressed completely in black, save for their white ruffs, they represent the cream of Toledan society. This gathering of sombre and attentive noblemen strikes one much as a Dutch group portrait would, but here it is the design of the group which is important and not the portraiture as such. There is something hard and at the same time magnificent about these faces, a hint of ascetic egotism and traditional love of metaphysics, a spirit capable of understanding that which is hidden from the senses. But let us continue.

The majority of those present at this ceremony are totally oblivious to the fact that an event of a very different kind is taking place in their midst. The two celestial envoys have arrived to undertake the burial of this faithful servant of the church, but only the burial of his earthly remains; above the count, now divest of his mortality and caught within a vortex of forms and clouds, is being received in solemn audience by Christ and His Virgin Mother. It is a scene in which the substantiality of form has had to give way to the insubstantiality of an ethereal vision. However, two of the assistants at the ceremony—both in the foreground—see what the others cannot see: they are the priest on the right, wearing a white surplice, and the young boy on the left—the one a man of profound faith, the other an innocent child. The priest is gazing upwards and is clearly struck with astonishment, while the boy is looking outwards and, as if wishing to draw the spectator's attention to the miracle, is pointing with his left hand to the two saints. It is the child's innocence which allows him to see the miracle; the only other person privileged to see what is taking place is the spectator who, thanks to El Greco's artistic mastery, is raised to a realm of pure spirit.

And this desire to lift man's spirit is the whole purpose of this strange painting in which El Greco, as in a generous bouquet of flowers, displays all that is best in the painting of his day: the Roman art of composition, the masterly Venetian treatment of colour, and the perfection of Dutch portraiture. Who, after the death of Titian, could have painted such sumptuous vestments as those worn by the two saints; who, after Tintoretto, could have captured with comparable skill the transitoriness of the moment; or who, since Michelangelo, could have solved with such daring the most complex problems of composition? Yet here is something more—an element of the miraculous, a spirit that transcends the limitations of earthly norms. But where does this event take place? If we did not know, we would hardly be able to guess: possibly in a church by night, but there is no hint of this in the picture. The solid, spacious structure, which, since Giotto, had formed the essential basis of all pictorial representation, has disappeared. We are thus left in doubt as to the depth and width of the area portrayed. The figures are crowded together as if the artist had arranged them clumsily, but the glimmering light and ethereal quality of the upper half of the picture create an impression of endless space. The basic idea of this composition is at once simple and old; hundreds of painters had already used it in portraying the Assumption. Yet here its character has undergone a transformation: El Greco has allowed the frame of the picture to cut across the figures in the foreground and, as we cannot see the floor of the church, these men seem to be borne up by some strange, miraculous power. In fact, they form the prelude to an enormous upward surge which, despite the gravitational pull of certain elements in the lower half of the picture, bursts like a flame through the isocephaly of the row of mourners. In the blaze of light above, El Greco both reaffirms and denies the traditional symmetrical arrangement of such pictures; while previous compositions had given pictorial expression to a material, architectonic rhythm, El Greco's does not. Indeed, he has completely abandoned this element, replacing the old, architectonic rhythm with one in which the perpendicular is given particular emphasis. Clouds and figures here obey different gravitational laws to those on earth, and the whole scene amounts to a splendid apotheosis; it is thus an unreal, dreamlike world subject only to the artist's imagination. The colours and individual shapes are intensified; they are no longer reproductions of things seen and go beyond the limits of normal observation. They are like a feverish vision in which the spirit has freed itself from earthly bonds only to lose itself in an astral world, which is both supersensual and superrational.

It was not without justification that El Greco's contemporaries called him 'the seer of spirits.' 'Ya era loco' (he was mad), explains the guide who today takes visitors to look at his painting of the count's entombment. This is a judgment which in the somewhat milder form of 'a noble but disturbed mind' has persisted right up to the present day, even in art books, if written by men with a scientific or materialistic turn of mind. It is with this 'madman' that we are about to concern ourselves—not, however, in order to defend him for that is no longer necessary, but only to examine the origins of his remarkable art.

As is well known, El Greco (or Domenico Theotocopuli, to use the artist's real name) was a Greek; he was born on the island of Crete which was then under Venetian rule, and so, like many of his countrymen, was educated in the great city of lagoons. There, he received his training in Titian's workshop and, although almost 90 years old, it was Titian who imparted to El Greco his profound understanding of colours. The young artist was likewise influenced by the aged Bassano, the painter of sharp contrasts of light and dark, and by Paolo Veronese, that master of delicate silver tones. Yet all this appears to have left El Greco dissatisfied. It was a time when Italian art had reached a turning point and was seized by a new spiritual impulse which, though having begun in Rome, was now affecting the work of many young Venetian painters. Thus, in 1570, we find El Greco in the Eternal City to which he had come with letters of introduction to the miniaturist Giulio Clovio. Then the trail is lost until 1577 when El Greco appears in Toledo, painting pictures which, apart from their technical mastery, have scarcely anything in common with the works of his Venetian youth. Here is a new El Greco, a man who had passed through what was then termed a conversion; and, as such a spiritual rebirth is the key to the work of any great master, it is essential that we search it out to its very roots.

We have no external evidence to aid us, there being neither dates nor paintings to help us piece together what happened to El Greco in the seven years between Rome and Toledo. However, and ultimately this is more important, we can gain a fairly clear picture of the new ideas and impressions he must have received during that time.

We must therefore turn our attention to Michelangelo, the greatest figure of the century and who, more than anyone else, was destined to anticipate the spirit of the coming age. As an old man he created works which, like El Greco's paintings, have for the most part been beyond the comprehension of the critics whose judgments are based on purely naturalistic standards. Thus, the works of Michelangelo's later life have often been considered either unfinished or the products of a senile mind. These include the *Pietà* in the Palazzo Rondanini, the *Deposition* in Florence cathedral and the master's final drawings of the human body. Also belonging to this period is a series of studies for a Crucifixion which tells us a great deal about Michelangelo's ultimate artistic beliefs and also represents his final bequest to mankind (Fig. 26). Why, in his old age, should Michelangelo have turned to this ancient and solemn theme which, for the essentially pagan art of the High Renaissance, had become distinctly unfashionable? One might suggest that he again wished to study the portrayal of the naked human form, a study which for over a hundred and fifty years had been the principal source of artistic progress in Italy. Yet how greatly these 'nudes' differ from everything the Italians had hitherto understood by that term, not discounting Michelangelo's own earlier works.

In a youthful study for *The Battle of Cascina*, Michelangelo had shown the highest possible fidelity to naturalistic representation and at the same time achieved, in the classical sense, perfection of bodily form. Art was knowledge and, having replaced revelation, was destined to show man his environment in its true context, i.e. a context of cause and effect. In the second phase of this development, which saw the creation of such works as the Sistine Chapel and the Medici tombs, Michelangelo transcended the individual human form and created figures which were at once superhuman and heroic—figures representing a godlike, Titanic race which had completely vanquished the old, supernatural powers. In the third phase of this development, to which belongs the *Last Judgment*, the artist's command of the human form was so great that he was able not only to transcend its inherent limitations but, at the same time, to make use of its postures and movements to express those sublime thoughts engendered by his rich experience. Yet this ultimate artistic apotheosis which, in triumphing over nature, had vied with the gods, was destined to disintegrate; never again did Michelangelo produce anything like it. The works of his last years appear to belong to another world. Everything which since the time of Giotto had come to be regarded as the essence of art, in other words everything which had found fulfilment in the early works of Michelangelo, now disappeared; gone is that artistic conviction which sought effectively to relate one form to another, spatially, physically and psychologically. Now one is almost reminded of medieval art. His *Crucifixion* is a simple, virtually formless triad of massive, unarticulated figures, formless, that is, if one thinks in terms of what had hitherto been regarded as form, namely the faithful reproduction of the material world. However, Michelangelo was no longer concerned with that; his figures are now block-like amorphous masses, as indifferent in themselves as stones by the roadside, yet vibrant throughout, volcanic and filled with a tragic element that springs from the very depths of the human soul. Anyone who understands these pictures must find all earlier portrayals of the crucifixion flat and superficial, for the source of Michelangelo's inspiration is not to be found in technical dexterity but flows from a profound inner response to the mystery of Christ's death, a death which redeemed the world. Michelangelo's intention here is to convey something of the force of that experience and to build his figures not, as it were, upwards from externals but outwards from inner depths, as if the body were possessed by the spirit. Hence the indifferences of these figures to every kind of deceitful, ephemeral beauty and their ability to fill us with a powerful sense of life and death.

Turning to the Rondanini *Pietà* we find that it is separated from the *Pietà* of his youth by far more than the experience of a lifetime. All that he once valued most highly now seems worthless: there is no marvellous construction of curves and the master makes no use of his supreme ability to model surfaces or draw his figures together into groups—skills in which he once surpassed the ancients. What now confronts us is a dead, loosely hanging mass devoid of both individualization and physical idealization, yet, at the same time, a deeply moving elegy; never was the dead Christ so effectively portrayed or grief so poignantly revealed, and surely no work of art has ever weighed more heavily upon the human spirit.

Thus, at the end of his life, Michelangelo turned away from the art of the Renaissance, away from a style concerned with the imitation and formal idealization of nature. He also rejected a purely objective view of the world, considering the emotions and experiences of the soul to be of greater importance to art than fidelity to sensory perception. His art thus became anaturalistic. Seen against a broad historical background, however, this was nothing new; looking at the course of art as a whole we see that anaturalistic periods were more common and more durable than those in which naturalism was encouraged. In fact, even in the latter, there invariably persisted an anaturalistic undercurrent, so that periods of naturalism appear almost like islands within a mainstream of artistic thought which regarded the representation of inner emotion as more important than fidelity to nature. And yet to some it must still seem incredible that, at the end of his life, Michelangelo should have turned away from what was not only his own style, but also a style which had helped Italy to achieve a position of prominence and, in so doing, to return to that anaturalistic attitude upheld by medieval Christian art.

It was essentially his spiritual development which brought about this change. In middle life Michelangelo possessed an almost god-like command over all aspects of art conceived in Renaissance terms, and he explored their fundamental problems, rather like a nineteenth-century Impressionist, to the absolute limits of artistic possibility. Michelangelo was undoubtedly fully aware of this and it must have troubled his sensitive spirit to know that one could not express everything that moved man simply by perfecting and intensifying material form. Indeed, he declared as much, in works such as his *Last Judgment.* However, eventually not even the naïve, classical joy of Renaissance worldly affirmation could satisfy him and his deep meditative spirit, following the general trend of the time, returned to the most profound existential questions: what is the purpose of life and what is the relationship between material, transitory, earthly values and those which are eternal and immaterial? Michelangelo grows immeasurably in our estimation when we think of him, the most celebrated artist in the world, lonely and in retirement, struggling to renounce everything on which his fame rested. *Non vi si pensa, quanto sangue costa* are the words the master himself chose to describe his situation and indeed it is difficult for anyone to realize what it must have cost him to break away from the material arts, that is, from painting and sculpture which, at least in that form understood by his contemporaries, could offer him nothing more. It is also impossible for us to conceive how hard it was for him to limit himself to creating, solely for the glory of God, a building whose giant dome was to tower over the sensual pomp of imperial and papal Rome; from now on, the only other works to which his old hands would occasionally turn were those drawings and sculptures which embody not the soul of a great victor but that of a humble seeker. And from these works it is not difficult to calculate exactly how much 'blood' and psychic energy had indeed been spent.

I have dwelt at some length on Michelangelo because his career followed a course of development that was mirrored both by contemporary art and culture, which is proof that it is not, as the nineteenth century imagined, the masses who determine our evolution or material and spiritual culture, but rather our spiritual and intellectual leaders. While even today the Sistine ceiling, the Medici chapel and the *Last Judgment* constitute a rich reservoir of artistic forms, the decisive impulse for Italian art, in the second half of the century, undoubtedly came from those last works of Michelangelo of which we have just been speaking. This fact is clearly revealed in the work of another great artist who also played an important part in El Greco's development — Tintoretto.

Tintoretto, too, had passed through a rebirth and had done so during exactly the same seven years as El Greco. People refer to this simply as the transition from Tintoretto's 'golden style' to his 'green style,' not bothering to wonder what such a transition might really mean. Tintoretto's early pictures rival those of Titian for sheer splendour of colour, yet this was eventually to disappear in favour of a sombre grey-green tonality from which only certain colours shine forth like incandescent flowers. The meaning of this innovation is clear. Hitherto, Venetian art had stood for the richest possible development of the sensual appeal of naturalistic colour, but Tintoretto now replaced this with a ghostly play of fantasy in which colours were either smoky masses or brilliant flashes of light reflecting subjective, spiritual states which have nothing in common with what we actually see.

But not only colour is at stake, for, as we see from a painting like the *Brazen Serpent*, the composition is now also curiously wrenched. The forms are bent and stretched without regard to normal pose or spatial disposition; they are interwoven according to laws perceptible only to a man who is possessed by a passionate intensity. We are confronted by a mass of twisted bodies and lines reminiscent of a witches' sabbath, strange shapes flash out of the darkness as if the figures had been torn asunder and everywhere there hover mysterious lights which, like will-o'-the-wisps, create a ghostly atmosphere. Tintoretto's *Ascension* (Fig. 27) also has this quality of a vision. In earlier representations, the most important elements had been the apostles and the landscape but now all but one of the apostles have, as it were, been thrust into the background. All sense of reality has gone; here, reality is what is in the mind of one man — the Evangelist, whom we find reading some distance away from his companions.

Thus the vision we see is the product of his mind. Christ ascending to heaven is neither near nor far, neither palpably flying upwards nor an optical illusion. He is rather a mental apparition untouched by natural laws and indifferent to reality. As so often in the work of El Greco, light and shade have ceased to perform their natural function; amid his clouds, colours and gestures they are no longer opposites but unite to give expression to dream-like images.

Perhaps Tintoretto's transition to this art of inner sensation can be seen to better advantage in the drawings he made at that time. They are utterly different from any other artistic product of the Renaissance, being the ecstatic record of the artist's visionary experience and containing his impassioned protest against the old conception of art. Indeed, they represent a struggle on the part of the artist for the right to portray things not as they appear to the conventional mind, but as conceived by his imagination and intuition.

From Michelangelo El Greco adopted anaturalism of form while from Tintoretto he took over anaturalistic colour and composition.

However, not even together can they explain El Greco's Toledan style. We are, therefore, forced to look even further afield and talk in terms of a general process, the centre of which was not in Italy but north of the Alps. *Nescio. At ego nescio quid?* These well-known words of the Jesuit Sanchez, which appear in his book on the highest and most universal knowledge, best characterize the situation—'to know that one knows nothing!' North of the Alps, especially in Germany, a ferment had been at work since the beginning of the sixteenth century; yet, whereas today movements are directed against capitalism, they were then aimed at the organized church and its widespread spirit of materialism. As we know, these efforts gave rise to the Reformation. However, discerning spirits soon realized that this reformation was little more than an unhappy compromise, seeking to bring the mysteries of revealed religion into harmony with reason. Thus, whereas the Reformation succeeded in banishing the cult of materialism from the church, it made no attempt to curb its development in the public sector. There had, in fact, been a change for the worse. Now, under the guise of 'good works,' both the individual and the state aimed at an optimum of personal gain and success.

This disillusionment led to scepticism and doubt as to the value of any theory or moral law based on reason, and to a keen awareness of the limitations of man's perception and the relativity of knowledge. One could speak of a political catastrophe following in the wake of a religious one, a catastrophe representing the collapse of the old, secularized dogmatic system of the church and finally embracing scientific and artistic issues as well. The traditional categories of thought had disappeared. Thus what we find expressed in the work of Michelangelo and Tintoretto is not something limited to art but the very criterion of their age. The roads which had hitherto led men to knowledge and helped them to create a spiritual culture were abandoned, the result being an apparent chaos, similar to that with which we are confronted today. Within the realm of art this period, which was by no means a self-contained affair but rather part of an extremely broad movement, the origins of which extend right back to the beginning of the sixteenth century and the influence of which can still be felt, has been somewhat unfortunately labelled 'mannerism.' This term was coined by art historians who, having had a naturalistic training, could not see beyond the fact that most of the artists of the period had, instead of turning to nature for their inspiration, relied entirely on a thorough revaluation of traditional forms. Thus, art was in almost the same position as it had been following the collapse of antiquity. However true all this may be, it tells us little about the essential character of this period. When an intellectual edifice collapses, especially one as large as that which had sustained the later Middle Ages, the Renaissance and the Reformation, devastation is bound to result. Like everyone else concerned with intellectual affairs, artists now lacked a code by which to judge their work. A dramatic upheaval thus took place, and amid a colourful mixture of old and new, philosophers, writers, scholars, politicians and, of course, artists searched for new supports and new goals. Artists turned either towards sheer virtuosity or to those new formal abstractions which had by then solidified into academic theories and doctrines. On the other hand, objectivity also gained in significance, at first in its grosser, sensual aspects alone but later also in its refined, artistic forms. At the same time artists began to employ a much wider range of subject matter in order to awaken interest, or rather, to underline the originality and subjectivity of their attitudes.

Out of this general ferment which, although of enormous interest, we cannot examine in greater detail, there gradually emerged two tendencies that were of vast importance for the future. Both were based on an effort to enrich man's life and understand its secret through psychological knowledge.

The first was both realistic and inductive, for it sought to achieve its goal by a careful observation not only of circumstances but also of those psychological conditions, whether personal or social, which control them. This was the tendency which ran through the work of Rabelais, Bruegel, Callot, Shakespeare and Grimmelshausen, and which in the centuries to follow was to become even more dominant, reaching its peak in the artistic realism of the last century, above all in the novels of Balzac and Dostoevsky.

The second tendency was deductive. It looked for inspiration to the world of feeling which it considered to be the source of all that is noble and enduring. It had as its centre the catholic countries, especially France and Spain, and was mainly evident in the field of religion. Strange as it may seem, it was here, rather than in protestant countries, that Luther's attempts to transfer religion to the sphere of contemplation and inner experience had most effect. Whereas in protestantism these ideas were inhibited by being part of an essentially pastoral teaching, they developed more freely in a catholic environment where the church limited itself to questions of dogma and ritual.

So it is that we find contemplation, meditation and ecstasy all flourishing during the second half of the sixteenth century, especially in France and Spain. In French literature they were to find perfect expression in St. François de Sales's *Introduction to the Devout Life*, a work containing a wealth of practical maxims, coupled with the most delicate psychological advice designed to evoke inner piety and raise the soul to a life based on eternal values and, within the framework of normal social life, help it attain that intensity of feeling which, according to Montaigne, provided contemporary catholicism with a rich substitute for all it had lost and which, having been adopted by the profane arts, was later to form a basis for the poetry of sentiment right up to *Werther* and *Childe Harold*. This new spirituality also left its mark on the graphic arts, as we see from the still little-known work of the French mannerists. Continuing in the tradition of the School of Fontainebleau, as exemplified in the works of Primaticcio, artists such as the sculptors Germain Pilon, Dubois, Freminet, the painter Toussaint du Breuil and the etcher Bellange exhibited a remarkable spiritual vitality, as can be seen, for instance, in Pilon's bust of Jean de Morvillie. This is a work of intense expression, the like of which had not been seen in art since the fourth century with its remarkable portraits of the emperors. Here is a likeness, whose physical attributes are merely a reflection of an inner fire, a likeness which is thus reminiscent of El Greco's self-portrait of some years later. These same artists also drew figures and scenes which might well have been illustrations to the work of St François de Sales. Bellange's *Three Maries at the Tomb* (Fig. 28) offers a fine example of this, especially the figure of Mary, which is full of the spiritual concentration of one totally absorbed in the miraculous. Her figure seems to say to us: 'I no longer belong to the world or to myself and only that which dwells deep within me is truth and blessedness.' These slim, elongated figures with small, delicately bowed heads, sweet expressions and nervous gestures re-appear in the work of El Greco. However, the fact that the whole emphasis of El Greco's paintings falls on the beauty of the soul offers even more cogent proof that he was familiar with the work of the French mannerists and had gained from them what the Italians could never have taught him, namely, the concept of a complete overcoming of the world through sentiment, which was the legacy of northern medieval Christianity. Inevitably this led El Greco to Spain where it had not only been preserved the longest but where, by the sixteenth century, it had gained a completely new impetus. This was the land of the Alumbrados, of St. Ignatius and St. Theresa, a land in which, despite the Renaissance, Gothic was still very much in vogue and in which medieval mysticism flourished, coupled with an intense subjectivity.

Two things characterized these noble spirits, introspection and complete control of the natural limits of thought and feeling. 'What I see,' said St. Theresa, 'is a white and a red, such as one never finds in nature, for they have a brilliance greater than anything one nor-mally sees, and pictures such as no painter has ever painted, pic-tures for which no models can be found but which nevertheless are the essence of nature and life and which contain the most exquisite beauty that one can conceive.' And what St. Theresa experienced in ecstacy El Greco endeavoured to paint, not as one who had joined her ranks but certainly out of the same spirit, a spirit for which inner experience had become the sole key to spiritual exaltation. In spite of its new goals, Italian and French art continued to objectify the world, whereas in Spain there was immediate acceptance of the fact that Renaissance concepts of truth and beauty had to be sacrificed in favour of a free expression of inner emotion. And this 'sacrifice' was made even before the time of El Greco, as we see in a work like Louis Morales's *Pietà*. Here the mannerism of Michelangelo has been wedded to an exaltation that is wholly Spanish. Works like this, at once phlegmatic and passionate, must certainly have influenced El Greco but what undoubtedly had the profoundest influence upon him was his spiritual enviroment as a whole. It was this environment which was able to lead El Greco beyond those new elements of expression, which he had picked up in Italy and France, to a point where he was able finally to subjugate natural objects to his own artistic inspiration. His figures became exaggeratedly long and gained an other-worldly appearance. His *St. Joseph,* in Toledo, around whose head we see Christ and a choir of angels, is no ordinary portrait such as could have been done by thousands of painters before or after him. What we see here is unreal, a pure idea, and does not refer us back to nature but to a life of inner experience. What does this painting convey to us? We see a man possessing little beauty of form, long suffering and worn by labour, a carpenter and yet at the same time we see something more — a man filled with supernatural goodness and humility. Here is one who, under the guidance of God, has grown to great stature, has become worthy to carry the Divine Child and capable of awakening feelings of perfect harmony in the heart of the observer.

El Greco often painted portraits in which the figures bear a striking similarity to one another, almost as if they were brothers, and this is as it should be for, looked at from a higher standpoint, they are indeed the same, being merely the masks and shadows of a deeper reality. But occasionally we find distinct portraits that can only be described as tragic, for example, that of Guevara, the Inquisitor. Standing before this picture, who is not reminded of that dream-like figure of the Grand Inquisitor in *The Brothers Karamazov?* This cowering figure with its cold penetrating gaze is not a particular individual but Fate itself. However, now, El Greco mostly turned his attention to biblical subjects, occasionally striking a note of fantasy as in his painting of *Christ on the Mount of Olives* (Fig. 29) which might well be described as a fairy-story in colour. In the background is dark, formless night, broken only by a shaft of light falling mysteriously on the city of Jerusalem; in the foreground there is a strange twilight in which glimmer fantastic colours. It is like a magic garden into which the celestial descends in the form of a cloud on which is kneeling the figure of a white angel.

Generally, however, it is the visionary character which predominates, as in the painting of *Christ's Resurrection*. The miracle has surprised the guards like an explosion; one is thrown to the ground while the others, struck with fear and wonder, run about wildly, throwing their arms in the air as if hit by a hurricane. Thus the whole painting achieves a magnificent upward thrust, which is made all the more intense by the contrast between Christ and the frenzied figures of the guards. The message of Christ's Resurrection thus comes across with far greater passion and conviction than in any previous work of art. Even more powerful, however, is El Greco's *Opening of the Fifth Seal*: the prophet sees the great day of wrath, sees how the souls of the martyrs, who have died for the Word of God, cry out for vengeance and are each presented with an immaculate white robe. What strikes one most forcefully in this painting are the contrasting sizes of the figures. In the left foreground, close to the edge of the painting, kneels the Evangelist, his hands raised to heaven, while towards the back, in various poses, some of which are reminiscent of the later drawings of Michelangelo, we see the figures of the resurrected to whom the angels are bringing robes. One could almost imagine that St. John were standing, for he is such a colossal figure in comparison to the others. He is not looking at what is happening behind him but towards heaven. Indeed, within him far mightier events are taking place, terrible events of which the figures in the background are merely a suggestion. He is a dynamic figure, the like of which was previously unknown to art and, at the same time, he represents the solution to a problem which, hitherto, must have seemed insoluble, for here is a massive form that is at the same time pure spirit.

Finally, another landscape by El Greco: *Toledo in a Thunderstorm*. However, this is not really a landscape at all but the revelation of a soul which has been torn apart by the demonic forces of nature, a painting in which the mood of the soul and the elemental drama form an entity. Here, with one mighty stroke, El Greco reveals the insubstantiality of earthly things and their metaphysical significance.

At about the time when El Greco painted these pictures, his Spanish contemporary Cervantes conceived Don Quixote, a character which Dostoevsky was to describe as the most beautiful in history, apart from Jesus Christ. Don Quixote was the pure idealist, as indeed was El Greco in the realm of art for his work represents the peak of a European artistic movement which sought to replace the materialism of the Renaissance with a complete spiritual reorientation. El Greco's victory was short-lived, however; from the seventeenth century onward the cult of materialism once again began to gain ground and all the more so as the popes of the Counter-Reformation thoroughly compromised on this point. From now on, the painter of Toledo was to be regarded as a madman and, because of a total failure to recognize his heroic qualities, Cervantes's hero was thought of merely as a comic figure. Nor is it difficult to see why, over the next two hundred years, El Greco was to become more and more neglected; these were years dominated by the natural sciences, by mathematical thought and a superstitious regard for causality, for technical development and the mechanization of culture—years dominated by the eye and the mind but demonstrating an almost complete disregard for the heart. Today, this materialistic culture is approaching its end. I am thinking not so much of its external demise as of its inner collapse which, for over a generation now, we have been able to observe affecting every sphere of cultural life, especially our philosophical and scientific thinking, until today it is disciplines such as sociology and psychology which take precedence. Indeed, even in the natural sciences the old, positivist suppositions, once regarded as absolute, have been fundamentally shaken. We have seen how both in literature and art there has been a turning towards a spirituality freed from all dependence on naturalism, a tendency similar to that of the Middle Ages and the mannerist period. And, finally, one can observe in all cultural sectors a certain unity of events which is apparently directed, by some mysterious law of human destiny towards a new, spiritual, anti-materialistic age. In the eternal rivalry between spirit and matter, the scales now seem to be balanced in favour of the spirit. It is thanks to this turn of events that we have come to recognize in El Greco a great artist and a prophetic spirit, one whose fame is assured for all time.

Translated by John Hardy

Julius von Schlosser

On the History of Art Historiography — "The Gothic"

The notion of a development of art in a three-staged schema: a Golden Age of Antiquity, a low point in the barbaric "Middle Ages," and a rebirth through the great masters of Tuscany, is already alluded to in the writing of Boccaccio and Filippo Villani.* In Boccaccio's novella of Messer Forese (*Decamerone* VI, 5), Giotto is the great restorer "who has brought back to the light that art which had been buried, for many centuries, under the mistaken notions of those who painted, more to please the eyes of the ignorant, than to satisfy the mind of the sages."

This concept, completely worked out into a historical construct (whose influence has not waned until the present day) appears in the short, albeit comprehensive chapter with which Lorenzo Ghiberti introduced his history of the Trecento, as the age of national rebirth. Since it cannot be ascertained whether he was familiar with Villani's writings, Ghiberti is in this regard, as in his artwork, to be considered as original, even though he evidently bases his contentions on local tradition. His view is the following. With striking intuition he recognized that Constantine's acceptance of Christianity heralded a new era; to this very day we still tend to regard the end of the actual Hellenic-Roman antiquity as marked by the great upheavals of the Diocletian era. What follows is not only the demise of all pagan art, but also the destruction of the entire practical and theoretical tradition of art (*volumi, commentarii — liniamenti, re-*

Filippo Villani wrote around 1400 a series of biographies of great men from Florence. The chapter on Giotto includes an outline of the development of Tuscan art, which states that the school of Giotto brought the reawakening of the arts after their long sleep during the Middle Ages. — Ed.

gole [treatises, commentaries—proportions, rules]). Here at the same time is established the historical moment at which the Renaissance, with Ghiberti himself in the lead, wished to pick up the thread again. A dim recollection of the eighth-century controversy about the use of images in Christian worship is evident, when Ghiberti remarks that under the pressure of iconoclastic edicts, the "temples" (that is, the churches, in a classicist manner of speaking that Leon Battista Alberti also always employs) remained bare and without adornment for six hundred years. In Italy, where the study of Roman law was particularly cultivated, the supplementary laws of the emperors of the fifth century directed against the pagan cult must indeed have contributed to this opinion. The regrets of this impassioned lover of art and antiquity are evident in the text, even more so in the inventory report that Ghiberti provides in the third commentary (Frey 2, 2f) about the classical statue discovered in the foundations of the houses of the Brunelleschi in Florence. Since it was found in a hiding place walled in by bricks, Ghiberti maintains that "qualche spirito gentile," moved by pity for such wondrous art, wished to protect it in this manner from complete decay.[1]

Following this deepest deterioration, indeed this complete cessation of all art, the modern Greeks, as degenerate heirs, feebly and coarsely (*debilissimamente e con molta rozzezza*) took up the practice of art again; this practice begins again with the 382nd Olympics after the building of Rome (circa 1157). Ghiberti is by no means here referring to the artistic tradition which, under the last Eastern Roman dynasty of the Palaeologs, continued to linger on in Byzantium from the time of the Latin conquest until Ghiberti's own time. He is of course referring rather to the "Byzantine Renaissance," much closer to him if only through the fact of his firsthand knowledge, an artistic revival that blossomed in Tuscany from the twelfth to the thirteenth century. The entire great Italian tradition of the mosaic in the early and late Middle Ages either did not exist for him, or—since he knew Rome—belonged in his view, to the "maniera greca."

Giotto and his students were the first to achieve once again, in one fell swoop, as it were, the *arte naturale* and the *gentilezza* resulting from true and beautiful proportions (*misure*)—truth and beauty here being understood in the sense of a later period—thereby reaching once again the lofty artistic heights of the ancient Greeks.

This is the leitmotif of the Renaissance, which from then on never vanished.

We know already that this historical construct, which inserted a barbaric "middle period" between the glorious, classical, and national antiquity and the rebirth experienced proudly as such by Ghiberti and his contemporaries, was essentially a product of Florentine humanism, a construct which could only have arisen on Italic soil. Ghiberti must, in his reading of Pliny the Elder, have stumbled upon passages in which he encountered similar ideas. Aside from the complaint which the conservative scholar of antiquity raises concerning the dying art (35,29: *hactenus dictum sit de dignitate artis morientis* [so much should be said about the dignity of the dying art]—a passage which Overbeck characteristically still placed at the end of his edition of antique sources), there is yet another statement (34,52): *Cessavit deinde ars (ol. CXXI) ac rursus olympiade CLVI revixit* (Art came to an end after the 121 Olympiad and came back to life again with the 156 Olympiad; Ghiberti translates "revixit" as "rinacque" = was reborn), which likewise suggests the notion of such an organic rise and decline.

We also find a related reference in the work of Ghiberti's contemporary, L. B. Alberti, who had but little interest in history. In the dedicatory note to his book on painting, addressed to Brunellesco, we encounter the notion that had already cropped up in the work of late-classical authors like Ammianus, that the world, having grown old and weary, was as little able to bring forth great men as it was to bring forth giants. In glowing terms, however, Alberti salutes the new generation of artists whom he finds at work upon his return to his native city in 1434—Brunellesco, Donatello, Masaccio, Luca della Robbia; their works seem to him to be worthy of comparison with those of antiquity. This is more than a writer's compliment, for the men that Alberti picked out with such a confident eye from among the mass of artists truly were the leading lights of Florence. As in the biography of Brunellesco (which we will soon have an opportunity to refer to) we find here, with Alberti, a statement made in reference to architecture, the art form closest to his heart, namely, the truly humanistic notion that the blossoming and decline of art went hand in hand with the political division of power. Thus architecture was born in Asia, experienced its youthful blossoming in Greece, but reached its maturity in the Roman empire and declined in turn with the decline of that political entity. As to the magnificent cathedral art of the Middle Ages, which in his own native region brought forth works like the Pisan and Luccan groups of buildings, the cathedrals of Orvieto, Siena, and finally Florence — all this was completely ignored in his major theoretical opus, as though these great buildings had never existed on earth. Alberti sought to associate modern architecture, as he himself attempted in practice, directly with antiquity. He stood completely cold-faced and unresponsive before the mighty conceptual wave from which the Romanesque and Gothic cathedral art had sprung, explaining it as caused by the influence of the stars or, in modern terms, and quite correctly, as the result of a mood-swing of humanity.[2]

Here as elsewhere, he betrays his distinct feeling of living in a new era; modern democratic Florence with the pagan profane spirit of its noble palaces arises before our very eyes in the open rebuke of that religiously restricted and suffused time: "as if humanity existed for no other purpose than to build churches." Thus in the same breath he makes short shrift of the Gothic pointed arch, almost as though it had nothing to do with the subject at hand, namely architecture, just because it was not classical and, moreover, of little practical value. So speaks the man who, in theory as well as in practice, prefigured the later Palladianism, the true restorer of Vitruvius, who realized his own ideal vision in San Francesco in Rimini, where the old basilica is disguised as a temple *all'antica*. This is one of the most authentic Renaissance buildings in existence: the sepulchre of the tyrant in the old sense who wishes, in death as in life, to be accompanied by his humanistic entourage.

Filarete is a second contemporary and countryman of Ghiberti. *
The precious-sounding humanist's name of this Florentine who left home early in his career already indicates his tendencies. To him antiquity truly constitutes the "classical" ideal, and the manner in which he parades his rather paucit learning accords completely with the plenitude of classical reminiscences with which he adorns his

---

*Filarete (Antonio Averlino, ca. 1400—after 1465); was an architect and sculptor who worked in bronze. Between 1451 and 1464 he wrote a treatise on architecture in the form of dialogues between himself, his patron, Duke Francesco Sforza of Milan, and this latter's son, Galeazzo. The treatise includes a description of the foundation of an ideal city, Sforzinda (see the quote from Book XIII on p. 211). — Ed.

own writings. As opposed to the *maniera antica,* which he accords
sole legitimacy, there is the *maniera moderna,* Filarete's term for
"Gothic" architecture; the latter is to him nothing more than a
contemptible "*praticuccia,*" upon which he places a formal curse.
The barbarian theory, which is not yet present in Ghiberti's
thought, appears albeit fleetingly, in the writings of Filarete. The
"*Ultramontani*" are to him the original perpetrators of this nonart;
this is the first trace of a view that would be so elaborated upon in
the following years. Brunellesco appears in the same way as a restorer of the *maniera antica,* just as Giotto was lauded by Boccaccio and
thereafter as the rediscoverer of the ancient "natural" spatial painting. But even the architecture of Giotto's day falls under the sway of
Filarete's curse; for he is absolutely convinced that the rebirth of
architecture is a brand-new achievement of his own generation.
This is evident in his comparison of architecture with literary language, which like the former had in his view only just in the last
thirty or forty years been reawakened and salvaged out of "barbarism," an extraordinary opinion, pointing in the direction of the
hybrid linguistics of the humanists, which culminated in the linguistic patchwork of the *Hypnerotomachia* or in the writing of Luca
Pacioli.* In general, however, Filarete looks down with great scorn
on his own time, a time in which no more Ciceros or Virgils will
arise; however, he himself in his Milanese buildings had to pay
ample homage to that *maniera moderna* which he otherwise liked
to belittle. Like Alberti, he too polemicizes against the pointed
arch, which he himself used or was forced to use. Its reputed great
solidity is in his view an illusion; besides, his ancients didn't know
it, reason enough to scorn it. Far more original is an aesthetic
objection to it, viz. that the eye encounters an unpleasant resistance
in the broken line of the pointed arch, whereas the sight of the
rounded arch is completely calming and satisfying. The Renaissance, striving after harmony and balance, speaks forth out of this
very remarkable statement. This accords with the fact that Filarete,
like his predecessors, perceived the loss of the classical sense of
proportion as the essential root of the low quality of "modern" art;

***Hypnerotomachia Polifili* ("The Dream Battle of Love of Polifilo"), an allegorical
novel by Francesco Colonna. Dealing with the rediscovery of classical antiquity and
written in a mixture of Italian, Latin, and Greek, it was published in Venice in 1499.
Fra Luca Pacioli (c. 1445–after 1509), famous mathematician, friend of Piero della
Francesca, L. B. Alberti, and Leonardo. — Ed.

ever since the end of the fourteenth century, artists as well as laymen agreed on the importance of rediscovering the lost tradition, that is, the artistic *rules* of antiquity. We recall the important roles that the terms *symmetria* and *misure* played in the thinking of Landino and Ghiberti; Filarete also insists that practical work alone, like that of Brunellesco, was not enough: the whole matter had to be codified. Here lies the point of departure for both the Renaissance study of proportions (with which in fact Filarete begins his first book), and also for the symmetry of the early Florentine Renaissance. This symmetry is clearly in intentional opposition to the picturesque freedom of the Gothic, which, however, is based on a deeper law, that of its organic growth from the inside outward, like the efflorescence of a noble tree. The striving after symmetry culminated in the "Fassadenbau,"* a form of architecture already current in Tuscany in the Middle Ages, and still a bugbear to this day; its influence is reflected, as though in conscious parody, in the architectonically disguised "Kunstschränke" (armoires) of the Augsburg workshops of the seventeenth and eighteenth centuries.

In Filarete's writing, as in Ghiberti's, we find a fleeting appearance of that important expression "rinascere," which was later established as the term for an already *ab ovo* existent notion. Here of course the word is still used in the author's own subjective sense. With clear comprehension of the significance of the new style, Filarete's princely patron says (Book XIII): *"mi pare rinascere e vedere questi cosi degni hedifici (sc. di Roma)."* (I seem to be reborn and to see those noble buildings [i.e., of Rome].) What Filarete (or the duke) means is really the rebirth of antiquity in architecture, which could be more clearly and strikingly demonstrated by comparison with the ruins than the rebirth of painting as practiced by the ancients ("al pari degli antichi Greci," as Ghiberti puts it)—a construct based exclusively on the classical literature of art, for this period could not yet have the faintest idea of what ancient painting really looked like.

These men could not realize, particularly in their opposition to the *maniera Greca,* that the Byzantine tendency in painting (as

---

*Fassadenbau: This untranslatable term of Schlosser's designates a building in which the architectural composition of the facade is largely independent of its interior, so that the facade masks rather than mirrors the interior space. — Ed.

opposed to the grandiose decorative style of Gothic stained-glass windows) preserved, in the *rilievo* of its modeling and in the depth of its rendition of space, a classical heritage on Italian soil. Thus the discrepancy, that the "Rebirth" in this humanistic sense was perceived and acknowledged first in the *imitative arts* (as in literature), then, a whole century later, in architecture, and again, almost two centuries later, in music—as a reaction to the last remnant of the "Gothic" in the arts of the Netherlands.

The theory of a Middle Ages in art, first summed up in brief by Ghiberti, was greatly elaborated in an excursus in the anonymous biography of Brunellesco, which has recently been ascribed again to Antonio Manetti;* it must in any case have been written by a younger contemporary of the great architect. It is one of the most remarkable documents of the Quattrocento, as it includes a complete outline of the development of architecture from the most ancient times to the new era of Brunellesco. The ideas elaborated here for the first time in such detail have become, especially through Vasari, common property of art history; for the above-mentioned *vita* of Brunellesco was one of Vasari's foremost sources of information about the Quattrocento. They are probably, at least in part, based upon classical ideas, as expounded above all in the introduction to the second book of Vitruvius; yet in their condensation and further elaboration they appear altogether original and new.

Just like the very first inventions of mankind, architecture also arises out of bare necessity; the human habitation is its point of departure, the twig-and-tree cabin its oldest product. Chance discoveries like the burning of lime lead to further technical advances. Following this exordium, the anonymous author offers a brief overview of the architectural history of the ancient Orient. A noteworthy peripheral look at the nomadic Mongols (*Tatari*) is probably based on the powerful impressions evoked by the written reports of medieval Italian explorers like Marco Polo. Then Greece steps forward as the heir to the culture of Asia; it is here that architecture first evolves into an art, whereas in the Orient—with the exception of the architectural works of the chosen and godly inspired people—it had served the purposes of pomp and ostentatious display

---

Antonio di Tuccio Manetti (1423–1491), a mathematician, is by now generally confirmed as the author of the life of Brunelleschi.—Ed.

rather than of art. Here too profane architecture is older than the true work of art, the temple; for the art of building precludes a knowledge of the art of carpentry, and the former evolved out of the latter. Centuries before Goethe's youthful essay (on Strasbourg Cathedral), the notion is already expressed here that even in the case of this quintessentially artistic nation, art was formative long before it was beautiful. In extensive experimentation, what is pleasing is separated from what is displeasing, what is meaningful and correct from what is deficient, until finally one arrives at the notion of the classical orders, the classic idol of the Renaissance, in which Renaissance man saw the fulfillment of his striving after harmony and regularity. We also find another notion which had yet been expressed in Ghiberti's writings. It is the belief in the inherent connection between absolute political power and the prospering of culture and art, an idea that is unmistakably derived from classical ethics and which lay particularly close to the Renaissance heart; it has its proponents to this day, although the highest evolution of German as well as Italian culture loudly contradicts it. It is architecture that follows the lead of wealth and princely splendor, thus artistic leadership passes from decaying and poverty-stricken Greece to the "*donna del mondo,*" the immensely expanding world power of Rome, and disappears in turn with the decline of the Roman empire. The classicistic foundation of this entire theory of the blossoming and decline of culture is evident.

The Romans are followed by the barbarians, Vandals, Goths, Longobards, Huns, and others who brought their own architects and masons with them into the conquered Roman provinces. These barbarians, themselves unskilled in any artistic practice, make use of the services of their neighbors, above all the Germans, who become their vassals. This is a strange conclusion *a posteriori* from the experience of the Renaissance itself; the artistic expertise of the German craftsmen still prized in Italy to this very day, the recollection of the clean, minute work of the German hand, of the goldsmiths, stonecutters, carvers, of the inventors and perfectors of the art of printing and engraving, so widespread, known, and sought after in Italy in the fifteenth century—all this is at the root of the aforementioned notion. This *barbaric,* this German, architecture— the *maniera Tedesca* of the later period—spreads throughout all Italy until finally Charlemagne chases out the last barbarians, the

Longobards, and also puts an end to their "collegi"—probably a vague reminiscence of the guilds of the *magistri Comacini**—and makes peace with the Roman popes and the sparse remnant of the *Respublica Romana*. *Karl* (whose Germanic nature has during this period already been completely superseded by the Charlemagne of the northern French *Chansons de geste,* ever popular in Italy, and the *reali di Francia†*), then hires Roman architects, in whose practice some of the good old traditions have been preserved, since they were born and grew up among the ruins of Roman splendor. With their help he rebuilds the fallen city of Florence, in whose oldest remaining buildings, erected in his time, San Pietro in Scheraggio and Santissimi Apostoli, at least glimpses of the ancient Roman manner become visible. What we have here are legend-tinted memories of two major facts of medieval art history: the restoration effected under the aegis of the reviver of the old empire, known to us today as the "Carolingian Renaissance," and the "Protorenaissance" of Tuscany (associated by an old local tradition with the mythic rebuilder of Florence), which ran parallel to the activities of the Roman Cosmati** and similar efforts in Umbria. The focus of attention is, as we know, the group of buildings around the Baptistery of Florence, which was thought to be a classical temple of Mars. How Brunellesco continued this national "classical" tradition has been elaborated at great length by Vasari in his second edition (Vita of A. Tafi).

With the demise of the Carolingian dynasty, the empire falls back to the Tedeschi, and the barely acquired "good" architectural manner is once again lost. This foreign German manner of building predominated then in Italy up until the time of Brunellesco.

The anonymous *vita* written by a personal friend of Brunellesco's, whether by Antonio Manetti or by someone else, is from all appearances not the work of a professional architect, but rather of a

---

Magistri Comacini: master stonecutters, masons, and builders from the region around Como, who in the eighth and ninth centuries were united in colleges and corporations by the Longobardian kings.—Ed.

†*Chansons de geste*: a series of eighty or ninety French heroic epics of the Middle Ages, which together constitute the national epic of France. *Reali di Francia*: legendary history of the kings of France, prior to Charlemagne, by Andrea da Barberino (first edition, Modena, 1491).—Ed.

**Cosmati is a modern term, derived from the frequent appearance of the proper name "Cosma"; it designates Roman craftsmen who specialized in marble decoration, from the early twelfth to the early fourteenth century.—Ed.

literate and historically learned man with the liveliest interest in art, a layman like those who held important positions in the art commissions in Florence. This work is clearly the product of the most impassioned partisan disputes over the dome of the cathedral; it makes no bones about its tendency and its opposition, namely against Ghiberti. The extraordinary compendium on the history of architecture once again mirrors the problems of concern to the followers of the two masters; the historical intuition is in places surprisingly brilliant and deep, very impressive from the distance of time. In Ghiberti's writings as well, the period from Constantine up until the rather wretched products of the *maniera Greca* is a period of deepest decline, which he however imputes to the complete loss of the classical tradition as a consequence of the alleged prohibition against the use of images in the early Christian church. According to his schema, he speaks only of the imitative arts and leaves the sphere of architecture untouched; it is Filarete who picks up the thread here. In Filarete's writing the *Ultramontani* appear as the originators of the bad "modern" manner, as a parallel phenomenon to the bad artistic manner of the modern Greeks. This construct is then developed into a complete system in the *vita* of Brunellesco. The synthesis and popularization of both views is finally the work of Vasari, who does however have one noteworthy predecessor.

The theory to which we have just been introduced had already by the beginning of the sixteenth century spread beyond its place of origin, Florence, and had taken root in that Roman circle that would have an important influence on the further development. Of this we have proof in the significant dedicatory epistle to Leo X,* whose inspirator, if not author, we have reason to believe was *Raphael* himself; this epistle was apparently intended to serve as an introduction to the artist's monumental archeological plan of Rome.[3] It also contains a summary discussion of the evolution of architecture, inspired by the author's enthusiasm for the Roman ruins, and by his Vitruvian studies. Here too, antiquity comes to an end in the times of Diocletian and Constantine, with the one exception that architecture still survives a while at its old high level of

---

*The alleged *Letter of Raphael* has been variously attributed to Baldassare Castiglione, Fabio Calvo, Bramante, and Peruzzi. In the second edition of his *Kunstliteratur* (1935), Schlosser endorses the opinion of F. Ertl, that it was in fact written by Castiglione. — Ed.

artistry, whereas sculpture and painting hasten hopelessly to their demise. This thesis is substantiated, interestingly enough, by reference to the surviving Roman monuments, the reliefs of the Thermae of Diocletian and the Arch of Constantine; as we know, it has been upheld to the present day. Then begins the unflagging decline of all areas of culture. Along with their destruction of the political framework of the Roman empire, the barbarians, Goths, and Vandals foremost, also destroy its great monumental expression, its architecture, and Greece herself, the matrix of the arts, perishes; the new *Greek* manner is nothing but a sad caricature of the old. Parallel to this new Greek manner, the Germans are evolving a style of the middle period, in which some manifest improvement makes it appearance, and which survives in several places.[4] By and large, however, this style is characterized by a depressing lack of proportions and taste, particularly in its abstruse and fantastic ornamentation, its queer caryatids and such aberrations. The static and aesthetic arguments in defense of the rounded as opposed to the pointed arch are already familiar from Filarete's writings. Curious here is the notion that crops up for the first time, that "German" architecture evolved from the primitive branch-huts of the forests of Germania; that the tied-together branches of the trees grown in the wild evolved into the form of the pointed arch. Further elaborations in the text show that this naturalistic theory is to be viewed as a counterimage to the account of the derivation of the Doric order from the original log cabin, as expounded by Vitruvius (IV, 2). We know what a long life this naive attempt at an explanation has had, namely, in German Romanticism, to whose fantastically dressed-up sense of nature and nation it was particularly well suited. The Romantics alluded to it again and again, and the sorry notion still crops up occasionally today.[5]

Thus Ghiberti's *maniera Greca* and the *maniera Tedesca* were presented as parallel developments, common sources of the new bad taste in art; with a bold conceptual leap over centuries, the blossoming of the medieval culture of the North and West, the high art of the French cathedrals (derived from the Celtic-Germanic spirit), and the chaotic beginnings of the art of the migration period were all tied together. The final codification and propagation of this developmental theory was effected around the middle of the sixteenth century through Vasari's great historical work (1550); his predecessors, Billi, and the Anonymous Magliabecchianus, concerned only as they were with the collection and sorting of material, had passed over these problems.

But Vasari found in two of his key sources, Ghiberti and the anonymous biography of Brunellesco, and probably in the prevailing scholarly opinions of his time, a foundation upon which to build; before him Rabelais had already adopted the Renaissance hatred of the Gothic barbarians and imported it to his native land.

Vasari's historical thesis is formulated in the *Proemio* to the first part of his work, and substantially expanded and deepened in the second edition of 1568, thanks in large part to the wealth of material he found in his reading of Paulus Diaconus's history of the Longobards (Kallab, *Vasari-Studien*, p. 34). In his depiction of the decline of Roman architecture he clearly follows the vita of Brunellesco; the reliefs of the Arch of Constantine serve him, also, as prime example in support of his argument. In the second edition of his work he includes a very substantial account of the history of medieval Italian art which is of no small interest. He remains entirely faithful in his fundamental precepts to the theories developed by Ghiberti and the author of the anonymous vita. The "barbarian theory" is expounded in great detail; it reads like a reminiscence in the part in which the Roman popes, in particular Gregory the Great, are accused of having with their interdiction destroyed the last remnants of pagan splendor; here Vasari displays a close affinity with Gelli. The Carolingian Renaissance in Florence is likewise discussed; the description of the Romanesque churches of Pisa and Lucca is Vasari's own original work; here too he claims to detect signs of substantial improvement in artistic taste. Finally, he does not overlook the Romanesque architecture in northern Italy, in Venice (San Marco) as well as in Lombardy.

If we lay bare the core inside these mythological shells, we must conclude that the Renaissance (in the person of its key literary proponent, Vasari) intuitively recognized the essence of the matter, even if it arrived at a rather one-sided evaluation of it. In the notion of the much scorned *maniera Greca,* as in that of the *maniera Tedesca,* lies the seed of the true perception that Byzantium and Paris were the two great poles of medieval artistic and cultural developments to the east and to the west, whose emanations intersected most decisively in Italy, the land in the middle, where the twilight of classical culture never completely faded. In his depiction of the "Middle Ages," that era branded already by Vasari (I, 253) with the long-surviving stigma of the *dark* ages, this latter can hardly lay on his colors thickly and harshly enough. He inventively heaps a selection of maligning epithets upon that "*infelice secolo*" with its "*goffezza*" and "*rozzezza*" (plumpness and coarseness). German architecture (which, by his reckoning, also begins with the migration period) is completely lacking in the characteristic Renaissance requirements, *misura, grazia,* and it possesses neither *disegno* nor *ragione alcuna* (Proem. I, 233). Its architectural manner is ridiculous, it reminds us more of a house of cards than one of stone or marble (Dell'architettura, c. III); the works of the Langobards are *di bruttissima e disordinata maniera,* the paintings and sculptures "baronesche" (clumsy). The wretched Greeks—*i quali piuttosto tignere che dipingere sapevano,* who were more housepainters than painters—restricted themselves finally to purely linear drawing on colored ground (*altro non era rimaso che le prime linee in un campo di colore,* I, 242); their figures, standing on their tiptoes with outstretched hands and wildly distended eyes (*occhi spiritati*), without modeling (*il non avere ombre*) or any psychical expression,[6] are just as childish as the sculptures, *cosi goffe e si ree,* that one could not even imagine anything worse, pure *fantocci* and *berlingozzi* (jumping Jacks and country bumpkins). In his technical introduction (*Introduzione alle tre arti del disegno, Dell'architettura,* cap. III. s.f.ed. Milanesi, I, 139 f.), he finally summed up his judgment, especially of this *maledizione,* as he condescendingly calls it. For the first time in the literature of art, it is the Goths who are cited as the actual originators:

> This manner was the invention of the Goths, for, after they had ruined the ancient buildings, and killed the architects in the wars, those who were left constructed the buildings in this style. They turned the arches with pointed segments, and filled all Italy with these abominations of buildings, so in order to not have any more of them their style has been totally abandoned. May God protect every country from such ideas and style of buildings! They are such deformities in comparison with the beauty of our buildings that they are not worthy that I should talk more about them. (Translation by Louise S. Maclehose.)

What Vasari presents is a complete distortion, but in the caricature there is much that is accurately observed. To the artists of the High Renaissance, with their altogether different problems of space and light, their tendency toward corporeal modeling and depth, this grandiosely decorative art of the Middle Ages with its strictly two-dimensional style must have remained a riddle. At best its technical proficiency (the mosaics of San Giovanni) occasionally elicited a cool word of praise. Vasari recognizes in his own time the high point of the reaction against the long-subdued *maniera vecchia,* which he sharply distinguishes from the true and good *maniera antica*[7] — that same *maniera antica* that Filarete had still perceived, as a living *maniera moderna.* The rebirth of architecture and the imitative arts did not occur simultaneously; as the latter had died out in late antiquity earlier than the former, so they were also restored one century earlier by Cimabue and Giotto. The *maniera Greca* is overcome earlier than the *maniera Gotica,* which Brunellesco, identifying completely with the native and Roman antiquity, finally brought down, fully conscious of the fact that he had thereby accomplished a feat similar to that of the aforementioned great restorers of painting, (V. di F. Brunellesco II, 337),

> Filippo had two very great purposes in his mind, the one being to restore to light the good manner in architecture, which, if he could effect, he believed that he should leave a no less illustrious memorial of himself than Cimabue and Giotto had done; the other was to discover a method for constructing the Cupola of Santa Maria del Fiore in Florence, etc. (Translation by Blashfield and Hopkins)

We can actually put our hands here on the classicistic foundation of this whole theory of the *rinascimento;* the great ideal of a true art, the *maniera antica,* stands here surrounded by its national halo, far removed from any other living and half-extinguished art. Vasari recognized the two great motivating forces of the new era in naturalism on the one hand, and imitation of antiquity on the other;[8] here, too, he was expanding older ideas. Niccolo Pisano reached out of the midst of the *maniera goffa* of the Greek sculptors back to the classical sculptures of the Campo Santo. Sculpture in general moves out in advance of paintings and has an easier time of it, because of its inherent naturalism. Vasari evolves here the basic themes of his much discussed Paragone (Life of Andrea Pisano, ed. cit. I, 482:

> It is, however, certain that if the art of sculpture incur the danger of losing its vitality, there is always less difficulty in its restoration than in that of painting, the former having ever the living and natural model, in the rounded forms which are such as she requires, while the latter cannot so lightly recover the pure outlines and correct manner demanded for her works.) (Translation by Blashfield and Hopkins)

Andrea Pisano also affiliated himself with the new manner of Giotto and with antiquity (ibid.). These are ideas in which, despite their one-sided tendencies, we do find some accurate observations, ideas that have had and continue to have an influence down to our day.

Vasari did not yet, it is true, use the catchwords "Gothic" (*maniera, stile Gotico*) and "Renaissance" (*rinascimento*), terms later taken into the language of all cultured nations, but he had already consolidated the entire theory of the Renaissance in its essence; *Goti e greci goffi* appear side by side as the carriers of artistic decay (V. di A. Pisano, I, 483).

This then is the structure that Vasari erected out of the building blocks handed down to him by preceding generations; as a result of the European renown that his historical work achieved, it had a decisive influence that still continues, at least in part, to this very day. The construct of three major artistic periods, as presented in standard art handbooks, is based upon the foundation of his ideas.

Before we further examine the evolution of these ideas, particularly insofar as they apply to the Gothic Middle Ages, we must consider the very complex question of the circumstances that gave rise to them.

The antipathy for the Middle Ages, as we encounter it on the special plane of art from Villani onward, is an old inheritance of Florentine humanism. Ever since Petrarch, humanism was in open feud with scholasticism (which had just found its greatest poetic proponent in Dante), and this in spite of their many persistent crosscurrents. In life we often observe an antagonistic relationship, in which the up-and-coming young generation almost always finds itself up against the "old fashioned," the immediately preceding generation of the father, which it must after all surpass, and in so doing, it not infrequently harkens back to the views and sensibility of the grandfather's time. Not for naught do we find in Italy the beautiful old custom that the grandchild takes the name of the grandfather, thus the third generation renews the first. So to the Humanists, ever since Petrarch, the period which we still refer to as the "Middle Ages," a term derived from their way of thinking—as though it were no independent period but a mere transitional stage—was solely a period of barbarism and spiritual darkness, and even to study its history was hardly worth the effort, on account of its poor historians. Beyond that dark period, in the distant past arose the wondrous edifice of classical culture, bathed in the magical light of fantasy, a culture to which the humanists reached back with all the more passionate longing, since antiquity embodied for them a national-political ideal of bygone national grandeur and universal expansion of power. Whosoever among the humanists, like, for instance, Biondo da Fiorlì, took up the study of the history of the Middle Ages, started out with all the odds against him and could only reckon with a limited interest and an even more limited fame—no small consideration in the fame-hungry Renaissance!

This antipathy derived from purely national-social motives. Vossler, in his great monograph on Dante, elucidated clearly how in the construction of the ideals of the high Middle Ages, the Italians stood by passively while the Celto-Germanic peoples to the north and west applied their best energies. During that period, the Italians remained dedicated to realistic fields, to mathematics, grammar, jurisprudence, in which they had recourse to their sharp reason. Thus even their national literature comes into its own later than that of all other Romance peoples, later even than that of the Germanic nations, but Italian literature immediately takes a modern thrust in its language, style, and character, so that it remains to an altogether different degree, close and comprehensible to the men of today, living with and among them; Old French and Middle High German, on the other hand, are dead languages today, only maintaining a shadowy existence in the scholar's study. Behind the strong "Tuscan" feeling of Florence always stood the idea of the rebirth of all of Italy. However many bridges still connect this *rinascimento* with the Middle Ages of scholasticism, troubadour poetry and the Gothic, it nevertheless has a different, specifically national character, and this rebirth marks the beginning, not only for Italy, but for all of Western Europe, of a new "modern" era. In recent times the term Renaissance has been frequently and often futilely bandied about in discussions; these old Florentines were altogether justified, from their own standpoint, in tracing their role as a civilized nation and as the first "modern" one among all others back to this "rebirth." (K. Burdach eloquently demonstrated how this idea sprang forth from the deep well of Italian religious and political thinking.) For here was a people that saw a high culture of long duration rise and decline in the wake of the onslaught of younger peoples from the north and east, peoples that had still to create their own new culture out of their primitive beginnings and the remains of the Mediterranean tradition. Just as the language of Italy remains closer to classical Latin than that of the former Roman provinces of "Romania," so much so that today without any undue effort one can still compose entire pages that are both Latin and Italian, so too does Italian culture have its roots deeply planted in classical soil; the fact that this exhausted, fallow ground required centuries of rest is but a function of the law of the natural order. What is classical is that peculiar individualism, so intimately mingled with a municipal and regional sense of self, which Burckhardt, with keen intuition, pointed out as one of the fundamental elements of the Renaissance. Classical is that *rilievo* in painting that Giotto salvaged from the much scorned *maniera Greca* (in complete contrast to the decorative flat style of Gothic stained-glass painting), and which, thanks to the Sienese, first triumphed in France, the country of origin of the Gothic. Finally, neither the spatial art of architecture nor homophony as the foundation of all Italian music can bely their classical origin, both being in sharpest contrast to the northern developments in these two areas.

Of all this, the Italians of the "rinascimento" could not of course have been aware; but it was the dark bond of blood relations that bound them to antiquity. In the *Hypnerotomachia* of Fra Colonna of Treviso, this Renaissance dream, dreamt amongst the ruins of the national Antiquity, found its passionate expression — so much so, that a tendency already in evidence with Boccaccio, namely, the disastrous attempt at an artificial archaization of the language, leads to a most peculiar hybrid, a latin *volgare*, as it were, with certain strains reminiscent of the naive clerical Latin of the old notaries. However, even Colonna did not put himself into such a profound opposition to common parlance, as Byzantine Hellenism vis-à-vis the "rhomaic" tongue of the people.

The ancient civilized nation had to give up its former dominance; it saw the appearance of hoards and hoards of foreign conquerors on its native soil, and even if the rulers from the north, following their age-old ambition, renewed the Roman empire, it remained nevertheless an empire in the foreign hands "of the German Nation." Later the linguistically related, albeit largely ethnically different French and Spanish peoples who settled in northern and southern Italy, drove the thorn even deeper into the heart of the entire Italian nation. Ever since that time, the flame of the "risorgimento," of the political rebirth of the nation, was never again extinguished; the best men of Italy kept it burning. The old Guelfic ideal of a universal papacy, which, since the exile in Avignon, had become a national institution, defended the cause of *Italy* against the Ghibelline dream of a medieval universal monarchy. Only in Italy could that heirloom of classical Hellas, the designation of all other nations as "barbarians," retain its meaning, a habit that persists, openly or clandestinely, to the present day.

The Italians of the Middle Ages must often have been overcome by a mood similar to the one so movingly described in the beautiful old local legend of de-Hellenized Paestum,* and which we find expressed for the last time in Dio Chrysostomus' speech† on the dying Greek colony of Olbia in the distant barbarian land. It is little wonder then that the hatred of the living heirs of antiquity for the foreign invaders, the Tedeschi, was projected back into an earlier period, that above all the oldest Germanic rulers of the land, the noble Goths, became the butt of this hatred, that *Gotico* became a term of contempt, a curse, and henceforth elicited a completely different resonance in the soul of the repressed and divided Italian

---

*In the 1st century B.C. the inhabitants of *Paestum* were completely "barbarized" in language and manners. But they celebrated once every year a festival wherein they addressed their gods by their old Greek names and reminded each other, weeping, that they had once been Greeks. See Athenaeus, *The Deipnosophists*, with tr. by Charles Burton Gulick, VI, Cambridge, Harvard University Press; London, Heinemann, 1950, pp. 409–411. — Ed.

†Dio Chrysostomus (A.D. 40–112), philosopher, writer on ethics and politics, friend of the emperor Trajan. — Ed.

nation than did, say, *"Gaulois"* or "Old-Frankish" among the French and the Germans. It is not for naught that Petrarch in his famous canzone *Italia mia* lauded the Alps as the dividing wall between his sweet homeland and the *"tedesca rabbia."*

In the history of Italian culture, the rise of the greatest and most national saint of the Italian peninsula constituted a juncture without equal; it is the moment in which Italy once adds her voice to the great European fugue of nations. How miraculous that Saint Francis had a name related to the heretofore dominant Frankish people; his sepulchral church in Assisi is the first monument of the "northern" style in Italy, and from' then on French and German architects were a presence in Italy up until the days of the Renaissance. We are well aware how their northern feeling had everywhere to establish a compromise with the southern classical sense of space; we also know with what national bias this "Gothic" movement evolved in the major cathedrals of central Italy, but also in Venice, and for how long it remained a dominant force, particularly in northern Italy. Finally, we still recall, as a satirical postlude to the great drama, the delightful and instructive late-Renaissance tale of the Gothic tailor Cremona in Bologna,* so charmingly narrated by Springer in his *Scenes From More Recent Art History.*

It is remarkable, then, how completely Italy broke, both in theory and practice, with its "middle period." Humanism, which celebrated antiquity, waving it about as a national-political banner, would have liked it best to completely expunge this past from the annals of history. The old conquerors of Rome, the Goths above all, were now viewed as the root of all evil—had they not brought down the Roman empire and even dared to storm the *caput mundi?* One of the most spirited champions of humanism in the Quattrocento, Lorenzo Valla, already employed "Gothic" as a derogatory term. In his book, *Elegantiae Linguae Latinae,* which sought to reawaken the purity of the "almost extinguished" old national language, he defends the "Antiqua" as the modern script in place of the "Gothic" monastic script. Such expressions are still in common usage today

*When in 1589 foreign architects submitted plans for the completion, in Renaissance style, of the Gothic church of S. Petronio in Bologna, the tailor Cremona made himself the leader of a popular movement, which opposed this project out of sympathy with the Gothic. See Anton Springer, *Bilder aus der neueren Kunstgeschichte*, 2d ed., I, Bonn, bei Adolph Marcus, 1886, pp. 375–402.—Ed.

despite their historical inaccuracy. However, the efforts to restore the monumental script *all' antica* constitute an independent chapter in the history of the Renaissance in which even the German Dürer had his part. This view has close affinities with the one already firmly rooted in Florence, of the death and rebirth of art; Valla likewise expressly extends his pronouncement to include "*illae artes quae proxime ad liberales accedunt*" (those arts which come closest to the liberal ones, i.e., painting, sculpture, and architecture).

Such views must then necessarily have had an influence on the theoretical appraisal of that architectural and decorative manner that truly did derive from the north—even if its influence manifested itself in a much later period. Despite its amazing adaptation to Italian conditions, this northern manner was nonetheless never perceived as an indigenous part of the Italian culture. The first guidebook to Florence flatly calls the old Cathedral facade a work *senz' ordine e misura* (without order and proportion)—the shibboleth of the Renaissance; its author, the *pretuccio* (phony) Albertini, pretends to be able to provide a "better" model. Even the works of the native sculptors, as soon as they take on Gothic decorative forms, appear strange and incomprehensible to these later generations; the magnificent marble altar of the Massegne in the Church of San Francesco in Bologna is scorned as a mere "opera Tedesca," without an artist's name, in the oldest guidebook to that city, Lamo's *Graticola* (1560). Hardly a decade earlier, Vasari had codified that harsh and presumptuous judgment which was, however, totally in accord with the development and mood of the nation. But characteristically, even before Vasari, Rabelais, the representative of a nation that had always for better or worse functioned as the leaven of Europe, brought these views as the latest fashion back home across the Alps; the French were the first and quickest to break with their "Gothic" past, their own product. In *Pantagruel* (II, 8) the Goths appear as the corruptors of "good" taste, in literature, that is.

A northern element did however survive in Italy for the longest time: the art of the Netherlands, in the broadest sense. In the past the new art had come from Tuscany via Avignon to France; simultaneously, as we have only recently learned, the other *ars nova,* the music of the sweet new style, came from Florence and achieved dominance over the *ars antiqua,* the Parisian mensural music of the high Middle Ages. From these roots, the northern French as well as the Netherlandish painting and music of the new style evolved; both came back to Italy in northern transformation in the fifteenth century and became, particularly in the northern and southern parts of the peninsula, the truly fashionable art of the Quattrocento, without thereby losing its foreign, and just for this very reason, its enticing character. Like Rabelais, Francisco da Hollanda had already brought the reaction against "Gothic" art, an art ancestral to him in a twofold sense, back to his distant homeland; those scornful comments which he ascribes to Michelangelo, and which almost bring to mind Louis XIV's ill-famed remark on the Dutch "*magots*,"* are of Italian origin. But when Netherlandish painters and sculptors of the sixteenth century were already studying under the Italians, and an entire colony of classicistic Flemings had established themselves in Florence, the Fiamminghi still had one bastion of their own left; sacred music. But when, once again in Florence, the last and decisive attack against the old "Gothic" *vocal polyphony* of the Dutch was carried through and the classical-southern-accompanied *monody* came to the fore, when, with direct reference to the authority of Vasari, this last remnant of foreign barbarism was cut to the quick and a completely new musical form, the opera, arose out of the dream of the reawakening of the classical musical drama—all this constitutes the last and by no means least remarkable episode in this century-long battle *for* Italy's own identity and *against* a partially imagined external enemy. In 1547, before the appearance of the first edition of Vasari's *Vite,* the first Italian epic written "according to the rules," Trissino's *Italia liberata dai Goti,* appeared, another Renaissance affair, like the renowned three unities of regular tragedy, which in itself is unthinkable without the precondition of Italian Cinquecento poetics.

The "stigmatization" of the "dark" Gothic Middle Ages, was, from Vasari onward, a foregone conclusion. In the *Vocabolario Toscano dell'arte del disegno* by Baldinucci (Florence 1691, p. 113), approved by the Crusca, we find, under the catchword "*Ordine Gottico,*" the following tirade that sums up everything to be said in Italy on the subject:

---

*Magots: Louis XIV is reported to have said, when presented with a painting by David Teniers depicting Dutch peasants: "Otez-moi ces magots!" (Take away those freaks!)—Ed.

It indicates that kind of building practiced at the time of the Goths, according to the German manner of proportion, which bears no similarity to the five good orders of classical architecture; it implies instead a design which is altogether barbaric, with columns which are over-attenuated, and disproportionately long, twisted and in more than one way unnerved, placed one on top of the other, with an infinity of little tabernacles, pyramids, ledges, lattice work, small keystones, foliage, animals, and vine tendrils—always heaping things upon things, without any rule, order and measure, that could be pleasing to good taste. (Editor's translation).

It is a solemn overall condemnation similar to the Neoclassicists' condemnation of the art of the Baroque.

It was of little account that insightful historians of the eighteenth century devoted to researching the Middle Ages, like Muratori in his *Annali d'Italia,* or the famous Scipione Maffei in his *Verona Illustrata,* raised protest against the non-historicity of this historical construct. Their protests remained scholarly objections that found little if any response among the public. In the north, in the France of Montfaucon and Mabillon, in spite of the dominant classicistic current, a more just, if fainthearted, appreciation of France's olden times arose. In his *Recueil historique de la vie et des ouvrages des plus célèbres architectes* (Paris, 1687), the learned court historiographer and historian of Saint-Denis, Dom Félibien des Avaux, wrote in detail and with obvious predilection on the architects of the Gothic period.

In the further course of the eighteenth century people had indeed become aware of the falseness of the historical construct; but matters only changed insofar as the old derogatory term "*Gotico*" was accorded a much broader meaning in the heyday of dogmatic classicism. This updated view was expounded in detail in the bible of German art lovers of that time, *Theorie der Schönen Künste* (The Theory of Fine Arts), by Johann Georg Sulzer, first published in 1771, as well as in its second edition, expanded by Eschenburg, issued in 1792. The book was sharply censored by the young Goethe. (See above pp. xx, 36, and 38.) "Gotisch" has here merely become a general term for bad taste as such, which of course the accursed Middle Ages possessed *in extenso*. It is worthwhile in this context to cite the key and major passages from this patriarchal compendium from Winckelmann's time, which, despite its wealth of material, has been all but forgotten (2nd part, p. 433):

> Gothic. Varied use is made of this adjective in the fine arts to indicate a barbaric taste, even though the meaning of the term is seldom exactly specified. It appears ostensibly to have been coined to designate a lack of beauty and sense of proportion in visual forms. The term derived from the fact that the Goths who settled in Italy did a poor job of imitating the works of ancient architecture. This would be the case with any as yet half barbaric nation that rapidly amassed power and wealth before it had time to even consider the culture of taste. Thus the Gothic taste is not unique to the Goths, but is common rather to all peoples who dabble in works of the visual arts before having acquired an adequate education in taste. Young nations fare the same as do individuals in this regard. . . . The Gothic is essentially a tasteless extravagance perpetrated on works of art not lacking in substance, and not always in magnitude and splendour, but lacking rather in a sense of the beautiful, the pleasant and the refined. Since this lack of taste can manifest itself in many ways, so too can the Gothic take on many forms.
>
> We therefore use the term Gothic to refer, not only to the ungainly buildings erected by the Goths, but also to the odd buildings overloaded with a thousand useless adornments, the first examples of which were most likely produced by the Saracens who settled in Europe. . . .
>
> In painting, that style which we call Gothic is recognizable in figures, before art had been restored through the study of nature and Antiquity at the end of the 16th Century. The painters before this time drew according to an ideal which was not elevated nature, like that of the Greeks, but rather, nature deformed with regard to proportion and movement. Limbs lengthened beyond the natural proportions, stiff or very affected poses and movements the like of which one would not find in nature, are characteristic features of Gothic drawing. It is evident that the Gothic painters drew their figures any which way they wished, and though these figures did have all the limbs of the human body, the draftsmen were obviously completely unconcerned whether or not they portrayed the true shape, the true proportions and movements, as in nature.
>
> Thus it would appear in any case that the Gothic taste derives from a lack of reflection prior to execution. The artist who does not consider precisely what the work which he is executing is actually supposed to express, and how it ought to be conceived, easily becomes Gothic. It is this very absence of

reflection in our time that still perpetuates the Gothic taste in ornamentation when such ornamentation is applied without any regard for the nature of the work so adorned. A tree carved in the form of an animal, a column that twists like a snail, a cup that stands on a very high and thin stem, and many other objects and implements adorned with a completely arbitrary taste are all Gothic in form.

In Eschenburg's supplements to the text, the old Renaissance idea of the derivation of the Gothic from the twig-and-tree cabin is introduced, that notion, in which, as I have already mentioned, the then incipient Romantic movement took such delight. It is easy to grasp the source of this entire untenable abstraction of the term "Gothic," the evolution of which we have outlined above. We can trace it back to the fatefully dogmatic doctrine of beauty as the hub of the entire artistic aesthetics; this doctrine was already firmly entrenched in the theory of the day.[9]

It is altogether in the spirit of these views, when J. J. Rousseau refers to the modern harmonic music as a "Gothic and barbaric" invention, first in the *Encyclopédie* and later in his *Dictionnaire de musique,* published independently in Paris in 1768. Rousseau has an ingenious, albeit purely intuitive grasp of the actual state of affairs. For the polyphonic music of the Middle Ages is, we now know, a product of the same spirit and the same Celto-Germanic race that gave rise to Gothic architecture. In Rousseau, the apostle of "pure nature" speaks forth, but also the classicist of classical-Italian cultivation, who—before Winckelmann—presents the simple greatness of homophony, in the classical sense, as "truly natural music," as opposed to that polyphonic development, which apparently originated in the British Isles, and without which our modern music would not be conceivable, a music that has indeed remained foreign and incomprehensible to this day to the popular consciousness of the "Greek" East.[10] Now that an age of the "exotic" appears on the rise, not only in the visual arts but also in music (where composers are reaching back to the diversity of the old keys), Rousseau's magnificent rhetorical tirade must bemuse us a little.

It was the young Strasbourg student Goethe who first challenged the rationalist abstraction upon which that theory was based; he sensed intuitively the artistic element in the old architectural manner. His dithyramb addressed to the *manes* of Erwin von Steinbach, that little text on German architecture, an early precursor of German Romanticism, was, as we well know, included by Herder in his *Blätter von deutscher Art und Kunst,* which appeared in 1773.[11] Consistent with his cool, critical manner, Herder immediately added the counterbalance; in a relatively poor German translation he presents an excerpt from a little book published in Livorno in 1766, which has today become rather rare. It is the *Saggio sopra l'architettura gotica,* by the learned Milanese mathematician Paolo Frisi (who himself supposedly descended from an old Strasbourg family named Fries), a purely technical and mathematical study of the statics of ogives and rounded arches, and the lesser solidity of Gothic vaulting, as opposed to its classical precursor, a theme which, as we know, was discussed quite often since the Renaissance. The condemnation of the Gothic is not lacking here either, in this case it is based on those technical arguments; the line of reasoning touches largely upon the famous architectural example from the author's own native city, the Cathedral of Milan.

Goethe himself, in the course of his development toward a mellow classicism, soon abandoned his youthful enthusiasm for the Gothic; his essay "Über Baukunst," composed later in life, scorns the Cathedral of Milan as a monstrosity, ascribing the character of northern architecture and decorative art to "multiplied minuteness," a phrase which embodies a true, albeit immeasurably exaggerated view that reflects the influence of a dogmatic prejudice. In much later years, once the vernal storm of the Romantic wave had already blown by him, he once again, in the quiet wisdom of age, weighed the pros and cons of the issue in his biographical-historical manner, true to the maxim which he had himself expounded in *Wilhelm Meister:* Not the truth, as one would suppose, but rather the problem as such remains in the middle ("Von deutscher Baukunst," 1823).

How the German Romantics, the Wackenroder, Tieck, Schlegel, Brentano, and Arnim, together with the philosophers, the collectors, and dilettantes of the Romantic period, in their way, once again revived and brought honor to medieval culture and art—this is well known and requires no further elaboration. It came from the seed strewn by the young Storm and Stress poets and writers of the eighteenth century, Goethe in the lead, the seed that sprouted late but opulently enough. Henceforth the historians, too, would approach the subject with altogether different devices and views than

before. The old *maniera greca* and *gotica* of Vasari survives up until
this time in the misleading conceptions of the "Byzantine" and the
"Gothic" styles. In his excellent discussion of the "common origin
of the architectural schools of the Middle Ages" (Berlin, 1831), the
great and brilliant art historian Rumohr argues against both termi-
ni, which he would like to replace by the terms "Vorgermanische"
(pre-Germanic) and "Germanische" (Germanic) architectural manner. The author of the little text that contained the first completely
unprejudiced and incisive evaluation of the medieval style in its
organic structure, with his far-reaching and critically sound attitude, could not possibly join in the Romantics' purely emotional
and nationally limited hymn to the "Altdeutsche"; but even he was
uncertain about the actual origin of the Gothic.

   The decisive voice came from the mother country of the Gothic
itself, from France. There in the second decade of the previous
century, through the efforts of such men as Gaumont, Didron,
Lenoir, that exemplary French school of archaeology evolved,
whose splendid descendant in our time was the short-lived Louis
Courajod. It was in their midst that the technical term, the "Romanesque" style, was coined, in insightful accord with the essentially related derivation of the Romance languages from vulgar Latin;
they proved likewise that the *style ogival*—we have no German word
for this good expression—first came into being in the heart of
France, and from there, made its way throughout Europe. This
confirms in a specialized domain what we already know about
France's leading role in the high Middle Ages. Through the art
historical handbooks of Kugler, Springer, Lübke, and Schnaase, this
theory was then spread, modified, and further developed in Germany, so that today we may consider it an established part of our
cultural heritage, and no isolated attacks of narrow-minded chau-
vinism can change this.

   We have come to the end of our discussion. For we are not here
going to further elaborate on those curious attempts to show the
name "Gothic" as justified because of its alleged connection with
the Visigoth building style in Gaul, nor shall we resurrect old nebu-
lous theories that derive the Gothic from the wooden architecture of
the Germanic-Gallic peoples. These are theorems that were already
propounded by Emeric-David and were defended again by more
recent scholars, like Rostières, and with particular passion, by

Courajod. Their inner inconsistency was demonstrated with incisive brevity by Brutail in his excellent book: *L'archéologie du Moyen age et ses méthodes* (Paris, 1900).

(1910)   *Translated by Peter Wortsman*

Notes

1. Giambattista Gelli (1498–1563) later presents this view in a more drastic form in his *Vite d'artisti fiorentini* (ed. Mancini, p. 35). (Here follows in the original a lengthy quote about the "superstition" of certain popes who ordered the removal of pagan statues as damaging to the Christian faith.)

2. The notion raised here by Alberti was pursued in an original manner by a bright mind of a later time, the aforementioned Gelli. He stands perplexed before old works, like the statues of San Paolo in Florence, as though faced with a psychological riddle. This man of a new era asks himself in vain how could the older generations, who after all had real people and classical statues to look at, take to such distortions (Vasari's *maniera goffa e rozza*) and be satisfied with them. He has recourse to a postulate that already foreshadows the doctrine of *corsi* and *ricorsi* of the great Neapolitan, G. B. Vico. It is, he argues, a law of nature that cultures which have reached their pinnacle succumb to barbarism and can only be regenerated by great geniuses. Thus he bypasses the heart of the matter; he is incapable of recognizing the unique and original qualities of medieval culture through his classicist spectacles. The fact that a Villard could translate a classical tomb into his Gothic style is in itself as little remarkable as that Dürer and the engravers of the eighteenth century could perceive the same classical monument in a Nürnberg manner or decked out in a rococo wig. It is only that we moderns still have the neoclassical tradition so much in our blood that we tend to feel more of an affinity with the latter two possibilities than with the former one.

3. Concerning this remarkable text, cp. now my *Kunstliteratur,* pp. 175 and 177.

4. Cesare Cesariano (1481–after 1540, an architect from the school of Bramante, who supervised the completion of the interior of Milan Cathedral; Ed.) saw nothing wrong in illustrating his Vitruvius Commentary (Como, 1521) with the ground plan and layout of his own Milan Cathedral, despite the fact that it was built "Germanico more." A note in an admittedly questionable source, the *Seconda Libraria* of the imaginative crackpot, Doni (Venice, 1555, p. 44), seems to confirm that the problem of the Gothic was the subject of extensive discussion in Raphael's Roman circle. Doni cites a number of theoretical writings of Bramante, among them a "*Trattato del lavoro Tedesco.*" However, we must not overlook Doni's tendency to invent many of the titles of the texts he cites, and that even blatant fabrications (like Dante's letter to C. da Polenta) have been traced back to him.

5. A recent example of this, hardly to be taken seriously, is the tirade in Muther's *Geschichte der modernen Malerei*, II, 324, written after all by an author who *wished* to be considered an art historian.

6. In this regard, we ought in particular to consider the description in the

Proemio to the second part of the *Vite,* in which Vasari characterized the achievements of the Giottesque manner (II, 101).

7. Vasari, *Preface to the Lives,* 17: "But in order that it may be understood more clearly what I call 'old' and what 'ancient,' the 'ancient' were the works made before Constantine in Corinth, in Athens, in Rome, and in other very famous cities, until the time of Nero, Vespasian, Trajan, Hadrian, and Antoninus; whereas those others are called 'old' that were executed from S. Silvester's day up to that time by a certain remnant of Greeks, who knew rather how to dye than how to paint" (Schlosser translates: "who were more housepainters than painters"). Cp. *Life of Niccolo and Giovanni Pisano:* "That old Greek manner, rude and void of proportion." (Translation by Gaston du C. de Vere.)

8. What Vasari has in mind is the *maniera antica* of Roman art, which as is well known, was held in equally high esteem until the age of Winckelmann; Ghiberti, himself owner of Greek antiquities, always with naive intuition sets greater store by Hellenic art. Note the very curious outline of the stylistic history of classical art that Vasari includes in his life of A. Pisano (I, 482 et seq.)

9. We can find a collection of source references in Lüdtke's essay, "'Gotisch' im 18. und 19. Jahrhunderts," *Zeitschrift für deutsche Wortforschung,* IV (Strasbourg, 1903) p. 133 et seq.

10. [Schlosser quotes here a long passage from Rousseau, *Dictionnaire de musique,* p. 241, article *Harmonie,* to the effect that harmony, unknown to Greeks and Orientals, is essentially unnatural, a "Gothic" and barbaric invention of the peoples of the North.]

In his diatribe against Rameau, Rousseau contends furthermore that the beauty of harmony is something that can only be learned, an appreciation of which must remain completely alien to the natural sensibility; the fact that harmony absolutely misses the true high principle of all art, namely, imitation, is, according to him, a consequence of the purely sensual basis of its perception.

11. Cp. Johann Gottfried Herder, *Von deutscher Kunst und Art,* ed. Hans Lambel, in *Deutsche Literaturdenkmale des 18. und 19. Jahrhunderts,* No. 40/41, Stuttgart, G. J. Göschen, 1892.

Aby Warburg

Italian Art and International Astrology in the Palazzo Schifanoia in Ferrara

The Roman world of forms of the Italian High Renaissance proclaims to us art historians the finally successful break of the artistic genius from medieval illustrative subservience. A justification is therefore in order, if here and now in Rome, at this very spot and before this expert and art-loving audience, I set out to speak of astrology (that dangerous adversary of free artistic creation) and of its importance in the development of style in Italian painting.

I hope that, in the course of the lecture, the justification will be provided by the problem itself, which because of its uniquely complicated nature, forcefully directed my attention — contrary, in fact, to my own initial tendency to focus on more beautiful matters — to the dim regions of astrological superstition.

The underlying issue is, how did the influence of antiquity affect the artistic culture of the early Renaissance?

About twenty-four years ago the realization came to me in Florence that the classical influence on the secular painting of the Quattrocento — particularly in the cases of Botticelli and Filippino Lippi — manifested itself in a refashioning of the human figure through greater mobility of body and dress, based on the example of classical art and poetry. Later I saw that typically classical superlatives in gestural language in the same way determined the style of Pollaiuolo's muscle rhetoric and, above all, that even the young Dürer's pagan fairyland (from *The Death of Orpheus* to the *Great Jealousy*) owes the dramatic thrust of its expression to such surviving, and basically very Greek, "Pathosformeln" as were passed to him through the art of northern Italy.[1]

The influx of this Italian style of classically inspired rendition of life-in-motion in northern art was hardly due to an indigenous lack of experience in dealing with pagan-classical subject matter; on the contrary, it became clear to me, in the course of inventory studies of secular art around the middle of the fifteenth century, that, for instance, in Flemish tapestries and paintings on cloth, figures clothed realistically in contemporary garb "alla franzese," were permitted, even in Italian palaces, to represent characters from pagan antiquity.

A closer study of the pagan store of images in the field of northern book art revealed, furthermore, in a comparison of text and illustration, that external appearances, which to us seem so irritatingly unclassical, did not distract the attention of contemporary readers from the key issue: the serious, even all too literal, intent toward an authentic illustration of antiquity.

So deeply was this peculiar interest in classical learning rooted in northern medieval culture that in the earliest Middle Ages we already find a kind of illustrated handbook of mythology conceived for those two groups of people most needful of them: *painters* and *astrologers*.

In northern Europe there appeared, for instance, that principal Latin treatise for painters of deities, the "de deorum imaginibus libellus," ascribed to an English monk, Albericus,[2] who must have lived as early as the twelfth century. His illustrated mythology with descriptions of twenty-three well-known pagan gods exercised an influence, heretofore completely overlooked, on the later mythographic literature, particularly in France, where French poetic adaptations and Latin moralized commentaries on Ovid afforded refuge to the pagan emigrants as early as the turn of the thirteenth to the fourteenth century.

In southern Germany there appears even as early as the twelfth century an assembly of the Olympian gods in the style of Albericus. As I showed in front of the fireplace in Landshut in 1909,* the mythological doctrine of his treatise still determined as late as 1541 the depiction of seven pagan gods.

*In 1909, Warburg explained to the participants of an art historians' congress the astrological imagery of the reliefs on the fireplace in the "Italian Hall" of the Residence in Landshut. See *Kirchliche und höfische Kunst in Landshut*, in A. Warburg, *Gesammelte Schriften*, ed. cit., pp. 455–458. — Ed.

What survives in Landshut is of course the seven planets, that is, those Greek gods who, later, under oriental influence, assumed the regency over those planets named after them. These seven enjoyed the greatest vitality among the Olympians, because they did not owe their selection to scholarly reminiscences, but rather to their own astral-religious attraction, which continued undisturbed.

It was believed, after all, that during all the periods of the solar years — months, days, hours — these seven planets prescribed human destiny according to pseudomathematical laws. The handiest of these doctrines, the regency over the months, assured the exiled gods a secure refuge in the medieval book art of the *calendaria*, which at the beginning of the fifteenth century had been illustrated by south German artists.

The *calendaria*, following the Hellenistic-Arabic conception, typically portray seven planet pictures, which, although they depict the stories of the pagan gods as a harmless collection of contemporary genre scenes, nonetheless acted upon the astrological believer like hieroglyphs of fate in an oracular text.

It is clear that from this kind of mythological tradition, in which the Greek gods and heroes had simultaneously assumed the uncanny power of astral demons, a mainstream would issue, in the course of which the pagans in their northern disguise would, in the fifteenth century, spread internationally. They could do so all the more easily, now that the art of printing, newly discovered in northern Europe, offered a new mobile vehicle for the transmission of images. Thus the very earliest products of book art, the block books (*Blockbücher*), included already descriptions and depictions of the seven planets and their children, which, in their explicit fidelity to the tradition, contributed in their way to the Italian Renaissance of antiquity.

It has been clear to me for quite some time that an in-depth iconological analysis of the frescoes in the Palazzo Schifanoia ought to reveal the twofold medieval tradition of the imagery of the classical gods.

Here we can document in every detail, on the grounds of the sources, not only the influence of the *Olympian* mythology, as transmitted from Western Europe by those learned mythographers, but also the influence of *astral* mythology as it had been preserved intact in text and imagery of astrological practice.

The series of wall paintings in the Palazzo Schifanoia in Ferrara represented images of the twelve months, of which, since their uncovery in 1840 from a whitewash, seven have been recaptured. Each depiction of a month consists of three parallel planes, arranged one on top of the other, each with its own pictorial space and figures of approximately half life-size. On the uppermost plane, the Olympian gods drive up in their triumphal chariots; the lowest plane presents the terrestrial happenings at the court of Duke Borso; we see him busy with matters of state, or setting out on a merry hunt. The middle plane belongs to the world of the astral gods, as confirmed by the respective sign of the zodiac that appears in the center, surrounded in each painting by three mysterious figures. The complicated and fantastic symbolism of these figures has heretofore eluded all attempts at explanation. By expanding our field of inquiry to the Orient, I will show that they are vestiges of surviving astral conceptions of the Greek world of the gods. They are in fact nothing else but symbols of the fixed stars, which, however, have lost much of the clarity of their Greek outlines after centuries of wandering from Greece through Asia Minor, Egypt, Mesopotamia, Arabia, and Spain.

Since it would be impossible, given the time allotted me, to interpret my way through the entire series of frescoes, I will limit myself to a discussion of the representations of three months, and will in most cases analyze iconologically only the two upper planes devoted to the gods.

I would like to begin with the first image of a month, that of March, which, according to Italian chronology, introduces the annual cycle. This month is dominated among the gods by Pallas, and among the zodiacal signs by Aries. I will then turn my attention to April, ruled by Venus and Taurus, and will finally focus on the month of July, because in that instance, an artist of lesser resistance allowed the learned program most palpably to shine through. Thereafter, an attempt will be made, by means of a glance at Botticelli, to understand the ancient world of the gods as depicted in Ferrara in terms of the history of style, as a transition between the international Middle Ages and the Italian Renaissance. But before turning to an analysis of the way in which the pagan deities are remembered in the Palazzo Schifanoia, I must attempt to sketch a rough outline of the instrumentarium and technique of ancient astrology.

The names attached to the two groups of stars (dissimilar in their apparent paths of motion) constitute the main tool of astrological divination. One distinguishes between the planets, with their seemingly changeable orbits, and the fixed stars, the positions of which, relative to each other, appear constant. The configuration of the latter group becomes visible to the human eye at either sunrise or sunset, depending on the position of the sun.

As long as astrology did indeed observe the heavens, it made the influence of the stars on human destiny dependent upon these conditions of visibility and upon the position of the stars relative to each other. In the later Middle Ages, however, real observation declined and was replaced by a primitive cult of star names.

Astrology is in essence nothing more than a name fetishism projected on the future. Whoever was born in April, and thus struck at birth by the rays of Venus, will, in accordance with the qualities ascribed to Venus in the myths, enjoy love and the light pleasures of life. Whoever came into being under the sign of Aries may expect to become a weaver—the legendary woolly fleece of the ram guarantees it. This month would likewise be particularly propitious for closing deals in the wool business.

Such pseudomathematical paralogisms have ensnared people for centuries and still do to this very day.

With the gradual mechanization of future-oriented astrology, in response to the practical demand, an illustrated handbook of astrology was developed for everyday use. The planets, which over the course of three hundred sixty days—a year, according to ancient calculations—did not offer sufficient variety, finally receded altogether from the picture, making way for an expanded fixed-star astrology.

The fixed-star heaven of Aratus (ca. 300 B.C.) is still today the primary aid for astronomy, since strict Greek science succeeded in intellectualizing the agitated creatures of religious fantasy as serviceable mathematical points. That jumble of humans, animals, and fabulous beings, though more than ample in our view, did not, however, offer Hellenistic astrologers a sufficient stock of hieroglyphs of fate for their daily predictions. Thus a retrogressive tendency to create new polytheistic entities evolved, a tendency which as far back as the first centuries of our chronology gave rise to the "Sphaera barbarica," written by a certain Teukros, probably in Asia Minor. This work is nothing more than a description of the fixed-star heaven, which with the addition of star names from Egypt, Babylonia, and Asia Minor, surpasses the star catalog of Aratus almost three times over. In his *Sphaera* of 1903, Franz Boll ingeniously reconstructed the "Sphaera barbarica" and traced the major stages of its fabulous journey to the Orient and back to Europe—an achievement of immeasurable importance to modern art history. He discovered, for instance, a small book illustrated with woodcuts that is in fact a reproduction of an astrological diary of the kind used in Asia Minor: the *Astrolabium Magnum*, edited by the German scholar Engel, and first printed by Ratdolt in Augsburg in 1488.[3] Yet the book was written by a world-famous Italian, Pietro d'Abano, the Paduan Faust of the Trecento, a contemporary of Dante and Giotto.

The *Sphaera barbarica* of Teukros comes down to us in yet another form, corresponding to the surviving Greek text, a form arranged according to decans, that is, thirds of months, each of which encompasses ten degrees of the respective zodiacal sign. This type came to the western Middle Ages via the star catalogs and *lapidaria* (books of precious stones) of the Arabs. So the "Great Introduction" of Abū Mā'sār (who died in 886), the main authority for medieval astrology, contains a synopsis of three different conceptions of the fixed-star heaven, each apparently quite peculiar and belonging to a different nation. Closer scholarly examination reveals, however, that these disparate parts can all be traced back to the Greek Sphaera of Teukros, expanded by barbaric additions. And the book's journey can once again be followed all the way down to Pietro d'Abano; having made its way from Asia Minor, via Egypt, to India, the Sphaera landed (probably via Persia), in the aforementioned *Introductorium majus* of Abū Mā'sār, which then was translated into Hebrew by a Spanish Jew, Aben Esra (who died in 1167). The Hebrew translation was then translated in turn into French in Mecheln, by the Jewish scholar Hagins for the Englishman, Henry Bates. And this French translation was finally the source of a Latin version completed in 1293 by Pietro d'Abano. The book was frequently reprinted, as for instance in Venice in 1507 (first edition Erhard Ratdolt, Venice, 1485). The *lapidaria* (books of precious stones), that teach the magical influence of the decan star groups on certain types of stones, also traveled the same route: from India to Arabia, and then to Spain. At the court of King Alfonso el Sabio of Toledo, Hellenistic natural philosophy experienced an extraordinary rebirth: In Spanish illustrated manuscripts, Greek authors revived, from their Arabic translations, authors who were to make the hermetic-healing or oracular astrology of Alexandria a fatal part of Europe's cultural patrimony.

Pietro d'Abano's *Astrolabium* in its most monumental edition has, however, not yet been included by Boll in the circle of his studies. The walls of the *Salone in Padua* are, as it were, large folio pages from an astrological fortune-teller's calendar for every day, inspired by Abano in the spirit of the *Sphaera barbarica*. I reserve the art-historical interpretation of this unique monument[4] for a future article, and I would like to direct your attention only to one page of the Astrolabium (Fig. 30), which will finally lead us to the Ferrara frescoes themselves.

We notice at the bottom of the lower half two small figures set in a horoscopic schema. The one is a man with a sickle and a crossbow; he is supposed to appear at the first degree of Aries, and is none other than Perseus, who indeed rises at the same time as Aries, and whose scimitar (Harpe) has been transformed into a sickle. Above him, we read in Latin: "At the first degree of Aries, a man rises, carrying a sickle in his right hand and a crossbow in his left." And below that, as a prophecy for those born under this sign: "He works sometimes, and sometimes goes to war." This then is nothing but trite name fetishism projected on the future! Above him stand three figures who in astrological parlance are called "decans"[5]; there are three of them attached to each zodiacal sign, hence there are altogether thirty-six decans. This arrangement is, in its system, thoroughly Egyptian, even if the external aspect of the decan symbol clearly reveals that it is Perseus once again, hidden behind the man with the cap and the scimitar; Perseus, who here dominates as *prima facie* not only the first degree, but the entire first ten degrees of the sign of Aries.

A glance at the genuinely classical Perseus in the Germanicus manuscript in Leiden proves without a doubt that in scimitar and turban of the first decan, the "harpe" and the Phrygian cap of Perseus have been faithfully preserved.[6] However, on an astrological marble tablet from Roman imperial time, the famous *Plani-sphaerium Bianchini* (Louvre; 58cm² = exactly two Roman ft.; found 1705 on the Aventine in Rome, and given by Francesco Bian-chini [1669–1725] to the French Academy), the Egyptian decans appear still in authentic Egyptian stylization; the first one holds a double ax.

Medieval loyalty preserved for us faithfully even *this* version of the decan with the double ax; the book of precious stones prepared for Alfonso el Sabio of Castille presents as the first decan symbol of Aries a dark-skinned man in a girded sacrificial apron, who is indeed holding a double ax.[7]

But it is only through a third version of the decan series, that of the aforementioned Arab, Abū Mā'sār, that we finally are guided directly to the mysterious figures of the middle plane in the Palazzo Schifanoia.

In the chapter of his "Great Introduction" relevant to our investi-gation, Abū Mā'sār gives a synopsis of three different fixed-star systems: the common Arabic system, the Ptolomaic, and finally the Indian system.

In the row of the Indian decans, one at first thinks oneself sur-rounded by phantasms of the most genuine oriental imagination (since, by and large, in this critical iconology the recovery of the original Greek image demands a constant stripping away of incalcu-lable layers of incomprehensible additions). Thus a closer examina-tion of the "Indian" decans reveals the fact, no longer surprising to us, that indeed Indian accretions have overgrown originally truly Greek astral symbols.

The Indian author, Varāha Mihira (sixth century), Abū Mā'sār's unnamed source, quite rightly describes in his Brhajjâtaka, the first decan of Aries as a man holding a double ax. He writes: "In the first decan of Aries, a red-eyed black man appears; he is girded about the loins by a white cloth; his aspect is both protective and terrifying, and he holds an axe upright. This is a man-Dreskana (decan), armed and answerable to Mars (Bhauma)."[8]

And in Abū Mā'sār (Boll, *Sphaera*, p. 497) we read: "The Indians say that in this Decan a black man with red eyes rises, he is powerful of build, full of courage and resolve; he wears a big white garment, fastened around the middle with a cord; he is angry, and stands erect, vigilant and attentive." Thus the figures all conform to the tradition, except for one nuance: in the Arab's version, the decan has lost his axe and kept only the garment girded with a cord.

Four years ago, when I read Abū Māʾsār's Arabic text in German translation (which Dyroff most ingratiatingly has added to Boll's book),[9] those mysterious figures from Ferrara, which I had pondered so often, in vain, for so many years, suddenly came to mind, and all of a sudden they made sense: one after the other[10] revealed himself as an *Indian decan* of Abū Māʾsār. The first figure in the middle plane of the March fresco had to show his true face: there he was, the black, angry, vigilant, standing man in his girded garment, whose rope belt he demonstratively holds up (Figs. 32, 33). And so the entire astral system of the middle plane could be analyzed unequivocally: The lowest level of the Greek fixed-star heaven had been overlaid by the Egyptianizing schema of the cult of the decans. This in turn was covered by a layer of Indian mythological transformation, which thereafter had to pass through the Arabic milieu, probably via Persian transmission. When the Hebrew translation had enacted a further obfuscation, the Greek fixed-star heaven finally incribed itself (through French mediation in Pietro d'Abano's Latin translation of Abū Māʾsār) in the monumental cosmology of the Italian early Renaissance—in the shape of precisely those thirty-six enigmatic figures on the middle plane of the Ferrara frescoes.

Let us now turn our attention to the upper plane, where the procession of the gods takes place.

Diverse artists of very unequal talent worked together on the entire series of frescoes. Fritz Harck[11] and Adolfo Venturi[12] have carried out the difficult pioneering work of stylistic criticism. We likewise have to thank Venturi for the discovery of the only original document, which identifies Francesco Cossa as creator of the first three representations of months (March, April, May), namely, a gripping and very informative handwritten letter dated 25 March 1470. In the upper portion of the fresco (Fig. 32) we see Pallas— somewhat ravaged but still clearly recognizable—with the Gorgon on her breast and the spear in her hand, seated on a festive chariot, drawn by unicorns, with the chariot's drapery flapping in the wind.

To the left, we see the group of Athena's disciples: doctors, poets, jurists (all of whom may one day be identified by more in-depth research as members of the University of Ferrara). In contrast, to the right we catch a glimpse of a Ferrarese needlework circle: three women embroidering in the foreground, three weaving at the loom behind them, surrounded by a crowd of elegant female spectators. To the astrological believer, this seemingly innocent gathering of seated ladies signified the children of Aries: whosoever is born in March, under the sign of Aries, will be favored with a pronounced talent for the artful handling of wool.

So *Manilius,* in his didactic astrological poem (the only major, systematically conceived monument of astrognostic verse produced by the Latin poetry of the Roman empire) described the psychological and professional character of those born under the sign of Aries in the following manner:

> et mille per artes uellera diuersos ex se parientia quaestus:
> nunc glomerare rudis, nunc rursus soluere lanas,
> nunc tenuare leui filo, nunc ducere telas,
> nunc emere et uarias in quaestum uendere uestes.[13]

The concurrence of our frescoes with Manilius's poem is (as all scholarship to date has failed to realize) by no means coincidental: Manilius's astral poem belongs since 1416 to those classics that were rediscovered and resurrected with loving enthusiasm by learned Italian humanists.[14] In a famous passage, Manilius presents the gods that watch over the various months as follows:

> lanigerum Pallas, taurum Cytherea tuetur,
> formosos Phoebus geminos; Cyllenie, cancrum,
> Iupiter et cum matre deum regis ipse leonem,
> spicifera est uirgo Cereris, fabricataque libra
> Vulcani, pugnax Mauorti scorpios haeret;
> uenantem Diana uirum, sed partis equinae,
> atque angusta fouet capricorni sidera Uesta,
> et Iouis aduerso Iunonis aquarius astrum est,
> agnoscitque suos Neptunus in aequore pisces.[15]

The seven extant triumphs of the gods correspond *verbatim* — as we shall see even more clearly in yet another instance — with this sequence, which moreover cannot be found in the works of any other writer. Pallas watches over March, the month of Aries; Venus, over the Taurus and April; Apollo, over Gemini and May; Mercury, over Cancer and its month, June; Jupiter and Cybele together (an altogether characteristic alliance, which occurs nowhere else), over the sign of Leo and the month of July; Ceres, over Virgo and the month of August; and Vulcan, over Libra, and the month of September. There can therefore no longer be any doubt as to which literary sources seem likely to have afforded the conceptual framework of the whole cycle of paintings. Hellenistic astral demons, in international medieval dress, rule the shady intermediary realm below; above, the Latin poet helps the pagan gods in their attempt to win back the ancestral heights of the Greek Olympus.

Let us now turn to April, the month ruled by Taurus and Venus (Fig. 31). Madame Venus, in her swan-drawn vehicle, with its drapery fluttering cheerfully in the wind, has nothing Greek about her outward appearance. Only her dress, her open hair, and the garland of roses seem to distinguish her from the crowd that is carrying on in an altogether worldly manner in the two love gardens to the right and to the left.

Indeed if we consider the Mars-Venus group out of context in their carriage, the shackled, swan-drawn troubadour who kneels so full of longing before his mistress evokes a Nordic Lohengrin mood, the like of which we find in a Netherlandish miniature illustrating the legendary history of the House of Cleve (compare the Chevalier au Cygne in the Ms. Gall. 19 of the Hof- und Staatsbibliothek in Munich). Considering the pronounced interest that the Ferrarese court showed for frenchified chivalric culture, an affinity with such soul fashions imported from the north would be altogether likely.

Nonetheless, Francesco Cossa portrayed Venus according to the strict dictates of learned Latin mythography:

The aforementioned Albericus prescribes in his book of divinities for painters the following figuration of Venus, which I can show you in an illustrated Italian manuscript.[16] The Latin text reads something like this in translation: "Among the planets, Venus holds fifth place. She was therefore represented fifth in line. Venus was portrayed as the loveliest virgin, naked and swimming in the sea [holding a seashell in her right hand]. Her head was crowned with a wreath of white and red roses, and she was accompanied by doves fluttering around her. Vulcan, the fire god, gruff and ugly, was betrothed to her, and stood to her right. But before her stood three little naked virgins, who were called the Three Graces; two of them had their faces turned to us, though the third showed us her back. Venus's son, Cupid, was also on hand, winged and blind, shooting with his bow and arrow at Apollo, whereupon [fearing the wrath of the gods] he sought refuge in his mother's lap; she reached out her left hand to him."

Let us now take another look at Cossa's Aphrodite: The wreath of red and white roses, the doves fluttering around the goddess who is riding on the sea, Amor, portrayed on his mother's belt, threatening a pair of lovers with his bow and arrows, and above all, the Three Graces, definitely modeled after a classical artistic prototype—all attest to a sincere desire for genuinely classical reconstruction.

We need only a touch of abstractive ability to recognize in a French miniature from the end of the fourteenth century the Anadyomene of Albericus traveling through medieval France. In the very same way, she climbs out of the sea in the "Ovide moralisé."[17] The situation and the attributes are clear: Amor may have transformed himself into a winged king on a throne, and the foam-born goddess may be grasping a duck in her pond, rather than a seashell; but the mythic rudiments are otherwise all there: white and red roses floating in the water, three doves fluttering about, and one of the Three Graces even seems to be moving into the prescribed reverse pose.

This Albericus-Olympos continued to hold sway well into the book illustrations of the fifteenth and sixteenth centuries, and likewise in the so-called Mantegna tarot-card deck engraved in northern Italy in 1465.

Let us now turn our attention to the Olympians as astral demons, the form in which they endure in the planet calendarii. Consider, for instance, the sheet depicting the fate of the "Children of Venus" on a page of a Burgundian block book from circa 1460, which is probably patterned after German prototypes.[18] The scene is not all that weirdly demonic here; the foam-born ruler of Cyprus has been transformed into the owner of a merry wine garden; couples bathe and frolic to musical accompaniment on a flowery meadow. Were it not for the presence of a naked female figure hovering in the clouds, with a mirror in her right hand and flowers in her left, set amidst her zodiacal signs, high up in the air, we would not recognize those figures down below on the earth for what they are: astrologically serviceable visual commentaries on the mythological qualities of the cosmic Venus, who reawakens the joy of life in nature and men every year.

Since in Ferrara, the twelve gods of Manilius occupy the planetary region, planetary astrology recedes here in favor of decan astrology. Nevertheless, we cannot help realizing that the love garden and the music makers in Cossa's fresco are inspired by the traditional representations of the "Children of Venus." Of course, Cossa's gripping sense of reality (of which the Galleria Vaticana possesses such an incomparable example in the Predella with scenes from the life of Saint Vincent Ferrer) overrides the inartistic element of literary infusion, which stands out all the more blatantly in those monthly depictions in the Palazzo Schifanoia, in which lesser talents were not able to defy the dry program by infusing it with life.

Such a lesser talent is the painter of the July fresco (Fig. 34). According to Manilius, the month belongs to the divine couple Jupiter-Cybele. However, according to the planetary theory of late antiquity, Sol-Apollo rules over July and the zodiacal sign of Leo.

Now, in the upper-left-hand corner of the fresco, we see monks kneeling in prayer in a chapel before an altarpiece; this image infiltrated the otherwise standard row of the twelve gods of Manilius from the planet-children cycle of Sol-Apollo. As early as 1445 these pious praying figures can already be documented as a typical element of the "Children of the Sun" in southern Germany.[19] The accompanying German verse in a planet block book reads as follows: "Vor mitten tag si dynen gote vil, dornoch sy leben wy man wil." (Before midday they serve God eagerly, but afterward they do as they please.)

However, apart from this infusion of an element from the Sol-Planet cycle, the divine couple Jupiter, and Cybele with her crenellated crown, rule, true to Manilius, over the Leo month of July; they share peacefully the throne of their triumphal chariot.

How seriously the artists and their learned advisors strove after a faithful resuscitation of the classical myth can be seen in the groups to the right: in the background, true to the barbaric legend, we find Attis reclining. And the fact that those holy men cloaked in Christian priestly garb, busy with cymbals and drums, are indeed intended as "Galli," and furthermore, that the armed youths in the background are meant to represent sword-swinging Corybants—this is confirmed by the presence, in the foreground, of the three empty chairs: an empty armchair to the left, two three-legged stools to the right. There can be no doubt that these seats, conceived in the contemporary style, are placed so prominently in the foreground as true, archi-classical symbols of a secret cult: they are meant to be the empty divine thrones of Cybele, of which Augustine still makes mention, on the express authority of Varro.[20]

The Albericus text is not the only source in which we find the Cybele legend, with all its barbaric details, albeit without this over-erudite painted reference to the divine thrones. Cybele was already introduced on an isolated page from a Regensburg manuscript of the twelfth century, together with several other very peculiar pagan figures. Behind Cybele, on her lion-drawn carriage, we notice two Corybants with drawn swords.[21] In this instance, the so-called Middle Ages were certainly not devoid of a will to faithfully reconstruct the archaeological fact.

The painter of the July fresco, whose lesser talent (unlike Cossa's figurative brilliance) does not allow us to forget the background in manuscript illumination, is an offshoot of a medieval aesthetic on its last legs. The wedding scene to the left is meant to represent the marriage of Bianca d'Este, a daughter of Borso's, to Galeotto della Mirandola. Galeotto was the brother of Pico della Mirandola, the brave forerunner in the struggle against astrological superstition, who, moreover, in a special chapter, attacked the absurd Arabic doctrine of the decans. We can well understand that a Renaissance man, whose most intimate circle was haunted by those astrological demons, would have defended himself against such barbaric idols of fate (Savonarola, another powerful opponent of astrology, was also born in Ferrara). To what extent, however, at the court of the Este the world of the ancient gods was still interlaced with classical notions and practices from late antiquity and the Middle Ages can be seen from the fact that as late as 1470 we find only the initial symptoms of a thorough artistic restitution of Olympus, namely, in the replacement of the planet gods with Manilius's twelve-god series.

Who then could have provided the learned inspiration? Astrology played an important role at the court of the Este. Of Leonello d'Este it is said, for instance, that like the old Sabean* sorcerers, he wore garments of the respective planet colors for each of the seven days of the week.[22] Pietro Bono Avogaro, one of the court astrologers, wrote prognostica for each year, and a certain Carlo da Sangiorgio used geomancy, the last degenerate offshoot of ancient astrological divination, to tell the future.[23] Not Avogaro, but the other professor of astronomy at the University of Ferrara, was the overerudite source of inspiration of the representations of the months in the Palazzo Schifanoia: Pellegrino Prisciani, the librarian and court historiographer of the Este. This we can establish on the basis of circumstantial evidence in original source material. It is true, in his prognostica, Avogaro also quotes repeatedly from Abū Mā'sār. However, Pellegrino Prisciani[24] (whose portrait is preserved on the title page of his *Orthopasca* in the library of Modena) cites in an astrological advice the very same odd triumvirate of authorities that we have just proven to be the major conceptual sources for our frescoes: Manilius, Abū Mā'sār, and Pietro d'Abano. I am indebted for the transcription of this heretofore unknown document, so significant to my research, to the archivist of the Library of Modena, Signor Dallari.[25]

Leonora of Aragon, the wife of the Duke Ercole, requested of Prisciani, who was the astrological advisor to the family, a reckoning of the best stellar constellations, under which all one wished for would of necessity be fulfilled. Prisciani observed happily that this very constellation was right now at hand: Jupiter with the dragon's head in conjunction with a propitious phase of the moon under the sign of Aquarius; he bases his learned decision on Abū Mā'sār's aphorisms and on the *Conciliator* of Pietro d'Abano. But the decisive final word he leaves to Manilius: (IV. 570–571) "quod si quem sanctumque velis castumque probumque, Hic tibi nascetur, cum primus aquarius exit."[26] This piece of circumstantial evidence may, so it seems, be confirmed once and for all in light of a second original document: the aforementioned letter written by Francesco Cossa,[27] which is a complaint about poor treatment on the part of the duke's superintendent of artistic matters. In this letter, the artist reaches over the superintendent's head to appeal directly to the duke

*Sabeans, semitic nation, documented in S. Arabia from the 8th century B.C. until the 11th century. Their religion was based on astrology. — Ed.

in the matter of poor treatment and payment. But the superintendent of art at the Palazzo Schifanoia was our friend, Pellegrino Prisciani. Francesco writes only that he is appealing directly to the duke because he does not wish to trouble Pellegrino Prisciani, "non voglio esser quello il quale et a pellegrino de prisciano et a altri vegna a fastidio," but it is clear from the context that he is bypassing the learned man because Pellegrino wanted to place him on the same pay scale as the other painters of the monthly representations, whom Francesco Cossa referred to as "i più tristi garzoni di Ferrara." We sympathize today with his justified, albeit fruitless, indignation.

I believe I do no injustice to the memory of Pellegrino Prisciani in assuming that the main reason he prized the other painters at least as highly as Francesco Cossa was quite simply because they depicted the subtleties of the learned program clearly and to the letter.

We must, however, not forget that Prisciani's program—however much it engendered in its pictorial execution, through an overload of details, an inartistic lack of unity—revealed the mind of a conceptual architect who knew how to handle tactfully the profoundly harmonious elements of Greek cosmology. If then, hazarding a rough sketch, we were to view the entire cycle of paintings, re-rendered spherically, we would be struck by the realization that the three-tiered pictorial planes in the Palazzo Schifanoia actually constitute a spherical system projected on a flat surface, in the layout of which the typology of the spheres of Manilius is combined with the Bianchini tablet.

The illustrated court and state calendar of Duke Borso symbolized the innermost core of the sphere of the earth. In the upper plane—in accordance with Manilius—the twelve Olympian gods hover as protectors of the months; of the twelve, the following are still extant in Ferrara: Pallas, Venus, Apollo, Mercury, Jupiter-Cybele, Ceres, and Vulcan.

In place of the planets, Manilius substituted and revered the twelve gods as regents of the twelve months. This cosmological theory is preserved in its essentials in the Ferrarese paintings. Only scattered remnants of the older medieval planetary astrology can still be found here and there; whereas the learned descriptive mythography—in particular, that of Albericus—gave rise to a pedantic overabundance of detail in the background.

The sphere of the zodiac is common to Manilius, the *Planisphaerium Bianchini,* and the cycle of the months in the Palazzo Schifanoia. In its elaboration of the decan system, however (which on the Bianchini tablet insinuates itself as a separate region between fixed stars and planets), Prisciani's Sphaera is consanguineous to the cosmos on the Bianchini tablet, for the Indian decans of Abū Mā'sār, who dominate the central plane in the Palazzo Schifanoia, revealed — albeit only after exact auscultation — that under the seven-layered traveling clothes of the weathered wanderers through time, nations, and peoples, there beats a Greek heart.

Tura's paintings in the library of Pico della Mirandola are unfortunately known to us only through descriptions. They would perhaps shed light on the evolution, as perceived in contemporary Ferrarese painting, of the major stylistic achievement that marks the turning point from the early to the high Renaissance: the restoration of a higher, classicizing ideal style for the representation of the major figures of ancient legend and history.

There seems indeed to be no bridge leading to this classicizing style of higher humanity from the frescoes in the Palazzo Schifanoia. We saw that in 1470, in the prose of a street procession, the representation of the legend of Cybele fulfilled the duties of medieval illustrative subservience — for Mantegna hadn't yet taught artists how the mother of the gods should be carried around at the triumphal pace of a Roman triumphal arch — and even Cossa's Venus was not yet disposed to rise out of the lower regions of costume realism *alla franzese* to the luminous ether of the *Venere aviatica* in the Villa Farnese.

All the same, a transitional stage does exist between Cossa and Raphael: namely, Botticelli. For even Alessandro Botticelli first had to free his goddess of beauty from the medieval realism of banal genre art *alla franzese,* as well as from illustrative bondage and astrological practice.

Years ago[28] I attempted to prove that the engravings of the so-called Baldini calendar are early works of Botticelli's; at any rate, they exemplify *his* notion of antiquity. In the context of our discussion, the calendar is of twofold interest: for its text, and for its visual representations. The text is a practical guide for believers in planet astrology; a more in-depth examination would show that it is a veritable compendium of Hellenistic applied cosmology—as transmitted, likewise, by Abū Mā'sār.

As to the calendar's visual aspect, the seemingly inconsequential fact that we also possess a later edition of the very same calendar affords us an insight of great value for the history of style; in a nuance of the external appearance of the respective editions, we can observe *in statu nascendi* the new stylistic principle of classically idealizing mobility. The first edition of this calendar, dated approximately 1465, follows exactly the typology of those northern pages with representations of the planets. A stiff little female dancing figurine stands in the midst of the retinue of Venus: a woman in Burgundian costume, who wears the unmistakable French *hennin* with a *guimpe* on her head, confirming thereby that Baldini-Botticelli must have followed a Burgundian version of a northern prototype. The second impression of this engraving, to be dated a few years later, reveals the tendency and nature of the change in style that came about in Florentine early Renaissance.

Out of the tightly entwined cocoon of the Burgundian caterpillar slips the Florentine butterfly, the "Nynfa" with the winged headdress and the fluttering garment of the Greek Maenad or the Roman Victory.

In our context, it now becomes clear that Botticelli's paintings of Venus, "The Birth of Venus" and the so-called "Spring," sought to restore to the goddess, who had been twice confined—by medieval mythography and astrology—her Olympian freedom. Venus appears ringed with roses, a freshly husked Anadyomene in a seashell on the water. And her companions, the Three Graces, remain in her retinue in that other Venus painting, which years ago I called *The Realm of Venus*. Today I would like to propose a slightly different nuance of the same explanation, which would have revealed, not least to the astrologically trained viewer of the Quattrocento, the character of the goddess of beauty and mistress of reawakening nature: "Venere Pianeta," the planet goddess Venus appearing in April, the month of her dominion.

Simonetta Vespucci, to the cult of whose memory, in my opinion, both paintings belong, did after all die on the 26th of April, 1476.

Thus Botticelli received his subject matter from the preceding tradition; however, he adapted it to his own unique creation of an idealized humanity in a new style that the reawakened Greek and

Roman antiquity, the Homeric hymn, Lucretius and Ovid (interpreted for him by Politianus, who was anything but a moralizing monk), helped him fashion. Moreover, he was enabled to create this style because it was classical sculpture itself that allowed him to envision how the Greek gods would in higher spheres dance their round to Plato's tune.

Dear fellow students! The resolution of a pictorial riddle was of course not the sole purpose of this essay — particularly in a situation such as this, in which, not being able to calmly illuminate the subject, one is forced to spotlight it cinematographically.

With this tentatively hazarded, isolated effort, I wished to permit myself a plaidoyer in favor of a methodical expansion of our art-historical discipline, in both its material and its spatial reaches.

Overly limiting developmental categories have until now hindered art history from making its material available to the, albeit as yet unwritten, "historic psychology of human expression." Because of its excessively materialistic or excessively mystical tenor, our young discipline denies itself the panoramatic view of world history. Groping, it seeks to find its own theory of evolution between the schematisms of political history and the doctrines of genius. By the method of my interpretation of the frescoes in the Palazzo Schifanoia in Ferrara, I hope to have shown that an iconological analysis, which, in refusing to submit to petty territorial restrictions, neither shies away from recognizing that antiquity, the Middle Ages, and Modern Times are in fact one interrelated epoch, nor from examining the works of the freest as well as the most applied art as equally valid documents of expression — that this method, by applying itself to the illumination of a single darkness, sheds light on the great universal evolutionary processes in their context. I was less interested in the neat solution than in the formulation of a new problem. I would like to put it to you in the following terms: "To what extent are we to view the onset of a stylistic shift in the representation of the human figure in Italian art as an internationally conditioned process of disengagement from the surviving pictorial conceptions of the pagan culture of the eastern Mediterranean peoples?"

Our enthusiastic wonderment at the inconceivable achievement of artistic genius can only be strengthened by the recognition that genius is both a blessing and conscious transformatory energy. The great new style that the artistic genius of Italy bequeathed to us was rooted in the social will to recover Greek humanism from the shell of medieval, Oriental-Latin "practice." With this will toward the restitution of antiquity, the "good European" began his struggle for enlightenment in the age of the international migration of images that we refer to—a little too mystically—as the age of the Renaissance.

Translated by Peter Wortsman

Notes

1. See "Botticellis Geburt der Venus und Frühling," 1893, pp. 19 et seq., 33 et seq. and "Dürer und die italienische Antike" in A. Warburg, *Gesammelte Schriften*, ed. Fritz Rougemont and Gertrud Bing, 2 vols., B. G. Teubner, Leipzig-Berlin 1932. Cp. also *Jahrbuch der preuss. Kunstlgn.*, 1902, p. 188.

2. See now Robert Raschke, *De Alberico Mythologo*, Bratislava, M. & H. Marcus, 1913. (Breslauer philol. Abhandl. ed. Richard Forster, 45.)

3. Other editions, 1494 and 1502, Venice.

4. Considering the exemplary, keen diligence of Italian photographers, it is incomprehensible that so few of the frescoes of the Salone have as yet been photographed; an insurmountable hindrance to the heretofore neglected comparative study! (Cp. now Antonio Barzon, *I cieli e la loro influenza negli affreschi del Salone in Padova*, Padua, Tip. Seminario, 1924.

5. See, in addition to Boll, *Sphaera*, the groundbreaking book by André Bouché-Leclercq, *L'astrologie grecque*, Paris, E. Leroux, 1899.

6. I shall offer the same proof for the other decans; so, for instance, the seated, lute-playing woman is Cassiopeia, cp. illus. in Georg Thiele, *Antike Himmelsbilder*, Berlin, Weidmannsche Buchhandlung, 1898.

7. See the illustration in the *Lapidario del Rey Alfonso X* (1881) and in Boll, p. 433.

8. George Frederick William Thibaut, *Grundriss der Indo-Arischen Philologie III*, 9, p. 66, drew my attention to the English translation of the *Chidambaram Jyer* (1884), which was then found among the literary remains of Oppert in the Hamburg State Library; I am grateful to Dr. Wilhelm Printz for the German translation.

9. Pp. 482–539. A complete edition of the text of the works of Abū Māʾsār, with a translation, can be counted among the most pressing needs for the study of cultural history.

10. A more in-depth discussion of this in a later study.

11. *Jahrb. d. Preuss. Kstsmlgn.* V, 1884, 99 et seq.

12. *Atti e Mem. Stor. d. Romagna*, 1885, p. 381 et seq.

13. (He will yield his produce for the common benefit,) the fleece which by a thousand crafts gives birth to different forms of gain: now workers pile into heaps the undressed wool, now card it, now draw it into a tenuous thread, now weave the threads to form webs, and now they buy and sell for gain garments of every kind.

(IV, 128–132) Manilius, *Astronomica*, with an English translation by G. P. Goold, Cambridge and London, 1927, p. 233. William Heinemann Ltd. and Harvard University Press.

14. Remigio Sabbadini, *Le Scoperte dei codici latini e greci ne' secoli XIV e XV*, Florence: G. C. Sansoni, 1905, p. 80, and Benedetto Soldati, *La poesia astrologica nel Quattrocento*, Florence: G. C. Sansoni, 1914.

15. Pallas is protectress of the Ram, the Cytherean of the Bull, and Phoebus of the comely Twins; you, Mercury, rule the Crab and you, Jupiter, as well as the Mother of the Gods, the Lion; the Virgin with her sheaf belongs to Ceres, and the Balance to Vulcan who wrought it; bellicose Scorpion clings to Mars; Diana cherishes the hunter, a man, to be sure, but a horse in his other half, and Vesta, the cramped stars of Capricorn; opposite Jupiter, Juno has the sign of Aquarius, and Neptune acknowledges the Fishes as his own for all that they are in heaven. (II, 439–447; l.c., pp. 117, 119.)

16. Rom. Vat. Reg. lat. 1290, written in upper Italy around 1420.

17. The poem was composed by an unknown French cleric (before 1307); cp. Gaston B. P. Paris, *La littérature française au moyen-age*, 4th edition, Paris, Hachette, 1909, p. 84. The illus. is taken from the Ms. 373, anc. 6986, of the Bibl. Nat. in Paris, fol. 207v.

18. Cp. Friedrich Lippmann, *Die sieben Planeten,* Berlin, Amsler & Ruthardt (1895), Tab. C.V.

19. Rudolf Kautzsch, "Planetendarstellungen aus dem Jahre 1445," in *Repertorium für Kunstwissenschaft*, 1897, p. 32 (et seq., esp. p. 37).

20. *De Civ. Dei* VII, 24: "quod sedes fingantur circa eam, cum omnia moveantur, ipsam non movere." (". . . seats are depicted surrounding her because, while all things move about her, she herself is unmoved." This version of the sentence is today considered as corrupted.)

21. Georg Swarzenski, *Die Regensburger Buchmalerei des X. und XI. Jahrhunderts*, Leipzig, K. W. Hiersemann, 1901, p. 172, described the exceedingly interesting page of the Ms. Mon. Lat. 14271 (fol. IIv), which Dr. Fritz Saxl brought to my attention; I plan to reproduce and discuss the page.

22. Edmund Garratt Gardner, *Dukes and Poets in Ferrara,* New York, E. P. Dutton, 1904, p. 46, makes reference to Decembrio, *Politiae Litterariae*, 1540, fol. I: "Nam in veste non decorem et opulentiam solum, qua caeteri principes honestari solent, sed mirum dixeris pro ratione planetarum, et dierum ordine, colorum quoque coaptationem excogitauit." (In his dress he not only cultivated elegance and opulence [qualities honored by the other princes as well], he even chose [astonishing fact!] the combination of colors in accordance with the planets and the order of the days.)

23. Cp. his report from the year 1469 in A. Cappelli, "Congiura contro il duca Borso d'Este," in *Atti e memorie della Reale Deputazione di Storia Patria per le provincie Modenesi e Parmensi*, 2, 1864, p. 377 et seq.

24. About him, Giulio Bertoni, *La Biblioteca Estense,* Torino, E. Loescher, 1903 (esp. p. 194 et seq.) and Messèra, Archivio Muratoriano, 1911.

25. R. Archivio di Stato in Modena-Cancellaria Ducale-Archivi per materie: Letterati-Prisciani Pellegrino.

26. "But if you would have a man that is pious, pure, and good, you will find him born when the first portion of the Waterman rises above the horizon." Manilius, ed. cit., p. 267.

27. Venturi, ed. cit. (note 12), pp. 384–385.

28. "Delle imprese amorose nelle più antiche incisioni fiorentine," 1905, in A. Warburg, *Gesammelte Schriften*, ed. cit., I, pp. 77–88.

Erwin Panofsky

Eros Bound:
Concerning the Genealogy of Rembrandt's *Danae*

I

According to a famous notice by Pausanias, there was a sculpture at the gymnasium at Elis portraying Eros and Anteros fighting over a palm branch,[1] the composition of which we can attempt to visualize from a relief in Naples.[2] Anteros, the godhead of "reciprocated love," is not in origin a mythological figure, yet his conception derived from a mythological need: the need to bind not only the one who loves, but also the beloved, to a celestial power, to see that he reciprocates the emotion directed at him.[3] The point then of the Elian pair is not a struggle *against* love, but rather a contest *in* love: the two genii will not allow that either one should surpass the other in the strength and purity of his passion. This is confirmed by such mythologemes as that Anteros was begotten by Venus because, prior to his appearance, Eros, the firstborn, refused to grow—or that Anteros is the son of Nemesis, who requests a just balance even in the realm of feelings, and when this wish remains unfulfilled, has her son take an oftentimes terrible revenge. (Hence the popular belief that Phaedra's fate was determined by Eros, whereas that of Hippolytus by Anteros, and the legend that the Athenian cult of Anteros was inspired by the memory of a youth who, because of his nonreciprocation of a worthy man's love, drove this lover into suicide, and who then himself had to follow him into death.) And if another ancient relief depicts the struggle between Eros and Anteros not as the portrayal of a fight over the palm branch, but rather as a torch race,[4] then this is all the more unequivocal proof that the ancient Anteros in his original significance was nothing else but Dante's "Amor che a nullo amato amar perdona."

Since the rediscovery of the aforementioned ancient sources,[5] this original conception of the figure of Anteros was also carried over into the store of intellectual and visual concepts of Renaissance and Baroque. In Cartari's "Imagini delli Dei degl' Antichi," and in its countless adaptations, we find the pair described by Pausanias interpreted and visually reconstructed as a representation of "Amore reciproco."[6] And as is well known, no lesser man than Annibale Carracci depicted them in one of the corner spandrels of the Galleria Farnese, which commentators appraised as the true "Cardines" of the total conception.[7]

Simultaneously, however, the very same epoch that gave new life to the ancient concept in its original sense turned this original meaning on its head by transforming Anteros from a rival striving for the same end into a hate-filled opponent of Eros. Thus the godhead who originally compelled the beloved to reciprocate love, and, whenever necessary, avenged the nonrequital, was turned into a power that quenches the passion of love. This memorable reversal could in part be justified on the basis of an ancient pronouncement, which, however, as we now know, came into being only because of a textual distortion. In Servius' very influential commentary on Virgil, the conception of Anteros got confused with the even later one of Lyseros (the "love dissolver"), so that the god of reciprocated love appears not only as he should, as "cui curae est iniquus amor, scilicet ut implicet non amantem" ("he who attends to unequal love, in that he involves the unloving one"), but also simultaneously as the "*contrarius Cupidini,* qui amores resolvit," as the "opponent of Eros who quenches the fire of love."[8] We don't know whom to blame for this error, whether an old scribe or Servius himself. It took at any rate the full force of Neoplatonic thinking for the Renaissance to derive its conception of Anteros from a single passage whose inconsistencies should have been manifest at a glance—a conception of the godhead that constitutes neither more nor less than his equation with *"divine" love, in contrast to the "earthly" variety,* with "Amore vero, santissimo, razionale, divino," in contrast to "Amore volgare e sensuale." The sum total of what the Neoplatonists and their Renaissance apologists had to say in praise of "heavenly love" was quite simply transferred onto Anteros—and this with an audacity that would seem incredible to the modern reader were it not for those countless paintings, poems, and treatises that remind us again and again of the irresistible suggestive power of the Neoplatonic concept of love. Even Greek epigrams (in which Anteros, true to his original significance, is celebrated as the God of reciprocated love) were reinterpreted by Neoplatonists so that the very power that vindictively arouses the responsive passion of the beloved is turned into an antidote to the passion of the suitor.

This new and unclassical notion of Anteros was actually first circulated by Andrea Alciati. In the 109th of his world-famous *Emblemata,* Anteros appears, without torch or weapons, as "Amor virtutis," crowned with four wreaths, which bestow upon a nonsensual love (that shuns the company of "Cypris vulgaris") the blessing of the four cardinal virtues. (Claudius Minos, in his authoritative commentary on the *Emblemata,* cites Proclus as a precedent who characterized Anteros as an "Amor divinus, animas a corporibus abstrahentem."[9] And in the 110th Emblem (Fig. 35) Alciati goes so far as to present a struggle between this neoplatonically distorted version of Anteros, and "common love" ("Anteros, Amor virtutis, alium cupidinem superans"), the outcome of which is that "Amor pudicus" succeeds in binding "Cupido venereus" and in burning the weapons of his now defenseless opponent.[10] The extent to which both the authentic ancient conception of Anteros and its Neoplatonic distortion continued to compete with each other some one hundred years later can be seen in the wavering position held by even as learned a scholar as G. P. Bellori in regard to the Eros-Anteros group by Annibale Carracci. While, still working on his lives of the artists, he interpreted the group, in its true classical sense, as an allegory of "Amor mutuo";[11] one can read in the vitae themselves: "Nel quarto angolo viene descritto Anterote, che toglie il ramo della palma ad Amore, nel modo che gli Elei collocarono le statue nel Ginnasio; il quale Anterote credevasi che *punisse l'Amore ingiusto*"[12] (clearly a reference to Servius' notion of "iniquus amor," here not meant to signify "unequal" but "sinful love.")

The Museco Civico in Pisa has in its collection a beautiful painting by Guido Reni, commonly know as *Amore Santo e Profano,* of which a preliminary sketch can be found in the Mather Collection at Princeton. Based on the illustrations to Alciati's 110th Emblem, we can conclude without a doubt that Reni's work ought correctly to be titled *Eros and Anteros*. In both cases we find the motif of the bound Cupid combined with that of the burning of his weapons, and in both cases, "another," a bigger Eros appears on the scene as the executor of the punishments. In purely iconographic terms, Reni's composition differs from its model merely in that the temporal sequence of the two executions has been reversed. In the Alciati woodcuts, Eros is bound once his weapons are already burning; in Reni's painting, the weapons, with the addition of music, that subtler tool of seduction,[13] are just being cast into the flames, while the "Amor caecus" (in the posture of Michelangelo's rebellious *Slave* at the Louvre!) is already tied to the tree.[14] Indeed there is no great difference, in purely conceptual terms, between a battle of Eros with Anteros (as Alciati and Reni understood it) and a struggle of "heavenly" versus "earthly" love. In representational terms, however, the Eros-Anteros depictions in the Alciati illustrations and in Reni's painting are characteristically different from those pictures commonly acknowledged as portrayals of the struggle between "Amore celeste e profano," and can in fact be traced back to diverse sources. Compositions like the two paintings in upright format by Giovanni Baglione,[15] in which the victorious "Amore celeste" has toppled "Amore profano" (both here of almost equal size) and strikes out to give him the death blow, should be viewed typologically as final derivations from the "Psychomachiae," which include, as the most typical instance of the conflict between good and evil, the renditions of the fighting Archangel Michael, as well as those representations in which the conflict has been transposed to the erotic realm. There, the simple contrast between chastity and lewdness (Cupid and "Castitas," and Venus and Minerva, or the like) was replaced early by the less palpable distinction between "higher" and "lower" love, as expressed, for instance, in the popular *Punishment of a Satyr by Cupid*.[16] All these "psychomachic" representations portray the conflict between the two opposing forces as the actual dramatic execution of a fight, in which the physical existence of the opponents is threatened "ex nunc," down to the roots. The depictions of the Alciati illustrators, and Guido Reni's Pisan painting portray, on the other hand, not so much the execution of the defeat as the symbols of the triumph; they can in fact be traced back to types of representation which, in contrast to the "Psychomachiae," display a more neutral, if you will, a more *abstract* character: the *allegories of chastity* of the fifteenth century, which, inspired by Petrarch's *I Trionfi,* are among the most widespread subjects of Quattrocento art. In some of these based directly on Petrarch, Cupid, bound and bereaved of his weapons, is being driven about on the triumphal chariot of Castitas;[17] in others, bound to a tree by several female "Virtues," he is more or less vehemently abused.[18]

There can be no doubt that the type of representation exemplified by the Alciati illustrations and by Guido Reni's Pisan painting continues directly the chastity allegories, still so popular at that time;[19] and this very fact presents the most eloquent testimony to the power of the revisionist drive to which the original notion of the contest between love and requital had to yield. It is nonetheless significant that the task of punishing the little personification of "Amor terrenus" no longer falls to a Christian virtue, but rather to the platonic Anteros, "Amor divinus"—that chastity is no longer enforced by a religious, but rather, by an ethico-philosophical authority.

II

These reflections bring us at last to the problem of Rembrandt's *Danae,* painted in 1636 (Fig. 36),[20] whose interpretations so far have for the most part failed because of precisely the motif discussed earlier: the motif of the gilded wood carving at the headboard of the pompous baroque bed, depicting a *Cupid with his two hands tied, weeping over his powerlessness.* The painting has been assigned just about all the biblical and nonbiblical titles halfway applicable to a young woman awaiting her lover: Sarah awaiting Tobias, Rachel awaiting Jacob, Hagar awaiting Abraham, Bathsheba awaiting David, Venus awaiting Mars. The look of unabashedly intense joy—which for its very frankness and intensity marks Rembrandt's painting as, in a higher sense, the most innocent depiction of love in all the history of art—has in fact been misunderstood to such an extent that it was interpreted as a representation of Messalina. Indeed it is surprising that Semele, Abigail, Mrs. Potiphar, beautiful Helen or Dido have not likewise been proposed.

I do not wish to get caught up in individual refutations of all those interpretations which I find fallacious (particularly since the critiques that all prior discussants have directed at one another are always quite convincing in their negative contentions). Instead, I shall substantiate immediately that interpretation, which has as yet not been maintained with great conviction, perhaps for the sole reason that it is the oldest and still the "most obvious" one to common sense—the interpretation as *Danae*.

The sources offer three assertions that could bear reference to the Leningrad painting: first, in the estate of a certain Jan d'Ablijn, appraised by two heads of the Amsterdam Lucas Guild on June 25, 1644, mention is made of "Een groot schilderij van Venus van Rembrandt";[21] second, in Rembrandt's own inventory of 1656, listed as number 347, we find "Een groot stuck synde Danae," without the artist's name being specified;[22] third, in the estate of the widow of a certain Eduart van Domselaer, appraised by two of Rembrandt's own pupils, Jurian Ovens and Ferdinand Bol on October 16, 1660, we find, in almost identical formulation: "Een groot Stuck Schilderij van Rembrandt van Rijn synde een Dané."[23] These three records might well all refer either to the same painting (that Rembrandt could well have bought back between 1644 and 1656); or else to three different paintings, of which then at least two would have to be lost; or finally, to two distinct paintings. In the last case, one would have to assume either that only the "Ablijn Venus" and the "inventory painting" are identical, or that only the "inventory painting" and the "Domselaer Danae" or, finally, only the "Domselaer Danae" and the "Ablijn Venus" are identical. Considering the scarcity of titles such as the aforementioned in Rembrandt's oeuvre, there is no reason to rule out all three references. Thus, whichever combinatory pattern we chose, we are nevertheless left with but two contemporary titles that could possibly apply to the Leningrad painting: "Venus" and "Danae." The title "Danae" derives from two of Rembrandt's own students; whereas, on the other hand, the title "Venus" was chosen by two guild masters who neither bore any direct relation to the artist nor were really competent in such matters. This allows us to conclude at least one thing: a Rembrandt *Danae,* a work, moreover, of considerable size, really must have existed. Furthermore, if we conclude that the Domselaer and the Ablijn painting are identical, the misinterpretation of a Danae as a Venus is more likely than the contrary, considering the fact that even

Correggio's Danae was mistakenly described as a Venus by Vasari.[24] Thus the title "Danae" is the best documented one; it is after all the title which has been inseparably associated with the painting since its reappearance.

What then caused the disbelief in this traditional interpretation? First, the absence of the golden rain. Second, the aforementioned motif of the bound Cupid, which the proponents of the Danae interpretation were in fact as little able to explain as were the proponents of other theories.[25] Thirdly, the allegedly more horizontally than upward-directed glance of the reclining woman.

The third counterargument is the easiest to refute. For even if the *head* is not raised sharply, it is neither raised markedly less than in the representations of Danae by Annibale Carracci and Titian, not to speak of Correggio, whose Danae is looking downward, as if lost in dreams. The *glance* of our Danae is unquestionably directed *upward*, toward the radiant light pouring in through the drawn curtain. Her eye follows the uplifted hand, which both welcomes the apparition, and wards off its blinding brightness. The bright light, we acknowledge, is definitely not a real golden rain — and here we touch upon the second objection, leaving the third, the ostensible inexplicability of the Cupid, to the final section of this essay. But this burst of light does herald the appearance of the godhead as such, and one might say, as with the magical light that emanates from the Christ figures in Rembrandt's Emmaus paintings, that the miracle is hereby all the more miraculously portrayed than if it transpired in all its streaming or ringing splendor. Correggio also depicts, not so much the golden rain as the soft-toned cloud at whose edge the honey-colored drops first gather and slowly start to fall — not so much the occurrence itself as the *anticipation* of the miracle. And if, so as to extend still more the span between preparation and fulfillment, and thereby to add all the more import to the moment of waiting, Rembrandt completely dispensed with the cloud, depicting only the supernatural radiance emanating from it, then he did nothing else but raise the palpable plastic materialization of the godhead to a purely visionary realm. In so doing, he was only reverting back, beyond Renaissance paganism, to a visual concept that had already been formulated in certain representations of Danae in the Middle Ages, a concept whose gradual renewal can already be observed in the late sixteenth century. This said, we are now well into what we might call the *Typengeschichte* (typological history) of the myth of Danae.

III

In contrast to most other key figures in pagan mythology, Danae was not handed down to posterity in the form of a "Catasterism,"* nor was she accorded in-depth treatment by Ovid, who only mentions her in passing.[26] Except for occasional references in the works of other classical poets (among which the one in Terence's "Eunuchus" retained a particular presence in the Middle Ages, thanks to a quote from Saint Augustine),[27] and except for short accounts in the well-known mythographic handbooks (Hyginus, Apollodorus, Fulgentius, the two older Mythographi Latini), the most detailed accounts are to be found in Horace (Carm. III, 16), and in still greater detail, in the relatively obscure Scholia to the "Argonautica" of Apollonios of Rhodes (IV, v. 1091). Danae is the daughter of the Argive king Akrisios, to whom the oracle prophesied that the son of his daughter would kill him. To keep her out of any man's reach, he locks her up in a fortified dungeon (since Horace, usually referred to as a "brazen tower") guarded by sentries and dogs, but gives her, according to the Scholia to Apollonios, the aged nurse (*trophos*) to serve her and keep her company. How Jupiter nonetheless succeeds in approaching her is well known, and the attendant events, the birth and secret upbringing of Perseus, the exposure and the miraculous rescue of mother and child are all not at issue here.

In classical paintings (sculptures, if there were any, don't seem to have survived), the decisive event was the depiction of a golden rain falling either through the ceiling beams (as closest to the myth), or from the clouds, or, finally, from the cornucopia of a flying Cupid, into the lap of the now standing, now seated, Danae. In some cases, the scepter-wielding Jupiter sits enthroned close by, comically uninvolved. A remarkable fourth-century A.D. graffito relief in the Kaiser-Friedrich Museum in Berlin may be considered both a vestige of the classical, and a precursor of the medieval, representations,

Katasterismos: placing among the stars. — Ed.

even though the piece could hardly have been known to later centuries. In it the cloud is replaced by the halo-ringed head of a god, possibly already pointing at the Christian theological interpretation, which will be discussed presently.[28]

In the Middle Ages, where the illustration of Ovid, otherwise the most fertile branch of tradition, bears no fruit, we find (albeit hardly before the fifteenth century) pictorial representations of the Danae myth essentially in three contexts: in a *fictional,* a *moralizing,* and a *theological* one. First, there is the medieval revision of the Trojan epics, written by Raoul Lefevre toward the end of the fifteenth century, commonly known under the title "Recueil des Histoires de Troye," in which the compiler incorporated a good part of Boccaccio's "Genealogia Deorum."[29] Second, we have the fourteenth-century "Fulgentius Metaforalis," by Johann Ridewall, one of the many moralizations of mythology to which that century gave rise.[30] And third, there is the "Defensorium inviolatae virginitatis Mariae" of Franciscus de Retza,[31] composed at about the same time as Ridewall's work.

The illustrations of the "Recueil" are the farthest removed from the original mythical meaning of the legend. In a comically naive continuation of the ancient notion that the motif of the golden rain symbolized the irresistible pull of gold and jewellery, "Le noble Roy Jupiter" appears disguised as a diamond dealer. As a "messagier apportant plusieurs joyaux et baghes" (which he procured from the purveyor to the royal court of his father, Saturn)—like Autolycus approaching the hut of Perdita—he approaches the "fortified tower," ringed by moat and rampart, in which the poor princess "Danée" is being held despite her wild protestations. And following an effective parley with her "Damoiselles" (for the nurse of the Apollonios Scholia had already multiplied early on into a small female retinue),[32] he succeeds at a second visit in getting into the tower, and with the aid of the nurse (here advanced to first lady-in-waiting) gains entry to Danae's bedroom, where now in the full splendor of his beard and ambrosian locks, he reveals his true identity as father of the gods and men.[33]

The illustrations of the "Fulgentius Metaforalis" accompany a text that reads as follows: "Situ sublimata, moenibus vallata, egestate sata, agmine stipata, prole fecundata, auro violata." That is, Danae stands or is seated atop a tower protected to no avail by a throng of armed guards, while the golden rain falls on her in tight drops. These depictions (whose tradition can still be noted in Gossaert's famous painting of 1527, now in Munich), are not intended, after all, to merely tell a story, but rather to offer allegoricized moral instruction. And in accordance with the spirit of an exegesis, in which Juno signified "Memory" and Paris signified "Justice," the story of Danae is understood as an allegory of "Pudicitia." Thus the type of representation corresponds almost verbatim to the Giottesque allegory of Chastity in the Lower Church at Assisi.[34] If the "Recueil des Histoires de Troyes" transforms the Danae legend into the gallant adventure of a knightly prince, and the "Fulgentius Metaforalis" focuses more on the moral import than on the mythic essence of the tale, it is the mystery of the procreative act as such that interested author and illustrators of the *Defensorium inviolatae virginitatis*. Here, where the whole point was to wrest from both the ancient legend and the entire natural order evidence for the possibility of virgin birth, Danae becomes a *prefiguration of Mary*, for as the accompanying text affirms, "Si Danae auri pluvia praegnans a Jove claret, Cur spiritu sancto gravida Virgo non generaret?"[35] So in this case, it is the illustrator's intent to draw the viewer's attention to the miraculous occurrence as such. Whether Danae is depicted, contrary to tradition, as lying on bedding in an open field, or, like Saint Catherine or Barbara, is seated at a barred prison window, all that is meant to be brought home is that here, too, a virgin is impregnated by divine and incomprehensible means. And the means that seemed to visualize the miracle most clearly was the same to which Rembrandt would turn two hundred years later, namely, *the substitution of the metallic rain by a burst of light,* the only difference being that in these primitive depictions, the light is perceived as falling from the planets of heaven, rather than as a visionary emanation.

IV

In the Italian Renaissance a cohesive pictorial tradition of the Danae myth developed only relatively late,[36] since on the one hand, the age, by its very nature, could not connect with depictions such as those mentioned above, and on the other hand, it had no access to classical representations of the myth. Thus the sole paths open to such a development were either an autonomous creation, or a *creation based on analogous mythological motifs.*

Correggio's painting in the Borghese collection is an "holdes Wunder" (a lovely miracle) which, except for a vague resemblance, merely in the figure of Cupid, to the Ignudo to the right of the Cumaea, can neither be explained by reference to earlier art, nor has it, as far as we can see, a following—unless we are willing to acknowledge a grossly pornographic work of Bonasone's (Engraving B. 153) which, judging from Cupid's manner of motion and a few other details, betrays a familiarity with Correggio's work—and a few late French imitations as legitimate heirs to the Borghese painting.[37]

Aside from few exceptions, such as the aforementioned Bonasone etching or a Veronese-like composition in Turin, related in motif to Titian's *Nymph and Shepherd* in Vienna,[38] the representations of Danae in the Italian High Renaissance can largely be divided into two groups, which soon after their creation variously commingle: a *Leda-type* and a *Venus-type*. The *Venus-type* is represented perhaps in its purest form by a painting in Lyon ascribed to Tintoretto, and by a work of Schiavone's in a private collection in Italy. Both paintings depict a slightly modified version of the reclining Venus, a form very popular in Venice, whereby the Schiavone even dispenses with the golden rain, portraying instead a Putto strewing gold coins from a mighty urn.[39] The *Leda-type*, on the other hand, was first given form in a fresco by Primaticcio in the "Galerie des Réformés" at Fontainebleau, which has been preserved in a Viennese tapestry copy and an engraving by Thiry (B. 40).[40] This type received a form of world-historical importance in the painting by Titian, which was executed in 1545 in Rome for Cardinal Ottaviano Farnese, and hangs now in the Museo Nazionale in Naples (Fig. 37). Conceived, as it were, under the eyes of Michelangelo and, it is said, highly admired by him,[41] this picture, which has been often copied and even more often paraphrased, combines a Cupid derived from the Eros Chiaramonti[42] with a Danae who—like Primaticcio's—is unquestionably derived from Michelangelo's *Leda* (and his closely related *Notte*). In her gaze, which seems to emerge out of profound dreams, we seem to sense something of the expression of Michelangelo's Adam. And the fact that here even Titian had to reveal himself as obligated to the work of others—even if those others were to be Michelangelo and Praxiteles—demonstrates with particular clarity that the subject of Danae initially lacked a tradition. But the treatment of the cloud from which the metallic rain pours down is altogether new and uniquely titianesque. No more the still container, in which the golden drops gather, Titian transforms the cloud into a *flashing, flaming apparition*. Nothing could have been farther from Titian's intention than to "dematerialize" the mythically concrete event by transforming it into a "luminaristic" phenomenon (it is far too dramatic for that, and a recently discovered later workshop copy even shows the face of Jupiter amidst the explosive discharge). Yet we can nonetheless foresee that this transposition of the motif into the realm of "lighting effects" could initiate a development that eventually would lead to the complete elimination of the actual cloud.

Nine years later, as we know, Titian executed, or rather, directed the execution of, several variations based on the original. In these later replicas (one must call them so, for the changes in the main figure are comparatively slight), the Cupid is replaced by the more profane figure of the aged nurse, which likewise appears in Primaticcio's painting. However, one should bear in mind that the nurse does not owe her appearance to a mere genrelike-satirical whim of the artist, but was requested outright by the account in the Scholia to Apollonios Rhodios, which had only now been rediscovered in their affinity to the spirit of the times, and which indeed encouraged a "worldly" interpretation of the scene. From then on the nurse became an almost indispensable companion of Danae; yet with regard to the Leningrad Rembrandt, we must acknowledge that it is just the later Titian composition, which—at least in those versions in Leningrad and Madrid—confirms the nurse's stewardly role through the presence of *pouch* and *key*.

In the course of the further development, individual aspects of both Titian compositions (sometimes the one, sometimes the other, and sometimes both together) are seized upon, but the michelangelesque boldness of the principal motif seems no longer tolerable, so that the portrayal of Danae gradually moves back again to the "Venus-type." And this happens as a rule in more or less blatant adaptation of the great model that Titian himself had created in his oft-repeated *Reclining Venus with the Organ Player*.

So Bloemart, Goltzius, and Wtewael combined this "Reclining Venus"—in more or less profound "Mannerist" transformation, however, in part also in reconstruction of the genrelike character of the interior, so indigenous to Northern art—with the old nurse of Titian's later composition (whereas the motif of Jupiter's head, looking down from the cloud as in a depiction of the Annunciation, seems to be derived from the above-mentioned workshop copy).[43] And so we come at last to *Annibale Carracci*, whose work in this as in so many other instances established the standard type of Baroque art. He simply transformed the same "Reclining Venus" into a Danae adapting the motif of the left arm propped up, with the hand grasping the bedsheet, the tilt of the head and the shape of the bedstead of the Neapolitan version of Titian's Danae (painting at Bridgewater House; Fig. 38).[*] The only feature that does not already figure in Titian's work is the sweeping gesture of the other arm, whose hand draws back the bed curtain. But the overall composition corresponds—especially in the adoption, even exaggeration, of the oblong format, in the elimination of the nurse, and the identical proportioning of the window frame—so closely to the *Reclining Venus with a View into a Landscape* (1555, Uffizi), that Guido Reni could retransform this "Danae," with only small changes, into a *Venus* (Dresden, Gemäldegalerie).[44]

V

This highly acclaimed work of Annibale's may well be considered the *actual prototype* for Rembrandt, who, as we know, owned not only the engravings by the Bolognese master but also copies of his paintings.[45] Evidently a gulf exists between Carracci's classicism, with its strict frontality and balanced correlation between figure and landscape, and the Baroque subjectivism of the early Rembrandt, reveling in the diagonal thrusts of the billowing curtains and the irrational eruptions of the light. It is true the gesture of the outstretched arm, which in Carracci's work merely draws back the

*According to D. Posner, *Annibale Carracci* (London, 1971), vol. 1, pp. 129–130, and vol. 2, p. 69 and plate 153a, this painting, now destroyed, was merely sketched by Annibale and executed by Francesco Albani.—Ed.

curtain, received in Rembrandt's painting the expressive significance of both joyous surprise and defence. Not only the figure's spirituality, but her physicality as well seems to have been reborn, regardless of the model, out of a "primary experience" (Urerlebnis) of Rembrandt's. And yet when viewed in the context of all other representations of the same theme, Carracci's and Rembrandt's compositions have so much in common that there can be no doubt about the connection.[46] It is a telling fact that Rembrandt's expressive impulse was ignited and nourished by Annibale's dispassionate classicism, rather than by the seemingly more congenial (in truth because of its profound otherness, unassimilable), excitement of a painting by Titian, infused with the pathos of Michelangelo. It was not ignorance, but rather an outright rejection of Titian's "Leda motif" that induced Rembrandt to follow Carracci: Not only did he reintroduce the nurse, absent from the Carracci painting (this could as well have been suggested to him by his Dutch predecessors); he also furnished her with the attributes of pouch and key, which, as far as we see, could only be due to a direct acquaintance with Titian's second version of his Danae. The genre figure of the later painting by Titian, stripped albeit of her gypsyish greed and ferocity, could thus enter Rembrandt's version for the very same reason that the academic Annibale Carracci had to eliminate her.

But aside from the "great compositions" of Carracci and Titian, Rembrandt knew still another less noteworthy Danae: that of Hieronymus Wiericx (Fig. 39). Wiericx's engraving (Mauquoy-Hendrickx, 1594) stresses, like so many Northern representations of the time, the realism of the interior, and adds the figure of the nurse; on the other hand, it treats the figure of Danae with such regressive mannerist stylization that she becomes — characteristically — in her overall appearance similar to Reni's Venus.[47] This engraving prefigured Rembrandt's painting in two characteristic features that are not to be found in any other depictions of the scene. For one, it is the *nurse* here, and no longer Danae herself who draws back the curtain. And secondly, the burst of light out of which Jupiter's head emerges is portrayed as an almost Dürer-like gloriole, so bright that Danae's head casts a dark shadow on the pillow. The assimilation and further development of the first motif gave Rembrandt the chance to transform the gesture of the outstretched arm, drawing back the curtain. Merely functional in the Carracci, it becomes in

Rembrandt's painting purely expressive. And the assimilation and development of the second motif paved the way for an even more profound "luminarization" of the miraculous occurrence. For Rembrandt — but only for him — it took just one more step to imbue the outstretched arm (which here is no longer engaged in concrete action and, in Wiericx's engraving, says both too much and too little with its beckoning gesture), to imbue this arm with that wonderfully complex expression of joy, fright, and defence. Rembrandt deepened the good-natured servility of an old nurse, eager to further the happiness of her beloved charge, into a quiet, motherly sympathy. And in place of that miraculous cloud, already so far altered into a luminous apparition, he let only its magical radiance shine forth. In Rembrandt, a Danae without a golden rain is no less unexpected than an "Arrival of the Women at the Sepulchre" without an angel, an "Agony in the Garden" without the chalice and an Andromeda chained to the cliff without Perseus and the dragon.[48]

Thus the genealogy of the Leningrad painting demonstrates that it stands, in spite of its profound originality, in a pictorial tradition which can be traced continually, beginning with Titian. It is hardly thinkable that a painting that combines details of three depictions of Danae; that contains a motif so typical (at least in northern Europe) as that of the old nurse;[49] that even in respect to its boldest innovation — the replacement of the golden rain by a mere radiance — is not without precursors and analogues: it is hardly thinkable that such a painting should not also depict a Danae.

But what is the significance of the bound Cupid? He cannot be a meaningless ornament. This is ruled out, not only by his conspicuousness, but also by the contemporary usage as evidenced in many parallel cases. So in a painting by Carlo Cignani, now in Copenhagen, the bed in which Potiphar's wife attempts to seduce Joseph is marked as a place of sin by a *torch-waving Cupid*. And we find similar confirmation in a particularly telling example, namely, a drawing of the calumny of Joseph (formerly in Oldenburg) from Rembrandt's own workshop; in this drawing the bedposts are shaped like a *nymph and a faun*.[50] It would be reasonable then to presume that these analogies would likewise call for the presence in Rembrandt's painting of a free, rather than a bound, Eros. But the drawing, formerly in Oldenburg, teaches us that, particularly with Rembrandt, the symbolic import of such "ornamentation" need not necessarily bear reference to the *scenic content of the moment,* but may rather shed light on the *entire character and destiny of the persons involved,* illuminating less therefore the momentary meaning of the action depicted, and more its psychological background. The bedposts in the shape of faun and nymph in the drawing do refer to Potiphar's wife, not in the sense that she is unchaste at this moment (for this, evidently, does not happen), but rather that she is unchaste by her very character and destiny. To put it more simply: the bed carvings tell us less about the way in which the bed is being used at the moment, but more about the purpose for which it was originally intended. And so too the bound Eros—whom, interestingly enough, Ferdinand Bol replaced with a Christian cherub in his reinterpretation of the composition as a *Marriage of Rachel,*[51]— characterizes not so much the mythic miracle taking place, or more accurately, announcing itself, as much rather the condition *preceding* this mythic miracle: namely, the *forced chastity* of Danae. She who had been condemned by her father, the "custos pavidus virginis abditae," to eternal celibacy; she whom, as we have seen, the Middle Ages would interpret as an allegory of "Pudicitia," and even as a parable of the Virgin Mary, and of whom it is repeatedly written: "Ad *castitatem* tuendam aerea turre inclusa,"[52]—her virginal bed could not have been more aptly designated than by a symbol which, as we have shown, has long stood for chastity, and moreover, a chastity dearly paid for by the "binding of instincts"; one might almost say, a chastity contrary to nature. And this is exactly how the seventeenth century understood the character of bound Eros. Even Annibale Carracci—and this should gratify those who would rather not credit Rembrandt with the spontaneous invention of an "allegorical" idea for a picture—expressed the concept of chastity in his Danae by a depiction of the aforementioned scene of the satyr flung to the ground, painted on the face of a large, smoking sacrificial urn—this latter perhaps not an unintentional allusion to the well-known motif in Titian's *Heavenly and Earthly Love.* Rembrandt simply makes the message that much clearer—and more human: His bound Cupid symbolizes the supposedly incontrovertible fate of a being, who, because of a selfish command, was denied fulfillment of her destiny, and could only be restored to this destiny by the intervention of a god. Bound and weeping, a symbol of reluctantly endured solitude, Cupid looms as a shadow of the past over a redemptive present, a present which from its very contrast to the past receives its justification and its radiant consecration.

Notes

1. Pauanias, *Periegesis* VI, 23, 3 and 5. Cp. to this and to the following the Anteros, resp. Eros articles in Roscher's *Mythologisches Lexikon* and in Pauly-Wissowas's *Real-Enzyklopaedie der klass. Altertumskunde.*

2. Salomon Reinach, *Rép. de Reliefs Grecs et Romains,* Paris, E. Leroux, 1912, III, p. 73.

3. Cp. this to the admirably learned compilation of L. C. Gyraldus, *Syntagmata,* XIII, in the Leyden edition of 1696, p. 410 and foll., which was generously used in Vincenzo Cartari's *Imagini degli Dei degli Antichi* (1556), which was alone available to me in the Venetian edition of 1674, p. 242 and foll., and in the Alciati commentary of Claudius Minos. (edition Leyden, 1591, p. 394 and foll.).

4. Reinach, op. cit., p. 219. It was common in antiquity to distinguish Anteros from Eros by depicting the former with folded wings.

5. Concerning the editions and translations of Pausanias (one of which was already begun in 1448, first edition of the original text printed in Venice, 1516), cf. Karl Bernhard Stark, *Systematik und Geschichte der Archaeologie der Kunst,* Leipzig, Engelmann 1880, p. 93 (kind reference of my colleague Prof. E. v. Mercklin).

6. Cartari, op. cit., p. 242.

7. Cp. H. Tietze in *Jahrb. d. Kunstlgn. d. Allerh. Kaiserh.* XXVI, 1906, p. 98, in which, however (despite the correct mentioning of the Cartari woodcut), there is no reference to the Eros-and-Anteros theme. I understand that Jean Seznec will undertake the still missing iconological examination of the Galleria Farnese.

8. *Servii Grammatici qui feruntur in Vergilii carmina commentarii,* ed. Georg Thilo and Hermann Hagen, Leipzig, B. G. Teubner, I, 1881, p. 559 and, above all, Praefatio, p. XII and foll.

9. Alciati, Emblemata, op. cit, p. 395. The relevant passages in Proclus, which Dr. Weil was kind enough to bring to my attention (*In rem publicam* I, p. 176, and II, p. 347, Kroll, above all however *In Alcibiadem,* p. 417, Cousin) all have nothing whatsoever to do with Anteros, but unequivocally refer to Plato's "Amor Divinus" or "Celestis" who, as *erōs monimos, energētikos, aulos, entheos,* embodies the opposite of fickle, material, passive, and wanton, sensual love. For this reference to Proclus, the Alciati commentator is likewise indebted to Gyraldus, who, however, is too careful simply to appropriate the version supposedly confirmed by Proclus.

10. Alciati, op. cit., p. 397 and foll.

11. Cp. C. C. Malvasia, *Felsina Pittrice,* 1678, I, p. 437 and foll.

12. Giovanni Pietro Bellori, *Vite dei pittori, scultori ed architetti moderni* (1672), Pisa, N. Capurro, 1821, p. 53.

13. For the symbolism of musical instruments and the *Libro di musica aperto,* cp. Cesare Ripa, *Iconologia,* s. v. "Scandalo."

14. The sketch allows us to recognize that the original composition placed the two figures closer together and thus was more closely related to the Alciati woodcut (this is confirmed by an obviously earlier sketch in Venice, ill. in V. Moschini, *Bollettino d'Arte,* 1931, p. 78. Between the Alciati woodcut and Reni's version, there

is a composition by G. Procaccini (drawing in the Albertina, No. B 86-2042; for the reference I am gratful to Dr. Heinrich Brauer), which already depicts the role reversal alluded to in the text.

15. Cp. H. Voss, *Jahrb. d. Preuss. Kunstlgn.*, 1923, p. 92 et seq. Malvasia, op. cit., p. 499 also makes reference to a painting of the same subject by Agostino Carracci.

16. Cp. instead of all other examples, the lovely drawing ascribed to Correggio, in Windsor, ill. in Adolfo Venturi, *Correggio,* German edition, Rome, A. Stock, 1926, pl. 175.

17. The number of representations is legion. In Schubring's Cassoni work alone, some twenty versions are presented (e.g., No. 325). At the same time there were of course depictions of the psychomachic struggle between Amor and Castitas, as in the well-known painting in the National Gallery (Schubring No. 326) and in Perugino's painting commissioned by Isabella d'Este.

18. Cp., for instance, Schubring No. 482, which is quite close to the well-known engraving, Internat. Chalkogr. Ges. 1889-5. Conversely, we have the engraving by C. Galle after Ag. Carracci, which shows Venus bound to a tree, while the kneeling Cupido is being lashed by Minerva (Malvasia, op. cit., p. 103).

19. Cp., for instance, Cesare Ripa, *Iconologia,* s.v.v. "Castita" and "Carro" (here the *Trionfi* of Petrarch). The large engraving B. 101 by Bonasone, done in 1563, gives a new, cheerfully frivolous twist to the motif of the bound Eros, showing the souls of happy lovers (the scene is transposed to Elysium) who, only as a joke, tied up the god of love and only jokingly pummel him with wreaths of roses; when Venus, enraged by her own amorous destiny, seriously castigates Eros, the souls of the lovers let him go free, ". . . E tornò poi/In questo mondo, a trionfar di noi." As we can well imagine, it was only a sentimentalized form of a similarly frivolous version that became predominant in the eighteenth century, as in an engraving by W. W. Ryland, based on a tondo by Angelica Kauffmann, in which the bound Cupid (motif taken from Reni!) is bombarded with flowers by two charming young ladies, while a third attempts to break his bow; or in an etching by Johann Heinrich Ramberg in which three little girls bind an Amorino with chains of roses. In an engraving by Marcenay de Ghuy after a painting by Lebrun, the motif is even used in a pictorial epithalamium: Minerva and a personification of Innocence clip the wings of the bound Cupid and Hymen triumphantly waves his marriage torch.

20. From the literature, I shall mention only W. Niemeyer, *Rep. f. Kunstwiss,* LII, 1931, p. 58 and foll. (interpretation as Hagar, according to which the nurse would then be Sarah and the Cupid would refer to the infertility of the legitimate marriage of Abraham); Werner Weisbach, *Rembrandt,* Berlin, W. de Gruyter, 1926, p. 242 and foll. (interpretation as Venus, according to which the Cupid would have to foretell the binding of the godly lovers by Vulcan); Shelly Rosenthal, *Jahrb. f. Kunstwiss,* 1928, p. 105 and foll. (interpretation as Rachel). Niemeyer's critique of the two last-mentioned interpretations (as also of the, at first glance, very convincing ascription of the scene to Sarah awaiting the arrival of Tobias) seems to me to be so conclusive that I would not want to add anything further to it. I cannot, however, adopt his own interpretation, for the very reason that it seems implausible to me that the old housekeeper (see text), who identifies herself through her attributes and posture, and whom both written sources and typological history confirm in equal measure as a nurse, should be the dramatic subject of the painting.

21. Cp. A. Bredius in *Oud Holland* XXVIII, 1910, p. 9, particularly emphasized by Weisbach, op. cit.

22. Cp. Cornelis Hofstede de Groot (ed.), *Die Urkunden über Rembrandt,* Haag, M. Nijhoff, 1906, No. 169.

23. Cp. A. Bredius in *Oud Holland* XXVII, 1908, p. 222, and C. Neumann, *Rembrandt,* Munich, F. Bruckmann 3rd ed., 1922, p. 444 (this note rightfully seemed important enough to Neumann to prompt him to abandon the interpretation he had earlier accepted "for lack of a better one," namely, that the painting depicts Sarah awaiting Tobias).

24. Vasari, ed. Milanesi, VI, p. 115.

25. Thus Somoff in the catalogue of the Ermitage under No. 802, in which he explains the bound Cupid as the "Symbole de l'amour vénal" (cp. the dissenting view of Niemeyer, p. 60).

26. Cp. Roscher and Pauly-Wissowa, op. cit., s.v. "Danae."

27. Augustinus, *Civitas Dei* II, 7: "Hinc apud Terentium flagitiosus adolescens spectat tabulam quandam pictam in pariete ubi inerat pictura haec, Jovem quo pacto Danaae misisse aiunt quondam in gremium imbrem aureum." ("So the young rake in Terence gazes at a certain picture painted on a wall: Where in the painting was the tale how into Danae's lap a golden shower fell. Dispatched by Jove, Men say . . . ") (Translation by George E. McCracken).

28. About the classical murals, cp. Salomon Reinach, *Rép. de Peintures Grecques et Romaines,* Paris, E. Leroux, 1922, p. 1 and foll. About the Berlin graffito (published by O. Wulff, *Amtl. Berichte aus d. Kgl. Kunstlgn.,* Berlin XXXV, 1913, p. 28) cp. Marc Rosenberg, *Von Paris von Troia bis zum König von Mercia,* 1930 (private printing), p. 59 and foll.

29. Cp. P. Meyer in *Romania* XIV, 1885, p. 1 and foll. and in particular, Heinrich Oskar Sommer, *The Recueyll of the Historyes of Troye,* London, D. Nutt, 1894.

30. Cp. Hans H. Liebeschütz, "Fulgentius Metaforalis," *Stud. d. Bibl. Warburg* IV, Leipzig, B. G. Teubner, 1926, pp. 56 and 116, also Fig. 8.

31. Cp. J. v. Schlosser, in *Jahrb. d. Kunstlgn. d. Allerh. Kaiserh.* XXIII, 1902, p. 311, as well as pl. VII and XXIII. For further reference see Marc Rosenberg, op. cit.

32. Cp., for instance, Mythographus II (G. H. Bode, *Scriptores rer. myth. lat. tres,* 1834), No. 110: "Adhibens puellas custodes."

33. Paris, Bibl. Nat., ms. fr. 22552, fol. 43, 45, 49. In a handwritten manuscript like Paris, Bibl. de l'Arsenal 3692, the various scenes (to which sometimes the scene of the incarceration in the tower is added, as, for instance, in Bibl. Nat., ms. fr. 59, fol. 42v) are all combined into one.

34. The source is evidently Augustinus, *Civ. Dei* XVIII, 13: ". . .finxerunt . . . Danaae per imbrem aurem adpetisse concubitum, ubi intelligitur pudicitia mulieris auro fuisse corrupta. . . . ." ("Whoever the men were who invented the legend that . . . Jove sought to share the couch of Danae in a shower of gold, in which we understand that the woman's chastity was corrupted by gold . . . " transl. Sanford and Green.) The fact that Jan Gossaert is indebted to the Fulgentius Metaforalis hardly needs to be substantiated: in his painting, the golden rain that pours down in heavy vertical drops likewise strikes a smartly dressed, seated lady, whose domed, semicircular bower still seems to presuppose, because of the character of the view outside the windows, a reminiscence of the "Situ sublimata" of the ancient text.

35. ("If, as is well known, Danae became pregnant through Jupiter's golden rain, why should not the Virgin, pregnant of the Holy Ghost, have given birth?") Hereto as source reference, Augustinus XX O, *de Civ. Dei,* VII (mistakenly cited instead of II, 7, cf. here note 27) "et Terentius in Eunucho et Ovidius Metamorphoseos."

36. In Schubring's work on the Cassoni, one sole and apparently rather dubious example is cited (No. 502/503), of which neither a more detailed description nor even a photograph was available. Baldassare Peruzzi's depiction of Danae in the small

frieze in the Villa Farnesina is essentially merely the Renaissance transformation of the medieval type of Danae as prefiguration of the Virgin Mary.
37. Cp. the paintings by Louis de Boulogne (illus. in "Les Arts," 1905, No. 43 and 45; the author thanks Frau Sittah Janssen for the reference) and P. Cazes, engraved by L. Desplaces. Correggio's *Danae* was, as we know, in the possession of the Regent Philip of Orléans.
38. Cp. Salomon Reinach, *Répertoire de Peintures du Moyen Age et de la Renaissance (1280–1580)*, Paris, E. Leroux, 1923, VI, p. 200.
39. Cp. Reinach, ibid., p. 202, as well as Froehlich-Bume, Dedalo X, 1929/30, p. 369.
40. Illus. in Burl. Mag. XXXVII, 1920, p. 131.
41. Cp. Carlo Ridolfi, *Le Maraviglie dell'Arte*, ed. D.v. Hadeln, 2 vols., Berlin, G. Grote, 1914, I, p. 178 and foll.
42. As already noticed by Crowe and Cavalcaselle, *Tizian* (German edition publ. by Jordan 1877, p. 470).
43. The workshop copy (which shows the Neapolitan version, albeit contaminated by certain features of the later version) is published as authentic by D.v. Hadeln in *Burlington Mag.*, XLVIII, 1926, p. 78 and foll.; two drawings by Wtewael (one of them probably not authentic) are reproduced in C.M.A.A. Lindemann, *Joachim Anthonisz Wtewael*, Utrecht 1929, Tab. LI and LII; the Goltzius painting (dated 1603) is published by O. Hirschman, in *Oud-Holland* XXXIII, 1915, p. 129 and foll. The latter, by the way, is not only noteworthy for its varied allegorical-genrelike and mythological enrichments, but also for the fact that the motif of the torso — above all, in the tilt of the head toward one shoulder and in the posture of the left arm — was modified after the example of a drawing by Sebastiano del Piombo, formerly ascribed to Michelangelo (*The Dead Christ*, Frey 21), a drawing, which, as the Munich Pietà of Willem Key proves (cp. E. v. Liphart, *Zeitschr. f. bild. Kunst.* N.F. XXIV, 1913, p. 208 and foll.), was known in the Netherlands.
44. Dresden, Catalog No. 324. Incidentally, Titian's Neapolitan *Danae* was also often copied as a Venus, as, for instance, by an Anonymous in Dresden, Catalog No. 288, and by Contarini in a work now in the Academy in Venice.
45. This according to the Inventory of 1656 l.c. No. 81, 83, 209, 232.
46. Subsequently I see that W. Drost has already pointed emphatically to the affinity with Annibale Carracci's Danae, in *Handbuch der Kunstwiss.*, *Barockmalerei in den germ. Ländern*, p. 159. However, one cannot agree with his aesthetic appraisal and, in particular, with his interpretation of Rembrandt's painting as a *Dalilah* (which is based only upon the fact that the blinded Samson of the Frankfurt painting is likewise being bound).
47. One might well contend that Reni is the only major Italian Baroque painter who was able to carry the positive innovations of Mannerism over into the Baroque. This fact not only stands out with beautiful clarity in the Eros and Anteros painting, but also in his Venus, who provokes comparison with her Carraccesque model, and in her tense slimness, her rhythmically tight contour, her almost gothicizing crossing of the feet, and her strangely opposite arm movements, may well remind one of Bronzino or Wtewael.
48. As to the absence of the chalice in the Gethsemane etching B. 75, cp. the excellent analysis by F. Schmidt-Degener in "Rembrandt und der Holländ. Barock," tr. G. Pauli in *Stud. d. Bibl. Warburg* IX, Leipzig, B. G. Teubner, 1928, p. 18 and foll. In the drawing *Women at the Sepulchre* (Slg. Koenigs), which W. Stechow brought to my attention (Rembrandt exhibition, Amsterdam, 1932, Catalog No. 321), Rembrandt intentionally removed the angel that was originally included, as Schmidt-Degener has also observed. Finally, the small Andromeda painting in the

Bredius Collection is particularly instructive in our context, in that we are here dealing with a creation of about the same period and type, and in that here, too, the moment of expectation, the eager concentration of Andromeda's psychic energies upon the arrival of a "redeemer" coming from outside the picture (in this case, Perseus approaching from afar), plays a decisive role.

49. Of those Danae depictions of "titianesque" derivation known to me at the moment, only three relinquish the nurse: Annibale Carracci's version, which obviously and for perfectly comprehensible reasons, is the first to eliminate again that all too "genrelike" motif; Carlo Maratti's version (engraved by Louis Desplaces) which, like so many other works by that master, is a mere variant of the Carracci painting, yet transfers the titianesque motif of catching gold in a piece of clothing from the nurse's apron to Cupid's shirt; and Giuseppe Diamantini's etching (B. 40), which, despite Baroque shifts and various additions and changes in details (such as that Jupiter here pours the golden rain out of an urn), can likewise be traced back unmistakably to Carracci's conception. On the other hand, the nurse is present (in addition to the aforementioned instances of Titian II, Primaticcio, Bloemart, Wtewael, Goltzius, and Wiericx) in works by "Tintoretto" (Lyon), Stefano della Bella (etching de Vesme-Massar 539), van Dyck (Dresden, Catal. No. 1039), P. Cazes, and L. Boulogne (here she is added in spite of the strong dependence upon Correggio), and lastly, in an etching by Oeser.

50. Published by E. Waldmann in *Monatshefte f. Kunstwiss.* I, 1908, p. 436 and foll., cp. now W. Valentiner in *Rembrandt, des Meisters Handzeichnungen, Klass. d. Kunst.* Vol XXXI, Stuttgart, Deutsche Verlagsanstalt (1925), No. 104. For the reference to this drawing, which is so important in our context, I am grateful to Frau Dr. Schubart; however, cp. also Schmidt-Degener, op. cit., p. 19.

51. Painting in Braunschweig, ill. in Sh. Rosenthal, op. cit., Fig. 4.

52. Thus the *Mythographus* III (ed. Bode, op. cit.), Chapters 3, 5.

Translated by Peter Wortsman

Photographic Credits

The editor and publisher wish to thank the custodians of the works of art for supplying photographs and granting permission to use them.

1. Bayerische Staatsgemäldesammlungen, Munich.
2. Bayerische Staatsgemäldesammlungen, Munich.
3. Bayerische Staatsgemäldesammlungen, Munich.
4. Bayerische Staatsgemäldesammlungen, Munich.
5. Bayerische Staatsgemäldesammlungen, Munich.
6. Bildarchiv Foto Marburg.
7. Deutsches Archäologisches Institut, Rome.
8. Städelsches Kunstinstitut, Frankfort/M.
9. Alinari/Art Resource.
10. Bayerische Staatsgemäldesammlungen, Munich.
11. Alinari-Scala/Art Resource.
12. National Gallery Publications, London.
13. Deutsches Archäologisches Institut, Rome.
14. Deutsches Archäologisches Institut, Rome.
15. Deutsches Archäologisches Institut, Rome.

16. Deutsches Archäologisches Institut, Rome.

17. Deutsches Archäologisches Institut, Rome.

18. Giraudon/Art Resource.

19. Copyright © Ursula Edelmann, Frankfurt/M. Courtesy Liebighaus-Museum alter Plastik, Frankfurt/M.

20. Deutsches Archäologisches Institut, Rome.

21. Giraudon and Musée Condé, Chantilly/Art Resource.

22. Giraudon and Musée Condé, Chantilly/Art Resource.

23. Philip Evola, from Wickhoff, *Gesammelte Aufsätze*.

24. Studio Koppermann, Munich.

25. Ampliaciones Reproducciones MAS, Barcelona.

26. Copyright © The Ashmolean Museum, Oxford.

27. Alinari/Art Resource.

28. Copyright © Graphische Sammlung Albertina, Vienna; Photo Lichtbildwerkstätte Alpenland, Vienna.

29. Szépmüvészeti Múzeum, Budapest.

30. Philip Evola, from A. Warburg, *Gesammelte Schriften*.

31. Alinari/Art Resource.

32. Alinari/Art Resource.

33. Alinari/Art Resource.

34. Alinari/Art Resource.

35. Philip Evola, from Alciati, *Emblemata*.

36. Courtesy of Egbert Haverkamp-Begemann.

37. Alinari/Art Resource.

38. Philip Evola, from Donald Posner, *Annibale Carracci*.

39. Copyright © Bibliothèque Royale, Brussels.

The Authors

JACOB BURCKHARDT (1818–1897), professor at the universities of Basle and Zurich. Burckhardt explored the history of art as part of the history of culture and civilization. His works include *The Time of Constantine the Great* (1852), *The Civilization of the Renaissance in Italy* (1860), *The History of the Renaissance in Italy* (1867), *Recollections of Rubens* (1898), and *History of Greek Culture* (1898–1902).

MAX DVOŘÁK (1874–1921), successor of Wickhoff at Vienna University. The title of his posthumously published volume of essays, *The History of Art as History of Ideas* (1924), summarizes the direction of his research. His other works include *Das Rätsel der Kunst der Brüder van Eyck* (1904), and Preface to *Oskar Kokoschka, Variationen über ein Thema* (1921).

JOHANN WOLFGANG VON GOETHE (1749–1832), the greatest poetic force of the Germans, was also a scientist, historian, and critic. He translated the autobiography of Benvenuto Cellini and wrote the first evaluation of *Winckelmann and His Century* (1805). His *Theory of Color* (1808) attempts to provide a scientific basis for pictorial aesthetics. In his middle years Goethe endeavored, through his periodical *Propyläen* and annual art competitions, to erect a Neoclassical bulwark against the rising tide of Romanticism. However, in his old age, his support for the restoration of the cathedrals of Strasbourg and Cologne, and his appreciation of medieval painting, mark a return to the enthusiasm of his youth.

280 ·   The Authors

WILHELM HEINSE (1746–1803) formulated, in opposition to Winckelmann, a vitalistic theory of art. His *Briefe aus der Düsseldorfer Gemäldegalerie* (1776–1777) contain the first modern appreciation of Rubens. Heinse's novel *Ardinghello und die glückseligen Inseln* projects an aesthetic utopia into the Renaissance.

THEODOR HETZER (1890–1946), student of Vöge and Wölfflin; professor in Leipzig. Like Wölfflin, Hetzer was interested, above all, in the formal characteristics of great art, and became a sensitive interpreter of Giotto, Raphael, Dürer, Titian, Poussin, Goya, and Cézanne. His book on *Titian* has been described as a "history of European coloring."

EDUARD KOLLOFF (1811–1879). Life and talent of this gifted art historian were wasted in a subaltern position in the Bibliothèque Nationale in Paris. His essay on Rembrandt (1854) established the historical rank of the master. In another essay, *Die Entwicklung der modernen Kunst aus der antiken bis zur Epoche der Renaissance* (1840), Kolloff anticipated, in his positive evaluation of late antiquity, the findings of Riegl.

ERWIN PANOFSKY (1892–1968), professor in Hamburg and at the Institute for Advanced Study in Princeton. In partial continuation of the tradition established by Warburg, Panofsky elucidated the humanistic content of a wide variety of artworks and wrote penetratingly about methods and aims of art history. He wrote *Idea* (1924), *Hercules am Scheidewege* (1930), *Studies in Iconology* (1939), *Albrecht Dürer* (1943), *Early Netherlandish Painting* (1953), and *Problems in Titian* (1969).

ALOIS RIEGL (1858–1905), curator of textiles at the Austrian Museum of Art and Industry, then professor at Vienna University. His work was directed toward the rehabilitation of previously underrated periods of art, and he explored philosophically certain supra- or sub-individual forces which, according to him, determine the evolution of style (*Kunstwollen* = "aesthetic urge"). Among his works are *Stilfragen* (1893), *Late Roman Art Industry* (1901), *Das holländische Gruppenporträt*, (1902), and *Die Entstehung der Barockkunst in Rom* (1908).

CARL FRIEDRICH VON RUMOHR (1785–1843), art historian, novelist, and author of a famous cookbook. His *Italienische Forschungen* (1827) are based on extensive archival studies and form a still useful history of Italian art from the early Christian period to the High Renaissance.

FRIEDRICH SCHLEGEL (1772–1829), poet, theoretician of literature and art, and initiator of the study of Sanskrit in Germany. In continuation of the ideas of Wackenroder, he laid down, in his *Gemäldebeschreibungen aus Paris und den Niederlanden* (1802–1804), that ideal of Christian, medievalizing art that informed the painting of the Nazarenes (Overbeck, Pforr, Fohr, Schlegel's stepson Philipp Veit, and others).

JULIUS VON SCHLOSSER (1866–1938), director of sculpture and applied arts at the Vienna Museums, successor of Dvořák at Vienna University. His main work, *Die Kunstliteratur* (1924), is an unsurpassed compendium of all the biographical, theoretical, and technical writings on art from the early Middle Ages to the end of the eighteenth century.

WILHELM HEINRICH WACKENRODER (1773–1798) wrote, with his *Effusions from the Heart of an Art-Loving Monk* (1797), the artistic manifesto of German Romanticism. He stressed religious inspiration, and the emotions as principal motive forces of artistic creation and presented the naive and pious simplicity of Old German painting as a model for the renewal of contemporary art.

ABY WARBURG (1866–1929), founder of the Warburg Library, which is now, as Warburg Institute, part of London University. This is the foremost research institute for the survival of classical antiquity in Western art and culture — Warburg's field of study. Warburg investigated first the classical antecedents for the depiction of life-in-motion in the idealized human forms and mythological pageants of the early Florentine Renaissance. Later, he detected the survival of classical mythology in medieval astrology, prophecy, and magic. His collected writings are published as *Die Erneuerung der heidnischen Antike* (1932).

FRANZ WICKHOFF (1853–1909) is generally considered to be the founder of the Viennese school of art history. His introduction to the publication of the fourth-century *Vienna Genesis* manuscript (1895) is the first full-grown history of Roman art; in it, Wickhoff refutes the notion of later Roman art as a period of decline. He wrote Renaissance studies, but also with appreciation about Impressionism, Gustav Klimt, and architectural engineering.

JOHANN JOACHIM WINCKELMANN (1717–1768). Founder of classical archaeology as a scholarly discipline and, through his essay *On the Imitation of the Painting and Sculpture of the Greeks* (1755), a pioneer of the neoclassical movement in art. In 1755 he became prefect of the pontifical antiquities in Rome and wrote, from 1756 until 1764, *The History of Ancient Art*, followed by books on unpublished ancient monuments, allegory, and classical architecture, and on the excavations at Pompeii and Herculaneum.

HEINRICH WÖLFFLIN (1864–1945), student of Burckhardt, professor in Basle, Berlin, Munich, and Zurich. Wölfflin aimed at a scientific description of the evolution of styles by way of detailed formal analysis of individual works of art. Among his works are *Renaissance und Barock* (1888), *Classic Art* (1899), *The Art of Albrecht Dürer* (1905), and *Principles of Art History* (1915).

ACKNOWLEDGMENTS

Every reasonable effort has been made to locate the parties who hold rights to previously published works and to the translations reprinted here. We gratefully acknowledge permission to translate or reprint the following:

"Zweiter Nachtrag alter Gemälde (1804–1823)" and "Dritter Nachtrag alter Gemälde (1804–1823)," by Friedrich Schlegel, from *Kritische Friedrich Schlegelausgabe, IV, Ansichten und Ideen von der christlichen Kunst*, ed. and pref. by Hans Eichner, translated with permission of the publisher, Ferdinand Schöningh Verlag.

"Über Murillo, 1843," by Jacob Burckhardt, from *Die Kunst der Betrachtung*, edited by Henning Ritter, translated with permission of the publisher, DuMont Buchverlag GmbH & Co. KG.

"Die antiken Triumphbogen in Italien," by Heinrich Wölfflin, from *Kleine Schriften*, edited by Joseph Ganter, translated with permission of the publisher, Schwabe & Co. AG.

"On the Imitation of the Painting and Sculpture of the Greeks," by Johann Joachim Winckelmann, translated by Henry Fuseli, in *Winckelmann: Writings on Art*, edited by David Irwin, reprinted with permission of the publisher, Phaidon Press Ltd., Oxford.

"On German Architecture," by Johann Wolfgang von Goethe, translated by John Gage, and "Observations on the Laocoon," by Johann Wolfgang von Goethe, in *Goethe on Art*, edited by John Gage, © 1980 John Gage, reprinted with permission of the publisher, University of California Press.

"Memorial to Our Worthy Ancestor Albrecht Dürer," by Wilhelm Heinrich Wackenroder, translated by Elizabeth Gilmore Holt, in *From the Classicists to the Impressionists: A Documentary History of Art and Architecture in the 19th Century*, reprinted with permission of the publisher, Yale University Press.

"On El Greco and Mannerism," by Max Dvořák, translated by John Hardy, in *The History of Art as History of Ideas*, reprinted with permission of the publisher, Routledge & Kegan Paul PLC.